BEYOND
BIOFEEDBACK

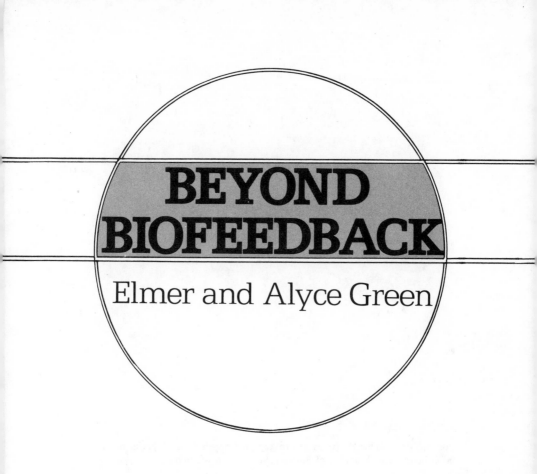

BEYOND BIOFEEDBACK

Elmer and Alyce Green

KNOLL PUBLISHING COMPANY, INC.

Portions of Chapter 15, pages 317 to 325, first appeared in a special report published by the Academy of Parapsychology and Medicine.

Manufactured in the United States of America
Fifth printing — 1989
Designed by MaryJane DiMassi
Cover art by Ann Nunley

Library of Congress Cataloging in Publication Data

Green, Elmer, 1917 —
   Beyond Biofeedback

   Knoll Publishing Co., Inc.
   Bibliography: p. 344.
   Includes Index.
      1. Biofeedback training. 2. Yoga 3. East and West. I. Green, Alyce, joint author.
II. Title. BF319.5.B5G73 152.1'88 77-3256 ISBN 0-940267-14-4

To Pat, Doug, Sandra, and Judy

Acknowledgments

Our thanks to Antoinette (Dolly) Gattozzi for her suggestions in organizing this book and for her editorial work cannot be expressed in words. Our association with Dolly has been longstanding. She participated in the research with Swami Rama, accompanied us in our study of yogis in India, and was an articulate and informative subject in pilot research with theta brain-wave training.

Our biofeedback research is made possible through the construction of a great deal of sophisticated electronic equipment by the biomedical laboratory of the Menninger Foundation. For this we wish to recognize the cooperation of engineer Rex Hartzell, who designed the circuits of our biofeedback machines and the portable psychophysiology lab for the India trip, and Duane Callies, Wendell Spencer, and Darrell Albright, who build and maintain these many devices.

We thank many Topeka housewives and college students for their help as biofeedback research subjects, but in particular we thank those non-Kansas subjects, Jack Schwarz of the Aletheia Foundation, Grants Pass, Oregon, and Swami Rama of the Himalayan International Institute of Glenview, Illinois, for their contribution to the "beyond biofeedback" parts of our voluntary-controls program.

As everyone who has conducted research knows, nothing much could be accomplished without financial help. Our thanks in this regard go especially to the Menninger Foundation for providing space and facilities, a biomedical electronics lab, and a supportive atmosphere for our activities since 1964. Other nonprofit organizations which have made sizable contributions to our support include the National Institute of Mental Health (research grants MH 14439 and MH 20730), the Foundation for the Study of Consciousness, the Institute of Noetic Sciences, the Joseph and Sadie Danciger Fund, the Millicent Foundation, the Stranahan Foundation, the van Ameringen Foundation, a donor who wishes to remain anonymous, and the Laucks Foundation. Mr. Irving Laucks provided funds to bring people from India and Japan to the first Council Grove Conference, in 1969, and later, at a very critical time, supplied travel funds for our study of Indian yogis.

In India, we are indebted to seventeen research subjects, and are especially grateful to Mr. Manoharlal Dudeja of Kanpur for solving many of our housing, transportation, and insurance problems, and for finding a most remarkable driver to chauffeur us around the country in a minibus. Mr. M. S. Khan (Chotey) of Kanpur had the reflexes of a road racer (he had won third in a grueling thirty-day all-India race), the patience of a kindly bus driver, the knack of a crackerjack mechanic, and the communications skill of a pantomimist. Although he was our driver, we were his guests in India, and he made India seem very hospitable.

Many friends, too numerous to mention, cared for us in Kanpur, Rishikesh, Varanasi, Calcutta, Waltair, Adyar, Pondicherry, and Hyderabad, but special thanks must go to Swami Rama, Mahatmaji of Bharat Mandir, and Uma Dutt Gaer, all of Rishikesh; to Mr. C. Giri of the State Yoga Organization, who provided yogi subjects and research space in Chandigarh; to Dr. K. Ramakrishna Rao of Andhra University, Vishakhaputnam, who obtained research subjects and opened his lab to us; and to Mahayogini Rajalakshmi of Tirupati, who provided research subjects and also took care of our team member, Judy, during a three-week bout with hepatitis. Concerning subjects in India, special mention should be made of Dr. Shukla of Benares Hindu University for his contribution to the theory of chakra energies and "coincidence control," and to Yogiraja Vaidyaraja for his unusual demonstration of metabolism control.

Jean Raymond of the Theosophical Society (Adyar), James de Vries (Auroville), and Drs. G. S. Melkote and V. M. Reddy of Hyderabad contributed in important ways to our research and/or provided opportunities to meet with psychologists and with physicians.

We thank Pan American Airlines for transporting our psychophysiology equipment to India without cost, as a contribution to our research, and especially for their great help and courtesies in India.

We cannot leave the India project without thanking Elda Hartley, Harvey Bellin, and Tom Kiefer of Hartley Productions (Cos Cob, Connecticut) for traveling with us to make a documentary film.

Special mention must be made of Dr. Dale Walters, our longtime colleague, who kept the lab work going while we were three months in India.

We gratefully acknowledge the many named and unnamed, whose wisdom and works have influenced our lives.

This book was typed and retyped by our secretary, Shirley J. Anderson, and some of her colleagues, in a remarkably short time. We thank them for their help, and promise to not write another book in the near future.

—ELMER AND ALYCE GREEN

Foreword

This fascinating book by Elmer and Alyce Green is an attempt to integrate a lifetime of scientific work, personal experience, observations, and reading relevant to the problem of the autonomy of mind and its control of matter, including the body. They do not limit themselves to systematic data, and their gracefully written descriptions are evocative, recalling related experiences of the reader, while their often highly speculative theoretical integrations present an important challenge.

The period of the sixties and seventies has been a time of breaking down rigid barriers to inquiry into parapsychology, from telepathy to healing and mental manipulation of objects. At the same time, there has been increased understanding of mental processes contributing to the cure of pain and other physical symptoms such as migraine headache and infection. Psychiatrists as well as general medical practitioners and anesthetists have applied biofeedback techniques experimentally, and now, in some cases, routinely, to help their patients without the use of drugs. While other books deal with this major development within a medical context, the Greens carry us further. They confront us with the implications of this now well-documented process, and invite us to consider its significance for philosophy and for our understanding of the basic nature of mind and of matter and of the unity which underlies them.

Elmer and Alyce Green are in themselves a unique combination of scientific commitment, pioneer daring, and creativity. Their book is a bold effort to progress along the cutting edge of contemporary scientific thought; readers interested in the intellectual wave of the future will be stimulated and nourished by their work.

—GARDNER AND LOIS MURPHY

Preface

When **Beyond Biofeedback** was first published, various examples of biofeedback research and clinical applications were given to illustrate principles of self-regulation. And as examples, they remain adequate. Since the *principles* of yoga and psychophysiologic self regulation have not changed, we will not here describe additional research and applications which have accumulated since 1977. If the reader wishes to obtain information on specific biofeedback projects and applications, however, it is available from the Association for Applied Psychophysiology and Biofeedback (known until 1988 as the Biofeedback Society of America). For this, please write to Executive Director, AAPB; 10200 W. 44th Avenue, #304; Wheat Ridge, CO 80033-2840.

There is one area of feedback training, however, on which we wish to focus additional attention. *Theta brain-wave training* has recently increased in importance for the development and enhancement of creativity. In Chapter 7 we speak of the general state of theta consciousness and benefits of theta brain-wave training, but after ten years of additional experience we have decided to make this training available not only to those in the helping professions, who usually explore unconscious processes only for therapeutic reason, but also to business men and others — for getting problem-solving help from their own unconscious and from the Jungian racial unconscious.

In line with this, in 1986 we (Elmer and Alyce, and also our colleagues Dale Walters and Rex Hartzell (the circuit designer and builder of our 3-band beta-alpha-theta brain-wave machine)) agreed to join Julian Gresser, an international lawyer interested in creativity and experienced in American-Japanese industrial developments, in his efforts to establish a company (Discovery Engineering International (DEI)) in which training in creativity would be paramount. Using our basic program, theta training would be made available to anyone in Japan or America (and other countries) who had specific problems to solve.

Of importance in EEG feedback training, the machine emits tones which can indicate the *simultaneous* presence of the three basic rhythms, a high tone for beta, a medium tone for alpha, and a low tone for theta. This simultaneous feedback is important, for all brain-wave frequencies can appear at the same scalp locus at the same time.

Beginning meditators who practice without EEG feedback, generally fall asleep when they reach this theta stage of consciousness (at least in the United States). But *sleep is the enemy*. The student must learn to maintain inner awareness during theta so that impressions, instructions, and information from the Ego can come to consciousness. This tendency toward sleep is combatted (or opposed, or reversed) by the low-frequency theta tone from the feedback machine. Loud enough to reach consciousness, the theta tone interferes with sleep. The beginning student at first responds to the tone with an "orienting response," thinking, "Ah, I have achieved theta." This kind of thought drives the left occiput back into alpha, or even into beta — stopping the theta tone — and the student must again quiet the mind and return to theta.

With practice, it becomes possible for the student to *hear without listening*. Eventually, theta tones are observed non-reactively and there is no orienting response. This means that the body, the emotions, and the mind have become *silent* — but consciousness remains. This important state of consciousness, Theta Reverie, opens the inner door to the unconscious, whose most important section is the superconscious mind, the Ego, the Source of Creativity. When the theta tone becomes consistently present but not focussed on, awareness of the Ego can consciously begin.

As an example of the relationships, a biophysicist whom Alyce and I met in India in 1973 (in the city of Chandigarh, during a research study of yogis) used this state to solve problems blocking his Ph.D. thesis. At his request, Alyce wired him up to our EEG feedback machine, and he demonstrated that he could consciously generate, within seconds, pure beta, pure alpha, or pure theta at will. This was unheard of. I asked how he could produce theta at will, and stay in the state as long as he wished, and he said he merely turned himself to the state of consciousness in which he had discovered, through years of meditation, that he could solve the most difficult technical questions — a level of mind that appeared to "know everything." I asked how he knew what theta was *in advance of his being wired up*, and he replied that from my description (the same as I have given above) he understood that theta represented, or was associated with, the deep state of meditative awareness which he had learned to enter at will. At the present time, [he says,] as Head of a Department of Biophysics in a large University, he uses this state when confronted with "insoluble" problems.

A question arises, though. "Why would the spiritual Ego be willing to help the personality ego? The latter is a limited, often-baffled creature which frequently has less-than-worthy motives." The answers seems to be that the Ego is concerned during ego life with [the ego's success in becoming a powerful] and transcendent personality. Apparently the only way this can occur, however, is for the ego to actively seek the aid of the Ego.

When this happens in full consciousness, the Ego not only will help solve problems, but will begin to shape the ego into a stronger and more representative image of Itself. According to Aurobindo, the Indian sage of Pondicherry, if the ego's motives are positive, the Ego will help. Otherwise, not. Also, says Aurobindo, in both Eastern and Western metaphysical theory the positive development of the ego is the Ego's goal in this transformational stage of planetary evolution. As long as our expansion in life, in business, in science, in the arts, in religion, contains elements for the betterment of all, Egos will help.

Whatever the truth of this metaphysical theory, theta training works as described above. I discovered these facts [about mind] for myself, starting with mental exercise, in somewhat the same way as the Indian biophysicist. Since 1939 I have used a meditation system premised on the idea that the above-described relationship between the lower-case ego and the capital Ego actually does exist. I learned this system from a [gurudeva] Teacher whom I studied with while a student in physics at the University of Minnesota. I did not know, though, until 1968 when Alyce Green, Dale Walters, and I were conducting brainwave research in the voluntary Controls Program at The Menninger Foundation, that the theta brain-wave corresponded in me to the state in which I was able to get creative solutions to technical problems in physics, and in psychophysics.

I ... described some of this in **Beyond Biofeedback**, recountingmy discovery of the over-arching mathematical law governing subjective visual intensity in response to objective flashes of light. This psychophysical relationship had been a puzzle and controversy since 1860, since the time of Gustav Fechner. I solved the puzzle by consciously and intentionally becoming physically, emotionally, and mentally quiet, and then invoking the aid of the Ego, [appropriate images and mathematical symbols then appearing in my mind's eye].

To find later that this state of quietness and attunement to the Ego could be approached through theta training [by everyone] was to me a great delight. It meant that the average person, without having to subscribe to a religion, or to a dogma, or to a meditation system, could learn to move into the state of consciousness in which the seemingly-infallible Source of Creativity could be invoked for the solution of problems. Since without exception every human skill that is learned is learned with feedback, it is not surprising that many people whom we have instructed in the use of Theta Reverie [in workshops for those in the helping professions] have made as much progress in a few weeks as many meditators make in two or three years.

In my experience, theta training is the most effective modern way for approaching the Source of Creativity. Being a consistent dreamer, in 50 years I had opportunity to examine over 50,000 of my own dreams, some actively solicited, and have carefully analyzed well over 300, using Freudian, Jungian, Assagiolian, and Tibetan symbology. The knowledge gained was invaluable, but for conscious immediate solution of problems, the Theta Reverie with its hypnogogic imagery has been most useful, more rapid and effective.

I have also worked with about six systems of meditation over the years. Each yielded important insights and led to greater understanding of the dynamics of mind, but no technique has been as useful to me as the ability to consciously enter the theta state, interrogate and program the unconscious, and receive hypnogogic imagery from the Ego, for guidance.

One more comment along the same line. Over the years I have participated in a variety of human-relations training programs. My first experience was in the Engineering Department of Minneapolis Honeywell. Later, as a Supervisory Physicist at the U. S. Naval Ordnance Test Station, China Lake, California, for five years I was a senior member of a multi-university training program focussed on the development of management skills for solving personnel problems, brainstorming for creative solutions of technical problems, etc. But none of theses experiences was in the same domain as Theta Reverie training for penetrating through personality barricades and [egoistic] obstacles which prevent people from dissolving their own personality problems, developing good will and group harmony, and maximizing their creative potential.

.... All that has happened, it seems, is that a way has been developed by means of which a modern, scientific, machine-oriented civilization can reap the benefits of its own spiritual nature without being blocked by preconceived and erroneous ideas imprinted by materialistic [dogma] or superstitious religion ...

All the best to you and the others in DEI/Japan. We look forward with enthusiasm and keen interest to the full development of you DEI salon [in which theta brain-wave training will be made available to Japanese clients].

> Sincerely,
> Elmer E. Green, Ph.D.
> Voluntary Controls Program
> The Menninger Foundation

With the above ideas of "Ego" and "ego" in mind, it is interesting to note that the principles of psychophysiologic self regulation have been known for at least 2500 years, especially as elucidated by Patanjali (Taimni, 1967). However, by translating his concepts to modern language, as we have attempted to do, (1) we can more easily understand how *involuntary* processes of body and mind, the major part of the "internal cosmos," are continuously influenced and controlled by VISUALIZATION, and (2) we begin to understand that the "external cosmos," outside our skins, also responds to visualization — though only shamans and occultist seem to have known much about the latter. Undoubtedly there is such a thing as "coincidence control."

From our viewpoint, the development of full human potential starts most easily with mastery of *body* energies (through internal control of images, emotions, and volition), and the process can be extended to energies which influence the outside world. It is striking that in yogic theory ten pranas (ten kinds of energy), which can be self regulated, control the world inside the skin — and the *corresponding* pranas affect the outside world. As below — so above! In ancient Greece the macrocosm and microcosm (that is, the "gods" — and us), and our relation to the "divine" pantheon, seem to have somewhat similar meaning, though little is said in Greek mythology about how to influence or control the gods, or escape their influence. Another similar concept was outlined by the Tibetan teacher of Alice Ann Bailey. He emphasized in Esoteric Astrology that our primary task in living is to free ourselves from the archetypal pressures and controls which are *symbolized* by the planets and constellations (in the clock of the heavens), and thus free ourselves from personality cycles — and eventually, when no longer puppets of the "lunar" archetypes, becoming co-creators with the "Solar" Archetypes who comprise the divine Being of this planet.

Be that as it may, it is our belief, our conviction, that through theta training, it is possible for anyone (who take a few weeks to learn how to enter Theta Reverie) to become aware of at least some aspects of the "planetary field of mind." In this regard, one reason for writing **Beyond Biofeedback** in the first place was to lay a foundation for the considerations of Chapter 14, The Field of Mind Theory. It would be useful if the concepts therein were seriously evaluated by students of the mind, for, if true, those yogic concepts and ideas make clear *why* we are our "brother's keeper," *why* an injustice done to anyone on the planet is an injustice to each of us, *why* the despoiling of the planet through industrial pollution is also a despoilation of each of us, and *why* anything done for the "least of these" is something done for All.

Best wishes for interesting explorations.
Elmer and Alyce Green
Box 829, Topeka, Kansas 66601

Contents

1 Introduction

This book is not a scientific document, or a review of biofeedback and self-awareness training programs, or an autobiography, or a travelogue, or a long essay on philosophy and metaphysics—but it is partially all of these. Every chapter bears on questions that all humans raise at one time or another: Who are we? What can we do to shape the events in our lives so that we can develop our talents and live joyfully? The two questions involve self-identity and volition—the subject of this book.

In working with patients we have noticed that our having developed a limited skill at physiological self-regulation encourages them. "If you can do it, maybe I can" seems to be their unexpressed feeling (something like the motto found at the front of a popular text on algebra: "What one fool can do, so can another"). We have decided, therefore, to tell not only about our research, but also about ourselves, and explain how the study of consciousness and volition became our main interest.

By the end of this book, we hope, it will seem obvious (or at least highly plausible) that psychology and parapsychology are part of a more general Psychology, that medicine and spiritual healing can be parts of a more general Medicine, and that physics and psychophysics are literally parts of a more general Physics.

In considering these pairs pragmatically—psychology and parapsychology, medicine and spiritual healing, and physics and psychophysics—it is necessary to give to *mind* a role in nature that has heretofore not been acceptable in modern science. Some scientists do not like this, but there is no way to avoid it. The evidence is overwhelming and can no longer be ignored. In the twenty-first century it will be taken for granted by every schoolchild that mind and matter, both inside and outside the skin, have something in common. In a way, this book is a preview of what we think will be scientifically studied in the coming century. A significant factor in that science will be "self-awareness."

If the old model must be scrapped, what is to take its place? Some scientists who realize that the old model is finished have viewed with alarm the chaos that the new ideas are injecting into scientific thought. However, the fact that mind can influence both body and nature does not usually have any revolutionary effect in our lives. If we fall off a ladder, we do not really care that Newton was not exactly correct. For all practical purposes he was right, and his description of the law of gravity fits the case quite closely. In the same way, even though our understanding of mind and nature and their interaction may open new possibilities for self-direction and volition, and for freedom of spirit, we still must send our children to school, pay taxes, earn a living, and do everything else that mundane life demands.

The most significant difference the new concept makes is in our self-image. As we begin to realize that we are not totally the victims of our genetics, conditioning, and accidents, changes begin to happen in our lives, nature begins to respond to us in a new way, and the things that we visualize, even though unlikely, begin to happen with increasing frequency. This also is what the book is about.

Biofeedback training has to do with the way in which the body responds to thoughts and feelings. "Beyond biofeedback" has to do with mind and nature. The body seems to be a special case of nature in general and is essentially a "test tube" in which we can practice the control of energies that are part of nature.

If these ideas seem unlikely, it is because we have been inhibited, repressed, and hypnotized by our cultural conditioning and education to see ourselves as powerless to control or change events in our bodies and lives. In psychology there has been a tendency to look on humans as "king-size rats," reflective only of genetics and conditioning. In medicine we have accepted the idea that the doctor must "cure" us. In order to be made well, we must undergo surgery, drug treatment, radiation treatment, or some other kind of manipulation by outside forces. We have not been informed that our bodies tend to do what they are told *if we know how to tell them.* The laws of nature are seen by most scientists—the priests of today—as not connected in any way with mind.

This matter-without-mind concept is mass hypnosis, mass illusion, according to people who have developed unusual physiological and psychophysical capacities, and only when we do not accept this limiting image of ourselves can we break the thralldom and begin to operate as free beings, capable of influencing to a significant extent the course of our lives.

Having said this, we recognize that freedom is nevertheless conditional. "Freedom" here means that fraction of control potentially available in us to help bring genetic predisposition and previous conditioning under self-control. At the beginning of training in self-regulation we may be programmed by genetics and conditioning to a large degree, but it is the extent to which we can modify the program that is important, and it is here that we begin.

Many adherents of the new existentially based psychologies, humanistic and transpersonal, have become aware of the fact that our civilization is in danger of destroying itself through acceptance of self-limiting ideas that have no basis in fact, ideas that developed from the work of existentially deprived researchers in behavioristic and experimental psychology and from theories developed from Freud's early views of the unconscious—views that clearly were influenced by Freud's view of himself. Freud and his coterie accumulated massive amounts of data in support of the theoretical position he developed, but later, when he showed interest in parapsychological processes, such ideas were rejected by many of his followers. Freud was more flexible than his admirers. He was reported to have said that if he were to live his life over again, he would also be interested in studying the parapsychological phenomena of nonsensory communication that he had experienced with certain patients.

Jungian psychology also reflected the experience of its founder, Carl Jung, but since from the very start his awareness included much direct parapsychological experience, he naturally had a different view of human beings than Freud did.

The point here is that the ideas people tend to develop of psychology and nature depend to a large extent upon people's own experiences. The theoretical ramifications of their philosophies, however large, seldom transcend the limits of their own existential base. So in order to make our position clear, we will interweave our own experiences and existential story with the academic and research story.

If there is a message in this book, it is that the development of individuals and of the race depends on the extent to which consciousness and volition are studied and used. Citizens of the future will be relatively free, we believe, from simple behavioristic concepts that promote a defeatist self-image. With a new view of themselves and nature, individuals will be able to develop more easily those capacities and creative potentials that lead from knowledge to wisdom. With that, we begin, and hope the reader will find the trip interesting.

2 Roots and Sources

The divorce between scientific facts and religious facts may not necessarily be eternal as it at first seems. . . . The rigorously impersonal view of science might one day appear as having been a useful eccentricity rather than the definitely triumphant position which the sectarian scientist at present so confidently announces it to be.

—WILLIAM JAMES

This book is a joint venture. From this point on, italics are used to indicate that the writer is Alyce and Elmer's text is in roman type. Everything that is written, however, is really a joint production. We have discussed, and sometimes debated, every idea in detail, regardless of who has written about it, and we have edited and modified each other's material freely.

In this chapter we share something of our personal backgrounds. Some of Elmer's experiences that led, while he was still in high school, to an interest in the unconscious are included here. Other experiences that are particularly appropriate to the development, or restatement, of the field-of-mind theory are included later, in Chapter 14. My background, which includes experiences with unconventional healing (often called "spiritual healing"), is also saved for inclusion later where it seems most appropriate.

Several years before I met Alyce in Minneapolis, my mother, father, brother, and I had become aware of what we referred to as "mental telepathy." Parapsychological events at our home in Duluth, Minnesota, now seem commonplace, compared to present-day reports, but at the time they were quite impressive. For instance, on more than one occasion my mother got inexplicably correct ideas about events in the lives of my brother and myself. It was disconcerting to us for her to know about someone we had met before we had told anyone about him. It was she who stimulated our interest in and awareness of improbable "coincidences." For a while I kept records of such occurrences. Record-keeping seemed to have an awareness-sharpening effect, and I was amazed to note how much I was functioning, or making decisions, with information that was normally unconscious.

On one occasion I had a dream in which, while walking on a feature-less gray plain under a uniformly gray sky, I met the brother of a friend, John Feran. This brother, Jerry, had joined the Navy and was stationed at San Diego, California. When we met in the dream I asked how he was feeling, and he gave me a long, detailed description of trouble he had been having with an infection in his leg. He was all right now, he said, but it had been a bad experience. I wished him well, and he continued on his way. The image of Jerry was so vivid that I was jolted from semiawareness into full wakefulness. The next day I told John about the dream, and he said that his mother was worried because Jerry's regular weekly letters had not come for a month. A week later John called and said a letter had just come from Jerry. He had been in the hospital for a month with an infected leg, resulting in thirty or forty boils, but he was almost well and was being discharged. He had been so uncomfortable that he could not even write home.

Events of that kind stimulated a lot of discussion in my family, and we often debated the meaning and interpretation of psychic experiences. We also argued about related questions, such as, What behavior is appropriate if you perceive that something of an unpleasant nature may happen to a friend? Should you say nothing? Should you say something? In another vein, What does psychism have to do with religion?

When I was a senior in high school my mother became very much interested in a series of talks on psychic phenomena, and she and I joined a study group conducted by Arthur Jay Green, a traveling lecturer. Arthur Green had been a religious minister on the West Coast for many years, and eventually, under the tutelage of Jacques Ramano, a renowned Englishman, he had begun the study of mind-body coordination. According to Arthur, Ramano had been trained by Sufis. He had run away from home when he was nine years old, shipping as cabin boy on a freighter bound for Egypt. In Cairo, Arthur told me, Jacques had jumped ship and met some Sufis who apprenticed him to a teacher. His last stage of training, at age sixteen, consisted of living alone and eating only dates at a secluded oasis until, among other things, conversational telepathic communication was established with his teacher. After that he returned to England, was educated as a chemist, and began teaching the Sufi philosophy.

Whatever the details of Jacques Ramano's early life, my mother met him when he toured the United States at about age seventy-five. She told me that he had the appearance of a much younger man. On a radio program before returning to England he impressed both the doctors who examined him and the radio audience, who could hear the *flub-dup flub-dup* heart sound amplified from a stethoscope, by obliterating his pulse.

One of Arthur's major precepts, learned from Jacques Ramano, sounds familiar today: "If you feel that you know a truth, you must be able to demonstrate it in your life to some degree. Otherwise, you don't really know it. You are only talking." Is it not interesting that this is what we were told forty years later by don Juan, the Yaqui Indian whose teachings were put in book form by Carlos Castaneda?

When I first met Arthur Green I was studying physics in high school and was thoroughly imbued and permeated with "the scientific method." At the same time, I was hearing Arthur Green say, "In addition to the scientific view of nature in physics and chemistry, we must add second-order corrections. These have to do with the power of mind to influence body and nature." To me, this was a startling idea. Arthur discussed the brain and its electrochemical impulses as if, in some way yet to be discovered, there were brain patterns associated with thinking and with telepathy. This was just a few years after Hans Berger in Germany had discovered brain rhythms in his own fruitless search for an explanation of "mental telepathy."

According to Arthur Green, the two most significant features of Sufism were control of the body, emotions, and mind and aligning oneself with nature. If these were done successfully, then one's visualizations of events tended to be followed by a compliance in nature. There was another kind of problem, however: the need to determine what visualizations could be morally constructed. In order to work morally with nature, "it is necessary to know what Nature approves of" and then to tell nature, through visualization, what nature wants. In this context, humans seemed to be transmitters of intention, the agents of action rather than the sole determiners of action. Again according to Sufi theory, everyone works at two paradoxical levels simultaneously: that of appearances and that of causes (though what we call causes them-

on spiritual development. After severing connections with the church, he traveled and lectured, as Arthur Green did, visiting many European countries and most of the United States. When Will J., as we called him, moved to Minneapolis in the fall of 1937, I joined his study group on Eastern and Western approaches to self-awareness.

Meeting him was an event of major importance. He was jovial, friendly, and warm, and seemed to know more about me than I had ever disclosed to anyone, though that fact did not seem to threaten me. He was a cheerful, pink-cheeked, white-haired, blue-eyed Irishman of about medium height but somewhat more than medium weight, who was extremely psychic when he wanted to be. One day when I visited him at the Curtis Hotel in Minneapolis, where he often stayed during lecture engagements, he walked to the phone and put his hand on it. In about five seconds it rang. He picked it up and, without saying hello, asked, "Did you just get a special-delivery letter for me from St. Louis?" There was a pause, and Will J. said, "Oh, I was expecting it, you know." Replacing the phone, he turned with a mischievous grin and said, "You have to be careful and not scare people." In a minute a bellboy came up with the letter and handed it over with an odd look. When the messenger was gone I asked Will J. how he had known that the letter had just arrived. "In the last fifteen years I haven't received a letter or telephone call or visitor without knowing it in advance," he said. The price he paid for that sensitivity was considerable. At one time, he said, his extrasensory awareness of the problems of others was almost more than he could bear.

In the same way, perhaps, it is sensitivity to the torments of others that often tortures the lives of psychiatrists. The psychoanalytic theory of transference, in which patients cast their angers and frustrations onto their doctors, may have a substantial basis in psychic energy that must be accepted or rejected or dealt with in some other way. A chapter could be written about this occupational hazard of psychotherapists, with reference to Jung, to Reich, and to the new generation of young therapists who speak of "bad vibes." Suffice it to say here that if extrasensory perception is a fact, as both Freud and Jung believed, then we might usefully entertain the idea of energy transfer between humans. If information is transmitted, then energy probably is involved, regardless of domain, whether normal or paranormal.

Will J. seemed to be a kind of Irish yogi, but he did not develop his skills through the long practice of austerity. Instead, they appeared spontaneously. A believer in reincarnation, he felt that by age sixteen he had merely "come to himself." His psychic talents had been developed in another life, he felt, and as Will J. he was merely remembering some of his previous abilities.

Whatever the explanation, I observed that he had unusual self-regulatory abilities. When he gashed his hand badly with a sharp kitchen knife, it healed completely in a few days, leaving no scar. His explanation was almost identical to what we heard again and again over the years, both in the United States and abroad: The body will do what you tell it, if you learn how to tell it. The way of telling it involves quietness plus a visualization of what you want the body to do.

I was studying physics rather than physiology, but there was no doubt in my mind that Will J. had unusual powers of physiological self-regulation. More significant to me, though, was his remarkable awareness of others.

Over the eight years in which he and I became very well acquainted, I began to suspect that unusual powers of control over normally involuntary *physiological* processes, such as self-healing, were accompanied by an awareness of normally unconscious *psychological* processes—awareness not only of oneself but of others, too. Dr. Erwood could go down a row of people in an audience and describe family members and events going back several generations.

Since I had through personal experience become aware of extrasensory perception (ESP), I took Will J.'s demonstrations of ESP more or less for granted. What seemed more interesting was the possibility of psychokinesis (PK). Was it possible, as yogis maintained, to influence the physical world by mind alone? I found myself more and more intrigued by the possibility of studying scientifically mind-matter events outside the skin. Control inside one's own body was a special case. Psychic healings were not really adequate evidence of the influence of mind over the physical world, because some persons with psychosomatic disorders seemed to recover from physiological malfunctions in response to a mere gesture from someone they deeply believed in: a doctor, minister, or other healer. Even if we were certain that tissues had been affected, how would we know whether the patient himself had not unconsciously brought about the entire change? Additionally, if ESP was possible, patients might unconsciously modify their own bodies at a suggestion from a healer, even though the healer might be far away. So-called healing at a distance might not be evidence of a direct relationship between mind and matter so much as evidence of a relationship between mind and mind.

The problem of proving energy transfer in a study of mind-matter relationships in living beings is formidable, because such phenomena are embedded in a welter of so-called spontaneous physiological and electronic "noise." It has always seemed to me that the most satisfactory demonstration of energy transfer would necessarily use some kind of inorganic transducer: an inorganic device for converting mental energy into physical energy, analogous to the phonograph cartridge, which converts mechanical vibration into electrical vibration. Further, it must be a device that any person who can focus attention can influence.

Psychokinetic phenomena, although rare, are excellent subjects for investigation, because results are observable. Any event in the nonliving physical domain that can be observed and correlated with a mental event is especially important for construction of a general theory of "mind," because organic transducers, such as plants, animals, and humans, have that mysterious ingredient called "life," whose properties are, at the least, enigmatic. If a human responds to so-called energy transfer, the theoretical significance of the event is ambiguous, because a number of explanations are possible. But if an inorganic body responds to energy that is manipulated, focused, or directed by mind, then a much cleaner theoretical position can be established.

Nowadays, with many research subjects, as demonstrated by Uri Geller, objects move and metals bend or break at the request of scientists. Critics may claim sleight of hand by research subjects, but no one who investigates denies that objects are bent. If you try to make your sleeping dog wake up by mental suggestion and he wakes up, it can be argued that he was going to wake up anyway, but with cutlery it is not easy to say that it was going to bend anyway, right at that time.

Parapsychological problems were marvelously intriguing, and I began skipping classes, spending my time reading the literature of the psychical research societies of Europe and America. What might have happened if I had continued that way I cannot say. What did happen was that I met Alyce in 1939 and had to face the fact that no employer would pay me to think about psychophysical energies. If we were to get married (which we did in 1941), I would need a job to support a family, so I turned toward more practical studies, and in 1942 graduated with a degree in physics.

I immediately took a job at Minneapolis-Honeywell, where I worked in instrument development and later as a technical representative with the Air Force during World War II. After the war I enrolled as a graduate student in physics at UCLA. On the side I began a study of the retina as a biological energy converter, still thinking, though, of methods for direct detection of psychophysical energies. Money was in short supply, for Alyce and I were raising four children by this time, Pat and Doug from her previous marriage and our own two, Sandra and Judy, so I left UCLA and took a job as a physicist with the Naval Ordnance Test Station (NOTS) at China Lake, California. Our business was research and development of guided missiles and rockets. My work involved optics, photography, electronics, computing, design of instruments, management of an optical-research group of about eight physicists, and management of a data-reduction group. When I left NOTS I was head of the assessments division, supervising the work of sixty-five mathematicians, physicists, electronics engineers, and statistics aides in evaluating optical and electronic data obtained in weapons tests.

During those years Alyce and I read continuously in the fields of metaphysics, parapsychology, and theosophy, searching for and constructing a framework of ideas that would correspond with our own experiences and at the same time be reasonable in terms of a possible science in which mind and matter were not forever separate. I took it for granted that I would return to UCLA for further graduate work in physics, but as time passed and information on sensory systems came to my attention (such as the excellent book by Frank A. Geldard titled *The Human Senses*, 1953) it began to seem that for the study of psychophysics I would need much more physiological and psychological information. Possibly I could get a Ph.D. in psychology while gathering the information. That would be especially useful, Alyce and I decided, in finding a position where we could conduct research of our choosing. Freedom is not easily obtained, even with a Ph.D., but we were more fortunate than most research couples in finding a good situation in which to work.

In 1958 we enrolled at the University of Chicago, Alyce as an undergraduate student in psychology and I as a graduate student in biopsychology. One of our reasons for choosing the University of Chicago was that Carl Rogers was there, and we looked forward to contact with him. He had developed a system called "client-centered therapy," in which the therapist is essentially a psychological mirror in which the client can confront himself; one might say that the therapist provides "psychofeedback," in contrast to biofeedback. But when we arrived at the university, Rogers had departed. Behaviorist experimental psychology and a positivist philosophy held sway. Having a philosophy of our own, we were able to take what was useful from these paradigms without being disturbed by their antihumanistic orientation. The same could not be said for many of the students, however. Some were disturbed because of the conflict with their belief systems, and some, we felt, were depressed because of the conflict without knowing the cause. It is not easy to be a graduate student, and it is especially difficult in psychology if you feel that there is something wrong with the interpretation of humans that you are obliged to espouse in order to get a degree.

The return to college was a challenge of the first magnitude. Although I was familiar with the elements of perception, it was necessary to fulfill academic requirements in biology, zoology, neuroanatomy, and especially in the neural basis of sensory discrimination. Going to school was also expensive. Not only were Alyce and I in college, but our youngest children were high-school students in the Laboratory School of the University of Chicago. Fortunately, I was able to obtain a predoctoral fellowship from the National Institute of Mental Health, which helped our finances.

I spent the first two years in the electrophysiology laboratory of Professor Dewey Neff, helping his graduate students trace audio signals through cat brains. These years of study and practice taught me that electrophysiology was a useful technique for mapping sensory-projection areas (such as brain areas that respond to visual and auditory information) but shed almost no light on the problems of mind and volition I wanted to explore.

As Alyce and I continued our own studies of metaphysical systems it became clear that for us the primary problem was not the classical mind-body problem (Is there a mind that has nonphysical characteristics?) but that of will (Is there a force called "volition" that operates in the domain of mind?). Volition, we have come to believe, is the key problem of our day, because control of the individual by society and by the state has taken away some of our own responsibility for our health, our education, and our activities.

When Dr. Neff left the university, I was fortunate enough to obtain the sponsorship of the late Ward C. Halstead. His Laboratory of Medical Psychology in Billings Hospital at the university was justly famous for scientific innovation. He was a pioneer in studying the relationship between brain damage and associated psychological deficits in humans.

My area of specialization, biopsychology, included the detailed study of the brain and nervous system, neuroanatomy and neurophysiology, and perception and behavior in humans and animals. My doctoral dissertation (1962a)—on pain perception in humans under conditions of sensory barrage, including vibration, noise, and flashing lights—clearly demonstrated that an important factor in the perception of pain is the focus of attention. When attention is directed away from pain, pain is not felt. Many people had experienced this, of course, but I was able to measure changes in pain threshold and relate these changes to measured amounts of distracting stimuli, with subjects' reports on their locus of attention as an independent variable. Attention per se cannot be defined operationally, but as one professor remarked long after the oral examination in which I defended my thesis, "We certainly know when we've got it."

About once a year while attending graduate school I thought about research on mind-body processes and wondered how best to begin a study of yogic-type skills without arousing opposition before the research had had a chance to prove itself. Then, in 1962, a fellow graduate student in the department told us about a book he had come across called *Autogenic Training* (Schultz and Luthe, 1959). The book was about a system of therapy especially applicable to psychosomatic (mind-body) disorders. Curious, the student had tried some of the techniques for relaxation and for warming the hands. The results had upset him: The techniques worked! His hand got so warm and swollen that he couldn't remove his ring for several minutes. That was impressive enough, for none of his previous studies had so much as hinted that a person could control the temperature of his hand at will, but what truly startled him was a sudden and profound change in sensations from his body when he used a relaxation exercise for inducing a feeling of heaviness. Surprising body-image changes often accompany deep relaxation; for example, many people experience sensations of floating just before falling asleep. We talked about the perceptual distortions that occurred, and I told him about some of the relevant things I had read about yogis, such as their ability to control heart rate, metabolic rate, peristaltic action (movement of the intestines), and awareness of pain.

This same graduate student was also a teaching assistant in one of my research courses, and I had considerable conversation with him about temperature control. I discussed with him the well-established accomplishments of certain yogis in Tibet who, even in the arctic winters of the high Himalayas, need only a single cotton garment because they can control their body heat (called Tumo, or Vital Heat). I also described the well-documented but not understood control of heat which allows "fire walkers" of various lands to walk across a bed of burning coals without damage to flesh or clothes. The idea of fire-walking interested him, but he found it quite unreal. His own success at warming his skin at will was bothering him, because the textbooks said it was impossible and yet it had happened. What should he think? In any event, our interest had been triggered by what he had said about Autogenic Training, so we got the book and studied it. It was clear that we were reading of a system of "Western yoga" that, because of its medical origin, would be scientifically legitimate to study.

Elmer's Ph.D. in biopsychology was awarded in the spring of 1962, at which time I received my B.A. degree in psychology. I completed course work toward a Master's degree in educational psychology and counseling, including courses and a practicum in client-centered therapy, which was still being offered by the department of education. Courses under Professors Philip Jackson and Jacob Getzells, authors of Creativity and Intelligence *(1962), a book based on their research, aroused my interest in creativity as a process. This, combined with an interest in Oriental civilization and philosophy (augmented by an excellent course in Indian civilization offered by the university), led to my choice of the topic "Creativity East and West: A Comparative Study" for the Master's thesis. My course work was completed but the thesis was scarcely begun when we left the university during the Christmas holidays of 1963 to find a new location in which to do the research we had planned.*

Before leaving the university, I solved a hundred-year-old problem in visual brightness, discussed in some detail later. I also designed an automated version of Ward Halstead's test battery for evaluating brain damage. While working on the test battery, over a period of months, he and I discussed some of the psychophysical-energy concepts that had led me into the field of biopsychology. Eventually we decided to establish a laboratory that would be devoted primarily to studies of the autonomic nervous system—the involuntary nervous system, which yogis reputedly could control. My research would start with a scientific evaluation of Autogenic Training. In order to get funds for this enterprise, I wrote a grant proposal for submission to the National Aeronautics and

Space Administration. After a long ten months of deliberation, NASA turned down the proposal. Meanwhile, however, I had begun to think that Halstead's interests and mine differed considerably and that we would not be comfortable working together. Alyce and I decided to leave Chicago and find a place where we could work on the kinds of projects in which we were most interested: projects that would explore both voluntary control of autonomic body processes and awareness of normally unconscious mental and emotional processes.

We felt that such a place existed, because I had already "glimpsed" it. Twelve years earlier, at NOTS, I had meditated on the question of where to work and had experienced a short hypnagogic "movie." The grassy fields and the buildings where I could have a laboratory were clearly seen, but they were obviously not in the desert. My immediate question about where to work had had the limited objective of determining what job to take at China Lake, but I had not specified this. If my question had been more specific (for instance, What would be useful to do immediately?), perhaps the hypnagogic image would have been different; ask a general question and you are likely to get a general answer. As it was, the green grass, the tree-covered hill, and the buildings and tall clock tower of the image I saw did not exist where we were living. If this image was significant, I felt at the time, it applied to a future possibility, and I merely stored it in my memory. These buildings and the clock tower, it eventually turned out, were located on the west campus of the Menninger Foundation.

Perhaps the reader will ask, How is this possible? What happened, anyway? I can only report that in answer to my mental question the image I described came into my awareness that day. I can also report that the image was correct. (This kind of experience—precognition—is perhaps more prevalent than psychologists realize. Certain kinds of perception seem to be independent of space and time, even though we may hypothesize that they are projected into the space-and-time brain when they are consciously perceived.)

After we decided to leave Chicago I focused attention again in this timeless domain, and saw some additional views of the laboratory. Again the institution consisted of a number of buildings spread out like a college campus over a grassy, tree-covered hill, but this time the large building with the clock tower, which could be seen from far away, was the most obvious feature. In one hypnagogic image I went into the clock-tower building and looked at a variety of American Indian artifacts in a small museum. There were also glass-covered cases containing manuscripts. In another image, my work was conducted in another building, in which activity was coordinated by a highly respected older man (who turned out to be Gardner Murphy). Much electronic machinery was involved, and though I could not see exactly how it was used, it seemed to relate to human behavior. A striking feature in one image was the appearance of small lines of light that came from far away and converged on my forehead. Each line, my mind "explained" in a subsidiary hypnagogic flash, was a connection with someone in the country who was involved in the same kind of work as I. It seemed that there would be a network of people all over the country working in the same general area. They would be aware of one another, and their work would be mutually supportive. It is possible for images to be wish-fulfilling, of course, but in my experience valid precognitive images have a kind of certainty connected with them. This feeling of certainty and validity leads, at least in my case, to a feeling of "Okay, let's see how the future unrolls." In this case, the images were accurate.

The question at the end of 1963 was, Where is that laboratory? We decided to start looking for it by going to New York City to spend the Christmas holiday with our daughter Pat and her family, then visiting labs on the East Coast and gradually working our way across the United States until we reached California (where we hoped it would be). While driving to New York, however, I began to think about the enormity of the problem of finding in any mechanical way the location of *the* lab. I suggested to Alyce and Judy, who was with us, that it would be more convenient if someone at the lab contacted us and steered us in the right direction. In one sense, our feeling at that moment was very similar to what we had felt on our departure from England to cross the Atlantic in our ketch *Daphne* a few years earlier. When we set out from land we had the sensation of leaving the familiar behind and trusting to our own continuous awareness in the present to lead us into all future harbors.

After the holiday season was over, while preparing to leave Pat's home, I received a telephone call from Dr. Philip Rennick of the research department of the Menninger Foundation. I was surprised to hear from him. He had graduated from Halstead's lab at Chicago a year ahead of me and disappeared from my ken. I was surprised that he could find me, because I had left no telephone number at which I could be reached after we left Chicago. Phil explained that he had received a

Christmas card from another of Halstead's graduate students, Jan Berkhout, who mentioned that I was leaving the university and was going to visit my daughter in New York and look for a job. They knew Pat's name, and the telephone company did the rest.

Knowing of my experience in electronics, Phil had suggested to Gardner Murphy, the director of the research department, that I might be the one to help solve a problem there. The problem was not extremely difficult, but at that moment there was no one there who could adequately bridge the communication gap between the biomedical engineers and the psychologists. Gardner Murphy wanted me to come to Topeka, Phil said, and talk about the possibility of joining the department. My response was that I would be happy to do so and would stop there en route to the West Coast. Phil suggested that since they were paying the bill I might as well catch a plane the next day and visit Topeka immediately. Although it didn't seem to me that the Menninger Foundation, which I knew was a psychiatric institution, would be a likely place to establish a psychophysiological research laboratory, I was intrigued by what Phil had said about bridging the gap between psychology and biomedical electronics, and agreed to visit Topeka for a day.

Phil met my plane, and we spent an evening discussing our experiences at the University of Chicago. In the morning he took me to the foundation. The closure between the timeless domain and the time-and-space domain often comes with a kind of jolt, a moment of truth in which time and space seem momentarily suspended. When I saw the clock tower on the grassy, tree-covered hill, it had a feeling of rightness. Nevertheless, I wanted Alyce to see the place before I made any commitment.

I met Gardner Murphy and other members of the research department, and we talked about the communications problem. Gardner offered me a job, and I realized that I would have a chance to build a laboratory and generate the kind of research projects I had described in the grant proposal to NASA. Alyce and I would be able to begin our own research.

It was, to say the least, a uniquely propitious offer: They wanted a laboratory and I wanted to build a laboratory. As a staff member of the department, I would be permitted to carry out whatever research I could obtain funds for. I explained to Gardner that I wanted to test the claims of Autogenic Training. Only two members of the research group had heard of Autogenic Training, but it sounded interesting to them, and Gardner felt that it would be an appropriate area of study.

The important thing was that Gardner gave me the opportunity to spend at least one fourth of my time right from the start on whatever I chose. In addition, he said, I probably would be able to work full time on my own projects once the communications problem had been solved. Earlier, I had considered joining the staff of a university, but rejected this possibility because, with a brand-new Ph.D., I would have to begin at the bottom of the academic ladder and work on tasks that senior people did not want to be bothered with. At age forty-four I had already put in about eighteen years of professional development—but that might be of little significance at a university. Gardner was offering the opportunity to work on projects of my own choosing, and it was an offer I could not afford to turn down. Kansas might not be the place where Alyce and I planned to live, but California would have to wait.

3 Autogenic Feedback Training and Voluntary Control

The task of . . . psychology . . . is to apply ruthlessly, and to the limit, every promising suggestion of today, but always with the spice of a healthy skepticism which will know how infinite are the nature of the macrocosm, and man the microcosm, how infinitesimal our knowledge of it and of him.

—GARDNER MURPHY

The eastern part of Kansas has an unusually fine climate. The winters are mild, and seemed almost balmy after our years in Chicago, Minneapolis, and Duluth. Really hot summer weather seldom lasts more than six weeks. The countryside around Topeka has a pastoral beauty beyond compare in the spring, and the falls are colorful and last until December. The land is gently rolling, with many trees. About thirty inches of rainfall each year gives it a lush green look until the ripening grain fields turn it to gold. Geese from Canada stop here in the fall and on their return flight in the spring.

The Menninger Foundation property where the research building is located is a beautiful three-hundred-acre park. The research building itself was completely rebuilt and refurbished in 1963, and when Alyce and I arrived in 1964 it was all new. It is one of the most graceful places in which to work that one could imagine. The mountains and the ocean of California are far away, yet it is hard to imagine a more fortunate set of circumstances than we found.

Gardner Murphy, the director of research at the foundation, was also the president of the American Society for Psychical Research. He was one of the few prestigious individuals in American psychology who was daring enough to say what he felt was true about parapsychology. According to a survey made about 1960, approximately one third of U.S. psychologists felt that there probably was a scientific basis for the re-a good idea that probably would work. Suddenly it struck me: He was proposing the same approach to self-regulation in a human being that we had used at the Naval Ordnance Test Station for self-control in guided missiles. If feedback proved effective in enabling control of unconscious muscle tension, possibly the same principle would also work with the autonomic nervous system.

Feedback of signals is used in every self-guided mechanism, without exception. For instance, consider a heat-seeking missile designed to chase and shoot down an aircraft with heat-emitting engines. The missile contains a scanning device that examines the field of view covered by its optical system and automatically measures the angular deviation between its heading and a direct course to the "hot spot" in the sky (the aircraft). The angular deviation is converted to an electrical signal, amplified, and fed to motors which automatically change the steering vanes, thus moving the "hot spot" toward the center of the optical field of view. When the missile is moving directly toward the aircraft, the "hot spot" is in the center of the scanning system, and whenever the missile deviates from that direct line a self-regulating correction is made, returning the "hot spot" toward center. Cycles of scanning, feedback, and correction continue until the missile reaches the vicinity of its target and a proximity fuse detonates the explosive charge.

Consider other examples. A furnace and its thermostat represent a complete, self-contained, self-regulated system of temperature control. Every self-regulating, automatic machine has a feedback loop by means of which the machine's behavior is continuously fed back to a control mechanism, which then "tells" the machine what to do next. In learning to drive a car, a person has continuous visual feedback. If the car heads for a ditch, this error is detected visually, and feedback of this information results in changes in the muscular system of the driver which affect the steering wheel so that the course is corrected. Learning to play a pinball machine involves three kinds of feedback: sight, sound, and vibration. Without vision *and* sound it is very difficult; without vision, sound, and vibration, it is impossible. Without feedback, nothing can be learned.

Gardner was suggesting a way of learning to control unconscious muscle tension anywhere in the body. The solution was to detect a person's tension, then feed this biological information back to the person, thus making him conscious of it. It is necessary to become aware of something before you can change it, control it.

This was so obvious that I was surprised that I had overlooked it in thinking about voluntary control of those unconscious body functions governed by the autonomic nervous system. Medical textbooks said that voluntary control of the autonomic nervous system was impossible, but I knew of no reason why control could not be established by increasing self-awareness through feedback. In fact, every yogi I had ever heard of was able to control his own autonomic nervous system to some degree. Moreover, if the data from Autogenic Training demonstrating autonomic control were reliable, a useful psychological method for developing conscious autonomic self-regulation already existed, and feedback should make Autogenic Training much faster.

In order to develop voluntary control of behavior, whether it be slowing the heart or playing a piccolo, it is necessary to become conscious of (or focus consciousness on) the present behavior and at the same time visualize (imagine) the desired behavior. The difference between the two, between the fact and the visualization, corresponds with the angular deviation detected by a heat-seeking guided missile—between the "hot spot" in the sky and the direction of the missile.

The guided missile is not conscious, of course, but its designers were conscious when they figured out how to make it work. In the same way, we must be conscious when we voluntarily *learn* any skill. Consciousness is necessary when we are learning to use deviations between performance and goal in order to change our behavior. After a body learns a skill, it can often perform as unconsciously as a guided missile (as when driving a car automatically while involved in a serious discussion). While designing or modifying behavior, however, consciousness is needed, and in order to become conscious of deviations between the facts of behavior and the visualization of behavior, we need conscious feedback.

But note an underlying principle: In both cases, conscious and unconscious, feedback is needed in order for a mechanism (organic or inorganic) to function properly in a changing situation. Our involuntary body processes are set up by nature with internal feedback loops (to regulate heart rate automatically, for instance), but if we want to gain voluntary control of any of these autonomic processes, we need conscious feedback. When the new behavior has become automatic in its own right, we can forget it and it will continue on in its proper new course. This is one of the goals of Autogenic Training which we wanted to study.

ness and warmth exercises were related to some unusually basic psycho-physiological processes, even though medicine and psychology were not yet aware of what they were. At the foundation, once the new psycho-physiological laboratory was set up, we at last had an opportunity to investigate Autogenic Training and see for ourselves what would result in the mind-body domain.

As mentioned before, Gardner's suggestion for using feedback for control of striate muscle tension (which normally is under voluntary control) had opened up the possibility in my mind of feedback for control of the normally involuntary section of the nervous system—the autonomic. I designed a "temperature trainer," a feedback instrument for training people to warm their hands, to be built by our Biomedical Laboratory. One of the questions Alyce and I asked was, Will biofeedback facilitate Autogenic Training? We planned to study that while testing Schultz's second standard Autogenic Training exercise, for control of warmth in the hands.

The first standard exercise, for heaviness in the body, obviously involved muscle tension, and I set up a muscle-tension feedback system (an electromyographic system, EMG feedback) with Dale Walters. Dale was a young graduate student whom Gardner had hired to help conduct muscle-tension research, and at first he was on loan to us, helping with the recording instruments while learning lab procedures. Later, when Gardner retired from the foundation and went to George Washington University, Dale, Alyce, and I became a solid team, and we worked together in every succeeding project.

Before speaking of our early studies of voluntary control in the autonomic domain, it may be useful to review the first study we conducted with muscle-tension feedback and explain some remarkable results. The muscles that are used in voluntary action are not activated by the involuntary (autonomic) nervous system, but are controlled by the voluntary (craniospinal) nervous system. For a long time one of the basic research questions was, Is it possible to imagine doing something without having accompanying muscular tension in the body? For instance, can we imagine rowing a boat without having any muscular activity whatsoever in our arms? (This question was once quite important. Theorists had proposed that unless we have muscle tension of some kind we cannot imagine, or think. In other words, we do not have muscle tension because we think or feel, but just the reverse—we think or feel because we have muscle tension. Thinking is in the body rather than the brain, they said.) With sensitive electronic amplifiers and filter circuits, it is possible to investigate such questions. Electrodes are placed on the skin over the muscles involved or inserted directly into the muscles, and whatever tension appears in those muscles is easily detected, measured in volts, and recorded.

The first experiment was to test the hypothesis that in order to imagine such things as rowing a boat, it is necessary to develop muscle tension in the arms. We were surprised by the results, which led us to the idea of *voluntary control of single nerve cells*.

This was pilot research, and therefore was not conducted with a homogeneous group of subjects. Instead, we used as subjects a number of male college students, other young men from our laboratory, and ourselves. (We feel that unless researchers include themselves in pilot research they really are not qualified to make many comments on the states of consciousness, or body control, experienced by their subjects. This is not our opinion alone. That many if not most of the members of the Biofeedback Society of America agree is a good indication that biological and psychological scientists are moving toward the existential evaluation of research findings in appropriate cases.)

The project was conducted as follows. An electrode was attached with salt paste to the forearm, and another electrode was placed over the bony hump on the back of the wrist. The voltage difference between the two electrodes was amplified and recorded on polygraph paper. The output of forearm muscle tension was displayed not only on polygraph paper but also on a meter. By looking at the meter, the subject saw what was happening in the forearm muscles; the meter provided external feedback of information from inside the skin.

Biofeedback means getting immediate ongoing information about one's own biological processes or conditions, such as heart behavior, temperature, brain-wave activity, blood pressure, or muscle tension. Information is usually fed back by a meter, by a light or sound, or subjects simply watch the physiological record as it emerges from the monitoring equipment. Biofeedback training means using the information to change and control voluntarily the specific process or response being monitored. (A similar procedure using animals lacks the voluntary element and is called operant or instrumental conditioning.) In other words, when the subject uses the position of the needle on the meter as an indicator of muscle tension and tries to change it, then the setup is being used for self-training. In such a situation it is obvious that the doctor or psychologist is not doing anything to the subject but is merely providing him with information that normally he does not have. What happens after that depends entirely on what the subject does—how he uses the information.

Subjects in our experiment were seated at a card table in a quiet, darkened room, with the illuminated meter before them. In a control room about fifteen feet away, separated from the experimental room by two walls and a hallway, the researchers communicated by intercom, giving whatever instructions were needed.

The subject's first task was to reduce muscle tension to very low levels, as indicated by the meter. Then the meter was turned off, and the subject was asked to imagine a physical exercise, such as rowing a boat, while trying to stay relaxed. After fifteen seconds the experimenter said over the intercom, "Now you may stop visualizing. When the meter is turned on, please reduce the muscle tension to as low a level as possible before the next trial." After about thirty seconds of feedback the meter was turned off again, and the second trial began with another phrase, such as "Now imagine that you are climbing a rope hand over hand." With the feedback meter turned off during the visualizations, the subject could not be certain whether muscle tension was involved.

Our purpose in alternating the tension trials and the relaxation trials was to get the muscle tension to very low levels before each visualization so that minute changes in tension could be detected. When muscles are tense, small changes cannot be detected.

Several subjects succeeded in reducing muscle tension so remarkably that I felt something was wrong with our recording machinery. At certain moments our polygraph record indicated zero tension. From my study of neuroanatomy, I did not believe that it was possible to have no tension in a muscle, yet this was what the record said. In addition, a rhythmic firing pattern indicated by a sawtooth wave (at seven spikes per second) was, I thought, due to some unusual malfunction in our electronic machinery.

The presence of these sawtooth records brought the experiment to a halt. Dale Walters and I spent three weeks with a high-gain oscilloscope, trouble-shooting every wire and piece of equipment. (An oscilloscope is essentially the same thing as a television set, except that you can examine many electrical signals and not merely the signal from a television broadcast station.) Eventually I was convinced that the seven-spikes-per-second phenomenon was actually originating from the subjects.

What could it be? When I first reported this finding to Gardner Murphy, he too was surprised and puzzled. One of the other researchers in the department bluntly said, "I don't believe it."

Whenever a scientist is confronted with such a situation, his next step, contrary to popular opinion, is usually to search the scientific literature in depth. Scientists are sometimes portrayed as people who know almost everything about what they are doing before they do it, but this is generally not the case.

I found a book written by John Basmajian, *Muscles Alive* (1962), in which he described a muscular firing pattern called "single motor unit firing" (SMU firing), and he made reference to two previous investigators who had also noticed this phenomenon. He pointed out that with the help of visual and auditory feedback it was possible for a person to reduce the tension in a muscle to levels far below what had previously been thought possible. He explained that the usual medical idea that muscles could not become that relaxed was due to a misinterpretation of research reports. He also mentioned that when the nerve supplying a muscle was cut, researchers found not a cessation of muscle firing, but instead spontaneous muscle firing that was considerably higher than zero tension.

In order to pick up SMU firing with a large surface electrode, it is necessary for all of the muscle fibers that can be detected by the electrode (perhaps several thousand of them) to remain still, except for the group connected with *one single nerve cell*. Each nerve cell that triggers muscle acts as a tiny electrical activator and is usually attached to a number of muscle fibers. Whenever the single nerve cell fires, on command from somewhere in the central nervous system, it activates the group of muscle fibers attached to it. (We might think of the nerve fiber as a twig to which are attached many leaves, with each leaf a single muscle fiber and the entire group of leaves a single motor unit.) Tension in a muscle bundle (which may consist of thousands of motor units) is controlled partly by the firing rate in individual nerve fibers and partly by the total number of nerve fibers that are firing.

As already mentioned, it is possible for a person to learn to control one single nerve fiber in a bundle of nerve fibers. Basmajian gave the name "single motor unit geniuses" (which he shortened to SMUGs) to those who could control the SMUs. Approximately half of his subjects were able to accomplish it; Basmajian was one of them. Interestingly, no one who can control single-motor-unit firing can describe how it is done. All that can be said is that you visualize what you want to have happen and then the body does it. The feedback helps you get a feeling for the process, so that you can repeat it, but it doesn't help you explain in words how it is done.

In Basmajian's research each pulse of the single-motor-unit firing was heard on a loudspeaker as a thump, and he soon noticed that with auditory feedback a person could learn to control the thumping pattern. For instance, if it was desired to hear *thump-thump* followed by *thump-thump-thump,* quite often it would happen. People found that they could manufacture doublets, triplets, and drum rolls at will. The important point of the research was the fact that *single cells were being controlled by volition.* This fact is remarkably significant.

From a medical point of view, the ability to develop conscious control of a single nerve cell has theoretical consequences that extend through all biofeedback research, whether in the domain of voluntary muscles or the autonomic nervous system or the central nervous system. The muscle tension developed by a single motor unit cannot be detected by sensory awareness, but with feedback we can control our instructions to the body and the conditions in the body that allow it to follow instructions.

We completed our research in short order once I was convinced that the polygraph record of seven spikes per second represented actual single-motor-unit firing. Surprisingly, seven out of twenty-one subjects learned to produce either SMU firing or zero firing during the twenty-minute period in which the imagining and relaxing trials took place. When the feedback meter was turned off prior to a new visualization, the subjects could usually maintain their low level of muscle tension in the forearm bundle—so there was no evidence that it was necessary to have tension in the forearm in order to imagine strenuous arm activity. Another interesting finding was that only one of the subjects was able to produce single-motor-unit firing without the aid of electronic feedback. Presumably, after training others might have been able to do so, but we did not test that.

The one person who was able to produce single-motor-unit firing without feedback was myself, after I had put my arm in a state of quietness that I had learned through meditative exercises back in the 1930s. With this experience of my own and the research data on SMU firing in mind, I was more impressed than ever by the fact that Autogenic Training provided a heaviness exercise as the first step in recovering from stress problems and gaining control of muscle tension. Great quietness in the muscle system is useful in preparation for the next step in Autogenic Training, in which great quietness in the autonomic nervous system is induced through the warmth exercise.

We began our research on Autogenic Training methods in 1966. I developed a set of phrases adapted from the first and second standard exercises, for relaxation and warmth, but condensed into one fifteen-minute training session. The subjects were thirty-three women from the local community. Each came to the laboratory for one session of guided practice in using Autogenic Training phrases to achieve relaxation of the whole body and warmth in the hands. The rationale for what they were about to do was explained in the following manner before practice began:

> *It is general knowledge that our bodies are equipped with regulating mechanisms and systems that work automatically—the breathing mechanism, the circulatory system, and so forth. It is also known that such systems can be influenced by various thoughts and experiences. For example, being startled can make you catch your breath . . . embarrassment may make you blush . . . thinking of someone squeezing a lemon may make your mouth water.*

> *Recent research has established that it is also possible to influence such autonomic processes intentionally, volitionally, by directing physiological changes via one's focus of attention.*

> *In attempting to make a physiological change through the focus of attention, it is important to realize that it is not accomplished by force or active will. It is done by imagining and visualizing the intended change while in a relaxed state. We call this* passive volition. *Relaxation is important because it is easiest then to have the casual, detached, and yet expectant attitude that is useful in bringing about the desired change.*

> *It has been found helpful to try to visualize clearly the part of the body that is to be influenced while using the autogenic phrases (which means "self-regulating phrases") that I will give you. In this way a contact appears to be set up with that particular body part. This seems to be important in starting the chain of* psychological *events that eventuate in* physiological *changes.*

> *These changes essentially result from the operation of the psychophysiological principle, which affirms, "Every change in the physiological state is accompanied by an appropriate change in the mental-emotional state, conscious or unconscious; and, conversely, every change in the mental-emotional state, conscious or unconscious, is*

accompanied by an appropriate change in the physiological state." This principle, when coupled with volition, allows a natural process—psychosomatic self-regulation—to unfold.

The autogenic phrases are useful in beginning practice. The idea is to visualize, imagine, and feel that the change is happening . . . and then just let it happen. Do not interfere with the body's tendency to cooperate. The aim is to train certain processes to cooperate in such a way that finally a very brief visualization will accomplish the intended physiological change.

Several physiological processes were measured during the practice session, including respiration, heart rate, galvanic skin response, and blood flow and temperature in the hands. One of the first things we learned in conducting research with a large number of wires and electrodes attached to the subject was that the wiring was a major psychological handicap in learning self-regulation. A wired-up subject, constrained in the experimental chair, suffered from what we came to call "the electric-chair effect." In order to overcome this undesirable influence, we constructed jackets in different sizes in which thirty-six wires were hidden in seams, with rubber "plug-in" blocks sewn under the sides of the collar (for head electrodes) and inside the cuffs (for hand and arm electrodes).

We wired the subject in a pleasant room, and afterward she walked with us to the research room. The subject could move so freely that, usually, she forgot about the wires. Just before she sat down, we said, "Just a second. We must plug in the jacket so we can get our records." A flexible cable led from the jacket to our recording devices. The experiment could begin with a relatively comfortable subject. For research in which physiological states are being correlated with psychological states, such arrangements are useful. We have found it is important not to treat the subject as an object.

After the session at our laboratory, subjects were asked to practice at home, twice daily, for two weeks. Then we had them come back for a final laboratory session, during which the same physiological measurements were recorded.

We were encouraged by what we learned in this study, and became eager to proceed with studies combining biofeedback and Autogenic Training phrases. Even without biofeedback, a number of the subjects were able to relax deeply, and several of them were able to raise the *temperature in their hands significantly as a result of this brief, two-week practice with Autogenic Training phrases.*

Our most interesting finding led to the use of voluntary hand warming for control of migraine headache. It came about accidentally. One of the subjects developed a migraine headache during both her laboratory sessions, brought on, she said, by fear that she would not succeed in warming her hands. During the second lab session, after the Autogenic Training practice and the ensuing fear and headache, we asked the subject to run through another simple test routine, which was part of the research design: to watch a small light for ten minutes in a totally darkened, quiet room. It was very relaxing. All she had to do was touch a switch if the light appeared to move. While this was going on, I was in the instrument room, studying the physiological records as they emerged on the polygraph. Suddenly, at about the ninth minute, I noticed a rapid vasodilation in both hands, and a corresponding increase in hand temperature of about $10°F$ in the next two minutes. When the test was over I went into the experimental room and asked, "What happened to you a couple of minutes ago?" She replied, "How did you know my headache went away?"

Needless to say, this startling answer raised some interesting questions. An opportunity to explore the phenomenon again occurred soon, when word of this research finding reached Lillian Petroni, the wife of a colleague in the research department. She asked if she could be "trained out of migraine." I felt it would be quite useful to try, but explained that positive results were far from certain. The principles of autogenic feedback training (which is what we call our biofeedback procedures coupled with Autogenic Training phrases) were explained to Mrs. Petroni, and she was conducted through a fifteen-minute temperature-feedback training session. I gave her a copy of the Autogenic Training phrases and one of the just-completed portable temperature trainers with which to practice at home. I asked her to practice every day for a week, then phone me.

She followed the training guidelines and got excellent results. After two weeks of practice with the meter and phrases, she had stopped taking drugs and no longer needed the machine to continue the control over migraine. She has remained free of migraine ever since (ten years). I believe that training in inner awareness and in control of relaxation in both the striate and autonomic domains gave her the ability to turn off chronic tension in the sympathetic nervous system (the "fight-or-flight" system, the body's activation and alarm system) and helped her develop a more relaxed style of living in which migraine had no place.

About a month after learning to control warmth in her hands, Lillian telephoned to say she had another problem: "Will temperature training cure cold feet?" I suggested she use the Autogenic Training phrases to focus warmth in her feet. It worked immediately, and her husband stopped by my office one day to thank me for solving a long-standing family problem—his wife's need to get up at two or three o'clock in the morning to warm her cold feet in a tub of hot water. Since that time we and others working with temperature control have helped many people with their cold feet. For those who have the problem, it is no joke!

Interested by the migraine finding, Joseph Sargent, director of internal medicine at the foundation, felt it would be useful to conduct a pilot study of headache patients in a clinical setting. In 1967 he began a study of temperature feedback for migraine control. Migraine headaches have been described in medical lore and in literature for two thousand years, and studied scientifically for the last forty years. Yet no effective treatment was known. Powerful drugs have been used, but they are not effective for everyone: Their side effects are often bad, and often dosages must be increased as the body adapts. It is estimated that as many as ten million persons in the U.S. suffer from migraine attacks. Because this type of headache poses such a difficult problem, Dr. Sargent felt that any new approach that might safely help merited study. He saw the use of Autogenic Feedback Training to normalize blood flow as such an approach (Sargent, Green, and Walters, 1972).

A vascular theory of migraine was set forth by H. G. Wolff (1963) and his colleagues, who were among the first to study migraine headache scientifically. They concluded that it results from dysfunction of cranial arteries. First, the blood vessels of the head become unusually constricted (vasoconstriction), producing the preheadache sickness, and then unusually dilated (vasodilation), which results in the headache itself. Something initiates the process that constricts cerebral blood flow, which quite often is a response to pressure or stress, and if an adequate supply of blood to the brain is endangered, other automatic processes that control blood flow start to unfold. One of their effects is to cause blood vessels in the scalp to dilate. If this physiological response is great enough and persists long enough, biochemicals are released which produce edema and other effects that are experienced as pain.

Some authorities feel that this view of migraine, consisting of phases of vasoconstriction and vasodilation, is not basic enough. They suggest that emotional factors that modify the behavior of subcortical brain structures have a causal role in migraine headache. This last fits well with our own concept of the psychophysiological causes underlying psychosomatic disease, as will become evident in our discussion in Chapter 4 of the rationale underlying biofeedback training: how and why it works.

One aspect of the general migraine syndrome—that is, the set of symptoms associated with migraine headache—is a decrease of blood in the hands. Voluntary increase in blood flow in the hands, learned through temperature feedback training, reflects a voluntary decrease of "nervous tension" (neural firing in the sympathetic section of the autonomic nervous system). This self-induced sympathetic relaxation in the hands is apparently a reflection of "relaxation" in the subcortical neural center that regulates blood-flow behavior throughout the body. It appears that the entire vascular system of the body tends to rebalance in response to hand-temperature training and the vascular dysfunction in the head is correspondingly corrected. In other words, this undesirable vascular response to stress, the general migraine syndrome, is brought under voluntary control as a "side effect" of hand warming.

More than two hundred patients have completed Dr. Sargent's ongoing migraine-control study. The standard procedure is as follows. For one month prior to beginning biofeedback training each subject charts daily the type of headache, severity and duration, presence or absence of associated symptoms, and degree of disability. The patient also records the type, strength, and total number of units of each medication taken in a twenty-four-hour period and lists any side effects associated with the drug(s).

Before a patient is accepted into the project, a detailed medical history is taken, a complete physical examination is given, and laboratory studies are made. In the initial session he or she learns the use of the temperature-feedback trainer and the Autogenic Training phrases for relaxation and warmth, and then takes the trainer and a typewritten copy of the phrases home, with instructions to practice daily, recording temperatures of the hand at the beginning and end of each practice period.

The patients continue to keep the daily headache and medication charts during training. They are seen at weekly intervals until a con-

sistent positive response on the meter and an associated awareness of warmth in the hands are achieved. Practice with the meter usually can be discontinued within a month, but daily practice without the meter continues, with the aim of learning to initiate relaxation and warmth in a few seconds to prevent or abort headaches. After training, participants return to the clinic at intervals, pertinent data are gathered, and a refresher practice session with the temperature trainer is offered. Medical follow-up continues for a minimum of one year, and is extended whenever possible to two to three years.

About 80 percent of the migraine-headache patients have obtained relief, ranging from slight to excellent. A few have reported a migraine-free life since completing the program.

Joe Sargent is an internist, and during the first two years of his migraine research, he and Peter Fleming, a psychiatrist, and I met each week at Joe's request to discuss problems with individual patients. For example, one of the early patients who had suffered classical migraine for many years quickly learned how to raise the temperature of her hands by as much as 25°F, and then she apparently began to lose the skill. As she progressed with her training and got some control over her headaches, she became disturbed by the fact that she was no longer able to make such dramatic changes in hand temperature. Together, we examined her records. What was happening was clear: As she learned to meet stressful situations in a more relaxed way, her vascular system was continuously rebalancing, and her hands had begun to be warmer *all the time.* This was a measure of success rather than failure, but she could no longer go from 70° to 95°F, because her starting temperature had moved up to the middle 80s. Since 95°F or 96°F is close to the top, a change of 10° was about as far as she could go. As her hands approached normal temperatures through her continued practice, she could expect to see less and less change on the meter.

A question that is often asked about migraine patients is, How many get no benefits from hand-temperature training? Experience is not uniform across the country, because different clinicians have different ways of training and different systems for evaluation. In the first group of thirty patients that Sargent, Fleming, and I discussed, however, three quit the program without really giving it a try. The usual reason was expressed by one patient after ten days: "This program isn't going to do me any good, so I'm quitting." Interestingly enough, a specialist in speech pathology heard this patient talking with Dr. Sargent during the first visit to the clinic and told Sargent that that patient had a rigid personality, would not learn anything, and probably would quit the project. Asked how he could know all that, the doctor answered that the patient had a "unilateral lisp," a speech defect that indicated a rigid personality (speech was deformed from tension in throat muscles). If that person had stayed in the program, we might have predicted that his bad speech habit, as well as his migraine, would have changed for the better.

Three more patients, all female, learned to warm their hands in two or three weeks, began to get their migraines under control, and then lost the ability. The migraines returned in full force, and they could no longer warm their hands. We hypothesized that the initial success was due to the fact that at a conscious level these patients wanted to get better. As soon as health improved, however, a psychological problem, one that used to be at an unconscious level, began to surface and could not be dealt with. Apparently, it was easier to have the pain of migraine than to become aware of the underlying problem that was linked to the migraine. Sargent's question to Fleming and me was whether the training program, if continued, would cause psychological problems. We concluded that, so long as we reviewed the cases every week, it was in the patients' interest to persevere.

These three patients agreed to try for a few weeks longer. Then, one day Joe phoned me about two of them, asking if I thought it was possible to recover from migraine in one week. Two of the women had come to him, individually, and said they knew why they had migraine: Each said she could not put up with her husband. Both were going to get a divorce. As soon as they made the decision, Joe said, migraine stopped and no more drugs were needed. Several months later I learned that they had followed through and gotten divorced.

The other woman in the "persevering" group also got control of her headaches. She came to Sargent one day and said that she knew what her problem was: Her husband, a politician, often brought company home unexpectedly. Migraine was her way of handling the situation— how could he bring company home if she had an incapacitating headache?

These three cases followed a pattern which has since been reported by numerous clinical researchers across the country. If a problem has a trivial cause, or a cause that is no longer of any significance in the life of the patient (the problem merely hanging on like a bad unconscious habit), it may be erased without the patient's ever becoming aware of its psychological component—its "cause." It is as though unsatisfactory neural wiring is simply rearranged by the training program. How it got that way in the first place is unimportant in these cases.

If the problem has a serious continuing cause, however, there is often a conflict of conscious and unconscious processes, as in the cases of the women who learned how to control migraine and then lost the ability. In persevering, each suddenly became aware of the problem. Persistence drove the unconscious problem to the surface, a decision was made, and that decision terminated headaches and the need for drugs.

Raynaud's disease is a vascular dysfunction characterized by reduced blood flow in the hands and feet. The smooth muscles of blood-vessel walls in the extremities suffer chronic spasms, often, it seems, in response to some long-ago traumatic or stressful situation. In severe cases the hands turn blue or white and are extremely painful in cold weather; if the disease progresses, deterioration of the flesh of the fingers occurs, gangrene follows, and amputation may become necessary. No truly satisfactory and effective treatment has been developed. The drugs used to prevent vasoconstriction are powerful, have distressing side effects, and are rendered ineffective by prolonged use; sympathectomies (cutting of the sympathetic nerves leading to the "diseased" limb to prevent constriction of the blood vessels) of necessity are often the treatment of choice in spite of several unpleasant side effects; amputation, sometimes necessary to control gangrene, is of course the last resort.

Since temperature training in the hands was proving useful in the treatment of migraine, which is a vascular problem in the head, it was reasonable to suppose that it might prove useful in the treatment of Raynaud's disease. Shortly after working with Lillian Petroni, Elmer tried this technique with a woman from out of town who stopped at the research building to see us. Although her purpose in coming to Topeka was to inquire about biofeedback for headache control, she complained that she had Raynaud's disease too. Elmer asked if she would like to try the temperature trainer for her hands while at the lab, and when she answered yes, he took her through a training session. To her surprise, her hands turned from a rather dull gray-blue to a normal pink color as she succeeded in warming them in the first session. That was our only contact with her, except for a letter a year later saying that her Ray-

naud's problem had been greatly reduced after using the Autogenic Training phrases.

Dr. Sargent did not have time to conduct a biofeedback research project for Raynaud's disease, but he did accept a few Raynaud's patients. His assistant, Barbara Pearse, had suggested an intensive five-day temperature-training program for migraine sufferers unable to take part in the migraine research project. Barbara, a warm and dedicated young woman, met with a surprising amount of success with this five-day training procedure, and was able to include a few Raynaud's cases.

One of these patients had suffered migraine headaches for many years, until she was in a serious automobile accident. Then the headaches disappeared and were replaced by Raynaud's disease. When she began her treatment, all her fingertips had sores on them. She was extremely nervous but was determined and diligent in practice. She completed her five days of training with a feedback meter and returned to her home in Iowa with instructions to continue to practice the exercises at least three or four times daily. Three weeks later she wrote to Dr. Sargent and Barbara saying that Iowa had had eight inches of snow and that for the first time in years she had been able to shovel the snow from her porch. She could warm her hands almost every time she tried and believed she was doing very well, adding, "This is the first time I have been able to type in six years, and am I ever rusty!"

In January she wrote again, saying that she was still progressing, that it had been twelve degrees below zero and her hands "have not turned blue—not once." She also felt that she was much calmer, and added, "For some reason I don't understand, I am regaining my memory." She had "lost almost all recall" following the accident. She told of crocheting an afghan, a sweater, and a skirt since Christmas, and ended her letter by saying, "My outlook is completely different. I really feel like a new person." This last remark is one that we and many others working in biofeedback hear frequently.

Biofeedback Training

The greatest thing, then, in all education is to make the nervous system our ally instead of our enemy.

—WILLIAM JAMES

Biofeedback training was developed by several researchers, working independently in different parts of the country, mostly during the 1950s and 1960s. What is unique about what they did? They developed a new way to use electronic technology. The development can be thought of as a technological breakthrough in the sciences that study man.

An outstanding feature of modern medical devices is extreme sensitivity, an outcome of the "explosion" of electronic technology during and following World War II. Such devices can detect, from the surface of the skin, exceedingly small electrophysiological signals. In the biofeedback training procedure, these otherwise inaccessible signals are amplified, filtered, and displayed with great rapidity (speed is another feature of electronic systems). Deeply buried information about some ongoing activity inside the skin can be delivered (fed back) to the subject while it is happening, second by second, for as long as is desired. Why is this so important? It turns out that enhancing a person's sensitivity to (or bringing to consciousness of) psychophysiological processes ordinarily too subtle to be sensed makes it possible to develop a measure of voluntary control over these processes. Another way of saying this is that, with the aid of biofeedback training, consciousness and control can be extended over normally unconscious and involuntary body processes. Biofeedback training is a tool for learning psychosomatic self-regulation.

It may be possible to bring under some degree of voluntary control any physiological process that can be continuously monitored, amplified, and displayed. Research in many laboratories has demonstrated voluntary changes in such diverse functions as blood flow, heart rate, blood pressure, brain waves, gastrointestinal functions, and air flow in bronchial tubes (for asthma control). Increased, and in some cases restored, control in paralyzed or spastic muscles has also been demonstrated. These developments are considered in some detail in Chapter 6.

The earliest use of biofeedback training was probably made long ago by yogis learning to regulate the basal metabolism rate. This was accomplished by regulating breathing—for instance, learning to slow it to one breath per minute. Involuntary jerking of the diaphragm (the autonomic response to anoxia) fed back to consciousness the action of a normally unconscious process. One of the goals was to teach the body to be quiet, which indirectly is a control of the basal metabolism rate. Slow breathing was found to be associated with quietness. If the diaphragm did not jerk, the yogi could assume that learning was proceeding correctly. As will be seen later, this procedure qualifies as a noninstrumented form of biofeedback.

Another noninstrumented kind of biofeedback was developed by Johannes Schultz in Germany when he taught patients to use feedback of heart rate in the third standard exercise (control of heart rate) of Autogenic Training. The instruction was to lay the hand on the chest over the heart until the heartbeat was detected, then tell the heart what to do, using the sensed beat as an indicator of progress. This feedback is vibratory (rather than visual or auditory), and it too qualifies as biofeedback.

Instrumented biofeedback for a variety of purposes began at least as early as J. H. Bair's 1901 report called Development of Voluntary Control. We thank Barbara Brown for discovering this early study and reporting it in her book New Mind, New Body (1974). Bair used an ingenious mechanical feedback device to train people to gain control of the muscles that wiggle the ears. As quoted by Brown, Bair said he undertook the study "because of the light its solution would throw upon the nature of the will" (emphasis added).

Another early report was made by Mowrer and Mowrer (1938), who had developed a way of controlling bed-wetting in children by bringing them to consciousness when wetting began. An alarm system triggered by urine was all that was needed.

Another kind of biofeedback was used by Lawrence Kubie (1943) in training patients to get into a state of "hypnagogic reverie" in order to get information from the unconscious "without the multiple distortions that occur in the dream process." Kubie fed back amplified breathing sounds as a monotonous fixating stimulus and observed a great quieting of the body as a result, a state conducive to gaining awareness of hypnagogic imagery.

An impressive early use of biofeedback was reported by Haugen, Dixon, and Dickel (1963) in training patients suffering from anxiety tension to control their electromyographic (muscle) behavior as seen on an oscilloscope. In conjunction with this, they used a form of Progressive Relaxation (Jacobson, 1938) for home training.

It was Joe Kamiya, however, who was responsible for triggering the current wave of interest in biofeedback possibilities when he began to report, in the early 1960s, that alpha brain-wave rhythms could be detected and self-regulated by college students. It was from Joe Kamiya, in fact, that Elmer first heard of brain-wave feedback, at a meeting of the Psychophysiological Research Society in 1965. This intrigued us because it suggested another physiological indicator that would be useful in research involving voluntary control of the nervous system, in this case the central nervous system. At a later meeting of the Psychophysiological Research Society (1968), Elmer and I met Barbara Brown and heard her describe her research with EEG feedback to investigate the subjective correlates of beta, alpha, and theta occipital brain rhythms.

In the mid-1960s voluntary-control studies using biofeedback techniques were blossoming all around the country. To name only a few: Basmajian (1963) and Marinacci (1968) reported on EMG research; Hnatiow and Lang (1965) on heart rate; Hardyck, Petrinovich, and Ellsworth (1966) on control of speech muscles during silent reading. At the Veterans Administration Hospital in New Bedford, Massachusetts, Dr. Tom Mulholland and his associates were using EEG feedback instrumentation in investigating problems of vision (1962, 1966).

Our own interest, as we have said, centered on the study of relationships in the mind-body domain. In 1965 we began our research on muscle tension and the control of skin temperature (blood flow) in the hands through the use of Autogenic Training phrases and visualization (which, when combined with biofeedback, became the basis of the migraine study described in the last chapter). In what follows we will describe how we apply biofeedback training in working with patients, and discuss the larger implications of our studies of autogenic feedback training for warmth control and various related questions that emerged in our laboratory and clinical work.

We wish to focus attention on what is known about mind and body coordination for two reasons. The first is to point out that much of the information is not new but is firmly based in medical and psychological science. The second and more important reason is to let people know how orderly, reasonable, and logical biofeedback is.

There is a usefulness in showing how biofeedback works that far outweighs all academic considerations: that of helping patients (trainees) learn voluntary control of internal states. For long-lasting results in biofeedback training, it is important that patients have a clear understanding of what *they* are doing and realize that neither the machines nor the doctors are making anything happen. *It is the patient who does it.* Often physicians do not explain what is taking place to their patients. Patients are often not capable of interpreting medical terms and understanding complex explanations, and busy doctors can seldom take the time to explain a problem in laymen's language. This is one of the undesirable side effects of scientific medicine. As it has grown increasingly sophisticated and specialized, it has forgotten its humanistic manners, as well as the role of the patient in his own healing.

In working with patients we have found it effective to explain Figures 1 and 2 to them, with the understanding that we do not expect them to remember details unless they want to, but we want them to realize and remember that the ultimate machinery for self-regulation is within each person. For instance, I talked with the first migraine patient with whom we worked, Lillian Petroni, for about an hour about the coordination between psychological and physiological processes before starting her on a course of temperature training. A brief training session followed; then she took the temperature trainer home to practice twice daily by herself. The point is that by the time she left my office with the machine, she understood that there was a psychophysiological process that she could influence and that the machine would help by providing immediate information about very small changes in skin temperature. The machine helped increase her awareness of warmth in her hands.

In about two hundred subjects tested in our laboratory, wired up so that we could measure simultaneously skin temperature and blood flow in the fingers, we have found a very close correspondence between temperature and blood volume. In general, if there is an increase in

almost continuously. There was so much movement that it was difficult to know what was responsible for it. Few subjects were able to correlate the behavior of the machine with internal cues until the machine was made less sensitive.)

If a person could normally sense a temperature change in the hands within four degrees, then the machine is approximately four hundred times more sensitive than the person, so that one's ability to notice changes in the warmth of the hands is increased four hundred times while watching the machine. Because of this, we sometimes refer to biofeedback training as consciousness training, or awareness training. This electronically enhanced sensitivity provides information that makes it possible to learn to regulate hand temperature.

Let us look closely at self-regulation of hand temperature. Just what is it that a person learns to control? At first glance one would say it is skin temperature. But just below the skin, it is blood volume that is being regulated, and this is directly proportional to the diameter of blood vessels. When blood vessels increase in diameter, blood volume increases, and within seconds the temperature of the finger begins to rise. The diameter of blood vessels, in turn, is regulated by smooth muscles in the vessel walls. In the hands this smooth muscle is controlled exclusively by the action of the sympathetic section of the autonomic nervous system, and this in turn is regulated from a center of vascular control that lies in an involuntary part of the central nervous system.

At the top of the control hierarchy, then, we find a regulator in the brain subcortex that normally functions outside the realm of consciousness, and in order to learn voluntary control of hand temperature, one must develop a kind of awareness of normally unconscious involuntary events. External feedback of temperature change activates the conscious visual cortex, and gradually one learns to correlate what one sees with *subtle internal sensations* that were previously unconscious. These sensations may not be describable in words, but when they come to consciousness it becomes possible to control them. When these sensations are controlled at will, then in some automatic way *the body changes to correspond with the consciously programmed sensation.*

There is another way to say it: The person visualizes and feels the desired change that will influence the meter and allows the body to carry out the instruction. The feeling seems to be the instruction. This feeling has been reported by many successful performers to be, at least in the early stages of learning, a composite of imagery, emotion, and body sensation, but after a skill is thoroughly learned, the body sensation can be "turned on" at will, often with no need for any particular mental image or emotion.

In order to organize the major ideas we are discussing, it is useful to refer to Figure I, a representation of the brain and nervous systems and their arrangement in conscious and unconscious domains. The solid horizontal line represents the average theoretical dividing line between conscious and unconscious parts of the peripheral nervous system (PNS). The central nervous system is divided into cortex and subcortex. (The subcortex section includes the spinal cord.) The peripheral nervous system includes both the voluntary craniospinal section, which operates our normal muscular apparatus of everyday life, and the autonomic involuntary system, with its two divisions, sympathetic and parasympathetic (not shown specifically), which control vital functions and constitute the logistic support apparatus that, when operating properly, keeps us alive without our having to think about it.

In the average person, activity in the voluntary nervous system (the craniospinal nervous system) occurs in the normally conscious domain and autonomic nervous activity occurs involuntarily and unconsciously. Control of the diameter of blood vessels is not an exception to this general rule, according to medical textbooks, yet with more than two thousand trainees we found that blood-flow control in the hands is a remarkably easy thing to learn.

The autonomic, or automatic, nervous system is controlled by subcortical brain structures. Visceral, circulatory, glandular, and other such basic processes are dependent upon the autonomic nervous system. Its two classes of activity, sympathetic and parasympathetic, act together; essentially, one controls the upper limit of physiological activity and the other the lower limit. For instance, if excitement speeds up the heart too much, a built-in control circuit (the parasympathetic) operates to slow it down. If it slows excessively, another automatic control circuit (the sympathetic) acts to speed it up.

Many of the involuntary processes of the body are regulated by these two control functions. Blood flow in the peripheral parts of the body, however—the arms and legs, hands and feet—is controlled only by action in the sympathetic section of the autonomic nervous system. The only way that one can warm the hands intentionally is to increase the blood flow, and the major way the blood flow can be increased (other things being essentially equal—for example, unchanged body position) is to decrease sympathetic firing. Sympathetic firing is controlled from the brain, at the hypothalamus, so in order to warm the hands volitionally it is necessary to turn down sympathetic tone at the source: the hypothalamic control center. Because this control center regulates blood flow throughout the body, when a person learns to warm the hands, vascular relaxation and rebalancing often occur over the entire body. Presumably, this is what takes place when the temperature-control technique is used to treat migraine and Raynaud's disease.

Learning to warm the hands at will, then, is essentially learning to decrease activation in the sympathetic nervous system. The stresses of life activate the sympathetic nervous system, also known as the "fight-or-flight" system. Such activation increases blood pressure and heart rate, bringing about general activation of the body. If the tension level in the sympathetic nervous system does not drop when the crisis has passed, when the need for activation is over, but instead remains high, then psychosomatic disorders may ensue.

The next few pages present a summary of most of the biofeedback concepts we have been discussing. In Figure 2 we have drawn a flow chart representing the significant events of self-regulation. This conception falls in the domain of cybernetics, a branch of science concerned with communication and control founded by mathematician Norbert Wiener thirty years ago.

Specifically, Figure 2 is a representation of processes that occur simultaneously in the voluntary and involuntary neurological domain and in the conscious and unconscious psychological domain. The upper half of the diagram represents the normal domain of conscious processes—that is, processes of which we normally have awareness when we wish it. The lower half of the diagram represents the normal domain of unconscious processes. As mentioned before, the neurological location of conscious processes seems to be in the cerebral cortex and the craniospinal apparatus. The normal location of unconscious processes appears to be in the subcortical brain and in the autonomic nervous system.

Electrophysiological studies indicate that cerebral perceptions of outside-the-skin (OUTS) events, such as telephone calls, upper left box of the diagram, have associated with them (Arrow 1) electrical activity in both conscious and unconscious structures that are involved in emotional and mental responses. The two boxes labeled "Emotional and mental response . . ." have been placed on the midline of the diagram, divided by the horizontal center line into conscious and unconscious parts, in order to show their two-domain nature. The lower left box, "Limbic response," is placed entirely in the unconscious section of the diagram, though some neural pathways lead from limbic structures directly to cortical regions, implying that information from limbic processes can reach consciousness, or that consciousness can reach down to information in the limbic system.

The limbic system is an important link between emotions and the body. It has been intensely studied in both animals and humans since J. W. Papez's historic paper (1937) outlining its function in emotional responses. Paul MacLean (1949) coined the phrase "visceral brain" for the limbic system, and others have referred to it as the "emotional brain." The relevant point is that emotional states are reflected in, or correlated with, electrophysiological activity in the limbic system.

Of major significance is the fact that the limbic system is connected by many neural pathways, represented by Arrow 3, to the central control panel of the brain, the hypothalamus (located on the center line at the bottom of the brain above the roof of the mouth). The hypothalamus weighs only about four grams (one seventh of an ounce), but it regulates a large part of the body's automatic neural machinery, and in addition it controls, to a large extent, the pituitary gland, which is attached to it. The pituitary, the so-called king gland of the body, is at the top of the hormonal hierarchy. Its action can precipitate or trigger off changes in other glandular structures throughout the body. With these concepts in mind, it is easy to understand how news from a telephone message can cause a person to faint, or to have a surge of blood pressure. To summarize, the perception of OUTS events leads to limbic-hypothalamic-glandular responses, and, of course, (Arrow 4) physiological changes (represented by the box at the lower right in the diagram) are the inevitable consequence.

To this point, the information is not new. Most of it was known by 1947. What *is* new is the fact that if a physiological change is detected by a sensitive electronic instrument and fed back to a person by a light or tone (Arrow 5), that person is thereby provided with visual or auditory information about inside-the-skin (INS) events, which can be used to learn control of the process. We can say the person perceives, in a certain way, what is going on inside the skin. The ease in learning and the degree of success are different for different people, but the fact remains that voluntary autonomic learning is possible.

Based on experience with hundreds of persons over a period of years, it seems to us that it is reasonable to conclude that biofeedback works because the feedback of INS information generates, results in, or causes a new emotional response (Arrow 6), a response to normally unconscious INS information. The new emotional response is associated with a new limbic response (Arrow 7). It combines with or replaces or modifies the original limbic response (Arrow 2). This new limbic response in turn develops a new pattern of hypothalamic firing and pituitary secretion, and a new physiological state ensues. Thus, a closed cybernetic loop is established. Closing the cybernetic loop seems to bridge the normal gap between conscious and unconscious processes, between voluntary and involuntary processes.

In learning voluntary control of normally unconscious processes, we do not become directly aware of the neural pathways and muscle fibers involved, any more than we become aware of what cerebral and subcerebral nerves are involved in playing ping-pong. But, as in ping-pong, when we get external objective visual feedback we can learn to modify the internal setup so as to bring about changes in the desired direction. Again it is worth noting that, without exception, *everything that is learned is learned with feedback of some kind,* whether it involves the cortico-striate system or the cortico-subcortico-autonomic system.

During the first interview with a patient, in order to help him understand what biofeedback training is about, we explain Figure 2. By the time that explanation is completed, the person knows about the mental-emotional apparatus and the physiological apparatus involved in making biofeedback work. He may not have faith in his own ability to learn conscious voluntary control of hand temperature, but we try to leave no doubt that the mind and body influence each other.

In discussing Figure 2 with patients, we generally say that our purpose in presenting this information is merely to let them know that the circuits and control systems are all there inside them. We talk about the workings of the involuntary nervous system, of which people are usually unaware, and which normally they need make no effort to regulate, and point out that the traditional difference between learning in the voluntary and the autonomic systems has hinged on the presence or absence of feedback of information to the cortex.

We use the example of an automobile and talk of the need for visual feedback in learning to drive a car. In learning to drive we get feedback by looking out the windshield, but with the autonomic nervous system we normally do not have feedback—a handicap in attempting to learn self-regulation. If we are given feedback of a normally unconscious involuntary process, in many cases it is possible to learn to control or regulate it, if we want to. "Wanting to" is essential, and we will say more about this later.

Often biofeedback is not needed for more than a few weeks. Most important, biofeedback is not addictive, because voluntary internal control is established, rather than dependence on an external agency. Drugs are often addictive, and dosages almost always need to be increased in order to compensate for the body's natural habituation. With biofeedback, voluntary sensitivity to subtle internal cues is increased rather than decreased, and therefore the use of feedback devices need be only temporary. This increased sensitivity, indicated by Arrow 8, is an essential step in closing the internal cybernetic loop. In other words, as voluntary sensitivity increases, the patient is able to become aware of what is going on inside the skin, whenever that is useful, and eventually no longer needs external feedback.

This freedom from the machine was illustrated in one of Bernard Engel's tachycardia patients, who, after some weeks of biofeedback practice, said that she did not need his heart-rate machine any more in order to know how fast her heart was beating (Engel, 1970). She was aware of her heart rate *any time she turned her attention to it*. In terms of the diagram, she used Arrows 5 and 6 at first. Then Arrow 8 began to develop, accompanied by the formation of Arrows 9 and 10. When these two were well developed, she no longer needed Arrows 5, 6, and 8, and the machine was no longer necessary. The internal control loop (Arrows 9–10–7–3–4–9) had been established. She could now modify her own dynamic equilibrium without external aids. She could adjust the homeostatic (physiologically self-regulating) balance point involving heart rate at will, by making internal changes. She learned to choose the psychophysiological states that were productive of self-regulation, such as a certain kind of breathing and a certain response—or lack of response—to environmental stress.

It is an important empirical finding that in self-regulating a physiological response to psychological stress, the biofeedback patient apparently handles the stress itself in a satisfactory way. This result probably stems from the fact, first recognized by Johannes Schultz, that when a patient's motivation and volition bring about recovery from a psychosomatic problem, there is little need for another symptom. Another way of putting it is to say that when autogenic feedback training is used, it seems as if the problem is erased from brain structures. The patient apparently self-deconditions both psychologically and physiologically.

Although volition has been an implicit ingredient in the previous discussion, it is now necessary to distinguish two types of volition associated with voluntary and involuntary parts of the nervous system. The normally conscious voluntary sections of the nervous system (the cortical and craniospinal in Figures 1 and 2) respond in particular to *active* volition, and the normally unconscious and involuntary sections (the subcortical and autonomic) respond in particular to *passive* volition. Active volition is the familiar type we use every day of our lives without thinking about it. Passive volition, on the other hand, must be consciously developed and used.

In Autogenic Training, reference is made to "passive concentration" as a technique for bringing about changes in the autonomic nervous system. In biofeedback training we have come to prefer the phrase "passive volition." Volition is definitely involved, though not the will of action. Instead, through visualization one simply tells the body what is wanted and allows the body to do it. The meter then moves to the left or to the right, or the light flashes or the tone sounds. Because the instruments reveal moment-by-moment physiological behavior, the effects of different strategies can be easily and rapidly tested.

If people try to force their hands to get warm with active willpower, the hands almost always get cooler. If a subject then stops this strategy, the temperature of the hands usually increases (which gives us a good opportunity to explain passive volition). One just tells the body what to do, usually by visualizing the desired state, then detaches from the situation—steps aside, gets out of the way, so to speak—and allows the body to do it.

Another example of the difference between active and passive volition is in falling asleep. If you try to force yourself to go to sleep you become more awake, and the harder you try the less you succeed, until finally you are exhausted and wide awake. With passive volition, however, you visualize and feel the body becoming quiet, the emotions becoming tranquil, and the thoughts stopping. Effort itself is turned off. Our normally involuntary and unconscious sections can often learn to behave in ways that are consciously chosen if we visualize what is wanted and ask the being (body, mind, brain, unconscious, or whatever) to do it.

A metaphoric way of putting it is to say that the cortex plants the idea in the subcortex and then allows nature to take its course without interference. That is passive volition. The operational idea suggested by "the cortex plants" is analogous to farming. There is an apt correspondence between inside-the-skin responses to our volition and nature's response to a farmer's volition. The farmer (a) desires and visualizes the crop, (b) plants the seed in the earth, (c) allows nature to take its course, and (d) reaps.

In a corresponding way we (a) desire and visualize a certain kind of physiological behavior (this is a conscious cortical process); (b) plant the idea in the unconscious, the earth of our psychological being (physiologically, the subcortical area); (c) let nature take its course (we must allow our psychophysiological machinery to function naturally, without anxiety or analytically picking at what we are trying to do, just as the farmer does not dig up his seeds to see if they are sprouting); and (d) reap mind-body stability.

In this context, our personal unconscious can be thought of as nature inside our skins. The paradox of passive volition inside the skin must be lived to be understood. When it is lived, inner harmony seems to be reflected outside the skin. Many biofeedback trainees have told us that people have said to them that they look different, they seem different, their personalities are different, they appear more poised. We try to guard against telling a new patient too much about this possibility, in order to prevent the creation of anticipatory resistance or fear in the patient. Furthermore, we wish to prevent a Pollyanna optimism or overblown expectation of change. A fear of change (even a change for the better) is experienced by most of us if change means giving up something we know for something we do not know. One psychiatric patient said to me, "How do I know I want self-control? Maybe life is better the way I am now."

In addition to being cautious (even though optimistic) when talking with patients, it is advisable when talking with colleagues not to give the impression of being an enthusiast. To be enthusiastic is permissible, but to be an enthusiast means that judgments are probably biased continuously in favor of beliefs. We try to remain on the conservative side, though it is not always easy.

In working with patients we do not often point out that the "detachment" to which we refer is a basic feature of yogic training. Yogis found out long ago that the autonomic nervous system does not respond to force. There are other similarities between biofeedback training and yoga. The most obvious similarity is that both are systems of self-regulation, in contrast to programming through hypnosis, symptom control through drugs, and direct surgical modification of the patient. In yoga, even though the student follows a system in order to learn self-regulation, he alone is responsible for its application. The same degree of responsibility is found in biofeedback training. The machines do nothing but detect physiological processes and present the information to a patient, but it sometimes takes two or three weeks before the patient is convinced of the passive nature of biofeedback machines, that they are simply like mirrors.

Psychosomatic disease can be thought of as a distortion of healthy mind-body functioning that begins when psychological stress is allowed to disrupt the neural and humoral sequences of homeostatic events. A mechanical structure, or physiological process, that is strained beyond its elastic limit often cannot regain its original shape or function when the stress is relieved, even if an outside force is applied in the opposite direction. For instance, sudden powerful psychological stress can strain the human psychophysiological apparatus beyond its limits of natural recovery. Reference to this phenomena is repeatedly heard in such phrases as "His hair turned white overnight" and "She'll never be the same."

It is not necessary for stress to be overpoweringly traumatic or unpleasant, however, for it to result in psychosomatic disorder. For instance, a verbal insult often results in nothing more than a momentary feeling of discomfort. But if its effects are allowed to persist, through brooding over the memory and reexperiencing the emotions, physiological changes are bound to take place sooner or later. Voluminous neurological and biochemical evidence scattered throughout the literature testifies that chronic emotional strain is accompanied by chronic changes in homeostasis.

The good side of this tight mind-body correlation is the implication that an emotional state may be volitionally selected for correction of an undesirable physiological state, such as a psychosomatic disorder or a drug-dependency problem. And now biofeedback (which shows the physiological response to a new emotional state) is available as a new and powerful tool for implementing psychophysiological self-regulation and psychosomatic health.

Later on in this book, in Chapter 6, we will present the many different clinical uses of biofeedback training that are being developed and again discuss psychosomatic health. Now, however, let us go beyond the immediate clinical applications of biofeedback training—exciting and important as they are—to consider other ramifications of self-regulation.

5 Volition as a Metaforce

It is here contended that such a special property (that a certain property of the cerebral cortex is different from properties found in matter in general) in outstanding measure is exhibited by the dynamic patterns of neuronal activity that occur in the cerebral cortex during conscious states, and the hypothesis is developed that the brain by means of this special property enters into liaison with mind, having the function of a "detector" that has a sensitivity of a different kind and order from that of any physical instrument.

—SIR JOHN ECCLES

Fundamental among [man's] inner powers, and the one to which priority should be given, is the tremendous, unrealized potency of man's *will*. Its training and use constitute the foundation of all endeavors. There are two reasons for this: the first is the will's central position in man's personality and its intimate connection with the core of his being—his very self. The second is the will's function in deciding what is to be done, in applying all the necessary means for its realization and in persisting in the task in the face of all obstacles and difficulties. . . . Therefore I believe that the right procedure is to postpone all intellectual discussions and theories on the subject and begin by *discovering* the reality and the nature of the will *through its direct existential experience.*

—ROBERTO ASSAGIOLI

As we worked with biofeedback and became acquainted with the voluminous literature on psychophysiological behavior in humans, it seemed useful to propose the principle mentioned in Chapter 3. We believe that this principle refers to a fundamental characteristic of human functioning. It affirms: "Every change in the physiological state is accompanied by an appropriate change in the mental-emotional state, conscious or unconscious, and, conversely, every change in the mental-emotional state, conscious or unconscious, is accompanied by an appropriate change in the physiological state." The principle is closed, by which we mean the body affects the mind, the mind affects the body, and then the new body state affects the mind, and so on. Whenever these psycho-physiological operations are coupled with volition, psychosomatic self-regulation occurs. This principle is supported by our own work and experience, and by other sources as well, including data gathered by many other scientists, physicians, and therapists who have worked with bio-feedback training over the last decade.

As we pointed out before, this closed-loop system is similar to a furnace and thermostat system. If you set the thermostat in your house at 70° during a spell of cold weather, the temperature will stay, within certain limits, at 70°. If the house cools off, the thermostat detects this cooling and turns the furnace on. When the temperature of the house reaches a degree or so above 70, the thermostat detects this and turns the furnace off. In other words, the furnace affects the thermostat, the thermostat affects the furnace, and so on. The furnace/thermostat system is built to be a closed-loop system for our convenience; we can choose to set the thermostat at some temperature and the system will remain where we put it. If we decide that 70° is not quite warm enough and change the thermostat to 72°, then we add a new factor to the temperature equation of our house: ourselves, our volition. The hand that resets the thermostat is the instrument of our volition. The furnace and thermostat system plus our volition make it possible to regulate the temperature of the house according to our desire.

Our volition also makes possible self-regulation inside our skins. In the furnace and thermostat system, our action is a metaforce so far as the limited furnace/thermostat system is concerned. That is, the hand resetting the thermostat acts as a force from another operational dimension, a dimension independent of the closed furnace-and-thermostat system. Continuing the analogy, we may think of our volition as a metaforce which can act to restore homeostatic balances within the neural and glandular systems of our psychosomatic being.

Volition is at the heart of the mind-body problem. Its existence, and the associated question of "free will," have been intensely debated for two or three hundred years. From an existential point of view, perhaps all that can be said about volition is that we feel as though we have it. All of us have a feeling of voluntary control, at least part of the time, regardless of our attitude toward the physical and metaphysical implications of that feeling. Few people realize, however, that the feeling or intuition of freedom has unusual significance with respect to the autonomic nervous system, the so-called involuntary nervous system. Our studies indicate that psychosomatic disease is rooted in the unconscious and that this domain is open to volition. This makes good sense if we think of volition as a metaforce with regard to our psychosomatic system. Unfortunately, most people are unaware of this possibility of self-regulation and tolerate their psychosomatic problems as if they really were externally caused diseases and not conditions brought on and maintained by unawareness and subsequent lack of control of self-destructive reactions to stress.

As mentioned earlier, we think it important to explain to our patients, before they begin biofeedback training, what they will be doing. Often the patient interrupts and says something on the order of "This is all very interesting, but how am I going to get control? How do I make it happen?" The question makes it possible to talk about the fact that although many well-known physical and psychological variables are involved in a healthy body and mind, the contribution of volition has been almost entirely ignored. What we are interested in is how to mobilize volition for mind-body coordination. If the patient is a psychologist or physician who wishes to analyze the nature of volition, we agree that it cannot be operationally defined and suggest that for the time being it be accepted as an existential fact. Most patients, however sophisticated, are willing to give it a try, if only because they are fed up with their physical state, which is obviously not under control.

Without the exercise of volition we are indeed compounded solely of our genetic predispositions and our cultural and environmental conditioning. Fortunately, however, this grim imprisonment is unnecessary. Some of our most successful people are those who learned to shape their minds and bodies to their wills, against high odds. Franklin Delano Roosevelt is one example. Ben Hogan, one of the all-time champion golfers, is another. When an automobile accident put Hogan out of action, one leg so severely damaged that doctors wanted to amputate, it was his will to refuse amputation and trust to his own healing powers. Eventually the damaged tissue developed a new vascular network. His desire to play golf would not let him stay down, and he became a Masters Champion. That galvanizing impulse guided by his visualization (of playing golf again) resulted in a yogic accomplishment of the highest level. In some way, Ben Hogan told his body what he wanted it to do, and the body complied. The question for everyone with mental, emotional, or physical problems is, of course, How do you tell it?

British medical doctors have known for a long time that some Indian yogis could demonstrate voluntary control of physiological processes that are by definition involuntary. It was reported by physicians in the last century, for instance, that certain yogis could stop their hearts, or could be buried for many days and when dug up "come back to life." These reports were not widely believed at first, but as decades passed and more reports came in, and the phenomenon of hypnosis came to Western medical attention, it became clear that the normally involuntary section of the physiological apparatus could be manipulated somehow by volition and mental instructions, primarily through control of visualization.

While discussing this point, one patient asked me, "This may be true, but how does volition get into the nervous system?" That is a tough question, the answer to which is not known. Why, when I want to use a pencil, does my hand reach out and pick it up? One way volition could get into the nervous system is to be there already (as the behaviorists would have it) as a chemical-neurological discharge system in unconscious brain structures, whose subthreshold operations automatically program us, in the same way that random processes and certain preset restrictions and rules make computer music.

Some theorists believe that this is an accurate description of how the neurological system works in human beings. They believe that somewhere in the brain, in unconscious subcortical structures surrounded by neurological and hormonal feedback loops, there is a "king cell" or "primary neural nucleus," whose random firing patterns trigger off cascading impulses through neural networks that have been genetically predetermined and then shaped by conditioning. The spontaneous activity in these subconscious networks takes account of all drives and primal motivations as well as innumerable other variables, and eventually projects neurological patterns into the cortex, at which point we say, "I just got a good idea."

This is the view from a hard-line behaviorist position. The theoretical position that seems more accurate to us, however, takes into account the data of parapsychology as evidence that mind has general characteristics (outside the skin) as well as special characteristics (inside the skin). We think the parapsychological data on psychokinesis (mind over matter outside the skin) are particularly compelling in this regard. For if anything can be made to happen in the world outside our skins by mind alone, then we must seriously consider that volition operates in the mind-nature domain as a metaforce similar to the way that we control the furnace/thermostat system.

What scientific evidence for psychokinesis is there? Plenty, we believe. For example, Dr. Justa Smith demonstrated (1972) with biochemical analysis that certain persons reputed to have healing powers can change the characteristics of enzyme solutions in test tubes. Uri Geller has demonstrated hundreds if not thousands of times that metals bend in his presence. Many people in England and on the Continent, and some in the United States, have found that after a demonstration by Uri Geller, they too can bend metal objects. Swami Rama caused a fourteen-inch aluminum knitting needle to rotate on a pivot in our laboratory. These are only a few of the recent events in the long history of documented psychokinetic phenomena. Probably best known in the field of parapsychological research is the work of J. B. Rhine and his team at Duke University, who amassed statistical proof of ESP and other parapsychological phenomena. The crux of the matter is that there is no way in which psychokinesis can be causally attributed to the movement of neurons or chemicals in our brains.

The point here and throughout this book is that humankind has more talents and more potential for self-regulation than we usually use or take credit for. It is not merely that parapsychological phenomena do occur, but that if psychokinesis is a fact outside the skin, then we might assume also that it is a fact inside the skin. *Mind over body, inside the skin, is a special case of mind over nature.* Even though very few people seem able to demonstrate the working of mind over nature, it puts into perspective the phenomena of self-regulation. Those who can make such things happen, such as don Juan and don Genaro in Castaneda's reports, Rolling Thunder in Doug Boyd's report, and Swami Rama in our reports, maintain that *all* people can demonstrate a measure of the same capacity if they choose to develop themselves. We believe that the concept of volition outlined here is the key to the construction of a new self-image for humans as a whole.

If we carefully examine the old reports about mind and also consider modern data, we can hypothesize that *mind is an energy structure,* without going into detailed discussion here. All of the unusual people with whom we have worked—such as Swami Rama, Jack Schwarz, and the American Indian medicine man Rolling Thunder—maintain that mind is an energy structure. By "mind" is meant, in this case, all of what has been referred to in the past as emotions, mind, and spirit.

Aurobindo Ghose, the great Indian philosopher who wrote *The Synthesis of Yoga* (1955), has an interesting way of putting it. He said that if you are embarrassed by the word "spirit," think of spirit as the subtlest form of matter. But if you are not embarrassed by the word "spirit," then you can think of matter as the densest form of spirit. In other words, in his estimation one basic energy appears in many different forms. Physical bodies, emotions, thoughts, and spirit are all interpenetrating energy structures in Sri Aurobindo's system. They are not separate from one another but appear differently because of some characteristic, perhaps analogous to density. They are unified only inside the skin of a living being. One compact way of saying this is: "All of the body is in the mind, but not all of the mind is in the body." That is, anything that is demonstrated in the body is in actuality accomplished in the mind. This is the basic position put forth in the yoga sutras of Patanjali, which date back to the second century before Christ. For Western science this concept had no significant support before the advent of parapsychological research some decades ago. (By the way, the concept of the body being a reflection of mind is certainly not the nonsubstantial concept of George Berkeley's philosophy, for it is definitely a concept which involves substance.)

This idea—mind contains body—is the reverse of the behaviorist position which maintains that the psychological state is always, and only, the consequence of preceding biochemical processes. There is no hard evidence to support this idea, yet it is a kind of faith with some. The idea that both the psychological state and the biochemical processes are particular conditions of an energy continuum in which mind is a substance or energy that is normally imponderable (that is, it cannot yet be detected with our standard nonbiologic measuring devices) is supported by at least four kinds of data: (1) self-regulation of nonsensory physiological processes, such as SMU firing, through biofeedback training (inferential support); (2) simple human awareness, in which we feel we make choices (existential support); (3) statistical data from ESP studies (statistical support); and (4) hard data from psychokinetic studies.

As Freudian and Jungian psychologies have well demonstrated, a limited behaviorist position is not without merit, for many, perhaps most, of our choices are obviously predetermined, not free. Many choices seem to result from unconscious processes, which may well be thought of as neurological potentials and biochemical gradients. But what is of vital significance to us is the fraction of opportunities that exist in which metachoices can be made—that is, choices made by a person from outside his or her own closed neurochemical system.

The image of man as a biochemical robot, without freedom or dignity, does not hold up in the light of modern psychophysics research. It is time for the idea of man as a robot to be replaced by a more comprehensive view. The development of a potent, positive self-image is particularly useful to all those who are depressed by circumstances and feel beaten. One thinks especially of paralysis victims, psychosomatic casualties, mental patients, prisoners, elderly poor people, and people dependent on drugs (including alcohol). The first need for them is to reject their old self-image and accept the possibility, however difficult to implement, that through the use of volition one can learn to modify mind-body processes.

William James is an example of one who, after much suffering, accepted such a possibility. He was never a robust person, and suffered a good deal of illness as well as much pain from a back disorder. His ill health was accompanied by mental unrest, indecisiveness, and depression. His concern about a relationship between his physical illness and his mental depression led in time to the study of brain pathology and to a lifelong interest in mind-body relationships.

James spent his twenty-fifth year (1867–1868) traveling in Europe for his health, visiting various spas, but he returned home feeling weary and depressed. Nevertheless, he studied for and completed his medical examination. In 1870 he suffered a breakdown, which he wrote of in his diary as "a great dorsal collapse—carrying with it a moral one. Today I touched bottom and perceived plainly that I must face the choice with open eyes."

The choice pertained to the question of free will—whether to give up the idea completely or to accept it and follow it. A year before he had written to a friend, "I'm swamped in an empirical philosophy. I feel that we are Nature through and through, that we are wholly conditioned, that not a wiggle of our will happens save as a result of physical laws . . ." Now he was in need of something that would allow him to draw on his willpower to pull himself out of his depression and pain.

It was at this time that he again took up a book of philosophical essays by Charles Renouvier that he had picked up in France just before leaving for home two years earlier. He reread Renouvier's definition of free will: "the sustaining of a thought because I choose to when I might have other thoughts." He decided to accept it, saying that his first act of free will would be to believe in free will; he would cultivate the feeling of free will, read books supporting it, and act as though its existence had been verified.

James recovered from his depression, and his health, although never strong, greatly improved. In 1872 he began teaching at Harvard and embarked on a long, creative, and productive career in philosophy and psychology.

Since the heyday of William James, at the turn of the century, psychology has suffered from its exclusion of consciousness and attention because they could not be defined in operational terms. The same is true of visualization, imagery, and, of course, volition. That is, these words cannot be defined in terms of physical procedures that lead to their measurement. However, they can be experienced. In Western psychophysics, a rapidly developing countercurrent of modern psychology, it is deemed necessary to explore both operational definitions and existential (experiential) definitions.

The tool of biofeedback instrumentation provides a powerful impetus to countercurrent studies, because it enables research to be done in a previously unresearchable domain. Now we are beginning to reinstate these abandoned concepts, gradually reintroducing operationalism into the domain of existentialism (and even seeing our colleagues on other fronts reintroduce existentialism into the domain of operationalism). In a manner of speaking, this is what science has always done. The scientists of the past whom we now most honor are those who successfully extended operational knowledge into the domain of existential knowledge. Gravity was an existential fact for everyone before Galileo came along, but only after he dropped his weights from the Leaning Tower of Pisa was it possible to delineate the characteristics of gravity in terms of physical operations and procedures.

Eventually, as more sensitive instrumentation is developed, we will move away from mainly existential definitions toward operational definitions. But for the present the science of mind-body coordination, which we might call the science of consciousness and think of as a mod-

---

ern branch of psychophysics, must deal with an existential dimension whose validity can only be approximated through consensus: the agreement of many observers concerning the nature of the inner terrain.

The fact that science has an existential as well as operational characteristic is not new. Percy W. Bridgman, an outstanding physicist in the first half of this century and winner of a Nobel Prize for his discoveries in the area of high-pressure physics, pointed out that all measurements are relative to the mental frame of reference of the observer—even such simple measurements as length and width. Every definition and concept in the field of physics involves, as he says, both physical and mental operations. It is worth noting that mental operations are existential by definition. In the domain of psychophysics many of the operations or procedures are existential only (rather than physical, as in most problems in physics), and we will soon have to cope with "existential operations," a seeming paradox; but the new tide of existential information, the expansion of consciousness into uncharted realms, will not disappear by being ignored.

Attitude is a critical feature in biofeedback training, because volition is influenced by what one believes (although the psychophysiological principle itself is entirely independent of *what* people believe or do not believe). This fact was first brought to our attention in Minneapolis about 1939 by John Seaman Garns, who phrased it, "Mind operates under its own conception of itself." John Lilly, in his book *The Center of the Cyclone* (1972), says somewhat the same thing: "In the province of the mind, what is believed to be true is true or becomes true, within limits to be found experientially and experimentally. These limits are further beliefs to be transcended." In discussing her concept of mind and matter, Mary Baker Eddy seemed to refer to the same general idea, and Charles Fillmore, the founder of Unity Church, on occasion used almost the same words as John Garns, and demonstrated many times the effects of basing his life on this concept.

The average person, however, was in a bind until the advent of biofeedback training. Consider some examples. One woman, who with the help of a biofeedback machine was learning to warm her hands, asked, "Do you have to have faith to operate this machine?" The answer was that to begin with faith was totally unnecessary, because the machine is a faith enhancer. No more faith is required to learn to operate it than to learn to drive a car. We do not have to believe or have faith that the car will turn to the left if we turn the steering wheel to the left. All that is necessary is to try it. Then we know.

Another woman, very pessimistic about her ability to succeed with any biofeedback machine, maintained before her first training session that even if everyone else could do it, she wouldn't be able to. She was "a born loser," and nothing would work for her. I taped the thermistor (the temperature-sensing element) of a temperature machine to the index finger of her right hand and said that the best thing to do was just begin and see what would happen. Although it is not necessary to use phrases for self-programming in order to begin, we have found that the use of autogenic-type phrases, combined with biofeedback, is very effective in initiating change. (Appendix I contains the list of phrases we use with all patients who are referred to us for biofeedback training.)

I began with the phrase "I feel quite quiet," allowed about fifteen seconds for her to repeat the phrase silently to herself, and then went on to the second phrase. By the time I had reached the twelfth phrase (or formula, as it is called in Autogenic Training), the temperature of the woman's finger had dropped 5°F. I stopped giving her the phrases, showed her the meter, and said, "Congratulations, you really have control." She looked at the meter and saw that the temperature had dropped —much to her surprise, because she had expected nothing at all would happen. "What do you mean? It went the wrong way." My reply was "On the contrary, it did exactly what you said it would. You said that if you tried to warm your hand it wouldn't work for you, even if other people could do it, and you proved it by making the temperature go down. Obviously you have a remarkable degree of coordination between conscious and unconscious processes."

She looked very flustered. Then she laughed and said, "Well, maybe I am doing something. Now I'll really try to make my hand get warm." Within three minutes her temperature had dropped another 2°F, and then she said, "Well, it moved, but it won't go up for me. I give up." Within a few seconds the temperature stopped decreasing, and within half a minute it started up. It went up continuously for about three minutes, increasing about 4°F. I said, "That's lesson number one. Give up. The involuntary nervous system can't be forced the way you usually force your muscles. You must learn how to visualize what you want to have happen and then allow the body to do it."

The rapidly rising temperature really impressed her, and she said enthusiastically, "Look at that. It's rising, it's really going up!" Within seconds the temperature stopped increasing and began going down again. That gave me a chance to say, "That's lesson number two. Don't get excited. In order to make your hands get warm you must keep your cool. First tell the body what to do, by visualizing what you want to have happen, then be detached and just allow the body to do it." I didn't tell her at the time that detachment was one of the primary goals in yoga. She was a scientific type, for whom the words "yoga" and "meditation" smacked of some far-off nonsense. Later, I did discuss meditation with her and suggested that anything that had lasted for so many thousands of years couldn't be all wrong.

There seems to be a hierarchy of effectiveness of psychological states with respect to self-regulation of physiological processes. The hierarchy might be arranged as follows: To hope, to hypothesize, to believe, to know—and biofeedback makes it possible to leap the entire distance at once. Anyone who tries a biofeedback machine has hypothesized something, and the experience of using the machine propels the person from hypothesizing to knowing. Hope is needed in order to initiate action, but it alone is not enough. The difficulty with prayer, for instance, is that it is usually loaded with supplication and with anxiety, doubt, and fear that the prayer will not be answered. This attitude is self-defeating.

The ability to leap from hypothesis to knowing is what makes biofeedback more effective than hypnosis. In hypnosis the subject or patient must have faith (at least at an unconscious level) in the ability of the hypnotist to program the mind and body in a satisfactory way. But many people do not believe at any level that hypnosis works, and as a result it is not effective with them. Even after a person has successfully used self-hypnosis for a period of months, quite often the ability to do it wanes and the problem returns. In our estimation, this loss of control is a result of mistakenly depending on someone else in the first place, instead of developing one's own volitional capacities.

It is worth repeating that, whether we are talking about prayer, meditation, hypnosis, Autogenic Training, or biofeedback training, the issue is the training of the unconscious. Psychosomatic disease strikes from or has a component in the autonomic nervous system—in other words, in the unconscious. Biofeedback is highly useful in training the unconscious, because it bridges the gaps between conscious and unconscious, voluntary and involuntary, cortex and subcortex, and even between reason and intuition. Speaking metaphorically, and perhaps literally, biofeedback seems to provide a means for bridging the functional schism between the left and right hemispheres of the brain.

It has been known for a long time that the left and right hemispheres of the human brain, though not the animal brain, have different functions. This was one of the primary findings of pioneer psychophysiologists such as Ward Halstead, who researched the effects of brain damage on psychological functions. Recently, a summary and synthesis of research in this field by Robert Ornstein, in his book *The Psychology of Consciousness* (1972), shows quite clearly that the left and right cortical hemispheres of the brain play different roles in the expression of personality. The left hemisphere is involved with ratiocinative processes, with thinking that is analytical, rational, logical, and discursive, and the right hemisphere with intuitive processes, with synthesis and gestalts, with perceiving the whole (which is something more than the sum of its parts), with music, art, and poetry.

Needless to say, it takes both kinds of functioning to make a whole, normal, healthy human being. However, people whose personalities reflect an equal balance of left and right hemisphere involvement are rare indeed. Most personalities reflect more of left than of right, or more of right than of left. If we plotted the distribution there would be two bell-shaped (Gaussian) curves, one to the left and one to the right of a point in the center of the base line, which represents the perfectly balanced personalities.

It has been suggested by some that consciousness resides in the left, ratiocinative half of the brain and unconsciousness in the right, intuitive half. This is incorrect. The domains of consciousness and unconsciousness which we have been speaking about are not physically restricted along left-right anatomical lines as much as along cortex and subcortex lines. In any case, it is self-evident that some fully conscious individuals are rarely logical, analytical, or rational, but are mainly intuitive and artistic, and vice versa. Some rare persons are consciously both rational and intuitive much of the time.

In India and Tibet the left side of the body is called the feminine side and the right side of the body is called the masculine side. Since the right side of the body is controlled from the left hemisphere of the brain and the left side of the body is controlled from the right side of the brain, the left hemisphere might be described as masculine and the right hemisphere as feminine. We must emphasize that all men and all women have all these characteristics to some degree, though these left-

and right-hemisphere characteristics do seem to be correlated to some degree with the sex of the body. Women are generally more intuitive than men, and men are often more analytical than women, but it is only a tendency and not a rule. Cultural stereotypes may enter in here, as well. All of us know couples in which the poetic, intuitive one is the husband and the practical, rational, down-to-earth partner is the wife.

In traditional Chinese thinking, all of nature consists of masculine and feminine energies, in the sense of the two sets of personality characteristics. The left cortex may be considered as the modern Western representative of the ancient Chinese yang energy or force, and the right cortex as representative of yin energy or force.

Everything in nature appears to be polarized. Magnets have north and south poles, electrical charges are positive and negative, and so forth. It is clear that without this polarity there would be no cohesion and thus no formation of structures such as cells. Later, we will discuss further the left-right dichotomy in cortical functioning and mention some of the theories that relate to synchronization of brain waves between the two hemispheres. For now, suffice it to say that with biofeedback training it seems that the two "halves" of a person's being tend to come into more harmonious relationship with each other and with the underlying subcortical structures that control the autonomic nervous system.

Harking back to our discussion of the need for both existential and operational data in modern psychophysics, we note that existential processes and phenomena are essentially right-hemisphere knowledge, and that which is operational is essentially left-hemisphere knowledge. The progress of science seems to be coincident with the development of left-hemisphere operations that analyze, define, and explain what was previously limited to right-hemisphere cognition.

It is often the case that people who are guided more by their left hemisphere than their right think that after they have successfully dismembered an existential state, they have explained it. This conceit is the one which Korzybski warned against in *Science and Sanity* (1948) when he pointed out that "the map is not the terrain." Every left hemisphere model of reality is only that—merely a model—and those predominantly left-hemisphere persons who deny their existential base often develop an antihumanistic bias because of the struggle within their own natures to remain uncontaminated by intuition.

On the other hand, the anti-intellectual posture of "right-hemisphere people" (to continue to use a shorthand metaphor), which can be found in some of the more extreme developments of humanistic psychology, is as far to the right (in cortex) as academic killjoys are to the left.

Biofeedback training often leads to a synthesis of these characteristics. Perhaps the most unexpected thing that many psychiatrists, medical doctors, and clinicians have observed in patients who used this training for self-regulation of physiological problems is that personality changes accompanied the physiological changes. If we look again at Figure 2, we can guess what happened in these patients. In order to change the physiological state, they had to change their emotional and mental states. They might have been unaware of the fact that that was what they were doing, thinking that they were changing primarily a physiological state, but their personalities began to reflect the changes. It is as if for each individual there is not only an ideal homeostatic balance in the physiological domain, but also an ideal homeostatic balance in the personality domain. Movement toward the establishment of healthy homeostasis in one tends to bring it to the other. If mind and body are integrated, how could it be otherwise?

The healing of the schizoid concept of mind-body duality means that a person can be psychosomatically healthy rather than plagued with psychosomatic disease. Psychosomatic disease is the evidence of our schizoid split, but its opposite—psychosomatic health—could become a general feature of human existence. If, starting in grade school, people learned not only that the mind and body always work together for good or ill, but that one can, with volition, induce them to work together for health, their choices could begin to make it so.

The Varieties of
Biofeedback Experience

"The trouble with Archie is he don't know how to worry without getting upset."

—EDITH BUNKER

... Tension is a habit. As we see it, the chronically tense person has practiced tensing and bracing innumerable times; "practice makes perfect," and hence he has become as proficient at it as he is at playing golf or typing if he pays much attention to those activities. He has not, of course, purposefully or knowingly practiced being tense, but the end result is the same.

... We daily see people who are braced as though a lion were lurking around the corner. It is our belief that they started reacting this way, as a rule, when they were quite young.

—GERHARD HAUGEN, HENRY DIXON, HERMAN DICKEL

Wilhelm Von Humboldt once ventured the optimistic belief that a time would come when it would be a disgrace to be sick and sickness would necessarily be regarded as resulting from perverse ideas. His friend Goethe expressed this more poetically: "What we nurture in ourselves will grow: that is nature's eternal law."

—HANNES LINDEMAN

In the following pages, we make no attempt to be inclusive with respect to either the kinds of problems that have been handled with biofeedback or the people who have been involved. Our purpose is merely to discuss one or two representative examples of research and clinical work in each of the major areas of biofeedback with enough depth so that the reader can get a good idea of procedures that are followed and results that are obtained. One of the best sources of information is the series of books called Biofeedback and Self-Control (*Chicago: Aldine*

Publishing Co.). The first annual and a reader were published in 1971 and in each succeeding year a number of significant and representative scientific papers have been collected and published.

We ourselves generally receive a few thousand letters and phone calls of inquiry each year, a large fraction from patients throughout the country. To them we send a paper or two related to their specific problems if possible, one or two general articles on biofeedback, and a form letter accompanied by a list of doctors in their area who know something about biofeedback and who, if unable to help directly, may be able to make a referral to another doctor who can help. Our list includes almost all of the states and is continuously growing as we add the names of participants in our biofeedback seminar and workshop, conducted weekly in the research department of the Menninger Foundation. The workshop lasts two days and is open to all in the helping professions, including physicians, psychologists, psychotherapists, physical therapists, teachers, social workers, ministers—in short, anyone who may be involved in the task of education, maintaining health, or restoring health. The names of the physicians, psychotherapists, and clinical psychologists who attend these workshops are added to the referral list. The list also includes others in the field whose work we know of through personal contact or through especially significant research or clinical reports that have come to our attention.

Elsewhere we have discussed the broad division of the nervous system into normally conscious and normally unconscious parts. The central nervous system (CNS) includes the brain's cortex and subcortex. The peripheral nervous system (PNS) includes the craniospinal section, for operation of the normally voluntary striate muscular apparatus, and the autonomic section, with its sympathetic and parasympathetic divisions, for operating the normally involuntary logistic support apparatus, which, when functioning properly, keeps us alive and well without our having to think about it.

An example of autonomic nervous system control is the regulation of blood flow through constriction and dilation of smooth muscles in blood-vessel walls throughout the body. Such regulation has generally been outside conscious control (except perhaps in the accomplished yogi). In fact, the functions under autonomic control are so far from conscious awareness that, like the jackass who needed to be whacked over the head "to get his attention" before being ordered into the barn, we must often be whacked by some major illness before we realize we must attend to autonomic functions that may have gone awry.

Considered below are some of the major areas of autonomic behavior in which biofeedback has had an impact.

Heart Behavior

The heart is a group of muscles. To a large extent it, like the muscle in blood vessel walls, is under autonomic (involuntary) nervous control. A number of variables combine to regulate heart behavior, including genetic and conditioned factors (the autonomic habits that the body has learned). Psychophysiological inputs such as fear and joy, and physiological factors, such as whether one is resting, jogging, whatever, also determine heart behavior at any given moment. Considering the great number and variety of determinants, and the complexities of their moment-to-moment interactions, it is easy to see why autonomic regulators evolved for control of the heart and circulatory system. Be that as it may, the point here is that because certain aspects of the heart's ongoing activity are readily perceived with the aid of biomedical instruments, it is possible to feed back to a person information about the behavior of the heart and thereby provide an opportunity to learn conscious control.

An early study investigated heart-rate stabilization (Hnatiow and Lang, 1965). The subjects were forty normal, healthy, male university students. Twenty of them (the experimental group) were asked to keep the heart rate as steady as possible during the experiment. They were instructed to watch the heart-rate display (synchronized with the output of a cardiotachometer) and told that keeping the pointer in the center of the display would help them in their task. The remaining twenty subjects (the control group) were instructed to keep their body processes at a steady level and to track the pointer visually. Pointer movements were not synchronized with the subject's heart rate but merely simulated cardiac change. The findings indicated that subjects who are given meaningful information can significantly reduce normal heart-rate variability.

The most comprehensive clinical research in the area of heart-rate control is that of Bernard Engel and his associates. An early study (1971) described work with patients suffering from premature ventricular contraction (*PVC*), which can be thought of as erratic heart rhythm. Eight patients took part in the study, and each was told the nature of the experiment in detail. They were informed as to the response being monitored and allowed to inspect their own records throughout the experiment. Visual feedback was provided by three lights: a green light to signal the patient to speed the heart, a red light signaling to slow down the heart, and a yellow light that stayed on whenever the heart rate was correct. Most of the patients participated in ten sessions, with about thirty-four minutes of each session devoted to each of four conditions: (1) heart-rate speeding, (2) heart-rate slowing, (3) alternate speeding and slowing, and (4) control of heart-rate variability. In addition, the patient was provided with information about the occurrence of each premature contraction.

All of the patients learned some degree of heart-rate control. Four were able to reduce the frequency of PVCs significantly and to maintain control without additional training during a three- to twenty-one-month follow-up. A fifth patient learned to recognize PVCs through "internal awareness" and to control them through resting. Three subjects did not learn PVC control in the forty sessions.

In another study (1975) Engel demonstrated that if the EKG (electrocardiographic) signal is displayed on an oscilloscope so that the flub-dup *action of each heartbeat is displayed as a visible spike-and-hump pattern (familiar to anyone who follows the medical dramas of TV), then it is possible to learn to control sections of the heartbeat. The salient features of the EKG signal are called the R wave and the T wave. Generally speaking, the R wave is taller than the T wave, but with certain heart peculiarities the R wave is too short, or sometimes is upside down relative to the T wave. Engel showed that simply by watching the oscilloscope and willing a change, subjects can learn to increase the height of the R wave.

This demonstration ranks along with Basmajian's single-motor-unit research as revolutionary, to say the least. It is theory-busting. If individual bits of heart behavior can be self-regulated through the feedback of information, what does this imply for the control of other organs in the body?

Recently we have begun clinical research with a few patients referred to us by Menninger doctors for biofeedback training. We have worked in an exploratory way with two heart patients, both of whom received help from training. The following is not a report but simply the story,* *in some detail, of the treatment and response to treatment of one of these patients. I hope that such an account, not to be found in professional journals, may prove to be both enlightening and useful.*

The patient was a woman with tachycardia and erratic heartbeat who came to see me in February of 1975. She had seen Biofeedback: The Yoga of the West, *a film about our study in India of a number of yogis who displayed unusual physiological controls and our research in our laboratory in Topeka, demonstrating that self-regulation of certain physiological processes can be gained with the aid of biofeedback. "Maybe I could be trained to help myself," she said. She told me that her heart rate was very high, normally about 100 to 110 beats per minute and racing at times from 120 to 150 beats per minute. (Normal heart rate is roughly 70 beats per minute.) This frightened her, as did the "extra" systoles (contractions) she sometimes felt. Before beginning training, she had had to be rushed to the emergency room as often as two or three times in a six-week period.*

I explained to her that it would be necessary for us to have a referral from her doctor before we could accept her as a subject. I briefly discussed the rationale diagram (Figure 2) with her and outlined what the training procedure would be if the referral was forthcoming. We would begin with temperature training in order to relax the autonomic nervous system, the system which controls heart behavior, and add EMG training for general relaxation. After she had learned to use these relaxation techniques in times of stress, she could begin work with the heart-rate feedback meter, practicing direct control of heart rate, learning to slow and speed her heart at will.

The referral from her doctor was received, and we started with the temperature trainer, teaching her to increase the warmth in her hands (which means, of course, increasing the blood flow to the hands). This necessitates relaxation of the autonomic nervous system—turning off the fight-or-flight pattern. After two sessions she took the temperature meter home with instructions to practice twice daily, recording beginning and ending temperatures and her answers to questions regarding her experiences during each session.

She soon learned to warm her hands from approximately 82°F to around 90°F, and later from beginning temperatures of 85–90°F to about 95°F. When she was proficient in warming her hands I suggested that she transfer the thermistor first to one foot, then to the other, in-

creasing circulation to her legs and feet. She could soon feel the increase in warmth in her thighs—which she said had a tendency to be cold— and in her feet. After about four weeks of training she reported that she no longer needed to have a hot water bottle at her feet at night.

During this time she also came to our lab twice a week to practice relaxation of the frontalis muscle in the forehead with the EMG trainer. The relaxation usually generalizes to the rest of the body, and she learned to relax very deeply. In addition to working with two biofeedback machines, she used some breathing exercises and Autogenic Training relaxation and warmth phrases whenever she felt her heart reacting to hurry or stress.

This patient cooperated beautifully and took an interest in making herself well. During March her reports indicated that she was able to use her training in many ways. A brief use of the breathing and relaxation techniques helped her control her pulse rate and handle pressures of hurrying and of parties and other social engagements. By nature an emotional person, she told of handling various reactions in calmer ways, having "a better temper." She reported waking at three o'clock one morning with a very severe headache. She sat up to reach for some medication on her night stand, then thought, "No, I'll use my exercises." In twenty minutes her headache was gone; she slept soundly and wakened refreshed.

This woman and her family had come to Topeka from a home "by the mountains and the sea" in a foreign land. She has been able to deal with old memories of her home and times there (such memories often flood up during deep relaxation) without undue emotion. More recently she has been reexperiencing happy memories of her family here, "good times with sun and in the garden." Such images come when she feels "between awake and asleep." On her record sheet she wrote, "I wanted to sing, I felt happy."

On April 10 she reported that she had seen her cardiologist and that the condition of her heart was improved. He was pleased that she had not had to go to the emergency room since starting her training. She told him that she could intentionally slow her heart, but when he said, "All right, show me," and placed his fingers on her pulse, she thought, "What have I done? Now I am frightened, how can I slow my heart?" She closed her eyes and thought, "Body, don't go back on me now," took several deep, even breaths, and then began repeating silently, "My *heartbeat is slow and calm, my heartbeat is slow and calm." Soon he stopped her, saying, "Yes, you are slowing your heart rate." In spite of the challenging situation, she had succeeded.*

Through the remainder of April she became increasingly aware of being able to handle her heart problem, expressed in such ways on her record sheet as "Extra systoles before my temperature training. I was afraid. I thought to calm down and I did it." Another time: "I have my pulse very high when I begin and I succeed in slowing it." One comment was amusingly Americanized: "I was uptight but felt loose afterwards." Some comments indicated awareness of psychological change: "I'm beginning to face my ideas and feelings" and, again, "This is useful for me. It makes me know myself, not only muscles and body, but also my mind."

Her relaxation sessions at the laboratory were also successful, the EMG feedback meter showing after several weeks of training that frontalis muscle tension at the beginning of her sessions was generally quite low and at the end of a session was lower still. Soon she no longer needed to use the temperature and EMG biofeedback meters. She was aware of and had internalized the subtle changes necessary for voluntary control.

In May, three months after beginning to learn self-regulation through relaxation, she began working with the heart-rate meter. Her heart rate away from the laboratory averaged eighty-five to ninety beats per minute. She practiced alternately slowing and speeding her heart in order to get an increased feeling of self-control. During practice sessions she was able to slow her heart rate into the low-seventies range. Her doctor decreased her medication slightly, and she was hopeful that at her next visit he would see enough improvement to decrease it further.

This patient is a prime example of something biofeedback researchers talk about but seldom put in their professional publications. As expressed by many patients or subjects: "Biofeedback has changed my life." Before beginning her practice session at the lab one day she said, "I must tell you something. Biofeedback has changed not only my emotions and my body, it has changed my mind," and she told the following story. Her husband, an important official in his company, had invited the president of the company and his wife and a few other important guests for Saturday-night dinner. In the discussion that followed dinner the president of the company had suggested a way of handling a policy matter that she felt was unwise. And then she did something that she

*said she never would have done before: She entered the conversation
and calmly discussed her feelings, which she felt were shared by many
others in the organization, and suggested an alternate course. "My husband looked at me with such surprise!" she said, but her idea was well
received and he was pleased. Without the "confidence of myself" gained
from biofeedback training, she said, she would not have been able to
express herself as she did.*

*One day she surprised me by saying she was no longer afraid of death.
When her heart raced and beat irregularly, she had been terrified of
dying; now she was not afraid.*

*Shortly after the dinner episode she came to see me, not at her ap-
pointed time and in great excitement. "Now look what biofeedback has
done!" she said. Amused, I asked, "What has biofeedback done now?"
"Just by chance," someone, seeing this bright, attractive woman and
hearing her charming accent, had offered her a job, and she had accepted. "Never without biofeedback," she said, would she have done
it. Feeling a bit concerned, I asked if her doctor knew. "Oh, yes, and he
said, 'Go ahead.' " I explained again what I had often explained before:
that whatever had been accomplished in her had been accomplished by
her, that biofeedback instruments are just sophisticated mirrors that
show us how we are doing when we try to make certain changes, and
that when we've learned how to make the changes we don't need the
mirrors any more.*

*Over a year has passed since we finished our work together. She con-
tinues to handle stress well and has again reduced medication. Although she previously had been afraid to fly she recently took the long
flight back to her native country for a daughter's wedding. She came to
tell me of the ease with which she had made the journey and had managed the excitement of the visit. Her husband met her in Miami on her
return to the states and they flew to Topeka together. The flight was
rough. She told me with great amusement that her husband had a drink
to steady his nerves and gripped the arms of his chair, while she—to his
great surprise—did her "biofeedback exercises" and went to sleep.*

Blood Pressure

One of the more difficult areas of biofeedback research has been control
of high blood pressure (hypertension). The absence of a satisfactory
noninvasive method of measuring blood pressure—the usual arm-cuff

---

procedure is cumbersome and inconvenient—has been a severe limitation. Recently, however, a technique using a constant cuff pressure has been reported by Schwartz and Shapiro (1973), and Brener and Kleinman (1970) reported a study in which blood pressure was measured with a cuff on the index finger of the left hand. These techniques provide a way to pick up the blood-pressure signal for biofeedback-training purposes.

Blood pressure is designated by two numbers, as in 125/75. These numbers refer to millimeters of mercury and indicate the pressure at the bottom of a vertical tube of mercury first 125 millimeters high then 75 millimeters high. The first number, always the higher, represents systolic blood pressure (measured as the heart contracts). The second number represents diastolic blood pressure (measured between contractions). A variety of internal sensing mechanisms located in blood vessels in the body and brain provide internal feedback of instructions to the central control area of the brain that regulates blood pressure. A very satisfactory, healthy blood pressure might read 115/65. A reading that would suggest caution is 140/90, and a dangerously high reading might be 200/110, although what is considered to need caution is somewhat different for different people.

Roughly speaking, it is easy to see from a mechanical point of view that if the hoselike network for distribution of blood in the body loses elasticity, then each pulse of the heart will generate greater pressure during each heartbeat than if the tubing were more elastic. Also, if the inside of the tubing gets plugged up with deposits so that the diameter is considerably decreased, then not only does the tubing wall become relatively inelastic, but the amount of blood that can get through the hose is significantly reduced. When that happens, automatic sensors scattered throughout the body send a signal to the control center that more blood is needed, the heart responds by pumping more forcefully, and blood pressure goes up.

Another important factor that is related to both migraine headache and Raynaud's disease, both of which are psychosomatic dysfunctions involving circulation in different parts of the body, is the increase in blood pressure caused by vasoconstriction. Decrease of blood-vessel diameter due to muscular tension in the smooth muscles of blood-vessel walls causes pressure to go up. If these smooth muscles are continuously activated by abnormally high sympathetic nervous tension, the effect is as though blood-vessel diameter had been mechanically reduced by internal deposits. Patients who suffer from "psychosomatic high blood pressure"—high blood pressure induced by excessive vasoconstriction due to improper response to some kind of life stress—often show a highly variable pressure. Their blood pressure is said to be labile—that is, it rapidly goes up and down in accordance with the patient's mood and the stresses of life.

Patients with blood vessels blocked by deposits are relatively non-labile. Blood pressure often remains high regardless of the patient's mood, and is not easily controlled by drugs. Labile hypertensives, however, are easily affected by drugs that alter smooth muscle tension. Unfortunately, these drugs affect smooth muscles all over the body. This is one of the side effects that often become so objectionable that physicians hesitate to increase dosages to the amounts necessary to control blood pressure.

Before turning to the research and clinical findings, it is useful to consider what systolic (pulse pressure) and diastolic (pulse relaxation) mean. When the doctor pumps air into the arm cuff, pressure builds up to the point where certain large arteries are squeezed flat and no blood flows through them into the arm. Using a stethoscope pressed against the arm next to the cuff, the doctor can hear the *swish-swish* of blood through the flattened arteries cease. Then he gradually allows the air pressure in the cuff to drop, watching a pressure indicator (called a manometer) and listening for the heartbeat sound associated with the opening of the artery. At the instant the pulse can be heard in the stethoscope, the doctor reads the manometer. This is the systolic pressure, the pressure resulting from the contraction of the heart.

As the doctor continues lowering the air pressure in the cuff below the systolic pressure point, a pulse sound remains audible until the cuff pressure is so low that it does not significantly compress the artery wall. When that happens, the sound disappears, and the doctor again notes the manometer reading. This is the diastolic pressure.

It is obvious that with a stiff and inflexible artery, a good deal more air pressure is needed before the artery is flattened to the point where blood will not flow. Similarly, an artery that is highly constricted because of tension in smooth muscles will not easily flatten, and will also take considerably higher air pressure before blood-flow sounds are stopped. Diastolic pressure also is higher in a nonelastic, thickened artery and somewhat higher in a vasotense artery. Diastolic pressure, however, is not as variable as systolic pressure. Physicians generally view the systolic reading as possibly including a significant stress component, while diastolic reading is generally considered to be indicative of a physiological state rather than an emotional-response state. This is what gave rise to the idea that the diastolic state would not respond in any significant way to efforts at self-regulation, though systolic pressures might. With biofeedback training or meditation practices, however, it has been found that both systolic and diastolic pressures can be reduced.

Before we report on our own exploratory work in blood-pressure control, let me mention two earlier scientific studies.

In the study by Brener and Kleinman, male college-student subjects watched a manometer on which systolic blood pressure obtained from a finger cuff was continuously displayed. (The finger cuff is used in the same way as an arm cuff but is considerably more comfortable.) The subjects were instructed to lower the pressure. Subjects were given twenty 50-second trials during each of two sessions and succeeded in lowering blood pressure 16 mm Hg (millimeters of mercury) during the first session and 12 mm Hg during the second session. Members of a control group were informed of the response being measured and were instructed to watch the feedback display, but were not instructed to lower their blood pressure. They showed no change in blood pressure during trials.

Schwartz and Shapiro reported the application of feedback technology in a study of systolic pressure in seven patients diagnosed as having essential hypertension (high blood pressure with no known cause). All patients were maintained on their prior drug schedules. Seven were given from five to sixteen adaptation sessions in a quiet, resting condition until there were no further systolic-blood-pressure decreases over five consecutive sessions. In other words, they were allowed to relax and adapt to the situation until their blood pressure maintained a constant level during five consecutive sessions. Then they received daily feedback sessions for decreasing systolic pressure until reaching the criterion of "no further decreases in pressure in five consecutive training sessions."

Five of the seven patients showed decreases in systolic pressure of 34, 29, 16, 16, and 17 mm Hg in differing numbers of sessions for each subject before reaching the criterion, respectively 33, 22, 34, 31, and 12 sessions. Two of the seven patients showed no significant decreases. Schwartz and Shapiro suggested that blood-pressure feedback com-

bined with other techniques designed to lower sympathetic activity (neural activity that causes constriction in smooth muscles in blood-vessel walls) might be a fruitful approach in blood-pressure control. In view of events that happened in our own laboratory, their suggestion seems a good one.

Prior to January 1975 we had not attempted to train people in control of blood pressure. We were busy with other research and with patients sent to us by Menninger doctors for biofeedback training in the control of muscle tension, anxiety states, and phobias. But in October 1974, an odd event occurred that led us to make a trial of peripheral warming for control of blood pressure—the same technique that we used for control of migraine and Raynaud's disease. Margaret Olwine, a medical writer for the Kansas City *Star* magazine, was writing a story on our research and visited Topeka to get information. She was impressed by our statement that we had trained more than two thousand people to warm their hands at will, and asked if she could undergo a training session.

Pat Norris, the director of our biofeedback seminar and workshop programs, ran Margaret through an autogenic feedback session with a temperature meter, and in about fifteen minutes Margaret had demonstrated that she could warm her hands. When the training session was over I suggested that since she planned to return to Topeka in about a week to get some photographs, she might like to take the temperature trainer back to Kansas City to get a little more practice with relaxation techniques, just as Sargent's migraine patients do. Alyce and I had already talked with Margaret over a period of two days, so I knew that she understood fully the theory involved.

I did not guess that she might attempt to learn to control her own blood pressure with the temperature machine, and she did not mention that she suffered from hypertension. If she had been a relatively sophisticated medical student, she might not have attempted it, but she reasoned that since blood pressure involves blood and control of temperature in the hands involves control of blood flow, there might be a connection between blood pressure and warmth in the hands. If she could warm her hands, the resulting relaxation might cause a lowering of blood pressure.

This approach to the hypertension problem proved surprisingly effective in her case. Margaret had been taking a drug for relaxation (Valium) under doctor's orders in order to control blood pressure, but when she left Topeka with the temperature trainer she decided to stop taking the medicine. That was possibly a risky thing to do and is something we warn people against, suggesting that they get their doctor's advice before making changes in a drug regimen. She did not notify her cardiologist of her intentions, but did make an appointment with him for a blood-pressure test on the day she was to return the meter to us in Topeka. Margaret practiced with the meter morning and night for one week, then went for her appointment. When the doctor took the pressure he was surprised and pleased to find that it was normal. She then told him that she was not taking her medication, and he said that perhaps something had changed and that so long as she hadn't been taking it and the blood pressure seemed normal, it would be useful to continue on a little longer and see if it remained that way. Then Margaret came to Topeka and told us about her experience with the temperature meter and her decreased blood pressure.

Three months later, at the annual medical symposium of the Association for Research and Enlightenment Clinic (ARE) in Phoenix, Arizona, where Alyce and I were conducting a biofeedback workshop for physicians, I happened to mention the experience of Margaret Olwine. One of the doctors present was especially interested in the case, and he asked me about Margaret as a person. First, was she a relaxed "believer," so that it would be easy for the vascular-relaxation effect to generalize over her whole body? Or was she a tense person who might learn to control temperature of just one hand, or one finger? I replied that by the time she returned to Kansas City she probably believed in the efficacy of biofeedback training and that she was the type of person who would likely relax throughout her entire body. Then he said that perhaps what had happened was that when she warmed her right hand she warmed her left hand also, and in addition increased the temperature in her legs and feet.

We have noticed that in many people who learn to relax a single limb through biofeedback training the effect generalizes over the body as a whole, so I allowed that this probably happened with Margaret, too. He told us then that when he was a surgeon at the Mayo Clinic in the old days before drugs became available for the control of hypertension, a surgical procedure for control of high blood pressure was to cut the sympathetic nerves in the legs. When the nerve supply to the smooth muscles in blood-vessel walls was severed, the muscles would relax, thereby causing dilation of the blood vessels and a large increase in the blood volume in the legs. The hydraulic change in blood volume in the legs would reduce the pressure throughout the body as a whole. In effect, he suggested about Margaret, "She merely gave herself a reversible sympathectomy." The members of the workshop laughed, but we thought his idea was interesting.

Two weeks later, when Alyce and I were back at our lab, a Menninger psychiatrist asked if we would attempt to train one of his patients to control a dangerous hypertension problem. I replied that if he had called three weeks earlier I would have been reluctant, but that since the events with Margaret Olwine and our discussion with the surgeon, we would be glad to give it a try, if one of our group had time to do the training. Alyce, who accepted this patient, found the case highly instructive. Since then George Eversaul, a clinical psychologist with a medical group in Las Vegas, Nevada, has told us that he has had similar results with hypertension control through temperature feedback training.

Elmer had already talked with the patient and provided her with a biofeedback rationale, similar to that shown in Figure 1, before she came for her first training session in mid-February. I went over the general principles again, explaining that she would use EMG training for general relaxation and temperature training for autonomic relaxation and blood-flow control. I then conducted her through an autogenic session with the thermistor attached to her right middle finger, but with the meter turned away so that during this first session she could listen to and silently repeat the autogenic phrases (see Appendix I) without being distracted by the meter. When the autogenic phrases were completed, in about twelve or thirteen minutes, we discussed the temperature changes, which I had recorded. Then the meter was turned so she could see it and she was instructed in its use. I left the room briefly, and she practiced warming her hands, using the phrases and meter by herself. She felt that she understood the procedure and took the meter home for twice-daily home practice. She was asked to come to the lab twice weekly for EMG practice and to complete an information sheet following each biofeedback session.

She was a good subject, but even so we were surprised by the drop in blood pressure and heart rate in just a few days. When she came for her first training session her blood pressure was 210/124 and her heart rate was 120 even though she was taking the following medication for blood pressure: Aldomet (250 mg), 4 per day, and Inderal (10 mg), 4 per day. For kidney infection she took Gantanol (0.5 g), 4 per day, and for high uric acid Zyloprim (100 mg), 4 per day.

This patient is a registered nurse, and she recorded her blood pressure and pulse before and after temperature-training sessions each day. The following results were recorded during the first week of training:

DATE	BLOOD PRESSURE		HEART RATE	
February	*Before*	*After*	*Before*	*After*
13	190/120	156/110	108	80
14	142/100	140/90	88	78
15	156/108	140/98	82	80
16	154/104	130/92	86	82
17	148/108	142/92	88	80
18	170/110*	150/100	104	80
19	150/100	148/94	80	78

* Patient's note on record sheet: "8:25 P.M. This was a very rushed day from 7:30 A.M. to 7:30 P.M."

She saw her cardiologist for a checkup at the end of the first week of training. Her blood pressure read 190/110 and her pulse was 88. She said to him, "I felt nervous. Give me just a couple of minutes and I'll lower it," and she did, to 150/98, with a pulse of 80. He reduced her medication by one Aldomet per day and said she might decrease by one Aldomet every two weeks unless her blood pressure went up and stayed elevated. Within a month she was down to one Aldomet and four Inderal per day.

Her rapid progress was halted when her husband died suddenly. Several weeks passed before she resumed biofeedback training. Steady progress again ensued. In six weeks medication was reduced to one Inderal per day. In ten weeks she was taken off blood-pressure medication completely. Her physician expressed surprise at her progress; he had thought she would never be able to be without Inderal. Interestingly, a long-standing kidney problem seemed to be correcting itself also. The pain was gone shortly after she began her training, and the infection was coming under control. On the same day the cardiologist stopped all blood-pressure medication, her urologist stopped her kidney medication to see if continued biofeedback training could complete the process of healing. The patient was free of medication for the first time in many years.

Toward the end of her training, she stopped taking before-and-after readings for each session. The following are the seven readings preceding July 25, when her doctor took her off all blood-pressure medication:

DATE	BLOOD PRESSURE		HEART RATE	
July	Before	After	Before	After
11	140/92	138/90	74	72
13	140/88	138/84	72	70
16	144/104*	140/100	80	78
18	144/94	140/90	76	74
20	142/92	140/90	76	72
21	144/92	140/88	74	72
23	144/98	140/96	74	72

* Patient's note on record sheet: "More comfortable, not so shaky." She had fallen down the basement stairs and feared neurological damage.

This was an imaginative and resourceful patient who used her training creatively. About two months after she began her training she took twenty-two Girl Scouts (her daughter's troop) on a two-day outing to Kansas City, the kind of thing she had not been able to do for several years. She took the temperature meter with her and managed to get in her practice sessions, and although she came home tired she felt it had really been a help. At another time she accompanied her high-school-age son to his bowling match at Wichita. Again she took the temperature meter with her. Not only did she practice in her hotel room, she took the instrument to the bowling alley and practiced during her son's competition. Even in such an exciting and tense situation, she was able to increase her hand temperature, indicating autonomic relaxation. Not only was it a help to her, she said, it was "a great conversation piece" at the tournament. During the summer she took the meter to a softball game at which her twelve-year-old daughter's team was competing for first place. Before the game her blood pressure was 160/108 and her pulse 100. She had rushed and felt excited, but was able to lower it to 150/100 with a pulse of 90.

Over a year has now passed since the patient started training, and blood pressure is steady at about 125/85. During this time she has encountered a number of stressful situations: the death of her husband and the settling of his estate, including the selling of the store of which he was part owner; the return to work as a psychiatric nurse after eighteen years; seeing her son through a bout with mononucleosis; meeting the many problems of house and children a mother who is alone must meet; and, finally, suffering a very painful dislocated shoulder. Yet during all this time, although her blood pressure has fluctuated occasionally, it has not been necessary to turn to medication again. She wrote to us saying that she found moments during the day to practice (no longer with a meter) and added, "I wonder what condition I would be in, physically and emotionally, without what I learned through biofeedback."

It seems obvious that this patient had not yet suffered any severe structural damage in the arterial system. Her labile pressures were an indication of stress-related problems. She was thirty-nine years old and had been suffering from hypertension since the time of her first pregnancy, sixteen years before. Another patient with whom I worked had a more severe problem. He was retired, sixty-seven years old, and had suffered from hypertension for many years. The training program was the same as that described above. It was observed, however, that even though readings of blood pressure at the beginning and end of a training session showed a consistent drop in systolic and diastolic pressures averaging about 12 mm Hg and 5 mm Hg respectively, no trend was visible from day to day, or week to week, over a period of two months. It would appear that much longer training would have to be undertaken (if at all useful) in order to reverse what physicians describe as structural changes that take place over the years.

It is worth noting that in addition to differences in blood-pressure lability, there was a marked personality difference between these two patients. The first patient was enthusiastic and eager to make changes, and the second was not even hopeful that anything would be accomplished. Could attitude make that much difference? At least in the case of a labile hypertensive, a positive attitude and the exercise of volition can be expected to favorably influence the course of events during and following biofeedback training.

I trained these patients in control of right-hand temperature, then left-hand temperature, and then asked them to transfer the thermistor from the hands to the feet. The increase in flow of blood to the periph-

eral parts of the body through temperature training is associated with an immediate decrease in sympathetic tone, so the suggestion made by Schwartz and Shapiro concerning the use of techniques for lowering of sympathetic activity does seem to indicate a fruitful approach to blood-pressure control.

In order to "prove" these theories, of course, careful research would be needed, but clinical results of the kind we obtained are useful because they suggest hypotheses that can be worked into experimental design immediately, thus saving a great deal of effort looking in blind alleys for the solution of problems. Almost all research progresses in this way. Researchers play around, so to speak, until they find a relationship among research variables that seems to imply cause and effect. The main result of these preliminary observations is to generate hypotheses for scientific testing. It may take a few years to establish the connection between temperature training and blood pressure to everyone's satisfaction, but such experiences as those related above help in determining which way to go.

Migraine Headache

Migraine has already been discussed as an example of biofeedback methodology in Chapter 3. A few additional observations about migraine and Raynaud's disease, also a blood-flow problem, may be useful. Of particular interest is the observation that family problems often seem to be involved in both migraine and Raynaud's disease. Family problems are so important, appearing again and again throughout the literature on psychosomatic disease, that we have focused part of Chapter 9 (dealing with homeostasis) on families in relation to illness. A readjustment must often be made in an entire family before a patient can truly recover from migraine. Homeostasis (change-resisting balance) in the family often makes it difficult to accept the former patient as a well member. Homeostasis can keep us sick as well as keep us healthy.

The patient who recovers without the permission (albeit unconscious) of the family, or without changes taking place in the personality structures and interrelationships of family members, often cannot remain well. The family seems to act like a large-scale organic entity that can develop an "immune reaction," not accepting the family member who has changed and whose personality has changed in the process of recovery, and may reject or isolate that changed person. Under such pressures the patient may revert to his or her previous condition and resume being sick.

Gastrointestinal Disorders

Some of the most unpleasant chronic psychosomatic problems that humans can suffer from are localized in the gastrointestinal (GI) tract. We are beginning to believe that each section of the tract can be independently trained out of its problem if researchers and clinicians can devise suitable devices for detecting the key GI signals and procedures for effecting appropriate changes in GI functioning. It is generally accepted by the public that excessive worry can bring on stomach ulcers; it is not so well known that anxiety states also can bring on disorders such as difficulty in swallowing and regurgitation of food, all the way down (literally) to spastic colon with uncontrollable, unpredictable diarrhea that can occur so suddenly that some victims are housebound for years at a time, afraid to leave their homes for more than a few minutes. Such patients, as Bernard Engel has pointed out, are highly motivated to recover. As he says, in certain circles it may be glamorous to have an ulcer, but not a spastic colon.

One interesting case (an example of straightforward conditioning rather than biofeedback) involved the use of conditioning procedures in the treatment of a baby only eight months old who was losing weight and wasting away because of inability to hold down his food. Shortly after eating, the food would be regurgitated. It was a spastic, reflexive behavior of the stomach whose cause was unknown. Rather than trying to instruct or communicate with the baby, Dr. Peter Lang decided to use a tiny but punishing electrical shock whenever the food began to be regurgitated. In a short time the baby's body learned that it was better to avoid the shocks than to regurgitate, and "the problem went away."

The first case we know of in which spastic colon was brought under control through biofeedback training involved an ingenious feedback procedure designed by psychiatrist James Howerton of Newport News, Virginia, in 1972. A physician who knew of Howerton's interest in feedback methods one day sent him a patient with spastic colon who had "worn out two internists and one psychiatrist" and was on a heavy drug regimen that was not bringing her problem under control. In addition, the drugs had kept her stuporous for many years.

Howerton thought of attaching the microphone from an electronic stethoscope to his patient's abdomen and training her to detect low-frequency rumbling sounds in the bowels and turn them off. At first the microphone did not seem sensitive enough. The patient's husband suggested that during training sessions a soup bowl be taped over the microphone in order to enhance or amplify low-frequency rumbles. That worked well, making the system sensitive enough so that, many minutes before the patient could feel any motion, she could hear the churning and bubbling. In other words, the microphone increased her awareness to a phenomenal extent. Howerton's instructions were simply to turn off the sounds. Within five months this woman was no longer taking drugs and was free of her problem. Howerton said she had a changed personality, an understatement in light of her years of suffering from spastic colon and drugs.

Seymour Furman (1973) reports the use of biofeedback training in the treatment of five patients suffering from functional diarrhea but manifesting no organic pathology. Commenting on the current treatment of such disorders, Furman says, "While the extent of disability can be overwhelming, the present status of treatment leaves much to be desired. Anti-cholinergic drugs, low-residue diets, and opiate derivatives for relief of abdominal cramps constitute the major modalities. Traditional insight-oriented psychotherapy and classical analysis have been unimpressive in relieving the presenting symptomatology."

The five patients were all female, ranging in age from fifteen to sixty-two years. Biofeedback was provided by an electronic stethoscope placed on the patient's abdomen as she sat in a semireclining chair in a pleasant, unstressful atmosphere. The amplified bowel sounds, played back through a loudspeaker, gave instantaneous audible feedback to both patient and operator, enabling them to converse without interrupting the signals.

In a series of thirty-minute sessions the patients practiced alternately increasing and decreasing peristaltic action (movement in the bowels). Imagery was used in achieving the desired response, and the patients were impressed by their ability to be aware of and control formerly subliminal sensations. They were praised for each success. All five patients were housebound to some degree, and had resigned themselves to this limitation of their freedom, planning their lives around their disability, making sure, for example, that a toilet was always quickly accessible. All reported that their symptoms were intensified by stress. Four of them had been under medication over a long period of time. The number of sessions required to achieve autonomic control varied among patients, yet all of them showed some degree of control within five training sessions. Furman states that although some of the patients did not achieve excellent control of peristaltic action, "Most impressive was the high correlation between the achievement of even partial or intermittent control and the remission of symptoms."

One case reported in some detail is that of a twenty-four-year-old married woman who had been given daily enemas for the first six months of her life and had never had normal bowel function. Shortly before beginning biofeedback training she was experiencing episodes of severe abdominal cramps and diarrhea as frequently as fifteen times per day on an average of two to three times per week. This patient learned control very quickly; after three weekly biofeedback training sessions she was able to turn peristaltic activity on and off at will. Furman describes her astonishing progress: "From the first feedback session . . . she has had three mild attacks, none lasting more than three hours. She was placed on a bowel regimen and has had one normally formed stool a day for the past three months. She has been relieved of her distress for six months now and has been asymptomatic for the last three months. For the first time, she has taken a job with confidence and enthusiasm."

Engel, Nikoomanesh, and Schuster (1974) report on the use of biofeedback and verbal reinforcement in treating six adult patients with severe fecal incontinence of from three to eight years' duration and a six-year-old child who had been incontinent from birth.

The treatment consisted of three phases. Phase 1 consisted of diagnostic procedures to determine the severity of impairment of rectosphincteric reflexes. The external-sphincter response was either diminished or absent in all patients. The nature of the normal rectosphincter reflex and the way his or her response differed from normal was explained to each adult patient. Electrical outputs from devices positioned at the internal and external sphincters were amplified and recorded by a direct-wiring polygraph.

In Phase 2 instantaneous biofeedback was initiated by allowing the patient to watch the tracings on the polygraph record of the sphincter *responses as they occurred. He or she was reminded of how they differed from normal, encouraged to modify them toward normal, told when the responses were poor, and praised when they were good. Verbal reinforcement was diminished as the patient learned what was expected and was able to affect the sphincter response.*

Phase 3 consisted of refinement of motor control of sphincteric response and weaning the patient away from dependence on the equipment by intermittently asking the patient to perform without feedback for a number of trials and then allowing him to again observe his performance on the polygraph.

Each training session consisted of about fifty training trials in a two-hour period, interrupted by a ten-minute break. During the three weeks between training sessions patients were asked to assess the effectiveness of the training in helping them to remain continent. This assessment continued after training was completed. Patients were interviewed every three months until they had maintained bowel control over a six-month period, after which they were interviewed yearly. Follow-up periods range from three months to five years.

All patients (except one) completed training within four sessions or less. Four have remained completely continent, one nearly so. One patient withdrew after the first session. The child was trained to relax her internal sphincter as well as to control her external sphincter. She not only learned continence but also to have normal voluntary bowel movements, which she had never had before training.

A biofeedback research project we have considered, but for which we do not yet have an adequate instrument for measuring and feeding back information, involves the control of stomach-acid level. Acid concentration, referred to as pH level, is an important factor in ulcers. In certain persons the stomach is especially sensitive to anxiety or stress, though in other persons it might be the skin or the heart that is especially sensitive. For the "stomach responders" a satisfactory device for measuring stomach-acid level could be particularly useful.

One of the main problems in pH feedback is that devices for measuring pH have to be swallowed with a wire attached, like an oyster on a string, so that they can be pulled up later. This procedure does not make it easy to get subjects. We would like to have an aspirin-sized transducer, or at most one no larger than three aspirins loosely attached together in a row, in which the first is the pH sensor, the second is a radio transmitter, and the third is a battery. Such a device could be swallowed

---

easily, and if it could be manufactured for fifty cents, or even a dollar, it would not have to be retrieved after being eliminated by the patient. The most inexpensive one we know of at this writing costs about fifteen dollars.

The patient would swallow the transducer; if he lay on his left side it would probably be retained in the stomach for an hour or so—plenty of time for a feedback session. A belt antenna would receive the pH signal, and an FM amplifier and meter, properly calibrated, would read pH level. The trainer could say to the patient, "Make the needle move in that direction." If the patient said, "How do you do that?" the trainer might say, if he wanted to be flippant, "Don't ask me, just take a deep breath and begin." In fact, this kind of statement could be used with all feedback patients. In practice, though, we find it more effective to suggest that the patient use the autogenic phrases of Appendix I as an internal road map for the first few sessions. This gives patients a way to start. Then they are encouraged to generate their own visualizations and use the phrases only when needed to reinstate a specific procedure.

If one of the big electronics companies that manufacture solid-state chips were to build a small, inexpensive pH transducer (and I do not believe it is much of a task), it would find immediate research use. Within a few years several million per year might be used in training patients to control undesirable pH effects due to anxiety reactions in the stomach section of the GI tract.

Asthma

One of the most interesting characteristics of asthma is that the blocking of air by the constriction of the bronchial airway is so easily triggered by emotional stress. In fact, some doctors say that all asthma is the result of emotional stress. Others maintain that it is a genetic problem aggravated by pollutants in the atmosphere, both man-made and natural (such as pollen). From a psychosomatic point of view, both positions are correct. Anyone who suffers from a psychosomatic disease presumably has a genetic predisposition; the disease merely strikes in the most susceptible portion of the neurological-biochemical system. Once a sensitivity to an irritant is well developed, dozens of biochemical processes are involved, and the chains of action and reaction inside the skin give rise to the idea, subscribed to by many physicians, that the entire problem is one of physiological reaction to the environment, without any psychological component.

In teaching psychophysiological control of asthma, we focus on the use of visualization to tell the body what to do and not on the cause that may be involved in the bronchial sensitivity. Hundreds of sufferers have been helped by learning the simple self-regulation exercises developed in Autogenic Training. The first two standard exercises involve the feeling of heaviness in the body and warmth in the arms and hands. The fourth exercise focuses on breathing and tries to reestablish the natural breathing rhythm associated with relaxation and freedom from stress. We have found that patients suffering from asthma often breathe improperly, sucking in rather than expanding the diaphragm as they inhale, and a step of first importance is to teach them to breathe properly.

An interesting example of the effectiveness of autogenic exercises occurred in our own department at the foundation some years ago. One of the biomedical technicians told me one day that his father, a farmer in western Kansas, had suffered from asthma for many years and had asked him if some of the things that were going on in our training program would be of value to him.

We had been planning for some time to use an electronic stethoscope to feed back bronchial sounds. It was our intention to install a high-pass filter (a filter that lets through only high-frequency sounds) in the amplifier in order to get rid of heart sounds and other lower-frequency noises as much as possible, so that the high-frequency wheezes often associated with bronchial problems could be amplified and fed back to the subject.

We had not had time to develop this instrument, even though it seemed such a logical thing to do, but I told our friend that even without the instrument many people had benefited from using the relaxation and breath-control exercises of Autogenic Training and that maybe his father would like to try them. After a visit to the farm, he told me that his father would very much like to try Autogenic Training. In order to simplify the commuting problem, I suggested that I teach him the relaxing and breathing techniques and he could teach them to his father. We did this, and within a couple of months his father seemed to be free of asthma. It was during a time of year, however, when pollen and dust levels were low. We all waited to see what would happen at wheat-cutting time in June.

That was a real test, and the father was much impressed when he got through the wheat season with little difficulty. At first he practiced faithfully and each day made an effort to quiet body and mind. He did not make it a "way of life," however; after the initial success he quit practicing even five minutes a day, and his asthma began to return. This is an important point. Many people are hopeful at first that self-regulation exercises will work as a pill—you do it a few times and your troubles are over. In the domain of self-regulation, however, nothing could be further from the truth. That does not mean that it is necessary to think about it all day, but it is necessary at least once a day to relax and tell the unconscious what you expect of it and how you want the body to behave. It is better still to find brief moments during the day (for example, while waiting at a red light) to practice these skills.

The use of biofeedback in the treatment of bronchial asthma requires a sensitive instrument for measuring bronchial function. Luce and Gattozi (1971) report the adaptation by Louis Vachon of such an instrument (developed by Robert Goldman at the Harvard School of Public Health). As the person breathes through the instrument it gives immediate and continuous feedback of respiratory resistance in the form of lights. Having tested its safety, Dr. Vachon began his research with asthmatic patients. Results were promising. A number of patients successfully learned to reduce their respiratory resistance. Luce and Gattozi note that patients could not describe how they did it, but several remarked that they did better "if they didn't try too hard."

Aman U. Khan (1973) used a similar biofeedback system in the treatment of asthmatic children. He based his strategy on the theory that asthma is originally triggered in many children by allergy and infection, but attacks may be provoked by repeated environmental and emotional stimuli until the child has been conditioned to respond to any number of such stimuli. Khan felt that the best approach would be the use of "counter-conditioning principles."

The child breathes into the biofeedback instrument and tries to turn on the feedback light, which is set to respond at gradually increasing levels of expiratory flow. The light and praise are used as rewards. The first five sessions are designed to "allow the formation of an 'initial link'" between bronchodilation and whatever internal and visceral cues are used to indicate it. During the final ten sessions the "link" is used to help the child overcome experimentally induced bronchoconstriction, induced by a stressful movie, suggestion, or if necessary by medication.

Khan follows completion of the training with a schedule of refresher sessions.

Another promising study of biofeedback training for asthma control in children (Kotes et al., 1976) used only EMG feedback for decrease of frontalis muscle activity. Results indicated that such decreases were related to increases in peak expiratory flow.

For self-regulation to be effective, it must become a way of life. Autogenic feedback training, meditation, or any of the yogic approaches are training systems for self-regulation in the entire body system, conscious and unconscious, voluntary and involuntary. Improved health lies in learning to coordinate the conscious and unconscious so that they work together for the well-being of the person. In many people the two sections of the being are at odds, and each is continually affecting the other in adverse ways. For instance, a poor self-image projected by the conscious mind continuously undermines the power of the unconscious to maintain emotional and physical health through normal homeostatic (self-balancing) procedures. If by chance the poor self-image is instilled by parents or early teachers and has sunk down to unconscious depths of the psyche in a child, then whatever that person attempts to do in later life will be negated by the program in the unconscious that interferes with success and the proper fruition of good plans. What is often not recognized by patients is that in bringing self-regulation into the autonomic nervous system, self-regulation is at the same time being brought into the unconscious sections of the psyche.

Sooner or later, it seems, almost everyone who seriously trains with biofeedback equipment comes to an existential awareness (in contradistinction to a simple cognitive awareness) of mind-body unity. Such people experience a degree of self-possession, which may irritate their colleagues who have not shared in this kind of awareness. The best cure for that is merely to try it. It does not take long for a hypothesis of self-regulation to become a certainty. The beneficial effects on one's self-image are tremendous.

Neuromuscular Disorders

Biofeedback training also is effective in the voluntary control of cerebrospinal and CNS functions. We might ask, Isn't that redundant, something like saying "voluntary control of voluntary behavior"? Yet if we stop to think about it, we realize that some CNS functions, such as

---

different kinds of brain rhythms, are not normally under direct volun-
tary control, because they have no sensory representation. Learning
control through brain-wave training not only breaks new ground in the
study of consciousness but offers the possibility of nondrug therapy
for epilepsy and other brain disorders.

It is also clear that normal voluntary control over striate muscles
(cerebrospinal control) can be lost, as with wry neck and tension head-
ache; or it may be obliterated if neuromuscular connections are struc-
turally damaged by accident or disease, or through atrophy from what-
ever cause. Electromyographic feedback holds promise for restoring
proper function and control in such cases.

For example, among the most dramatic reports in the EMG literature
are Basmajian's accounts, to which we have already referred, of volun-
tary control of individual motor units through auditory and visual feed-
back from indwelling electrodes placed in the large muscle at the base of
the thumb (abductorpallicus brevis). Such delicate control was learned
that subjects could produce various rhythms of single-nerve firing—
gallop rhythms, drum beats, doublets, and roll effects—after only sixty
to ninety minutes of training. Basmajian called attention to the practical
application of EMG training in rehabilitation of nonfunctional muscles
due to paralysis or atrophy, and opened up a field of research and clini-
cal practice.

Recent evidence of interest in EMG feedback training is the estab-
lishment of a new Sensory Feedback Unit in the ICD medical service
(a private rehabilitation center in New York City). The director is
Joseph Brudny, M.D., who conducts clinical studies in sensory feedback
therapy (his term for biofeedback therapy) at New York University
Medical Center. The unit treats incapacitated victims of stroke, cerebral
palsy, spinal-cord injuries, and other CNS and neuromuscular disorders.

As noted, in normal motor activity there is internal sensory feedback
from muscles to the brain as well as control instructions from the brain
to the muscles. When such sensory feedback is disrupted by accident or
disease, the brain motor centers, though intact, fail to function properly
or may not function at all. If the disrupted sensory information can be
substituted for, or augmented, by external feedback—visual or auditory
EMG feedback—then patients, through practice, can learn self-regula-
tion and often can establish a new internal sensory loop. When this is
accomplished, artificial external feedback is no longer needed.

Brudny told us that he has worked with a large number of torticollis patients, though he has not reported all of the cases in the scientific literature. In one of his first reports (Brudny, 1974) he tells of the use of both auditory and visual feedback displays in training nine patients to control this striate-muscle problem. After ten weeks of training, seven of the nine patients learned to control muscle spasms without external feedback. Psychological gains of self-assurance, overcoming depression, and resumption of social contacts were observed in these seven subjects.

In a later report, Brudny, Korein, et al. (1974) discuss the treatment of thirty-six patients suffering from spinal-cord injuries, hemiparesis, torticollis, and dystonia. Thirty-four of the patients responded with varying degrees of improvement. A case reported in some detail is that of a twenty-eight-year-old electrician with a spinal-cord injury that resulted in paraplegia and marked weakness in both arms. For three years he had received conventional therapy but had remained a total-care patient. Brudny initiated sensory feedback therapy, he noted, ". . . with two specific goals: relaxation of the right spastic biceps and proration of the forearm for use of a wrist-driven splint. Within two weeks the patient achieved both goals, step by step. The same progress took place concurrently in the left arm without sensory feedback therapy." Two years later the patient still retained these functions and could feed and groom himself, type, and drive an electric wheelchair.

The researchers comment: "New rehabilitation techniques could influence the quality of life of a severely disabled stroke victim, paraplegic, and cerebral palsied child. The nature of care will also improve when greater awareness of available rehabilitation potential becomes known to the government and the public."

Tension Headache

In the control of muscle-contraction headache, more commonly known as tension headache, the earliest and best-known studies are those of Budzynski, Stoyva, and associates at the University of Colorado (1970, 1973). The work of two British researchers in the late 1950s had demonstrated, through the use of a then-novel EMG integrative circuit, that the resting levels of the muscles of the forehead are higher in tension-headache patients than in normals. Since the usual immediate cause of pain in tension headache is sustained contraction of the muscles of scalp and neck, Budzynski and Stoyva hypothesized that if patients could learn to relax these muscles the pain would be alleviated.

Their early studies indicated that individuals can learn to lower the tension level of the forehead muscle, the frontalis, through EMG biofeedback training, and that the relaxation tends to generalize to other muscle groups, particularly in the head and neck. A pilot study with five tension-headache patients using EMG feedback from the frontalis muscle resulted in a reduction of headache frequency and severity. The researchers decided to do a controlled study (1973) to rule out the possibility that the positive results were mainly due to placebo effects or the effects of suggestion.

Eighteen patients who had suffered severe headaches for from six to nine years were selected for the controlled study: two men and sixteen women, ranging in age from twenty-two to forty-four. A base-line headache level was established for each patient, and pretraining EMG levels were assessed in two no-feedback sessions. The patients were then randomly divided into three groups. Group A patients were given EMG biofeedback training, receiving auditory feedback from the frontalis in the form of clicks. The click rate was proportional to forehead tension: Increased tension produced a faster rate and reduced tension produced a slower rate. Group B received what Budzynski et al. describe as "pseudo-feedback." Muscle-tension signals produced by Group A patients were tape-recorded and played back to Group B patients. Members of Group C received no training, but were asked to continue keeping headache charts.

Instructions to Group A included an explanation of tension headache; a statement of the goal of the study (to learn to relax so tension would no longer cause headaches); an explanation of the clicks that would be used to give information about the level of tension in their foreheads; and suggestions for using the information to achieve relaxation. Instruction to Group B was the same except the patients were not told that the clicks they would hear would give them information about their tension. They were told only that keeping their attention focused on the clicks heard through the earphones woud help to keep out intruding thoughts, and so help them relax.

Clearly, Group B did not get biofeedback, nor in actuality can it be described as "false feedback" or "pseudo-feedback"; the clicks were used simply as an attention-focusing device. Biofeedback by definition is the feedback of (one's own) biological information. Group B patients, told simply to listen to the clicks, were not told that the clicks reflected (fed back) tension levels in their foreheads. This was because "they could easily have determined that this was not true" (*emphasis added*). *This statement by the researchers raises an interesting point. We believe it is not possible to design a satisfactory "false-feedback group" in biofeedback research. Subjects can be fooled for a short period of time but not for a long-term training period. This also raises a question of ethics on two counts. First, to indicate to a patient that you are feeding back information about his or her body process when you are not is to lie to that person. Secondly, biofeedback is not like a sugar pill; it is not a "nothing." If a person is attempting to change a physiological function and the information which is fed back to him or her about that function is unrelated to what is really happening, this will lead to confusion, dissatisfaction with the process, and—if the subject suspects the truth—distrust.*

To return to the study, Groups A and B received sixteen sessions of training. They were also asked to practice relaxation outside the laboratory twice a day for fifteen to twenty minutes each time, in the same manner as in the lab but without instruments. Persons in Group C (the no-treatment group) were told their training would begin in two months.

Training sessions were followed by a three-month period during which Group A and B patients kept charts of their daily headache activity. At the end of the three-month follow-up they returned for three no-feedback sessions to test their ability to produce low EMG levels. The mean frontalis EMG level for the A group was 3.92 microvolts and for the B group 8.43 microvolts (on a time-integrated scale).

Drug usage had declined dramatically in all Group A patients in the three-month follow-up period. Decreases in medication were reported by only two Group B patients.

At the eighteen-month follow-up only four of the six Group A patients could be contacted. Three who had shown significant decline in headache activity during training had also maintained a very low level. The fourth patient had not shown a significant reduction during training but nevertheless reported a reduced level of headache activity. Only one member of Group B reported a significant decline in number and severity of headaches.

Eight members of the B and C control groups accepted the delayed offer to receive EMG training. Overall results indicated a 75 percent decline in headache activity.

Budzynski et al. make an interesting observation, based on verbal reports, that patients passed through several stages in their ability to

---

use a trained relaxation response to reduce headache. In Stage 1 the patients were unable to prevent or abort headaches; in Stage 2 they became more aware of tension preceding a headache and could relax to some degree, but could not abort the headache; in Stage 3 patients increased their awareness of tension, were more able to relax, and could abort light-to-moderate headaches; in Stage 4 patients could relax automatically in the face of stress. This ability became a habit, resulting in a changed life style, in which headache activity was greatly reduced or eliminated.

Among many others who have used EMG feedback in the treatment of tension headache are Wickramasekera (1972) and Gladman and Estrada (1974).

Anxiety Tension States

The first and one of the most interesting reports on the use of EMG feedback was written by Haugen, Dixon, and Dickel, and was called *A Therapy for Anxiety Tension Reduction* (1963). An interesting thing about the three authors was that they were all psychiatrists who explained to their patients, suffering from fears and anxieties, that before their cases would be taken up it would be necessary to learn a series of exercises for muscle-tension control.

The patient was wired up so that muscle tension was displayed on an oscilloscope. The patient was then given a tranquilizer and allowed to see the remarkable decrease in muscle tension as the drug took effect. The doctor asked, "How do you feel?" and patients generally said they felt wonderful and wished they always felt that way. Then the doctor explained that the kind of muscle-tension reduction they saw on the oscilloscope, resulting from the use of a drug, could be learned, and that the level of relaxation shown on the oscilloscope could be achieved without drugs after they had practiced the exercises for a few weeks.

Each week the patient returned to the clinic and was wired up so that he could see on the oscilloscope how his muscle-tension program was progressing. After the patient learned how to relax at will, usually in about five weeks, the doctor would say something like "You have now learned the relaxation system and we are ready to take up your problem," the original psychiatric problem. But about 90 percent of the patients replied that the problem didn't seem so overpowering now, that perhaps they had been merely too anxious, or the problem no longer existed, or the problem "seems to be going away," or "I was just too tense, and now I'm all right."

Epilepsy

In the series of research projects which we began in 1967, college students who received feedback of brain rhythms learned to control to a certain extent their EEG patterns. The results of that research, which focused most recently on the development of awareness of imagery associated with theta brain-wave patterns, will be discussed in detail in the next chapter. Attention here is on central nervous system control in epilepsy.

When physiologist Maurice B. Sterman agreed to test a hydrocarbon fuel for the U.S. Air Force for its convulsive effects on the nervous system, he did not guess that the research would lead him into a study of brain-wave feedback training for control of epilepsy in humans. Sterman is chief of neuropsychology research at the Veterans' Administration Hospital in Sepulveda, California. Prior to the Air Force study, he and his colleagues had demonstrated that cats can be conditioned to increase the percentage of a 12–15 Hz (cycles per second) brain-wave rhythm which appears in the EEG record from electrodes placed over the cat's sensorimotor cortex. Sterman called this pattern the sensori-motor rhythm, or SMR. The cats received a bit of milk every time their brains produced SMR, and they quickly learned that the milk appeared when they were totally immobile for a brief period. Each cat apparently developed a kind of "superstitious" behavior in learning to immobilize, for each seemed to associate a different posture with the reward. For example, one would stand with arched back and eyes fixed straight ahead, another would assume a half-sitting posture against the wall of the chamber—but the important point is that in each case SMR occurred with immobilization, as did the milk reward. This experimental design is called "instrumental" or "operant" conditioning, because it is necessary for the cat to produce the proper EEG signal in order to be given the reward.

With the SMR study completed, Sterman began the Air Force research on hydrazine compounds. These compounds were to be used as propellants in the Apollo and other man-in-space programs, and it was necessary to find out at what concentrations they would be toxic to the nervous system. As in his SMR work, Sterman used cats as test subjects,

---

but before the study was completed he found that additional cats were needed. The SMR-trained cats were still in the laboratory, and so he began testing five of them with the convulsive agent. To his surprise, two of the five did not develop convulsions at the concentration level which caused seizures in untrained cats and the other three showed longer periods between administration of the compound and the seizure, although they suffered nausea and other symptoms produced by the chemical.

This striking and serendipitous finding led Sterman to wonder if epileptic humans could learn to enhance SMR activity, and if seizure activity would concurrently decrease (1974). Encouraging results with the first epileptic patient stimulated Sterman and his laboratory crew to explore further, and they enlarged their sample to include four patients with dissimilar types of epilepsy. Feedback consisted of an interesting array of lights and slides and a tone to inform and motivate subjects. A home trainer was designed to allow the trainee to practice SMR enhancement away from the lab. During many months of training it was found that seizure activity indeed decreased as the brain-wave training progressed. This work stimulated researchers in other laboratories, and to date Finley, Smith, and Etherton (1975) and Lubar and Bahler (1976) have used SMR training with ten subjects, seven of whom have had substantial reductions in seizure activity. Four of these seven patients have had reductions in medication, a much-desired goal in training. Kaplan (1975) attempted to train two epileptics in SMR enhancement. Being unable to demonstrate the presence of SMR in these subjects, she tuned her brain-wave filters to feed back 6–12 Hz activity from the same sensorimotor location, but of greater amplitude than the tiny SMR pattern. With this change, one of the trainees who stayed with the study began to experience fewer seizures, but unfortunately a medication change during training made the results equivocal. Two new trainees, however, experienced significantly fewer seizures at the end of training.

These studies, as well as work in our laboratory with four epileptics (J. A. Green, 1976), indicate that brain-wave training can be effective in seizure reduction with some patients. Certain trainees feel that they can produce the normal trained-for brain wave at will and by doing so can sometimes abort an oncoming seizure when a warning sensation or imagery, called an aura, precedes the seizure. Other trainees are uncer-

tain how they produce the desired brain wave, and yet they too have fewer seizures.

In our lab each trainee was informed of the abnormal activity by a tone or light, with the instruction to keep that tone or light off while maintaining the "good" brain-wave signal. One trainee in our laboratory received feedback for low-amplitude beta activity. She discovered that she could turn on the tone indicating the presence of beta when she created in her mind a "strong" bright image of the sun. Later she found that she could use this image to counter abnormal spikes and slow waves occurring in the EEG record. Of our four trainees, only this subject learned to recognize the state of her brain by her mental state, and to make changes in the state of her brain by making changes in her mental state. Several months after completing her training, she reported that she could block seizures if there was time during the aura to activate her mind. She also reported that her memory was better and her reading faster. Most important, fear of the impending seizure, which previously swept over her during the aura, is gone—she knows that she is no longer a helpless victim.

The research frontier of brain-wave training for seizure control is being extended through the development of training techniques and the understanding of the neuronal mechanisms underlying particular brain-wave patterns and seizure change. Sterman, and more recently Wyler (1976) at the University of Washington in Seattle, used cats and monkeys to study subcortical and cortical structures and to delineate neuronal pathways that may be involved in seizure activity and in its control.

The clinical frontier of EEG training for control of epilepsy is being explored by Fernand Poirier in his Clinique d'Epilepsie in Montreal (1972, 1973). He has worked with over a hundred patients, and focuses on results (rather than research) through varying his training methods as necessary to adapt to the patients' own idiosyncrasies. For instance, sometimes he tells patients that they have a choice of having seizures or not; he may show them polygraph records of their "good" and "bad" brain waves. He uses exercises at home, and makes use of the placebo effect in any way he can, through encouragement, instructions, or whatever. With such a wide variety of factors, it is not possible to know for certain what is responsible for the many successful cases he has reported. It will take years of clinical observation, perhaps, to pinpoint *the most important factor, or it may be found that all of them make their contribution to Poirier's effectiveness.*

Brain-wave feedback for seizure reduction can be classified as training for control of the central nervous system, because the EEG signal triggers the lights or the tones that feed back the brain-wave information to the subject. Exactly how the patient learns to produce a brain-wave pattern that is inconsistent with epilepsy is not easy to say, any more than it is easy to say how Basmajian and his SMUGs learned to control single-motor-unit firing, but the fact remains that it is possible. This is exciting from a theoretical as well as a medical point of view.

Cerebral Palsy

In some respects the control of spastic behavior and of cerebral palsy seems related to the control of epileptic behavior, but those particular maladies are being studied primarily through the use of EMG feedback rather than EEG training. This brings up the question as to whether epilepsy might be handled through the kind of immobilization achieved in learning single-motor-unit firing in particular muscle bundles, but information does not exist on this point, to the best of our knowledge. In fact, many of the questions about the use of biofeedback for control of specific problems and whether alternate kinds of biofeedback might work for the same problems have not been studied. Several generations of graduate students will have to ponder these questions before the full potentiality, and also limitations, of biofeedback training are understood.

One of the most exciting developments in the field of mind-body coordination is the work of Moshe Feldenkrais. Part of his work is in the field of biofeedback, but it is different from all others because he himself is the instrument for detection of subthreshold processes in the striate musculature of patients, and he himself feeds back the information until the patient becomes aware of it inside. At a conference in London, the May Lectures of 1974, we talked with Feldenkrais and watched him demonstrate his training procedure with a victim of cerebral palsy. This patient, about forty years old, had learned to walk in a very crippled way with the aid of special crutches. He was severely handicapped even though he had received a great deal of physical therapy and had trained various muscle groups in his hips to take over or compensate for leg muscles that were not under control. In certain positions his legs would jerk uncontrollably and he would have to change posture forcibly.

While the patient lay on a conference table in front of us, Feldenkrais explained that the man's problem stemmed from the fact that when he was a child no one realized that he needed special training to develop consciousness in his diseased muscles. Instead, everyone said that his cerebral palsy meant that his body would be out of control in some respects for the rest of his life. In addition, they said that he would have to train other muscles to take over functions that could not be controlled in the normal way. Here is an example of a cybernetic feedback loop that was not being completed. Conscious and unconscious sections of the nervous system were not being hooked together in order to develop control of the body. Instead, other muscles were being trained to take over the work that was not being done.

Having made his explanation, Feldenkrais slapped the bottom of the man's foot with his hand, and the foot responded in a series of convulsive jerks. Then, with the fingers of his left hand pressing into the calf muscles and his thumb on the shin bone, Feldenkrais made an exploration of the muscular bundles in the calf, occasionally slapping the bottom of the patient's foot. After six or seven repetitions of slaps and jerking, Feldenkrais said, "There it is," and to the patient, "Do you feel that pulsing muscle in the calf?" The patient said, "No." Feldenkrais again slapped the foot and said, "Do you feel that in the calf?" At first the answer was negative; then, in a surprised voice, the patient said, "I feel that." Feldenkrais asked him what he felt, and the patient said he felt a trembling in his calf muscle that he had never felt before. Feldenkrais said that was what he had been looking for. He had finally located the muscle group that was out of control. There had been no feedback from that particular muscle bundle in this man's life. The muscle could jerk, but there was no associated internal (existential) awareness, only external awareness of the difficulty, and without internal awareness nothing could be learned.

Is it not interesting that this is exactly analogous to a psychosomatic problem in the vascular system? The patient is aware of the behavioral problem *but has no internal awareness in the control circuits associated with it*. It is very clear that body consciousness must be developed in order to bring the body under control, whether the problem is a spastic colon or spastic leg muscles.

It is worth noting that each muscle bundle has associated with it a large number of sensory detectors in the tendons which join the muscles to bones. These sensory detectors, called "tendon organs," feed back tension information; whenever a muscle tenses due to nerve firing, a special set of sensory detectors fire nerve impulses back to the spinal cord and up to the brain. This is feedback of information from the striate muscular system. This is one kind of proprioceptive feedback (feedback to the brain from internal body organs) that usually we are not very much aware of, because the operation is so automatic. Nevertheless, muscle-tension data are continuously fed back to the CNS. In cerebral palsy, Feldenkrais said, the proprioceptive feedback system is not sensitive enough. The feedback signal is weaker than that required to provide awareness of what a particular muscle group is doing. When Feldenkrais pressed on the muscle bundle with considerable force, the twitching of the muscle group was felt by the patient as a throbbing in his calf.

Feldenkrais said to the patient, "Are you sure you feel it?" The man said, "Yes." When Feldenkrais slapped the bottom of the foot again, it remained stationary, surprising everyone, including the patient. Feldenkrais brought that particular muscle to awareness by pressing on it with his fingers. With practice, and with an increase in awareness in that body location, he said, that particular muscle group would no longer fire in an oscillatory, uncontrolled manner. He had merely provided a feedback learning situation, and the body had done the rest. In addition, it was not necessary to press continuously on the muscle in order to maintain the awareness.

How remarkably similar this is to what has been found in the use of biofeedback machines. Consciousness does not need indefinite or permanent use of biofeedback machinery. In the same way that the biofeedback machinery works itself out of business, so also Feldenkrais practitioners work themselves out of business. As body consciousness develops, treatment is no longer needed.

When I commented to Feldenkrais that in actuality he was supplying a very neat form of biofeedback, his eyes lit up and he said, "Yes, that's it exactly." Someone in the group asked how he happened to develop this kind of training program, and he replied that it came about from doing a little bit of intelligent thinking about how control systems work, and how the voluntary and involuntary parts of a human work in establishing control in all parts of the body. In other words, if you know enough about biological principles and biological machinery, it is possible to devise training programs that will do what people here-tofore thought impossible. In his opinion, much physical therapy is aimed in the wrong direction. It does not train the patient to become aware of what the problem is, but instead tries to make other muscles compensate for the lack that exists in awareness. This was backward, he said. What we must do is bring nonfunctioning and mal-functioning muscle groups to consciousness so that internal feedback loops (direct awareness) can be established. That theoretical position is, to us, highly persuasive.

Fortunately, Feldenkrais spends a good deal of his time training doctors and practitioners. His discoveries will not die away, but will spread and find application in many striate-disease conditions.

In thinking about the remarkable findings of Basmajian and Feld-enkrais, it now seems obvious that the detection and feedback of firing patterns in deeply buried muscle bundles (accomplished with needle electrodes, as in the work of Alberto Marinacci, 1968) will make it possible for some patients to extend control over behaviors that cannot be reached with surface electrodes or finger tips. For instance, many problems in vision are caused by malfunctioning muscles that surround the eyeball. Consider the mechanical side of the visual process. Each eye is held in and controlled by a matrix of six muscles, and the two eyes must work together. There is a coordination center in the brain that makes the two eyes work together in harmony. When we consider the beautiful behavior of our two eyes in looking to left and right, up and down, near and far, and consider the coordination that must be developed among muscle groups, we can get some idea of the complexity of the control machinery involved. If there is a problem in proprioceptive feedback, however, then visual information alone cannot enable the two eyes to work together. The reason that eye exercises often are successful in eliminating cross-eye is not merely because the muscles are strengthened, but because the exercise "brings them to consciousness." Once the muscles are in consciousness, the feedback control loop is closed. In infancy the world is first seen doubled; then internal awareness and control are developed. This awareness is not necessarily conscious, in the sense of thinking. Few who have learned to align their eyes are fully conscious of doing it, and fewer still know the technical details of what they are doing, any more than pinball players are aware of the intricate meshing of internal and external feedback.

This is the exact procedure we follow in learning to play a musical instrument. First, external feedback (through eyes, ears, touch sensors, etc.) provides information about external behavior. Second, the internal feedback signals from the proprioceptive system are *made* to match the external signals, and the skill is learned. In correcting cross-eye, learning is usually automatic, but anyone who has closely watched a baby struggle to pull its eyes together and seen the eyes "snap" into place knows that effort (volition) is involved, however unthinking the act may be.

Why do we need such a complex process? The reason is that we have never seen, heard, or touched the external world. We are aware only of electrical signals from inside the CNS, and for binocular vision it is necessary to make the internal and external signals coincide. If this is done, we say that learning has taken place. Note that, in exact correspondence, the computer "brain" of a guided missile does the same thing as the human brain. In an elementary way, it matches two signals. One is the internal program (electrical instructions) that must be complied with, and the other is the signal (or group of signals) from sensing devices (accelerometers, heat detectors, etc.). It is easy to see that a human who visualizes learning a skill is establishing a set of neural instructions that are to be matched. The difference between Heifetz and the average violinist is in the care with which the visualization is first constructed and then complied with.

Unused muscles tend to atrophy, waste away. Consciousness in them disappears. But if feedback is reestablished, they often return to consciousness and regain their intended functions.

The Future of Transducers

In thinking about the many different kinds of feedback devices—for vascular control, striate-muscle control, gastrointestinal control, bronchial control, heart control, brain-wave control—the question naturally arises, Are there certain biochemical or physiological processes yielding information that could be fed back that a person could not, under any circumstances, gain control over through practice? No one knows the answer to that question. Many biofeedback devices that could be built have not yet been attempted.

For instance, there is no technical reason to prevent the implantation of a tiny temperature-sensing device in the body to transmit by radio signal (telemetering) the temperature of the surrounding tissues. That temperature indication would represent, reflect, or be regulated by two major factors: local metabolic processes (reflecting heat production in cellular activity) and local blood flow. If such a temperature sensor were implanted in a tumor, a patient might use the information, in conjunction with a visualization in which the blood supply to the tumor was cut off, to cause the tissues to cool and the tumor to starve. Alternately, in exactly the opposite direction, the patient might visualize an increase of blood bringing leukocytes and immunological materials to the area to attack the tumor. In that case one would expect that there would be an increase in local temperature. The Simontons' work with cancer (discussed in Chapter 8), if instrumented, could also be expected to show an increase in local temperature.

Concerning tissue cooling, the following case of cancer control is surely an example, even though the cancer was not monitored with a telemetering temperature detector. Some years ago Dr. H., a physician with whom we were acquainted, who wishes to remain anonymous, and another doctor had an opportunity to use hypnosis in the control of pain and bleeding in a terminal cancer patient. Because the cancer was on the bladder, it was possible to get information about what was happening without the use of instruments. The cancer was thought to be operable, but a preliminary operation showed that metastasis had occurred. Cancer cells had escaped from the bladder and were distributed throughout the whole body. Small cancerous areas were growing in the lungs, and possibly in almost all of the body organs. The case was considered hopeless, and no operation was performed for the removal of the bladder cancer. The man was sent to the cancer ward to await death.

This patient proved to be an unusually good hypnotic subject and could easily go into deep amnesic trance. Whatever the doctors suggested with respect to reduction of pain immediately happened. One day it occurred to Dr. H. that this particular patient would be a good one with whom to try blood-flow control through hypnosis. Because of urinary complications, a catheter had been installed to relieve pressure in the bladder, and the blood-and-urine mixture in the transparent catheter tube gave an immediate indication of the amount of hemorrhaging in the cancerous area. While in deep trance, the patient was told that a control center in the middle of the brain regulated all the blood vessels of the body. Could he find it? After a short time he said yes. When asked what it looked like, he described something like a boiler room full of pipes, or perhaps the inside of a submarine. There were valves, switches, and control levers for regulating pipes of all sizes.

Dr. H. told the patient that one of the pipes controlled blood flow in the cancer on the bladder and that if he could locate that pipe and its control valve, it would be beneficial to turn it off. Soon the man reported that he had found the valve and pipe—it was labeled—and after a few seconds he said that he had turned it off. The two doctors were very much impressed when in a short time there was a sharp line of demarcation between clear urine and the previous mixture of urine and blood coming down the catheter tube. They decided not to discuss this event with their colleagues at that moment, and especially not the ward doctor, who seemed to be uncomfortable about the idea of using hypnosis for any purpose. Their ostensible purpose in visiting the patient each day was for the control of pain, but each day they hypnotized the patient and repeated the suggestions for blood-flow control as well as pain control.

The bleeding was almost entirely stopped within a week, and the patient's appetite returned. After another week the patient said that he wanted to go home, and because he seemed so much better he was allowed to go home for two days. When he returned to the hospital the doctors continued working with him, and now they asked for his report on the internal condition of his body. He said that the growth on the bladder, which he had described as being about the size of a grapefruit, was shrinking and now was only about the size of an orange. Since his health continuously improved, his stays at home became longer. Eventually he reported to the hospital only once a week. Then a time came when he was away for a month.

Because of an unfortunate ending, this case did not reach the medical literature. When the patient returned after his month away, the ward doctor made a cystoscopic examination of the patient. During the examination he accidentally ruptured the wall of cancerous tissue remaining in the bladder. Urine escaped into the visceral cavity, and the man died of peritonitis within a few hours. Autopsy showed that the cancer on the bladder had shrunk to the size of a golf ball and the metastasized cancers had all disappeared.

It seems probable that if a temperature-sensing transducer can be implanted in a tumorous mass, through visualization and feedback the body can learn to starve out or attack and destroy that tumor. Most people whom we train in hand-temperature control are encouraged to use the autogenic phrases for only a few days and then to switch to some visualization which they prefer—for example, lying on a beach with their hand in the warm sand, or holding something warm in the hand, like a cup of hot tea.

One trainee, a medical student, objected to these suggestions. He said that the proper visualization was to imagine that you were going oudoors in *cold* weather. The blood-flow control circuits of the body would then automatically increase the peripheral circulation to compensate for the cold. We have all seen this effect in the rosy cheeks of children playing outdoors in the winter. I suggested that he use this visualization for himself, though it might be too complex for the average person, and it worked. This indicates that the primary feature of the visualization is the end result that is desired. *A mere visualization of an increase in blood flow to a tumorous area, if it did not contain the idea of attack and destroy, might not hinder the growth of the tumor.*

To continue the discussion of instrumentation, other transducers that have not been tried, to the best of our knowledge, might be implanted for telemetering the concentration of various chemicals in the body. For instance, a diabetes patient recently came to us and said that he had read of a device that could be installed on the arm to continuously monitor blood-sugar level and inject insulin automatically at the correct rate for maintenance of proper blood-sugar balance in the system. Would it not be possible, he asked, to use the first part of that device as a transducer and construct a feedback meter that would indicate the blood-sugar level? If so, then he could use it to practice various self-regulation exercises and might be able to get his diabetes under control. This idea seems well worth trying.

Robert Keith Wallace, in his Ph.D. research in physiology at UCLA (1970) has demonstrated that the rate of basal metabolism can be influenced through meditation. When the meditators switched from a simple resting state to a state in which they used their meditation procedure, the basal metabolism rate dropped significantly. This is a good indication that blood-sugar control might be possible.

Because of developments in blood-sugar transducer designs reported by the Diabetes Foundation in 1975, it may be possible to implement such a biofeedback project. One transducer is a small battery-powered detector that is implanted in the abdominal wall. It detects blood-sugar levels and continuously releases insulin into the

---

body. If the insulin-releasing section of the unit were replaced by a telemetering transmitter for radioing out information, the device could be used for biofeedback practice. According to Diabetes Foundation reports, the batteries can last for a year. There are at least a dozen medical centers in the U.S. where biofeedback researchers could conduct this kind of research.

Another transducer system that already exists, but which has never been used for biofeedback, so far as we know, is the kidney machine used for purifying the blood in patients whose kidneys no longer function adequately. After the patient is hooked up, the doctor watches the output indicators. He does not turn the machine around, however, and say to the patient, "Visualize the kidneys functioning so as to make the meters move *this* way. Take a deep breath, relax, and try."

If we were training patients with impaired, though existent, kidney function, we would start with the standard Autogenic Training exercises and later switch to the type of organ-specific formulas that Luthe and Schultz refer to. Many cases of organ control are discussed in the literature of Autogenic Therapy (Luthe, 1969). The addition of biofeedback would accelerate the process of gaining control.

I discussed this possibility with two doctors in Boston who use kidney machines. One laughed and said that if he tried to do such a thing he would be thrown out of the hospital. The other raised what he thought was an insurmountable problem: "How can biofeedback repair a damaged kidney?" The answer to that question may not be so difficult.

Neal Miller and Leo DiCara (1968) have already demonstrated that rats can control kidney functions, and anything a rat can do we ought to be able to do better, if we can only get our voluntary and involuntary nervous systems coordinated. As for how biofeedback might repair a damaged kidney, such damage is usually biochemical, and biochemicals are controlled by hormones. Each hormonal system has its own homeostatic balances, but these can be regulated in some measure by pituitary hormones. Since pituitary function is controlled by hypothalamic firings, which in turn are responsive to neural processes in the limbic system (the emotional brain), the kidney could have been damaged originally by a chronic undesirable *attitude*.

If a kidney can be damaged biochemically, why can it not be repaired biochemically? After all, growth and repair are biochemical processes. Our problem may be simply to learn how to restore normal healthy homeostasis in the body. The kidneys in some patients suffer from loss of blood—perhaps a kind of Raynaud's disease in the kidney. Patients are immediately aware of Raynaud's disease in the hands, but a loss of blood in the kidney might be interpreted in several ways, depending on what biochemical and purificatory processes were disturbed.

Research in Autogenic Training has shown a number of biochemical changes correlated with the basic standard exercises in which the patient learns to control heaviness and warmth in the limbs. For example, in his book Autogenic Training *(1965) Luthe reports on a research project with thyroid patients who were taught the standard relaxation exercises of Autogenic Training. During the training period, which averaged about seven months, both protein-bound iodine and serum total iodine were measured. The main finding was that the hyperthyroid patients (those who show excessive thyroid activity) came "down" toward normal; hypothyroid patients came "up" toward normal. This is an interesting and significant result in relation to stress. Stress affects people in different ways, depending upon their genetic structure and previous conditioning. In some people blood pressure will drop when there is stress, and in others blood pressure will rise. In some people there is an increase in thyroid activity in response to stress, and in others there is a decrease. What Luthe demonstrated in the case of thyroid malfunctioning was that through the use of identical exercises for hypo- and hyperthyroid patients, the body tended to return to normal.*

The importance of this for biofeedback applications is that we do not need to detect the concentration of every chemical in the blood in order to control it, or control the blood flow in every organ in order to restore it to normal. As Luthe pointed out, often it is necessary only to restore the system to homeostatic balance through learning how to self-tranquilize the striate and the autonomic nervous systems, and various disorders fade away. For handling many psychosomatic problems (and few diseases seem to be without a psychosomatic component), such a procedure seems ultimately logical. Benson's recent book, The Relaxation Response *(1975), emphasizes this point.*

It is too early to draw definite conclusions, but these kinds of findings give strong support to the idea that every physiological symptom has a psychological correlate, and it is becoming increasingly clear that if either can be handled, then through reflexive action a change will be found in the other. A confluence of organ changes would explain some of the claims of yogis that cause skepticism (or laughter) in Western-trained physicians. Some yogis say that a certain procedure will alleviate ——— (and then they name about fifteen diseases) and another procedure will alleviate ——— (another fifteen or twenty diseases). The claims may be somewhat exaggerated, but it is useful to note that if the yogic procedure in question is prohomeostatic (Luthe's term for "leading toward healthy homeostasis"), then it could well be understood that possibly fifteen or twenty diseases might be influenced. They all could reflect conditioning or stress imbalances in a section of autonomic function whose return to normal would make the procedure seem almost a panacea. Clinicians who use autogenic or biofeedback training, like yogis, sometimes have difficulty explaining the variety of results achieved. Luthe, for instance, in reviewing the literature pertaining to iodine metabolism, mentioned that "A number of authors . . . noted independently that [during Autogenic Training for thyroid problems] secondary manifestations such as sweating, hyperkinesis, fine tremor, hypermetabolism, nausea, vomiting, diarrhea, irritability, palpitations and other cardiac complaints gradually tend to subside. . . ."

Occasionally I had heard half-joking remarks about researchers in biofeedback sounding like snake-oil salesmen. It didn't bother me until one of our own doctors cautioned against the concept of biofeedback as a panacea. Then I gave it serious thought. Why did biofeedback prove helpful in the treatment of so many and varied disorders? Suddenly I realized that it isn't biofeedback that is the "panacea"—it is the power within the human being *to self-regulate, self-heal, re-balance. Biofeedback does nothing* to *the person; it is a tool for releasing that potential.*

From our point of view, it seems most reasonable at this stage of development to invent and test as many different kinds of transducers as possible, and at the same time to study in every possible biochemical and neurological system the effects of simple autogenic procedures. Only in this way can we discover how best to use biofeedback, Autogenic Training, self-hypnosis, Transcendental Meditation, and all other techniques for self-regulation.

A simple conclusion that can be made at this point is that never again will we be able to accept the simplistic notions that the body is a mechanical device having no mental input and that the best way to handle every disease is through drugs, surgery, mechanical procedures, or radiation therapy. Those forms of treatment have their place, but the terrain must be shared with self-regulation techniques that everyone can, to some extent, learn to use.

Theta Training:
Imagery and Creativity

It has always seemed to me that symbolism should be restored to the structure of world education. The young are no longer invited to seek the hidden truths, dynamic and eternal, locked within the shapes of behavior of human beings.

—MANLY P. HALL

Brain-wave Research

By conservative estimate, more than a million miles of EEG strip-chart records have been generated by an army of researchers and clinicians since Hans Berger discovered in 1924 the tiny oscillating voltages (on the order of fifty microvolts) that emanate from the human brain. Almost all of this mileage was associated with trying to find the relationship between various brain rhythms and observable human conditions, behaviors, or diseases. For instance, data have been accumulated on the correlation of various brain-wave patterns with age, basal metabolism, cataracts, dementia, epilepsy, etc., but until Joe Kamiya's research began, little information had been obtained on states of consciousness and essentially no information on a person's ability to select and produce brain-wave patterns at will.

In 1958 Joe Kamiya was struck by the possibility that if a person were continuously informed about his own brain rhythms, as seen by an electroencephalograph (EEG machine), maybe he would be able to turn them on and off at will. He added a relay circuit to an EEG machine to turn a tone on whenever alpha rhythm was present in the occipital cortex (the "visual" cortex at the back of the head) and found that college students rapidly learned to control the tone. This led Joe to begin studying the states of consciousness associated with different kinds of brain waves. Eventually he studied brain-wave patterns in Zen meditators and proposed that it might be possible to develop a "psychophysiology of consciousness" (Kamiya, 1962, 1968).

Barbara Brown's brain-wave research in the early 1960s also focused on the kinds of awareness associated with different brain-wave patterns (1970, 1974). One of her most interesting studies on occipital brain-wave patterns and psychological states involved the use of colored lights that were turned on and off by specific EEG frequencies. The subject's task was to discover for himself the subjective states that would operate the lights. By the end of the decade many psychologists were studying states of consciousness and brain-wave patterns.

Before discussing brain-wave training, it is useful to mention some basic facts about brain rhythms. Brain-wave patterns have no sensory concomitants—that is, there are no sensory processes by means of which we can detect the presence of brain-wave activity. We can detect tense muscles, cold hands, or a pounding heart, but there is no way to sense brain-wave activity. What we sense and control is not the brain wave itself, but a state of consciousness, a concatenation of subtle existential cues.

In actuality, that is the way we control all normally unconscious processes. For instance, even though we can usually tell the difference between hot and cold hands, the way we learn to warm our hands or any part of our body is through imagining a feeling of warmth permeating the part of the body in which blood flow is to be increased. Learning to control brain-wave patterns or blood flow in specific body regions (or in specific organs such as the liver or pancreas) does not depend on normal sensory feedback, but on the development of awareness of subtle internal sensations that normally we do not notice until a feedback device tells us what is happening. Through the use of this increased awareness we train our bodies to function more optimally. That is why we often refer to biofeedback training as "awareness training."

The major part of brain-wave research has been concerned with the voltages in the occipital part of the head, at the very back of the skull. The brain surface that lies just beneath the occipital area of the skull is of particular interest, because it is the "visual-projection" area of the brain—the cortical area to which are projected all the visual signals that come from the rods and cones of the eyes. This very complex pattern of neural impulses is *our view of the outside world.* As mentioned before, no one has ever seen the outside world. All that we can be aware of are our interpretations of the electrical pattern in the brain.

Our only view of the world is on our own living internal television screen. The occipital cortex is essentially the screen, and the eyes are two cameras that give us information about the frequencies and intensities of light. When the eyes are open we say we are looking at the world, but it is the occipital cortex that we actually "look" at. What we "see" are millions of brain cells firing in appropriate ways to display the retinal activity. Everything we have previously seen has an effect on what we presently see. I may say "I see a chair," but what I actually see is the retinal picture apparently mixed with my previous images of chairs. Perception is not exact and accurate, as most people believe, but is different for each person, in part because of the contribution of different past experiences.

Figure 3 shows the four major types of brain-wave patterns: beta, alpha, theta, and delta. The lowest frequencies, in the delta band, are longest and slowest. They range from about 0.5 hertz (cycles per second) to 4 Hz. When people produce delta in any significant amount, they are generally found to be asleep or otherwise unconscious. The next higher band of frequencies, from 4 to 8 Hz, makes up theta. Theta rhythms are usually associated with near-unconscious or subliminally conscious states. They often appear as a person becomes drowsy. The presence of theta is often accompanied by hypnagogic or dreamlike images.

The hypnagogic image (from Greek hypnos, *"sleep," + agogos, "leading") is one that comes into consciousness as a person is falling asleep. It was well described by Frederick Myers in about 1898. It is not a daydream-type experience, but a projection of impulses from unconscious sources. Unlike in a daydream, the content is not consciously followed but seems to appear suddenly out of nowhere, and therefore is often surprising or startling. Myers gave another name, "hypnapompic images," to the kind that comes to mind just as one is waking up from sleep. Increasingly, however, the term "hypnagogic" is used to designate both types.*

Alpha rhythms, from 8 to 13 Hz, are associated with a more aware state than theta. Thus, although most untrained people are not able to maintain full consciousness during theta production, virtually everyone maintains awareness during alpha. Occipital alpha generally appears when a person closes his eyes. It is estimated that 90 percent of the human population produce brief bursts of alpha hundreds of times each day when they close their eyes for a second or two, and also when

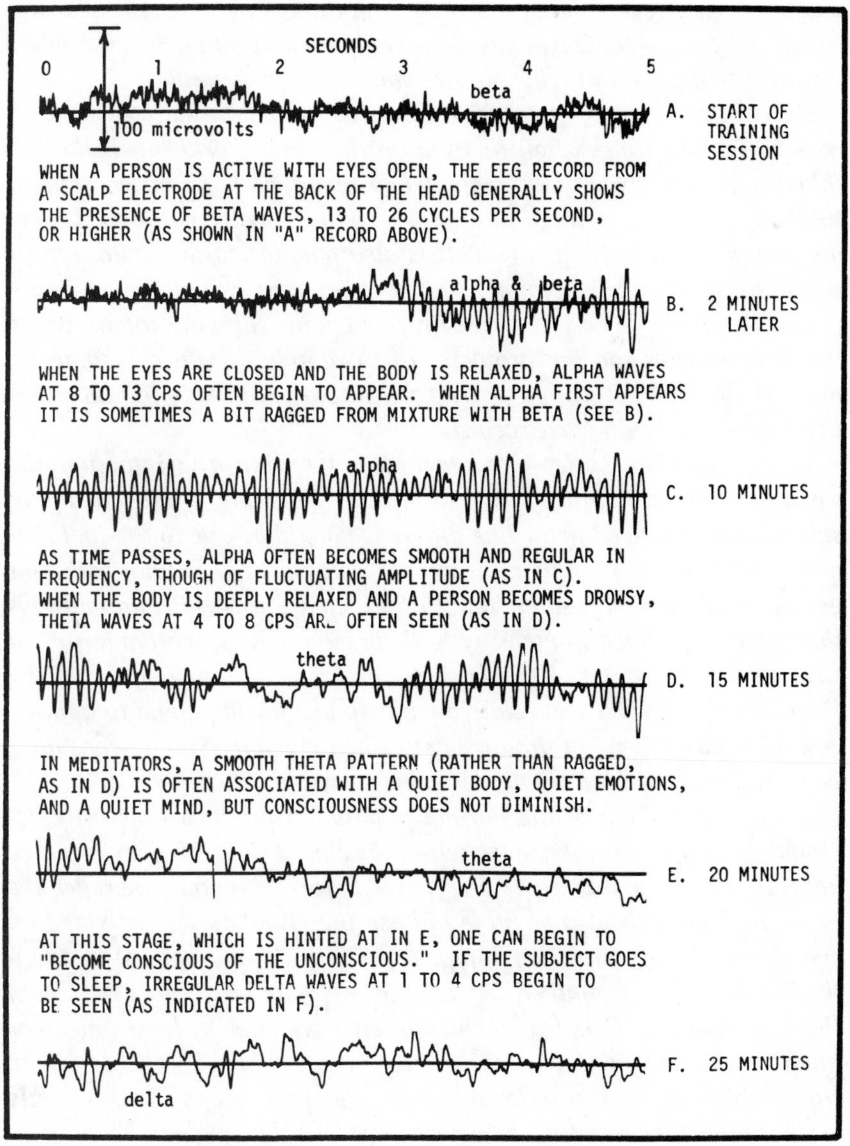

Figure 3. **EEG patterns.** These were obtained from the strip-chart record of a theta-feedback research subject at approximately the times indicated at the right.

their attention is focused on some interior image or daydream, even if their eyes are open. If you notice someone's eyes become glazed while you are speaking, you can assume that person has slipped into alpha and no longer hears what you are saying, though he may still hear the sound of your voice. During eyes-open alpha, a person is generally not paying attention to what the eyes are pointed at, so to speak.

By contrast, beta (13 to 26 Hz and higher) is usually associated with active attention, often focused on the outer world but including thinking concretely. For example, when reading a book or watching a football game, occipital brain-wave activity usually contains a predominance of beta frequencies. It is also possible to find beta almost continuously in the occipital brain-wave record when the eyes are closed. Such is the case if a person is anxious, thinking intensely, or trying to solve a specific problem. For example, if you ask someone mentally to subtract from 393 by 17's, you are not likely to find alpha in the occipital brain-wave record.

One researcher noticed that people who were asked to find the square root of a number "in their heads" generally produced alpha; subtraction produced beta. The difference could be due to the fact that most people know how to subtract and can be active in that task, but generally cannot remember how to find square roots. Presumably, as they tried to go back in memory to their school days, searching for instructions long unused, the cortex (which is called the "analyzer" by Russian researchers) was relatively inactive, allowing alpha to appear. A mathematician might produce beta when given the square-root task, because he would not have to search his memory to do it.

About 10 percent of the normal population produce very little occipital alpha when awake, even with eyes closed; instead, they produce beta almost continuously. As mentioned before, this could be reflective of anxiety, but it is also possible to keep the visual cortex activated by ceaseless thinking and imagining, especially if the imagery is attentively watched or examined. Related to this may be the fact that from the hundreds of EEGs from schizophrenic patients, at least one clear finding has emerged: Such individuals often produce very little alpha, from which some researchers deduce the presence of a constantly restless inner world.

The occipital-brain-wave research might be quickly summarized as follows. When consciousness is alert and focused, beta is found.

When consciousness is alert but unfocused, alpha is found. When a person becomes drowsy, or moves into a state of consciousness which Alyce and Dale Walters and I call *reverie,* theta waves tend to appear.

In deep sleep, delta waves appear. Another kind of sleep often associated with dreaming, called REM (rapid eye movement) or paradoxical sleep, shows a brain-wave pattern that looks like that of the awake brain, although the person is asleep by all behavioral signs. Within this framework of the four major types of occipital brain rhythms and their accompanying states of consciousness, let us review some very interesting research findings that were reported in the early 1960s in Japan and India. These studies asked, What is the brain-wave activity of a person who is meditating?

Kasamatsu and Hirai (1963) studied the brain-wave activity of Japanese Zen monks, a few of whom were regarded by their fellow monks as masters of *zazen* (the Zen Buddhist way of meditation). They found that (a) as the subject began to turn his attention inward, long trains of alpha rhythm appeared, (b) as time passed the dominant frequency of the alpha pattern began to decrease toward the alpha-theta border region (8 Hz), and (c) some subjects (those considered most accomplished at reaching a state of deep meditation) produced long trains of theta waves. When in this state of meditative consciousness, Zen masters are said to be in a state of "knowing" rather than "thinking." Does this have implications for a left-right theory of consciousness in which left hemisphere "thinks" and right hemisphere "knows"? We will discuss this later.

In India, Anand, Chhina, and Singh (1961) studied people practicing a yoga way of meditating. They observed that the meditative state could be intensely focused, or closely controlled, so that it could not be disrupted with flashing lights, sounding gongs, vibrations, or the touch of a hot glass test tube. In other words, the state of inner concentration was profoundly detached from sensory stimulation. These researchers also noted that during such deep-meditation periods, theta waves were appearing in the occipital brain records.

Such reports suggested to us that being in a theta state might have special significance—provided, of course, that the person producing theta remains conscious while doing so. In many types of meditation, consciousness is supposed to be focused on the inner terrain, not on the outside world. We were very much interested, therefore, in studying brain-wave patterns of ourselves and others who visited our laboratory and looking more closely at theta states.

Reverie and Creativity

I myself had been using a kind of meditative reverie to solve problems for a number of years, first as a student studying physics at UCLA and later when I got stuck on a problem at the University of Chicago. What was my brain-wave pattern? When Dale Walters and Alyce wired me to some psychophysiological recording equipment, we discovered that whenever I slipped into a state in which hypnagogic images appeared, they were accompanied by theta in the polygraph record and by an immediate, almost total relaxation in the blood vessels of the hand. In other words, in my case deep relaxation was associated with the presence of theta and with the presence of hypnagogic imagery.

As already mentioned, Alyce was preparing a monograph on creativity and had done a great deal of reading on the subject. She found that many artists and scientists who have been unusually creative in their fields have written about their experiences. Many described a kind of reverie or near-dream state in which intuitive ideas and solutions (in contradistinction to logical problem-solving solutions) come to consciousness in the form of hypnagogic images. Was it possible, we wondered, that they had been in a theta reverie when their creative ideas came to awareness?

Considering what we knew, Alyce and I began thinking about the possibility of developing "psychophysiological training for creativity." Deep relaxation plus theta feedback seemed a good place to begin. No matter how startling the notion might at first sound, there is reason to believe that a person can learn to be creative. Creativity does not have to be something you are born with (either you have it or do not have it), but might be something that you can learn through theta training, training to control your focus of attention in a particular way. Perhaps everyone is innately creative and merely needs training in order to increase the objective evidence of it.

It is worth mentioning again that brain waves as such are not known to have any sensory representation whatsoever. What can be detected and manipulated are such factors as focus of attention, thought processes, and feelings. The research program we developed in our laboratory is one of thought, emotion, and attention control. In our work, brain-wave control and voluntary changes in hand temperature or muscle tension are thought of primarily as physiological concomitants of psychological processes. It is desirable, we believe, to remain aware of the primacy of the psychological state in discussing this type of research, even though it is convenient to use shortcut phrases such as "alpha training," "temperature training," and "EMG training."

It might be objected that temperature and muscle-tension training both involve sensory information that we normally get through the neural system itself. That may be true, but what we learn to control are certain existential states, not temperature, blood flow, or muscle tension per se. It is the central nervous system that is trained, rather than blood vessels or muscles.

Before discussing our brain-wave training projects, it is interesting as well as useful to examine some of the existential reports of people who have used imagery creatively. William Blake, John Milton, and Samuel Coleridge are classic examples of artists and poets who received inspiration through imagery while in unusual states of consciousness.

Many people have described the states of reverie, dream, or near-dream in which creative solutions and inspirations came to consciousness. For example, Jean Cocteau (1952) wrote to his friend Jacques Maritain, "The poet is at the disposal of his night. He must clean his house and await its visitation." He explained, "The play that I am producing . . . is a visitation of this sort . . . one morning, after having slept poorly, I woke with a start and witnessed, as from a seat in a theater, three acts which brought to life an epoch and characters about which I had no documentary information. . . ." This experience led to his play The Knights of the Round Table.

Robert Louis Stevenson's ability to command "the brownies" of his mind to furnish him with a story while he slept is well known. Well known, too, is Poincaré's description of a vision he beheld as he lay in bed awaiting sleep: mathematical ideas rising in clouds, dancing before him, and colliding and combining into what he recognized as the first set of Fuchsian Functions, the solution to a problem he had been struggling to solve for some time.

L. E. Walkup (1965) studied creative scientists. In his paper "Creativity in science through visualization" he says ". . . creative persons appear to have stumbled onto and then developed to a high degree of

---

perfection the ability to visualize—almost hallucinate—in the area in which they are creative. And their visualizations seem to be of a sort that lend themselves to easy manipulation in the thinking process. This is illustrated by reports by many of the great inventors of the past and it is easy to demonstrate that individuals differ enormously in the kind and degree of their ability to think in such manipulatable visualizations. If correct, this aspect of creativity suggests many research attacks and many potential changes in education for creative activity."

The chemist Friedrich Kekulé (d. 1896) was especially proficient at creatively using the image-making faculty of his mind. At a dinner given in his honor he told of a series of deep dreamlike reveries in which atoms "gamboled" before his eyes, leading to the development of his theory of molecular constitution:

> *"One fine summer evening I was returning by the last omnibus, 'outside' as usual, through the deserted streets of the metropolis, which are at other times so full of life. I fell into a reverie, and lo! the atoms were gamboling before my eyes. Whenever, hitherto, these diminutive beings had appeared to me, they had always been in motion; but up to that time I had never been able to discern the nature of their motion. Now, however, I saw how, frequently, two smaller atoms united to form a pair, how a larger one embraced two smaller ones; how still larger ones kept hold of three or even four of the smaller; whilst the whole kept whirling in a giddy dance. I saw how the larger ones formed a chain . . . I spent part of the night putting on paper at least sketches of these dream forms."*

He also described the reverie that led to his most famous discovery, which Arthur Koestler (1964) called "the most brilliant piece of prediction to be found in the whole range of organic chemistry": the discovery that some organic compounds occur in closed chains or rings. In this instance, Kekulé told of growing weary of working late on the writing of a textbook; then:

> *"I turned my chair to the fire and dozed. Again the atoms were gamboling before my eyes. This time the smaller groups kept modestly in the background. My mental eye, rendered more acute by repeated visions of this kind, could now distinguish larger structures, in manifold conformation; long rows, sometimes more closely fitted together, all twisting in snakelike motion. But look! What was that? One of the*

snakes had seized hold of its own tail, and the form whirled mockingly before my eyes. As if by a flash of lightning I awoke. . . ."

And again he spent the remainder of the night working out the theory from the imagery. It is small wonder that he urged his contemporaries, "Let us learn to dream, gentlemen."

Rollo May (1959) tells of a scientist who dreamed a sought-for formula, wakened, and in his excitement hurriedly scribbled it on a paper handkerchief—only to find he could not read it the next morning. Each succeeding night he concentrated on redreaming it, and after several nights he did. This time he got up immediately and carefully recorded the formula, for which he was awarded the Nobel Prize.

There are literally hundreds of such anecdotes, showing that reverie, hypnagogic imagery, dreaming, and creativity are closely related. Various designations have been given to the state we call "reverie"—for instance, the "fringe of consciousness" (James, 1950), the "pre-conscious" (Kubie, 1958), the "off-conscious" and the "transliminal mind" (Rugg, 1963), and "transliminal experience" (MacKinnon, 1964).

Reports such as these from the literature on imagery in creativity encouraged us to conduct the pilot theta studies described below. We hoped to develop a new method for enhancing hypnagogic imagery.

Three Meditators

The brain-wave activity of three subjects who were self-trained over a period of fifteen to thirty years in "internal scanning techniques" (a kind of meditation) was recorded in our psychophysiology lab. Two of them demonstrated an unusually high percentage of theta waves in their EEG records during periods of deep reverie, occasionally producing long trains of theta waves. Both reported the presence of hypnagogic or dreamlike images, which they said were customary in their meditation experience. The third subject was able to reduce his normal alpha frequency from 9.5 Hz down to about 8.3 Hz (near the alpha-theta border) during a series of trials. He reported this as a mind-quieting, imageless stage preliminary to a deeper state of consciousness. Hypnagogic imagery was not part of his normal experience, he said.

States of Consciousness and Reaction Time

Dale Walters designed what was essentially an experiment in sensory deprivation, in which we studied reaction time and states of conscious-

---

ness. In this study, reports of hypnagogic imagery were frequently associated with drowsiness and the presence of theta waves. The images were called to conscious awareness by the reaction-time stimulus, the bump of a lightweight button on the subject's finger. One subject, for example, reported that the stimulus caused him to become suddenly aware of "little pictures" in his mind he had not known were there. He described a "void" from which the pictures "popped" when the stimulus was given. Without the stimulus, he said, he would not have been able to remember what was in his mind. This was an almost classical description of the usual way in which hypnagogic images appear, coming suddenly to mind from some unknown source.

Two Theta Trainees

A number of people had contacted us to ask if they might come to Topeka and work with us in some kind of experiential-growth-training program. We liked the idea, and I took on the task of working out a program. Eventually we put together the following elements in this exploratory project: assigned reading in yoga philosophy; discussion; yoga training, consisting of postures, breathing exercises, concentration, "traveling through the body," and meditation; autogenic feedback training, including temperature feedback and, most important, theta feedback.

The two women whose theta experiences are recounted below were our guinea pigs. These excerpts are from their diaries. First J.H., a woman in her mid-twenties, who wrote as follows.

> *The alpha-theta patterns, which began with alpha and went into theta, were not associated with images; my mind was fairly active and during completely thoughtless periods there was neither alpha nor theta. After several minutes of a lot of alpha and theta I began to feel quite disassociated from the sound, as though out there was all the activity, and my brain was completely passive. With this feeling came the disassociation with my body, which got a little scary, though I did not move or open my eyes to come out of it. During this session I also noticed that having sounds to passively attend to seemed to produce more—my mind was less likely to follow thought after thought when there were sounds to occupy it.*

From an entry ten days later:

There are so far two main differences between the alpha state (lots of alpha and little theta) and the theta state (lots of theta and little alpha). . . . In the alpha *state I am still making thoughts occur, but they have the feeling of being somewhat less attached. Images which occur in this state go along with the thoughts, and were put there in my mind by my conscious image-making faculty. In the* theta *state thoughts are quite detached—they feel as though they are flowing along, and there are vague images which also have this quality, and in retrospect I am not sure if the images actually went with the thoughts—I don't have the feeling in theta that I put the images into my mind. . . .*

FEELING OF PERCEPTUAL CHANGE: In alpha, though my eyes are closed, I feel as though if my eyes were open I would be looking out through them—I feel this physically—*and it feels as though my consciousness were attached to things outside my eyes, things external to me. When I begin to go toward theta it feels as though my focal point is changing from being in front of my eyes, to* behind *my eyes—I feel this physically, and have wondered if my eyes are turning* in—*anyway, I have the feeling that perception is inside my head, and does not extend past my eyes. Sometimes this occurs with a slight falling feeling—it's interesting that this usually comes when I'm about to fall asleep when I'm home in bed.*

J.H.'s report indicates that she attempted to observe herself very closely in the training sessions. She had not yet realized that it is necessary to turn off the analyzing mind to observe, to be the "witness," as it is often called in the literature of Asia. Six days later she described her first subjective experiences of what she felt to be a "theta state":

. . . The processes were detached thoughts and a stream of very vague images running along simultaneously with the thoughts BUT not connected with them—at least that is how it seemed at the time. These images were simply floating by—they were light, with no color, and I think that they were objects, figures, and faces but they were not clear and had no outlines, and they were meaningless—also they went by against a dark background. The vagueness of these images is not merely faulty memory—I remember being aware at the time that they were very vague.

As her sessions went on it became evident that when she was producing a great deal of theta she was unaware not only of the theta feedback but also of her internal experience, in spite of the fact that she had

---

the feeling that the stream of "disassociated thoughts and images" was constant.

Although she felt she had not learned any control of theta, her diary two days later says:

> This was a strange session—it does seem that I am learning to get into the theta region without first a long period of alpha. Subjectively, I feel more internal sooner, though perhaps this is because the beginnings of these last sessions have been relatively quiet and peaceful.

A diary report from her last four days of theta practice indicates J.H.'s growing recognition that theta is still somehow escaping her:

> I attributed the amount of alpha at the beginning of this session to be due to the fact that I was sitting up, and didn't feel as inward as in the previous sessions. I was surprised during the session to hear so much alpha and theta, and I noted that I was continually thinking, in an active way, which previously (in the early sessions) would have stopped alpha. I found that I was able to carry out thoughts with no interruption, unless I really focused my mind and forcefully created thoughts—then alpha would stop.
>
> Although I was under the impression that I was thinking throughout this entire session, with no lapses in consciousness, I must have been wrong—I simply can't believe that I produced so much alpha and theta —I wasn't aware of it all, I'm sure. Also the time seemed shorter than it actually was.

This subject's failure so often to hear the theta tones, to have many minutes of almost constant theta with no awareness of that fact and with little ability to draw up into conscious awareness what was going on just below the normally conscious level, contributed to our decision to design some way of bringing subjects to awareness during or just after theta bursts.

In the two weeks immediately following the completion of her participation in the program, J.H. reported experiencing three very vivid spontaneous hypnagogic images when she was relaxing, something she had never experienced before.

The second subject, A.E., was a woman in her mid-thirties. She is a professional writer, and her ability to express herself in writing makes *the reports from her diary especially interesting. About ten days after entering the program she wrote:*

> The alpha-theta meter presents me with an interesting problem: Finding, then staying on that thin edge between low-frequency alpha consciousness and high-frequency theta semi-consciousness. . . .
>
> It seems rather easy for me to produce plenty of alpha—the machine is a positive chirping bird if I leave the alpha signal activated. So, some days ago I decided to work only with the theta signal. The first experience of that was long, long silences with an occasional bleep of theta. . . .
>
> One session, however, was especially imageful and there were perhaps a dozen theta signals. But I was not confident that the images I recalled were indeed those associated with the theta burst, for there was an abundance of images outside the theta bursts, in what I expect would be low-frequency alpha periods.

Eleven days later her diary entry said:

> There are three things worth noting, and I shall do so briefly, for none of them was very strong or vivid, and I would rather not try to flesh them out with my waking consciousness.
>
> First, there was a relatively strong physical sensation of a warm pressure or weight that seemed, somehow, to come from inside my body even though I can best describe it as pressure on my body. I felt it on my arms and hands especially and perhaps elsewhere on my upper torso. It lasted, or I should say, I was conscious of it only a minute or so, but during that time it was very real and marked. It occurred again several moments later, but not so strongly, in the area of my knees and lower thighs. Aside from awareness of the sensation itself, no thoughts or images occurred concomitantly.
>
> Second, twice I felt vaguely afraid. But so vague that I cannot say anything more about these faintest of stirrings. . . .
>
> Finally, one image presented itself. A frightful one that did not, however, truly frighten me. The distorted face of a man; wrinkled and lined by folds of flesh; his one eye was like a very old apple that has turned pale brown and shriveled. It stood out of his eye socket. I saw no other eye. This image lasted several seconds, it seemed, and I got a good look at this face; it was alive, the changeless grimace seemed alive somehow, and the head turned somewhat. As I say, I was aware that this was a

hideous image, yet I was not afraid so much as curious to watch it to see what it might do.

When A.E. first began training with the alpha-theta feedback meter she was able to practice no longer than thirty to forty minutes at a time. As she became more comfortable in it she extended the time to an hour and sometimes even longer. About seven days after the preceding entry, she asked me if she might try a session without feedback. Her report follows:

> It was decided that I might try the theta feedback without the auditory signal, as I thought that I had enough experience with feedback to be able to recognize the subjective quality of theta to some extent; further, I was pretty sure that the signal interrupted the theta state and that without the tone it might be possible to stay in the state longer and have a better chance to bring something back from it. Accordingly, that evening I worked without the tone. Not much happened—that is, there was no more theta than I usually have and I remembered nothing concrete about the session. Here I would like to make a general comment: I was still feeling this mood of mild depression and I think that such a mood is antagonistic to internal awareness. . . . Even though I consciously wanted to explore my theta material, some other part of "I" did not want to do so and the second "I" won out.

Two days later she again tried a theta practice session without feedback, and, as she says, with more success:

> I did theta practice without feedback for the second time, and on this occasion was more successful. I began with regular breathing, saying Sa-Hum, and visualizing the chakras—this for perhaps seven or eight minutes. I felt myself to be relaxed. Some time toward the end of the period, I vividly experienced this scene: I was in a curious place. It was a corridor, well-lighted, that ran a straight length outward and somewhat downward. Off the corridor on the left (something like a New York City railroad apartment) were rooms, also lighted as far as I could see, in which I felt there must be people and scenes. I saw into only the first of these rooms, and I saw myself and someone else, together but doing I know not what. I really peered into the room for a few seconds, then withdrew and stepped back into the corridor. I had something in my hand . . . it may have been a rag doll, and there were coins on the floor . . . big shiny ones, not like money as we know

*it, but more like big ancient coins of gold and silver. Suddenly, as the
conscious-I became aware of this scene (as if the conscious-I said, Oh,
look at this, this is a theta scene, I'm sure!), the I-in-the-scene looked
up at the conscious-I and halted what she was doing, as if she were
being spied upon; she stopped and looked at "me," seeming to say,
Well, so what do you want; yes? can I help you? You are interrupting
me but I will attend to you so you will go away and I can go on with
what I was doing. . . . That is what her look seemed to say. And for a
brief instant there were three of me: One in the room, one looking into
the room, and one looking at the first two. In this moment the scene
froze, then faded. A few minutes later I ended the theta session and,
looking at the record, I'd say it was pretty sure that this experience
transpired simultaneously with the few minutes of closely spaced theta
activity that show on the polygraph just before the end.*

*To sum up this week's practice with theta: I think that I have a fair
idea of the theta experience. When it comes in just a brief flash, presenting just one image, say, like the Indian warrior, I think I can
recognize it as theta. I feel slightly more confident about identifying
more durable images, such as the corridor experience.*

*During our discussion of this theta session A.E. expressed the wish
to visit that corridor again; her verbal report of the experience seemed
to me to have a sense of "unfinished business." Twelve days later, just
two days before the end of the program, she did return to the corridor, and experienced even more vivid imagery:*

*Today's session bore more tangible fruit. I did not feel that special
at-easeness, as a matter of fact, but, during the last seven to eight minutes of the forty-minute session there came a series of images that were
associated with my hearing the theta signal. They were as follows:
I saw myself as a tiny mannikin standing before a huge blank wall;
that won't do, I told myself, you mustn't stand off and look at yourself
trying to "go blank"; get down there into the figure, be the figure. And
then I traveled down and merged with the figure so that "I" was staring
at the blank wall. . . . Then I saw a door, tall and wooden, standing
slightly ajar in the midst of deep, velvety blackness. Brilliant light
streamed from the other side of the door, radiating into the velvety
blackness and clearly illuminating the form of the door, its hinges,
frame, knob. The image persisted; I found it very attractive, still, sol-
emn, flowing, beautiful . . . then I had the idea of going through it, that
there I might find the corridor. So I went through and there indeed was*

the corridor and the other me frozen into the exact same attitude of "Yes, what is it?" in which I had left myself some days ago. . . . Again I tried to be active: Don't just look at her, I told myself, be her; so I went over and tried to merge with this figure of me as I had done earlier with the mannikin. Okay, now, I said, let's look again into the first room, c'mon, look; and let's look more at the corridor . . . but I couldn't do so; I couldn't make out anything in the room and, instead, the me-of-the-corridor just sank down slumped against the wall—exactly like a limp rag doll: She was inanimate, without consciousness. . . . So I didn't push any more . . . I just let it be. . . . And then I became aware of a huge eye; a beautiful eye, filling my entire visual field. It lingered quite a while; it just looked, its lid blinked naturally; but what was most beautiful, most enthralling, was the pupil: It was golden —an alive, moving, vibrating, changeful gold. I looked at the eye, and it at me, quietly, solemnly, benevolently, compassionately, beautifully —for a long time. . . . And then it was gone, and perhaps five minutes later I ended the session.

These last two reports are examples of what, when speaking or writing of our theta feedback-training research, Elmer and I have called theta-reverie experiences, or hypnagogic-imagery experiences. They go far beyond a simple hypnagogic image. As we have gathered such experiential reports from various biofeedback-trainee students, colleagues, and patients (for occasionally hypnagogic-imagery experiences occur during very deep relaxation in temperature and EMG training sessions), they have been a part of our learning, a part of our expanding realization of the fascinating possibilities within a human being.

Theta Pilot Group

We learned many things about training for hypnagogic imagery from our exploratory observations. We felt confident, for instance, that in order to maximize its effectiveness a training program ought to include autogenic phrases, breathing exercises, and alpha-theta brain-wave feedback. We had also discovered that we were going to need some sort of an alerting device that would prevent a person from going too deep into theta and thereby into unawareness of any associated imagery.

One way we knew of to maintain consciousness while reclining comfortably in a quiet, dimly lit room (in a situation highly conducive to sleep) was to keep the forearm and hand erect, balanced vertically on the elbow (Muldoon and Carrington, 1958). If the state becomes too deep, so that awareness slips away, the arm falls and (usually) brings the person back to consciousness. We liked the arm-balancing idea and used it in constructing a sensitive alerting device. This was a finger ring with a built-in mercury switch that closed a circuit if tilted more than twenty degrees in any direction, setting off a door chime to bring the subject back to consciousness.

While the ring was being constructed we wrote a proposal requesting support of our theta work from the U.S. Office of Education (Department of Health, Education and Welfare). I wrote the specifications for portable brain-wave trainers into this proposal. The machines would feed back different tones to indicate the presence of beta, alpha, and theta frequencies. It was our intention, though, to try these machines first with a special pilot group of ten meditators.

These portable brain-wave trainers were scaled-down models of the large laboratory brain-wave analyzer we had built in 1969. The lab machine, much too complex for general use, can feed back information in three brain-wave bands simultaneously. This feature had proved very useful, and we wanted that ability in the portable machines.

The lab machine also has the interesting characteristic of being able to feed back stereo information. Brain-wave data from two electrodes —left occiput and right occiput, for instance—can be separately fed back to the left ear and right ear through earphones. In addition, the actual frequencies in each EEG signal are analyzed into beta (13–25 Hz), alpha (8–13 Hz), and theta (4–8 Hz) and multiplied in each frequency band by 200 in order to bring the brain-wave frequencies up to the audible range. For example, because the lower limit of hearing is around 25 Hz, the average alpha frequency (10 Hz) would be inaudible without amplification. Multiply by 200, and the average alpha feedback tone goes to 2000 Hz, which lies in the range of the human hearing spectrum.

Each wave in a series of alpha waves is of slightly different duration. Thus, even though 10 Hz is the average frequency, what is actually observed in a train of alpha waves, wave by wave, is more like 10 Hz, 9.5, 10.1, 10.7, 9.0, 9.2, 11.2, 10.8, 9.1, etc. When multiplied by 200, these alpha waves generate a series of musical tones that sound quite like flute music. The volume of the music depends on the amplitude (height) of the individual waves.

Beta waves have a piccololike sound in our lab machine, and theta feedback sounds quite a bit like an oboe. When all three bands contain EEG signals at the same time (a common occurrence) a pleasing trio is sounded stereophonically. A standing joke in the lab is that we are going to teach someone to play "The Star-Spangled Banner" for visiting members of Congress, who might then be more inclined to provide research funds.

Notwithstanding such a delightful possibility, we had to sacrifice certain features of the lab machine in the design of the portable trainer. What is retained from the lab machine is a "presence indicator." That is, whenever alpha is present above a certain minimum amplitude, which we can select and preset, a 900-Hz tone sounds. The same is true for theta and beta, with frequencies of 400 Hz and 1900 Hz respectively. The feedback tones are individually pleasant, but intentionally set at non-harmonizing frequencies; harmonizing tones tend to mask one another, and often the subject cannot determine if alpha and theta are present at the same time.

Our plans to run a pilot project did not work out as scheduled, because the construction of the portable machines (going on apace in our biomedical electronics lab) was delayed by "bugs" arising from problems with electronic filters. We were obliged, therefore, to rely on the lab equipment, which we could use only sparingly—for each pilot subject, once a month for half an hour.

We chose psychologically verbal adults for the theta pilot group, because we felt that work with such subjects would more quickly lead to new insights. In the exploratory setting we created, we hoped they would help us develop and refine a method for bringing about a state of reverie, elicitation and recall of imagery, and for investigating the relationship of these variables to creativity. This method we would later apply in research with the college-student subjects we had in mind for the formal project.

This pilot group consisted of rather special subjects. It included ourselves and several others who had participated in the yoga classes of Swami Rama (discussed in Chapter 11). Perhaps this mutual background had something to do with our finding that, despite the limited amount of biofeedback practice, production of theta did increase in the group. Another finding, quite unexpected, may also be related. Three of the eight subjects who completed the study had ESP-type experiences during lab sessions. These experiences will be described below, but because we were not conducting ESP research we did not pursue the matter at that time. ESP events were also found with three of twenty-six college students we later trained in the full-scale research on theta reverie. Those findings will be mentioned below in our report on that study.

For training purposes we used Autogenic Training exercises to achieve relaxation of the body and a quiet, inward-turned state of mind. To this we added the practice of certain breath-control techniques: hyperventilation to activate the nervous system, followed by other types of breathing to still body functions and concentrate or focus attention.

For lab training sessions, we used alpha and theta feedback from the left occiput with the left ear as reference.

The subjects came to the laboratory for alpha-theta practice and testing approximately once a month, for a total of seven sessions. They were wired up and taken to the experimental room—a quiet, dimly lit, and safely comfortable place. The first session was devoted to familiarization with the laboratory and the procedures used, the second session to learning the relaxation and breath-control techniques. In the next five sessions the subjects received alpha-theta biofeedback training.

During these sessions, after a preliminary period of relaxation and breathing exercises, the subjects lay down on a couch, the brain-wave feedback equipment was turned on, and they began a thirty-minute period of biofeedback practice, listening for the tones that would tell them when the desired brain rhythm was present. After the first two sessions, only theta feedback was given, because the subjects had little difficulty in increasing their percentage of alpha and we were particularly interested in investigating theta.

Each subject's task was to report what was happening subjectively when the theta tone sounded (specifically, any imagery, visual, auditory, or somatic), unless, or until, the tone sounded so often that it was too disturbing to report each time. In the latter case the subject was asked to report occasionally any imagery or internal happening that seemed especially interesting or important. Often more complete and meaningful imagery would be reported after a series of theta tones. If, however, the subject failed to report for a long period of time during which theta was intermittently present, the experimenter watching the polygraph record assumed that the subject might have drifted too deeply into reverie to hear the tones and signaled over the intercom, asking quietly, "What is happening now?" Some subjects answered, "I wasn't aware of anything." Some said, "I know something was happening. There were images, but I can't remember them." Occasionally a subject said he did not want to be disturbed but would report later, and did so during the interview at the end of the session.

Home practice consisted of the use of the Autogenic Training and breathing techniques discussed above, without feedback, ten days out of each month. Home practice seemed to be important. We think it may have been responsible for the production of a goodly amount of theta (ranging from 10 percent to 75 percent over ten-second epochs) in some subjects who had formerly not been theta producers (they had essentially zero percent theta in the occipital EEG lead).

Results of this pilot research indicated that for almost all subjects the production of theta brain waves increased. Since theta waves are usually associated with unconscious or near-unconscious processes, it was particularly encouraging to find an increase in both the ability to be aware of images when in the theta state and the ability to hold them long enough to report on them. This increase in awareness of images and in the ability to remember them was important, because a major problem in studying hypnagogic states is that the material experienced is generally rapidly forgotten.

The ESP-like events that occurred might not have been noticed except for the fact that subjects were told to make spontaneous reports if an image seemed interesting, and also were asked, over the intercom, to report whenever their brain waves showed a long-lasting theta state. I was involved in the three events we did notice.

In the first, a young woman was the subject. While she was lying on the couch in the experimental room (fifteen feet from the control room and separated from it by a hallway), a research assistant came to the control room and said that I was wanted upstairs for a long-distance telephone call. I left the lab (in the basement of the research building) and went upstairs to my office, on the other side of the building. There I found that Swami Rama was calling about a research plan.

When I returned to the control room a few moments later, I heard the subject saying that she had thought of Swami Rama and suddenly had an image of him in the experimental room. He did not say anything, just smiled and stood there for a couple of minutes, and then disappeared. Was her thinking of Swami Rama a simple coincidence? Possibly.

The next ESP-like event occurred when Dale Walters was the subject. In the middle of the session a loud crash and thump from the floor above sent me upstairs to ask for quiet during the experiment. When I reached the first floor I found that three workmen had just brought in some large plants in heavy pots for an interior garden they were constructing in the building. One of the plants was intended for a trellis, but at the moment its bright green leaves and supple branches were lying across and trailing over a low fieldstone wall. I told the workers that we were running an experiment, and they said they were through for the day anyway.

When I returned to the lab, Alyce asked me what had caused the thump. When I told her about the plants, both she and our research assistant laughed. Dale had just said, before I entered the room, that he had the image of a plant, and that suddenly he *was* the plant, "a very green plant," that was lying on or falling over a low rock wall.

The third ESP-like event happened to me while I was a subject. I had reported a series of images in which Marolyn Moore, our research assistant, was continuously arranging and rearranging some blocks of colored paper on the wall. When I reported these images I mentioned that the blocks seemed somehow to represent time, and that Marolyn was compressing and stretching them in a variety of ways to make them fit in a given place.

When I went into the control room to see my brain-wave record, Alyce told me that after I had reported on Marolyn's arranging of paper blocks, Marolyn had said that during the entire run she had been preoccupied in trying to figure out a sequence of dates and events in connection with her wedding. That morning a letter had arrived from her fiancé, who had formerly worked for us but now was in the Navy. He had explained that their dates would have to be changed because his leave time had been rescheduled. When I reported the blocks related to time, Marolyn was juggling various dates, announcements, showers, visits from relatives, and the wedding date in her head, trying to fit them into a schedule.

Before leaving the subject of these ESP events, I should mention an amusing incident which had occurred a few months earlier, when I was a subject in an experiment in which a light was supposed to flash whenever I produced alpha. Marolyn and her fiancé, Jim, and Alyce and Dale Walters were operating the control room and were upset by the fact that fifteen minutes had passed and I had produced continuous beta, not a single burst of alpha. Jim said then, "Let's make him produce alpha. I will say three, two, one, and then everyone think 'alpha.'" They did that, and at the very moment of their "alpha" I produced a one-second burst of alpha.

After five more minutes without another alpha burst, they did the same thing again, and I produced another one-second burst.

After another five minutes Jim said, "Let's do it again, but this time let's think 'chicken.'" They did that, but they couldn't fool me: I continued producing beta that time.

We mention these results because we believe that events of this kind are not rare, but almost commonplace. Most people have them on occasion, and it seems of some value to admit and accept them. Then, perhaps, we can get on with the job of discovering their significance for psychology and physics. If we still hope to understand ourselves someday, we will have to include *all* the data. Coincidence could explain some of these events, but beyond a certain point it seems a rather farfetched explanation.

Reverie-and-Imagery Project

With the pilot group, we developed the features and methods to be applied in the more formal research with college students. A change was made in our alerting system. The arm-up technique was found to cause tension and irritation. In order to get around that problem we used resetting alarm clocks, which ring unless a bar on top is pressed periodically, advancing the alarm setting by seven minutes.

Money was eventually obtained to support the project, but it was granted by the National Institute of Mental Health rather than the Office of Education. We were happy to receive the NIMH funds, of course, for dollars all have the same color. If our work with college students was promising, sooner or later it would come to the attention of educators.

The research was carried out both at our lab and at Washburn University in Topeka. Our subjects were young male students, juniors and seniors at the university. The program consisted of two parts, as follows.

Part I was a five-week period in which we trained students to increase the time spent in those states of consciousness associated with eyes-closed alpha and theta brain rhythms. We had our portable brain-

wave trainers; for feedback we used auditory signals as described above, with different tones signifying the presence of different brain waves—low for theta, higher for alpha. The subject's task was to increase the amount of alpha and theta and to become aware of and report inner experiences. Imagery was not mentioned at this time. Subjects were told that we were investigating the possibility of building a better bridge between conscious and unconscious processes and gaining some control of that bridge.

When a subject met with us for a laboratory session he was first wired up. Two electrodes were placed on the surface of the scalp at the back of the head in the left and right occipital areas. Feedback was from the left occiput, to match the capability of the portable trainers, although brain rhythms were recorded from both left and right. Various other physiological transducers were attached to record other measures we wished to obtain: skin temperature and blood flow in the hands, heart rate, breathing rate, galvanic skin response, and skin potential.

Ready to begin in the training room, a quiet, dimly lit room furnished with a reclining chair, the subject commenced with a short period of autogenic relaxation and rhythmic breathing; then he received simultaneous alpha and theta feedback for fifteen minutes, followed by theta feedback alone for thirty minutes. The session ended with an interview (tape-recorded), in which the subject described his experiences during the feedback period.

Subjects came to the laboratory for a training and physiological-recording session every other week. In intervening weeks they came to report and discuss what had been experienced during practice alone, away from the laboratory, with the portable brain-wave trainers. Washburn University had given us the use of three small rooms in which our subjects could practice. We equipped them with portable brain-wave feedback machines, reclining chairs, and illuminated clocks. Each subject practiced for about an hour a day on each school day, except on the day when he came for a laboratory session. He kept a notebook or diary in which he recorded his experiences during the practice session. He also recorded his alpha and theta times, which automatically registered on timers attached to the feedback meters.

Part 2 followed the same procedure and was again a five-week training period. During this period, however, we asked our subjects to be especially concerned with increasing the amount of theta produced, *and with becoming aware of and reporting the hypnagogic imagery associated with it. Hypnagogic imagery was defined as imagery that comes suddenly into the mind from some unconscious source; it could be visual or auditory or somatic, a fragrance or a taste. All these are images, in the psychological sense.*

We found it necessary at this time to introduce the resetting alarm clocks for practice sessions at the university, to help subjects avoid slipping into sleep. In their sessions at the laboratory during Part 2, subjects were interrupted from time to time during their feedback practice by the question "What is happening?" asked over the inter- com. They responded by telling briefly what they were experiencing just before the interruption. They might be asked this question when mainly beta waves were present, or alpha or theta or any combination of these. We were, of course, especially interested in the imagery associated with theta waves, but we also wanted to know what was going on in consciousness when other kinds of brain waves predomi- nated. Notes were made of their verbal reports. During the interview at the end of the session subjects were asked to elaborate on the imagery and the experiences reported during the session. The imagery was coded for clarifying (by a "blind" judge) as to its main characteristics on a scale adapted from the Wallach and Kogan (1965) studies of creativity variables. It was also classified under seven major categories: mental events, physical (bodily) events, symbolic content, personal content, transpersonal content, and extrapersonal content. These were matched with the brain waves present at the time they were asked to report. At present, one third of the reports have been classified.

Most subjects were able to increase their production of alpha waves quite easily. Theta was more difficult but also was increased. Most interesting to us was the great increase in the ability to be aware of, hold on to, and report the hypnagogic imagery.

In addition to its potential for facilitating creativity, the significance of the study of hypnagogic imagery through theta training lies in what might be learned from the images. Hypnagogic imagery has an autono- mous character, seeming to follow its own course independently of the experiencer's will. In fact, attempts to observe it too closely or control it voluntarily usually make it disappear. One must learn to stand back and be a witness.

Some psychiatrists and neurologists have thought theta to be associ- ated only with psychopathology, but this may be because they have observed it mainly in patients. Our studies focused on normal, healthy subjects, and used biofeedback methods to explore the relation between specific internal states, or states of consciousness, and specific brain-wave patterns. We found theta to be associated with a deeply internalized state and with a quieting of the body, emotions, and thoughts, thus allowing usually "unheard or unseen things" to come to consciousness in the form of hypnagogic imagery.

Peter McKellar (McKellar and Simpson, 1954), while under the influence of mescaline during an experiment, used the analogy of hypnagogic imagery to communicate what he was experiencing to the experimenters. He thought it the closest analogy to something they might have experienced. We agree that the changing shapes and colors, the bizarreness of some of the images, the vividness of the experiences, and the many body changes described by our subjects do resemble to some extent the accounts of psychedelic and hallucinogenic experiences. Three of our subjects spontaneously told me, during interviews following a lab session, that they would not use marijuana or LSD again. They found more enjoyment in hypnagogic experiences and liked not only the feeling of being in control, but also the knowledge that what they were experiencing was not stimulated by something they had taken. We had made no inquiries as to whether prospective subjects ever used psychedelic drugs, but we did require their agreement not to use them for the duration of their participation in the project.

McKellar suggests that the scientific investigation of hypnagogic imagery is a route by which knowledge of abnormal experiences (whether psychotic or psychedelic) may be gained by the study of normal experiences. That is, we may learn about abnormal experiences by studying the seemingly abnormal experiences that occur to perfectly normal individuals during hypnagogic imagery. Alan Richardson, in his book on mental imagery (1969), cites research demonstrating that "confusion between the inner world of images and the outer world of percepts is present in individuals who are neither neurotic nor psychotic but well within the range of healthy psychological functioning."

We had not anticipated, in our research, the relatively high frequency of subject reports indicating that integrative experiences leading to feelings of psychological well-being were associated with extended alpha-theta practice. Training sessions during the first week or two left a few subjects feeling sluggish, fatigued, or nervous, but these effects were only temporary. One subject, for example, after a few weeks of practice reported having more energy, saying, "I don't feel drained all the time. I am able to encounter things easier because it doesn't seem like I'm burning up the nervous energy I seemed to burn up before. I seem more relaxed in my everyday approach to life."

Another subject said, "I have experienced generally, after sessions, a kind of speeding up. I feel good inside, physically things are in order, and I just feel sharper, sharper. I've noticed that the sharpness doesn't last, but with me it's a very precious experience. I have trouble feeling that way." Another described it as "I'm getting clearer and clearer." He described an experience he had: "It seems like last Saturday night something happened to me. Something clicked and I've felt different ever since, I'm calmer and I feel more inner peace. I just kind of slipped into a state of mind and I haven't left it much since—if you look at my notebook you'll see that this week things are picking up. I can get into myself much better." Other subjects put it in other ways: "I feel good, good after a session, like whatever I have to do, I can do"; "I feel so put together"; "I feel so with it."

Improvement in difficult interpersonal relationships was spontaneously reported, two with fathers, one with a roommate, due, the subjects felt, to growing tolerance and understanding on their part of the other person's point of view. Two students reported girlfriends liked them better—found them more interesting and easier to talk to. Several reported being more at ease in the classroom with their peers and with their professors.

There were many reports of rewards in school work. One subject, who worked an II-P.M.-to-7-A.M. shift on a job which allowed him to study, said, "I had this zoology test coming up. I studied all night. Then I practiced alpha-theta from nine thirty to ten thirty, and I had my zoology test at eleven. I had been, you know, tense, but everything went fine. That was funny for me. I was tense about the test, I'd been up all night, and yet I was able to relax and I did just fine." Another time, during the interview following an alpha-theta session in the laboratory, this same student reported that he had gathered a great deal of material for a paper that he was writing. Then a bout with the flu delayed him, and he got tense about the whole situation. There was no time to draw it all together, and besides, he'd forgotten everything that he'd read. It had become an "insurmountable problem," he told me. Then, during the alpha-theta session, he became very relaxed and had a feeling of detachment about the whole thing. In his words, "thoughts are so different when you're quiet like that." His mind began drifting through the articles he had read, and, he said, "everything just seemed to fall together."

Another student described his increased ability to concentrate in the following manner: "I had a test Monday morning. I stayed in on Sunday evening. I was going to study a little. It was about eleven or eleven thirty, and I was going to just skim over things. I sat down, and the next thing I knew it was six o'clock in the morning and I'd been studying right straight through. You know, I was so much into it, I didn't know it. I find myself totally involved now in what's happening. I'm able to let myself get out of the way and enjoy things more mentally, and because I can do it mentally it's more relaxing for me physically." Several subjects mentioned the feeling of greater involvement in whatever they were doing and also in their surroundings—for example, their increased awareness of nature: the varied colors, the wind, the trees, the sky.

Archetypal images (to use Jung's term) were the common experience of a number of our subjects: images of tunnels, the experience of going through a dark tunnel, or a tunnel lighted by sunlight at its end; images of stairs, and of climbing up or down; images of a cave or a pyramid. Images of a pair of eyes, or of a single eye, were reported by several subjects, as was the image of a wise old man in the form of a teacher, a professor, or a doctor. A book containing knowledge was another recurring image. As reported by one student, "I was in an office and I was asking someone for information; I needed to know something. Then this guy I had never seen before came from behind some file cabinets. He was a great big man, and he shoved this paperback book at me and said, 'The answer to everything you want to know is right in here.' I paged through the book backwards. There were all these Greek words, hand-script words, and in the middle there were pictures. You went through the book and you came to the section of all these picturelike things. All the words and symbols. When I looked at the words I knew 'That is the truth.' That's what I was after."

Quite early in the training there were reports of increased dreaming (or, rather, increased awareness and recall of dreams) and of imagery of past events occurring during practice sessions, some of them recalling forgotten events of childhood. They were not like going through a memory in one's mind but rather like an experience, a reliving. For example, this from a transcribed report: "Last Friday I got into some-

thing different during my practice, a kind of detachment. I began first sort of thinking of a bicycle I wanted to buy. And then I thought of a bicycle I had when I was a kid. And then zap, I was back in my child-hood, into a whole set of childhood feelings connected with sounds, with smells, how the gate sounded, all kinds of things. The smell of the back yard. The whole neighborhood. It must have lasted fifteen to twenty minutes, and I don't even know if I was getting feedback or not. It was strange, I was just totally lost for a while in that experience. Really absorbed, really startled by its clarity. It wasn't like, you know, you can remember about how the back yard looked, or you can think it looked like this, but when you start getting the smells and the sounds, that's different."

Such recall of early events brought to mind an article I had read some years before, "Imagery: The Return of the Ostracized," by Rob-ert R. Holt (1964). Holt stressed the importance of imagery and mem-ory, concluding with:

> *I want to mention briefly one speculative implication of the work on imagery, which to me opens the most exciting vistas. . . . Several lines of evidence are beginning to suggest that the capacity for an astonishingly complete recording of experience may be virtually uni-versal, and that the problem is primarily one of getting access to the traces . . . the vehicle of the extraordinary recall is imagery. . . . The indirect means of imagery may furnish the key to the fabulous store-house of memory, if we can learn how to make use of this neglected capacity.*

Theta training for hypnagogic imagery may be a way of opening the door to this "fabulous storehouse of memory."

As mentioned above, the state of deep quietness of body, emotions, and mind achieved in theta training seems to build a bridge between conscious and unconscious processes and allows usually "unheard things" to come to consciousness. Occasionally this included extra-sensory experience.

Elmer has already described those that occurred in the pilot group and noted that ESP was not a part of our theta-research project. Thus, when a subject reported an image related to something that was hap-pening in the control room which he would have had no way of know-ing through the usual sensory channels, we spoke of it among ourselves but no indication was given to the subject during the end-of-session interview that the image in question was unusual in any way. I recall two extrasensory images that were very simple and clear-cut, and the experiences of a third student which were quite complex.

The first occurred when, in the midst of a theta training session at the laboratory, a visitor stepped into the control room where Dale, Regina (our research assistant), and I were conducting the experiment. He had been in the room less than a minute when the subject reported over the intercom from the experimental room, "I just had an image of a man—a tall man with dark hair, and he was wearing horn-rimmed glasses." Our visitor was a tall man with dark hair, wearing horn-rimmed glasses.

The second occurred near the end of the research program. We had decided to have a spaghetti party at our home when the research was finished, to give subjects an opportunity to share their experiences with one another and ask questions that could not be answered during the course of the project. No mention of this had been made to the subjects. When several of us were discussing the party in the control room during a session, trying to decide on a suitable date, the subject reported over the intercom, "I had an image of being invited to something. It seemed like somebody—I don't know—I think it was Mrs. Green—was handing me an invitation to something." There was little chance that he could have heard us (there are two doors and a hall between the control room and the training room), but since we were not in separate buildings one can wonder if subliminal perception could have given him information that appeared to come from a nonsensory source.

Be that as it may, the extrasensory experience of the third student, a senior at Washburn University, is not easy to explain by a subliminal sensory process. It also happened near the end of the research. On a day when he came to discuss his week's practice sessions at Washburn, he reported the following events. During a theta session, just before noon in the early part of the week, he had an image of going home for lunch and hearing his roommate say, "You got a letter from Pittsburg [Kansas] and one from Wichita. You've been accepted for grad school at Wichita!" It was so real that he thought, "What's he doing opening my mail!", which brought him so completely out of the quiet state that he decided to end his session and go home for lunch. When he opened the door to his apartment, his roommate greeted him, letters in hand, saying, "Hey! You got a letter from Pittsburg and one from Wichita. You've been accepted for grad school at Wichita." "Did you open my mail?" he asked. "No," his roommate replied, "I just bent the envelope like this and peeked through the window and saw where it said you had been accepted."

The subject went on to tell of other strange things that had happened during the week. Several times he had known who was calling him before he picked up the phone, when calls were not expected, and in one case when it was someone who had never called him before. He ended with "I don't like this. I don't believe in any of this stuff." This student was a bright, practical person with a good sense of humor, but he was a psychology major in a behaviorist-oriented (Skinnerian) psychology department. He had no frame of reference into which he could fit what had happened. We talked for a while, and he accepted my suggestion to do some reading that might make the things that he had experienced seen more reasonable.

This student reported one further ESP experience that was precognitive. It was a few days after the conclusion of the training sessions. He came for a last conference, and I sensed that he was disturbed when he came in. He paced back and forth across the room, then told me that three nights before, just as he was falling asleep, he had had a sudden sharp image of Governor George Wallace being shot. It startled him, but he had shrugged it off as a bad dream, and in the hurry of the many pregraduation things to do during the next days, it had slipped his mind. While driving to the research building for his meeting with me, he had turned on his car radio and heard the announcement that Governor Wallace had been shot. He didn't want to know such things in advance, he declared. What was his responsibility? he asked. I answered that this is a problem to be considered. However, knowing the general nonacceptance of psychic phenomena, it was my feeling that he had no responsibility to tell anyone what he had "seen." Had he tried to do anything in that case, probably he would have been regarded as strange, sick, or maybe even dangerous.

We talked about such phenomena simply happening in one's life. If they happen, it may be useful to learn what one can from them rather than to deny them. But it is not necessary to seek them. Being psychic is often a nuisance, a distraction, and that is probably one reason why teachers down through the ages have recommended that one not strive for such powers. As one teacher put it: Seek ye first the kingdom of heaven which is within you and all else shall be added unto you.

I spoke with this student by telephone about six months later. He *was doing well in graduate school and was still using the relaxation and quieting exercises to advantage. He reported no further ESP experiences, but he no longer says "I don't believe in that stuff."*

We anticipated that there would be an increase in the ability of subjects to become aware of imagery, and that anticipation was borne out by results. But we had not expected, as previously mentioned, the relatively high frequency of subject reports (from twenty out of twenty-six subjects) associating "integrative experiences" with extended theta training. Such experiences led to feelings of physical and psychological well-being.

Is it not interesting that, on the one hand, many outstandingly creative people have reported that their greatest insights in physics, chemistry, mathematics, or esthetics were associated with reverie and hypnagogic imagery and, on the other hand, the imagery and insights reported by college students in the theta training project involved changes in their personal lives? The reason may be that we are all creative but in different ways.

The problems that students are most concerned with are not often the relatively abstruse, impersonal problems of classical creativity studies, but pertain to interpersonal relations (with teachers, girlfriends, roommates, parents), intrapersonal difficulties (feelings of guilt, insecurity, lack of confidence and self-identity), and attention problems (lack of concentration and inability to organize).

If our students had been mature Poincarés or Kekulés, their imagery might have been mathematical or chemical, but, not being at that advanced intellectual stage, and not being emotionally invested in such problems, they reported imagery and heightened awareness centered on themselves and personal problems in living. These also are amenable to insight, intuition, and creativity. As noted, we believe they are common property of humankind. It is in this sense that we say we are all creative.

The Use of Hypnagogic Reverie in Psychotherapy

A number of psychiatrists and clinical psychologists at the Menninger Foundation (and also across the country) have since become interested in knowing more about these integrative experiences. They have helped us implement a clinical research program with their patients, using a theta training program almost identical to that developed for the college students. Our basic rough hypothesis was, and is, "If psychiatric patients are trained in theta reverie, using insofar as is possible the same training technique used with college students, they will tend to have the same kinds of integrative experiences as college students." This unqualified statement may not be fully correct, but from a scientific point of view it provides a base for constructing research aimed at testing the idea.

Upon this base Alyce, Dale, and I have designed a research project called "Brain-wave Training for Mental Health." Twenty psychotherapists, representing a variety of approaches to physical and mental health, and about one hundred patients at the foundation will be part of this project. Although pilot work with patients has already given us positive indications of integrative experiences, far more work needs doing before conclusions can be drawn.

Theta training, as we use it clinically, is a blend of yoga, Autogenic Training, and biofeedback training—namely, a breathing exercise, relaxation and visualization, and a knowledge of results. The body, the emotions, and the mind are trained simultaneously, and brain-wave feedback tells when the desired state is prevailing. In order to produce theta consciously it is necessary to have a quiet body, tranquil emotions, and quiet thoughts *all at the same time.* We surmise that it is this state that leads to integrative reverie. Fortunately, the theta training technique is relatively simple and can be used as an adjunctive procedure by any clinician, whatever his or her theoretical orientation.

We wish to point out again that the idea of using reverie in psychotherapy is not new. In the world of psychoanalysis, Lawrence Kubie was impressed by this state of consciousness in the earliest years of his long and distinguished career. In 1943 he wrote:

> The hypnagogic reverie might be called a dream without distortion. Its immediate instigator is the day's "unfinished business," but like the dream it derives from more remote "unfinished business" of an entire lifetime as well. . . . Whatever the explanation . . . with [hypnagogic reverie] significant information about the past can be made readily and directly accessible, without depending upon the interpretation . . . of dreams. . . . It is probable that in this partial sleep, in this no-man's land between sleeping and waking, a form of dissociation occurs which makes it possible to by-pass the more obstinate resistances which block our memories in states of full conscious awareness, and which contribute to the distortion of memory traces in dreams. . . .

Kubie induced a state of hypnagogic reverie by feeding back breathing sounds, a "monotonous fixating stimulus." He notes that hypnagogic reverie can also be induced by total muscular relaxation. Both procedures have been used by yogis to attain a deep focus of attention.

We are familiar with two important contemporary approaches in the field of psychotherapy which make use of imagery and the reverie state with which "personal integration" is often associated. Roberto Assagioli's Psychosynthesis techniques (Assagioli, 1965) and Ira Progoff's "Dialogue House" techniques, reviewed in his recent book (1975), both use guided imagery. Induced imagery and reverie are being increasingly used in a variety of applications: for the treatment of acute neurotic disturbances (Beck, 1970; Leuner, 1969; Van der Berg, 1962); for removal of psychosomatic symptoms (Goldberger, 1952; Chappell and Stevenson, 1936); for inhibition of anxiety (Wolpe and Lazarus, 1966; Paul, 1966); for removal of amnesic blocks (Kubie, 1943); as a treatment method with emotionally disturbed youths (Trussell, 1974; Twemlow, 1974); and as a facilitator of integration in the therapeutic process. Desoille (1966) and Leuner (1969) also have advocated the use of guided imagery as a therapeutic method.

From what we have said, it is perhaps not surprising to note that David Foulkes, one of the foremost sleep researchers, found that subjects with the most "hypnagogic-type" imagery were psychologically healthier, had more social poise, were less rigid and conforming, and were more self-accepting and creative than those who report no hypnagogic imagery, who typically were authoritarian, rigid, conventional, and intolerant. These findings are consistent with the results of sensory-isolation studies in which occurrence of imagery appears to be related to intellectual flexibility and emotional freedom.

The following quotations summarize our own point of view on the benefits of using imagery as a standard tool in all psychotherapies.

> *Much light has been thrown on the understanding of normal personality by studies of the abnormal; hypnagogic experiences may illustrate the opposite process, namely a normal phenomenon illuminating the study of the abnormal . . . hypnagogic images may well provide a promising field of investigation as clues to the understanding of the individual personality and its emotional preoccupations. [McKellar, 1957]*

Censorship over verbal material is keen. Censorship over images is often less meticulous, and the patient may convey information without acknowledgment or without having to recognize officially the implication of the images. . . . Image formation is closely linked with emotion . . . and may propel towards expression of previously restrained emotions. . . . [Horowitz, 1970]

Referring to his experience with a patient, Kubie (1943) wrote, ". . . it is impossible adequately to convey . . . the free affectivity of the memories recaptured and revivified in these hypnagogic reveries."

The preceding discussion suggests that creativity is not limited in application to scientific or esthetic processes and problems. Creativity has applications in all areas of life, in domains physical, emotional, and mental. As people experience integrative changes in their lives, they experience a new kind of body consciousness very much related to their total well-being. In terms of physiological processes, creativity would appear to mean physical healing, physical regeneration. In the emotional domain, one might expect to find creativity manifested in improved relationships with other people as well as greater tolerance, understanding, and love of oneself and of one's world. Classical creativity in the mental domain involves new and valid ideas or syntheses of ideas, not primarily by deduction, but springing by intuition from unconscious sources. These too must be manifested; there must be a communicable product to complete the creative act.

8 Body Consciousness

... But in what figure shall we conceive the perfection of the body? ... An awakening in as great an entirety as possible of the body consciousness and an education and an evocation of its potentialities. ... Wherever limitations recede, the body becomes more plastic and responsive and in that measure a more fit and perfect instrument of the action of the spirit.

—SRI AUROBINDO

Among the professionals and students of the Humanistic Psychology and also of the Transpersonal Psychology persuasions, there is much discussion concerning body consciousness and its significance vis-à-vis emotional and mental awareness and total psychophysiological well-being. Opinion ranges all the way from "only body consciousness means anything" to "body consciousness is of no great importance." We think that both positions are right, and also wrong—an interesting paradox, but not a contradiction.

To explain that, we refer again to Aurobindo's concept of "interpenetrating energies," which was discussed in Chapter 5. In thinking about body consciousness, we again find it useful to follow Aurobindo in regarding matter as the densest form of spirit and spirit as the subtlest form of matter. His idea of "transforming" the body—making it a perfect tool and instrument—bringing in "overmind" and "supermind" energy, has room both for knowing the importance of the body and for realizing its relative insignificance. We think this seemingly contradictory statement expresses an important fact of nature.

It is easy to get into a metaphysical debate on this point. Most people are not aware of the basic neurological and existential facts that physiological psychologists take for granted. And those who are knowledgeable, including many psychologists who specialize in the study of sensory perception, do not take into account the basic existential significance of extrasensory perception. Consequently, there has been much confusion and conflict about body consciousness, leading some-times to extreme positions such as the puritan ethic and its opposite, the cult of the body.

Western science in the last two hundred years has conclusively demonstrated that there is no way to experience the world directly. In his eighteenth-century masterwork, *Critique of Pure Reason,* Imman-uel Kant established the idea that the causes of our sensations lie outside of us; we will never be able to know these causes directly, but only through the interpretation of our senses. A Kantian way of saying it is that in knowing something, "It is not the mind that conforms to things, but things that conform to the mind."

Don Juan, the Yaqui Indian teacher of Carlos Castaneda, main-tained exactly the same thing. Castaneda put it (1972): ". . . for a sorcerer, the world of everyday life is not real, *or out there,* as we be-lieve it . . . the world we all know, is only a description" (emphasis added).

About 450 B.C., Empedocles and some of the other early Greek thinkers had the idea that a ringing bell emitted little ringing bells that were conducted directly to the mind "through the door of the senses." Even as recently as one hundred fifty years ago many "scientists" still needed to be convinced that the sensory mind of the body never came in contact with the world, but only with the nerves that are agitated by energy from objects in the world.

One of the most well-demonstrated and accepted facts of modern neurology is that sensory consciousness depends on neural activity in the brain. For example, the rods and cones of our eyes pick up signals from the outside world and convert them to electrical impulses in fibers of the optic nerve. Then, through neural relays acting like telephone wires, signals are sent to that visual section of the brain previously referred to as the occipital cortex, the surface of the brain at the back of the head. If that piece of cortex is damaged, vision is damaged. If any of the nerve pathways or the optic nerve or the retina itself is damaged, vision is damaged. The important point is that the eye is an energy transducer. It converts electromagnetic energy of certain wavelengths (described as red through violet) into nerve pulses. These pulses form an intricate code in the occipital brain.

It is not the eye that sees, it is the "perceiver" in the brain, commonly called the *sensorium*. It is not the ear that hears, it is the sensorium. It is not the finger that feels, it is the sensorium. An example of this, which we have all experienced at one time or another, is getting hurt while playing a game and being unaware that we are bleeding and hurting until somebody points it out. Only then does the wound begin to hurt.

Taking all this into consideration, what is body consciousness? It seems that the correct answer is: awareness of all those sections of the sensorium which receive signals from the body. If all the sections of the body, including the voluntary and involuntary organs and tissues, are represented in the brain, as they seem to be, then the phrase "getting control of the body" really means "getting control of the central nervous system."

Looked at in this way, we have two obvious boundaries. The first boundary, the skin, separates us from the external world. The second boundary is inside, where the central nervous system meets the peripheral nervous system. The two boundaries are represented by the two circles of Figure 1. The peripheral nervous system interacts with the world outside our skin, and the central nervous system interacts with the peripheral nervous system.

If the central nervous system is then the "true" (relatively true) *inside* world, the peripheral nervous system is only a transducer zone and motor zone (operating the voluntary and involuntary parts of the body), and it too is in fact part of the outside world. Because of this, it is somewhat inaccurate and misleading to speak of "body consciousness." Not only are we not the world outside our skin, we are also not the world between the skin and the central nervous system. It is useful to keep this perspective in mind, so as not to get tangled in problems of identity.

For example, paraplegics who have lost all sensory and motor connections with the body below the neck are still subject to emotion, thought, pain, and pleasure. Who are they really? Certainly they are beings of (or, if not "of," then at least associated with) the central nervous system. We will say more about "Who am I?" later, in an in-depth look at our field of mind theory. Remember that when a sensory nerve is severed or otherwise damaged there is loss of sensation of some kind. If that severed nerve end is stimulated electrically, the person will report sensation in the body region that has been isolated. "Phantom limb" is a case in point. Many persons who have suffered loss of arms or legs report sensations, often pain, in the missing limb. They "feel" the limb, even though they know it is gone. What they are feeling often can be traced to excitation in the severed nerve trunks. Incidentally, such sensations, including pain in phantom limbs, are usually difficult to bring under control.

Parenthetically, it is worth noting that a neurosurgeon, Dr. Norman Shealy, in his Pain Rehabilitation Center in La Crosse, Wisconsin, has developed techniques for the control of such pain, and other kinds of pains too, through the use of techniques of self-regulation including autogenic-like training and biofeedback training. Dr. Shealy told us recently that he had trained four paraplegics, persons with severed spinal cords and therefore paralyzed, who suffered intractable pain presumably due to irritation of nerve endings, to control their pain through learning to "turn on alpha," the kind of brain-wave pattern usually associated with detachment, with attention turned away from the outside world. It is not easy when in pain to produce alpha in the occipital cortex, because the activating nature of the pain signal prevents relaxation, but if a person can nevertheless learn to produce alpha, the pain seems to recede. Sensation is still present "as a signal," but the agony does not appear. Pain control is to a large extent attention control. Shealy points out in *Occult Medicine May Save Your Life* (Shealy and Freese, 1975) that after attention control becomes automatic, the pain is automatically under control.

Having pointed out that body consciousness is really awareness in the central nervous system, we will nevertheless continue to use the term "body consciousness," to use the familiar shorthand that everyone uses when we say "My finger hurts." It is too cumbersome to say "Agitation of free nerve endings in my finger are being projected into brain areas that, when activated, and when attention is properly focused therein, give a feeling of pain."

We now turn to an important tenet of yoga. If a certain kind of body consciousness is developed—if one can become conscious in normally unconscious parts of the body, at will—then a large number of problems that afflict bodies begin to come under control. The examples cited on the following pages support the idea that body consciousness is an essential ingredient in becoming aware of certain normally unconscious processes. To become aware of the unconscious in a specific way is often the first step toward mind-body (psychosomatic) health.

An entertaining example that comes quickly to mind was provided by a professor from a university in Arizona. He was attending a Members' meeting of the Menninger Foundation and took the opportunity to visit us while in Topeka. After a few minutes of conversation it emerged that he had an excellent understanding of the role of consciousness in controlling normally involuntary physiological processes.

He first told how, about twenty years before, his stressful life had resulted in a stomach ulcer. His doctor said that surgery was necessary, but he decided that if he could become aware of his stomach psychologically, not just as a pain, and tell it what to do, he could handle the ulcer by himself. He didn't explain this to his doctor but was able to postpone the surgery for six weeks. By that time the ulcer had disappeared. We were reminded of Ira Progoff's Dialogue method for "contacting" offending and offended body organs.

His most ingenious use of consciousness was in the eradication (absorption) of hemorrhoids. His theory was almost identical to that of Johannes Schultz. It was necessary to "make mental contact internally with the part, to know it from inside," not just feel the pain. But how to make mental contact with a hemorrhoid? How to enhance internal awareness? Knowing that consciousness had to be increased in the offending part, he built a small battery-operated shocker that produced electrical stimuli of sufficient intensity to "focus consciousness" on a particular hemorrhoid. Wiring himself each day was no easy task, he said, but the device was easy to use. He merely pushed the stimulus button that he carried in his pocket and visualized the body absorbing the hemorrhoids. Within a few weeks they were gone, never to return. Of course, one might say that it has now been discovered that shocking a hemorrhoid will cause it to retreat, and the other nearby hemorrhoids will follow, but that was not my visitor's idea of what happened.

After hearing that story I wanted him to try hand-temperature control using the temperature-feedback meter without the benefit of autogenic suggestions, to see if he could do it the first time, without suggestion or previous training. I attached a thermistor to the middle finger of his right hand and showed him how the machine worked, then asked him if he could make his hand get warm. Within four minutes he had increased the temperature 7°F. That was a simple task. Then I said, "How about trying something more difficult? Make one hand warm and the other cold." He thought that would be interesting, so I attached another thermistor to the middle finger of the other hand, and he tried to produce a temperature difference between the two.

Usually a small temperature difference develops just from the attempt to make a change, but the difference in temperature between the two hands remained almost stationary, within about 0.2°F. After three minutes I was about to say that he shouldn't be disappointed, that this was not really an easy task and took some time to learn, when suddenly the temperature needle began to move rapidly, showing that the right hand, compared to the left, was getting cold. In one minute the temperature dropped about 5°F. "What are you doing?" I exclaimed. He laughed and said that he had goofed at first. When nothing happened after a couple of minutes, he realized that his visualization was wrong. His refrigerator had a hinge on the left, and he always opened the door with his left hand and took out the ice-cube tray with his right hand. In his imagination he had tried to put his left hand on the ice cubes, but his body knew better than that and wouldn't respond. After he corrected the visualization the temperature difference between the two hands changed rapidly.

He had discovered for himself a fact that we usually bring to people's attention during workshops: It is body *feeling* that is visualized, not an abstract idea. Autogenic phrases are used not as magical formulas but as a kind of map, a set of basic guidelines for the mind and body. Phrases are of no particular use after one knows how to do it. There is a body feeling associated with warmth in the hands that can be turned on at will, and when it is turned on the hands actually get warm. There is an increase in blood flow. After sufficient practice with a temperature trainer, a person can say, "That is the feeling of warmth." It may be a different feeling for different people, even as the smell of a rose seems to be different for different people, but each person who learns how knows what is meant. Almost everyone with whom we work eventually substitutes his own unique visualization and feeling for the autogenic phrases that are used at first.

The professor's examples indicated again to us that, more than any other factor, a certain body feeling is necessary for the control of normally involuntary body processes. The problem is to learn how to turn on appropriate body feelings at will. Although psychologists have long thought this impossible, it is now clear that it is impossible in the same way that it is impossible to control the autonomic nervous system—that is, it is an error in the textbooks. Students and practicers of yoga, on the other hand, have known for centuries that such control is possible and can be acquired. This was demonstrated in our lab.

The yoga teacher of Rishikesh, India, Swami Rama, was our "Swami in residence" in the fall of 1970. We thought it would reduce culture shock if he lived at our house, and were pleased when he accepted our invitation. To provide him and us with additional interaction, we organized a yoga study group. We also hired as a research assistant our son, Doug Boyd, to help Swami Rama with any adjustment difficulties and with the details of schedules, appointments, correspondence, etc. Doug had just returned from eight years in Korea and was especially capable of working with Asian people. Doug published his recollections of his association with Swami Rama in Topeka and other yogis he met later in India in his book *Swami* (1976). In Chapter 11 we will discuss the results of our research with Swami Rama. What we wish to talk about here is an exercise in body consciousness that Swami Rama gave the yoga study group, and later also demonstrated in public.

The group met twice a week for three hours of discussion and practice of a variety of yoga exercises. Swami Rama called one of these "traveling through the body." A person lay on the floor, and the Swami touched with a yardstick the body areas numbered sequentially in Figure 4, allowing about fifteen seconds between points. As he touched each spot he said the corresponding number. After each person had gone through the exercise once, with another person touching the body area in order to help focus consciousness, it was thereafter done mentally. It is merely necessary to lie down flat on one's back and to say to oneself, "One," visualizing as clearly as possible a *feeling* of being in the forehead; "Two," visualizing as clearly as possible a feeling of being in the throat, etc. The effects of this exercise were always interesting, and sometimes were remarkable. Eventually we ran each member of the theta pilot group (described in the previous chapter), studying brain-wave patterns as they went through this procedure while lying on a couch in our laboratory. They said each number aloud to help us (in the recording room) keep track of their progress.

It is not easy to remain conscious and go all the way through the numbers in a quiet, inner-focused way. Attention is theoretically not allowed to wander from the body point associated with a number, but that is easier said than done. Sometimes subjects would forget where they were and we would have to tell them what their last number was. Of particular interest to us was the fact that over a period of five months in which our subjects practiced this procedure among others ten days per month (or more if they desired), there was a significant

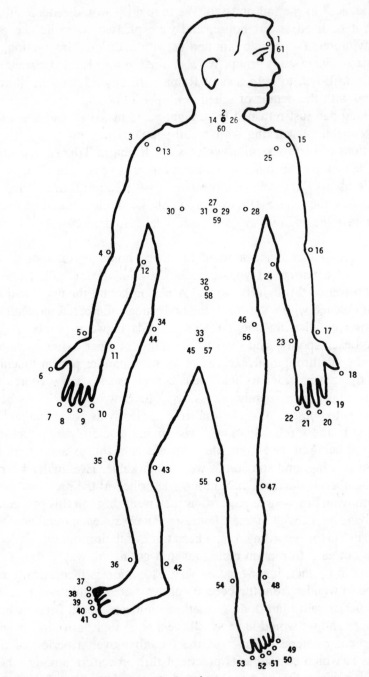

Figure 4. **Traveling-through-the-body points.**

increase in the amount of theta production from the occipital cortex during these "travels."

Swami Rama always asked each person he worked with in the group to describe the experiences or images that occurred during the traveling through the body. As time passed I realized that he was teaching, in a very simple way, a kind of yoga that had much esoteric significance in some of the Indian literature. The basic idea is that each section of the body is alive with a life of its own, with its own physical needs and emotions. We human entities are in actuality composed of all these pieces. That is, we are a composite, being made up of a multitude of unconscious beings about whom we must become conscious if we are to bring them under control. This concept is almost the reverse of the one held in Western science and medicine, which generally do not allow that the various sections of the unconscious are autonomous entities, working for themselves, as it were, as unconscious parts of our psyche. Perhaps the closest modern idea is Gordon Allport's concept of "functional autonomy" of personality traits (Allport, 1950).

And is this not remarkably similar to what don Juan called "the sorcerer's explanation" of personal identity? In *Tales of Power* (Castaneda, 1974) he said to Carlos after a certain shocking experience, ". . . you realized your true nature. *You are a cluster*" (emphasis added). Later he said, "When the glue of life binds those [autonomous] feelings together a being is created, a being that loses the sense of its true nature and becomes blinded by the glare and clamor of the area [of life]."

Swami Rami did not explain any of this to the group but always asked for their experiences each session. I finally asked him one day why he didn't explain to the members what traveling through the body was for. I gave my interpretation of the exercise, and he agreed that the basic idea was correct. He did not want to tell anyone, he said, because then it would be impossible to find out what really happened in anyone's experience. Swami spoke of the autonomous entities as if they were real. The training in body awareness was training in becoming conscious of them, so that they could be instructed or regulated in whatever way seemed useful. After becoming conscious of body parts by traveling through the body, it is much easier to talk to the body for therapeutic purposes. If he explained this, he said, all that he would get back from the students would be what he told them. Or, if they had had some experiences on their own, they would be mixed with his descriptions so that he would be unable to decide what was really happening.

In his book *Man: The Grand Symbol of the Mysteries* (1932), Manly Palmer Hall discusses the concept of the human body as a Noah's Ark of living "forces" that make up our nature. In a physical sense these living forces are our bodies. In the psychological sense they are our minds, conscious and unconscious.

Ralph Hefferline's work (1962) at Columbia University, conducting a survey among college students about awareness of body parts, has a significant relationship to the yoga exercise of traveling through the body. Hefferline wrote: ". . . on the assumption that the condition of the musculature could be taken to be part of the world of things and events and thus susceptible to observation and verbal report, I prepared mimeographed instruction sheets entitled *Informal Experiments in Self-Awareness* and distributed them to undergraduates enrolled in courses in abnormal psychology. In the course of about seven years, sets of reports were collected from more than a thousand students." (A version of this material, together with verbatim excerpts from written reports submitted by students, was published as the first half of a collaborative book entitled *Gestalt Therapy* [Perls, Hefferline, and Goodman, 1951].) Much to his surprise, he found that some students were totally unconscious of entire sections of the body. The following descriptions of procedures and results is paraphrased from Dr. Hefferline.

As part of the assignment the subject was encouraged to make what amounted to a systematic proprioceptive (muscle tension, tendon, and joint senses) survey of his own body, conducted in private with minimum external distractions. A person presumably should be able to discriminate the tension condition of all or of any part of his skeletal musculature. The first impression of a subject is likely to be that he can do this. He can feel, he says, every part of his body. When further inquiry is made, it often turns out that what he took to be proprioceptive awareness of a particular body part was actually a visualization of the part or a verbal statement of its location. Or else, to become aware of the part, he may have had to intensify sensation by making actual movements.

With further work, if he can be persuaded to continue, the subject may report certain parts of his body to be missing. Suppose it is his neck. He may have internal awareness of a mass that is his head and a mass that is his trunk, with what feels like simply some empty space between. At this stage the subject is apt to remember more important things to do, and his participation in the silly business ends.

Some subjects, however, apparently made curious by blank spots and hopeful of recovering some lost degree of freedom in their system of voluntary control, do whatever is involved in paying closer attention to and acquiring interest in this peculiar private situation. A blank spot, they say, may gradually fill in. Or it may suddenly become the locus of sharp pain: "electric" sensations, or the unmistakable ache of muscular cramp.

Then what formerly was a blank may become as demanding of attention as an aching tooth. Further and more detailed discriminations may be made. It may soon become imperative to relax the cramp, but the subject says that he does not know how to do so; he is concerned with so-called voluntary muscles, but these are reportedly not under voluntary control. The subject is somewhat in the position of the elementary psychology student who is assured that he has the voluntary muscles needed to wiggle his ears. The difference, of course, is that in the case of ear-wiggling he has never acquired control, whereas in the case of the cramped muscles he has somehow lost control. When the problem was how to regain control—in those days before EMG (muscle) feedback made the process relatively simple—a variety of approaches could be tried. One way that Dr. Hefferline suggested was to continue to pay sustained attention to the blocking, regardless of discomfort, and to be on the alert for subtle changes of any sort.

"Another instruction," he wrote, "is to increase the clinch deliberately, if possible, and then, while relaxing from this added intensity, to learn something about relaxing still further." (This is the method made famous by Edmund Jacobson in *Progressive Relaxation.*) Hefferline continued: "When a muscular block is definitely resolved, it is frequently claimed by the subject that there occurs vivid, spontaneous recall of typical situations, perhaps dating back to childhood, where he learned to tense in this particular manner. . . ."

This phenomenon of sudden recall is commonly reported by biofeedback clinicians, as in the case of Rosencranz's patient who recovered from Raynaud's disease. After warming her hands 20°F, she began to weep, recalling the blocked emotional trauma when her son packed up and left her, twelve years previously. Through temperature training she released a chronic spasm in the vascular system. Associated with that release of vascular tension was a release of emotional tension.

Dr. Hefferline commented: "Such subjective accounts of proprioceptively controlled events, although they may be revealing and fully convincing when made at first hand in observing one's own behavior, are obviously not to be taken at face value as scientific data. . . . A first step in this direction, it is believed, is the attempt to achieve quantitative measurement of proprioceptive stimuli and to lay foundations for a method of checking verbal report against instrumentally obtained data."

Note that biofeedback instruments are useful not only in developing self-control of body behavior through developing awareness of changes in body processes, but also in supplying the "instrumentally obtained data" that Hefferline called for in order to corroborate verbal reports objectively.

Hefferline noted that since the "uncontrollable tensions" he studied were in voluntary muscles,

> . . . one might presume that the individual, if his attention were directed to the conflict, might deliberately terminate the conflict in one direction or the other. Paradoxically, he can do this only indirectly, by the roundabout procedure of making a kind of proprioceptive inspection of this situation in the *internal* environment and then, with persistence and some luck, discovering *how* he maintains the muscular conflict. It is usually only after some increased mobility develops—the typical accompaniment of discrimination of slight changes in the contracture— that the question of why is likely to receive an answer. [Emphasis added]

Is it not interesting that an EMG biofeedback meter does exactly what Hefferline says is necessary? It provides "discrimination [awareness] of slight changes in the contracture" and this results in the development of awareness in the "internal environment."

We have devoted much of this chapter to the nature of body consciousness, the awareness of all those sections of the sensorium which receive signals from the body. This awareness is important because it allows for psychosomatic integration and health. Now let us talk about some techniques for developing body consciousness.

Except for the striate muscles, normally the body doesn't pay much attention to what we want it to do. Putting it another way, we could say that normally the involuntary section of the nervous system pays very little attention to the voluntary parts; the subcortical sections generally ignore the cortical sections. Or we could say that normally the unconscious pays very little attention to the conscious. In hypnosis, the hypnotist talks directly to the unconscious of his subject and the cortex gets out of the way, sometimes so far out of the way that the subject cannot remember anything that happened during the hypnotic session. The question is, How can a person talk directly to his own unconscious? Under what conditions is the body listening so that it will accept instructions and carry them out?

We found an informative event described in the biography of Edgar Cayce, *There Is a River* (Sugrue, 1942). Edgar Cayce, who died in 1945, had a remarkable ability to go into a trance and diagnose physical, emotional, and mental disorders in patients of whom he had no knowledge except for their names, ages, and whereabouts. This event took place at a time when Edgar was working with a group of doctors in a medical therapy team. They were applying his readings to patients whose illnesses he had diagnosed. The author, Thomas Sugrue, tells how a friend one day found Edgar lying immobile on the floor, with doctors trying to revive him. One had injected adrenalin and another had injected some other drug. The friend recognized that Edgar was merely in a trance state, and, very upset at what they were trying to do, kneeled down at Edgar's side. Bending near, he heard Edgar whisper to him, "Tell the body to reject the medicine."

So he told the body to reject the medicine, and soon the injections came back up out of the muscles and formed little lumps under the skin. The tissues apparently had not absorbed the fluids, and the muscles had constricted in the proper sequence of motor-unit firings so that the liquids were forced up through the punctures in the tissues. The medicines could not get through the skin without help, however, because the holes had crusted over. Edgar soon revived.

This story was a strange one for someone like myself, who had memorized much neuroanatomy and neurophysiology and thought in terms of neural circuits and control loops. How could telling the body to reject the medicine make it happen? How could the body prevent the medicine from infiltrating the tissues? The main technical question in my mind concerned the muscle-firing patterns that must have been required in order to bring the fluid back to the surface. How could such a sequence be initiated and carried through merely by telling the body to do so?

As it happened, I had a chance to experiment with this process myself. When I was cutting my lawn one day, the mower slipped into a ditch, and when I jerked it out I sprained my right shoulder. The shoulder ached for a couple of days, but I thought it would recover quickly

---

because it was only a strained muscle. The ache continued for weeks, however, and then began to get worse. Four months later the pain had seriously increased, and I was bothered by it much of the time while awake. I asked our staff doctor at the foundation what my problem was. He said it probably was bursitis and that injections of cortisone into the shoulder might help. When I jerked the lawn mower out of the ditch I had probably broken one or more small blood vessels, he said, and some bleeding had occurred between the sheaths that hold the muscles in bundles. When a person is young, such an injury is rapidly repaired and the chemicals released between the sheaths are absorbed back into the body, but when a person gets older this often does not occur properly, and a residue of calcium crystals is left. These grainy crystals continuously scratch the sheaths and the bursa, the lubricated-bearing surface over which tendons pull. They become irritated and inflamed, and the free nerve endings in those tissues are agitated each time the limb is moved. In some patients the shoulder aches continuously.

I declined the cortisone injection with thanks, saying that I was quite busy but that if the problem persisted I might be back. I did not want to explain that I wanted to try to handle it in my own way. We can experiment with a problem that is not an emergency, treating it as a challenge in the mind-body domain. (If a problem is acute rather than chronic, however, Alyce and I make use of whatever medical aid we can get.) A chronic physical problem can provide an excellent laboratory-type setup with which to try various procedures. We had already developed ways of handling some physical disorders, such as the flu, and bursitis would provide a different kind of problem.

The bursitis did not yield to any of the visualization techniques that I had used in the past, however, and I began to think (in part of my mind) about the solidity of calcium crystals and their lack of responsiveness compared to normal tissues. I was in a sterile visualization bind. Mulling over the problem, not working on it very much, I thought about the Cayce story and the physiological state in which his body was told to reject the medicine. Cayce's body was unusually passive when his friend told the body to reject the medicine. Was the state of deep trance useful? Perhaps when the body is deeply passive it is quiet enough to hear what it is told.

I decided to try to get into that immobilized state consciously and then tell the body what I wanted it to do. Although I had had experience, from occasionally waking from sleep in that particular state, it was extremely difficult to produce it at will. My usual meditation did not generate such a trancelike condition, and I had almost given up hope of using that technique when, about three A.M. one night, I was brought to consciousness by the pain of the bursitis and realized that the body was in the desired state. How fortunate. I was fully conscious, but felt unable to move. From previous experience I knew that with great effort I could force the body to move, to wake up, so to speak, but for the moment I was in a conscious natural trance state. Immediately I began constructing a visualization in which large increases in the flow of blood and lymph in the shoulder were a major feature. After about thirty seconds I realized that I did not know what chemicals were needed to dissolve calcium crystals, so I instructed the body to mobilize whatever biochemicals were needed, manipulate the concentration levels as necessary, bring the needed acids, enzymes, or whatever, and dissolve the crystals, restoring the tissues to normal. I held the visualization successfully for two to three minutes and then suddenly realized that my attention had wandered. I was thinking of something else. My first thought was "Oh, yes, I'm supposed to be thinking about my shoulder." So I put my attention there. To my surprise, there was no sensation of pain. That was a relief, and I immediately went to sleep. In the morning I was able to raise my arm over my head for the first time in three months, and the pain was almost gone. In the next three weeks the pain faded away completely, never to return.

These events occurred a few years before Swami Rama taught us the traveling-through-the-body exercise. Nevertheless, I recognized the feeling of internalization that I had during the traveling exercise as being of the same quality, though not the same depth, as the trance state in which the bursitis problem had been solved.

It is interesting to speculate about what actually happens in a case such as I have described. It is necessary to remember that from a neurological point of view, all perception is in the central nervous system. My visualization was, therefore, in the right-shoulder control areas of the central nervous system, but the blood flow and chemical changes, or whatever, took place in the body outside of the central nervous system.

Visualization seems to be the quickest and surest way of programming the body, perhaps because it involves a global instruction rather than a neurological instruction. The difference between these types of instruction is comparable to the difference between current computer languages and the primitive computer languages we used in 1948. Most computers solve problems with diodelike circuits, which are either on or off. In this on-or-off feature, the computer is very much like a brain, in that individual nerve cells either fire or do not fire. In general, they do not partially fire but fire full force, just like diodes.

In the early days of computer use at the Naval Ordnance Test Station, a group I supervised had to solve a problem in which there were 1,800 mathematical steps. It took six months of work to generate the program and make it work. In order to write it all down in binary language, each diode step of the process had to be handled individually. Nowadays a computer programmer does not bother with the actual language the computer uses to solve problems, but instead uses a command language, such as Fortran One, Fortran Two, Cobal, or some other such language. A command language involves a mathematical structure in which the computer is told what to do in terms of what is desired—for instance, "Take the fourth root of x." It is easy to use. A program that took us six months to write might take only two weeks now. The important point is that the command program tells the machine itself to generate the binary language needed for operating the diode circuits and getting answers.

In much the same way, the binary neurological machinery of the body follows *command visualizations*. We need not program each nerve directly, even though that may be possible, as single-motor-unit research has demonstrated. Instead, we visualize what we want to have happen globally and the body converts the command visualization into the individual neural process for execution. The body seems to know what to do if the person knows what is desired. In an example mentioned previously, a medical student, in order to warm his hands, visualized going outdoors on a cold day so that his body would compensate for the imagined cold weather by increasing the peripheral blood flow. His body knew what he wanted, and that visualization worked for him. For the average person, however, as we have mentioned before, the usual visualization is one of warmth, such as lying on a warm beach with the sun shining on one's hand, or holding something warm in the hand.

The body does not seem to care about the scientific accuracy of the command, or about the results per se. It simply carries out commands. Negative, destructive commands are followed, it seems, with as much success as positive commands. It is this very fact that gives rise to the peculiar physiological behaviors called psychosomatic diseases. Pa-

tients' visualizations of success or failure, sickness or health, and ideas
about their body and mind together determine to an important extent
what happens to them.

The root of psychosomatic disease lies in unconscious and involun-
tary domains. It is the unconscious that gets the message from oneself
and from other people and the environment. If we accept the external
commands, we tend toward being field-dependent. It is our task with
biofeedback training to become field-independent. That is what we
mean when we tell patients that it is not life that kills us, but rather our
reaction to life. The statement implies that the reaction can be con-
trolled. Using biofeedback, we show that the reaction can definitely be
controlled; we can increase our measure of field-independence. In
Chapter 9 the intricacies and implications of field-independence will
be considered in detail.

This chapter on body consciousness would not be satisfactory without
a discussion of the work of cancer specialists Dr. Carl Simonton and
his wife, Stephanie, of Fort Worth, Texas. They have been able to teach
cancer patients how to use visualization to aid in recovery from cancer.

But first let us go back a bit. Through the Library of Congress and
the libraries of Harvard and MIT, Erik Peper, the 1976 president of
the Biofeedback Research Society, made a computer search of the
medical literature to find all reported cases of spontaneous remission
from cancer. About four hundred articles were found and compiled as
a bibliography. When Alyce and I examined this list of references, as
well as other reports, we noticed that people had "spontaneously" recovered from cancer with a variety of methods. Some went to Lourdes
Cathedral, others to Arizona for a "grape-juice cure," and still others
to the mountains, to live at high altitudes, where the negative-ion concentration is supposedly "high enough to cure cancer." Since "spontaneous remission" is a medical term meaning "we are ignorant of the
causes of recovery," and since all recoveries are related to *something,*
the question is, What factor or factors did many or most of these people
have in common? The only common factor that I could find was a
change of attitude in the patient prior to "spontaneous remission," a
change involving hope and other positive feelings.

We were interested, therefore, to hear Carl and Stephanie Simonton
report (1975) that their survey of the literature had led to a conclusion similar to ours. They reported that the literature unquestionably
recognized a relationship between emotions and stress on the one hand

---

and malignancy on the other. Changing attitudes became one of their major tools in bringing recovery from cancer. The other major tool they use is visualization.

After discussing the possibility of a cancer type of personality, comparable to a heart-disease type of personality, the Simontons pointed out that cancer patients usually resist very strongly the idea that their own personality and their attitude are in any way part of the problem. Speaking relatively, the heart-disease personality is far more socially acceptable than the cancer personality, which includes a strong tendency, they say, toward self-pity and a poor self-image.

It seems necessary to change this attitude and self-image and also to supply the patient with a visualization in which the body is told what to do in order to achieve a slowing or remission of the disease process. Totally intermixed are the belief system of the patient, the belief systems of the family and others who mean something to the patient, and the belief systems of the physicians and therapists. It is clear that the belief system of the patient is inside his skin and the belief systems expressed by others come from outside the patient's skin. To the extent that outside beliefs influence the patient's well-being, a degree of dependence (*field-dependence*) is involved. That is, if the patient allows the attitudes of the doctor or the family to influence the disease, then he is acting in a dependent manner.

A major handicap in cancer patients, the Simontons noted, is a self-image which pictures them as victims of the disease. An almost insurmountable problem arises when, as they say, the physician's belief system parallels the patient's belief that "the disease comes from without, that it's synonymous with death, that the treatment is bad, and the patient has little or nothing that he can do to fight the disease."

But some cancer patients are able to fight back, to defeat the disease process. The Simontons reported that such patients had a common weapon: "visualizing themselves being well." Analyzing such cases to learn what such patients' thoughts about themselves were, from the time they were given their diagnosis to the time they were free of the disease, without benefit of medical treatment, the Simontons found none who had not used visualization to help himself. Their visualizations were uniquely personal, and all were very positive.

The mirror-image negative effect from negative visualization appears to be valid also. Dr. Simonton includes "type of visualization" in diagnosing. Too often, he said, a patient sees the cancer as "some big powerful thing, and the treatment as some little weak something that doesn't do much. He sees his white blood cells, his own immune mechanism, as really non-existent, and he is trying to coax it into working. These are to me very bad signs. I say they are bad signs because patients who verbalize this, in general, are doing very poorly at the time of their telling me this."

Stephanie Simonton works with groups of patients, helping them to become aware of their own roles in the development and course of their disease. She notes that at the outset she and Carl try to understand the patient's belief structure in order to adapt the treatment to the patient's needs and values: ". . . if we get into a conflict with their beliefs, they constantly fight us, and will almost get worse in spite of us, or *to* spite us." It is important to point out that patients are treated with radiation therapy or chemotherapy, or whatever is appropriate, *and* with psychotherapy. Most of them, having reached Dr. Simonton's clinic through the usual medical referral channels, do not know that they will have a chance to receive psychotherapy along with physical therapies. More than 80 percent of them refuse to participate in any form of psychotherapy. They will not attend group-therapy sessions. There is also the problem of *secondary gain,* the benefits—such as increased attention and escape from underlying interpersonal problems— which the patient derives from his or her illness. Says Stephanie Simonton, "They will not use the relaxation visualization techniques we prescribe. Many of them not only refuse to talk about it, or allow us to talk to their families about the psychological aspects of their disease, but they might even go back to their physician and ask to be referred to another doctor. That was a shock to me, yet as I continue to work with the patients, I begin to understand more of this. . . ."

The Simontons' approach to cancer, which is successful with certain patients, clearly illustrates many of the points we have made regarding body consciousness and visualization for changing body processes.

Homeostasis

The greatest discovery of my generation is that human beings, by changing the inner attitudes of their minds, can change the outer aspects of their lives. . . . It is too bad that more people will not accept this tremendous discovery and begin living it.

—WILLIAM JAMES

While I was still in the business of testing rockets and guided missiles for the U.S. Navy at China Lake, I had an unusually good opportunity, starting in 1950 and ending about 1955, to learn some things about human relations. The Harvard Graduate School of Business Administration had developed its casebook for the study of human relations in companies, and Robert Tannenbaum at UCLA was developing his theories of group interaction. Perhaps because life aboard ship tends to focus attention on interpersonal problems, the Navy carried out an experimental on-the-job group relations training program in the test department at NOTS. In addition to having materials and also workshop conductors from Harvard and UCLA, our management group studied Carl Rogers's *Client Centered Therapy* (1951). It was not intended that we should become therapists, of course, but the principles of right human relations and a humanistically oriented therapy like Rogers's are similar in many respects (and, as will be discussed below, also have a powerful effect on inside-the-skin problems). It was then that I began to understand our own family better and to realize that each person's development and balance involves the whole family. The family consciously *and* unconsciously helps and hinders. Since children are continuously changing, it is necessary continuously to shift family relationships until the children, who start out totally dependent on their parents, end up as independent as good friends usually are, even though a special relationship still exists.

Many of us who participated in the program at China Lake were very enthusiastic at first about the possibility that training in right human relations would not only help solve problems between and within small groups, but would also be applicable on a national scale and even on aň international scale. Eventually we noticed, however, that individuals who returned from high-intensity group-relations workshops and laboratories were not successful in changing their organizations. In fact, relationships often tended to worsen. Sometimes the "enlightened" member no longer could exist in the group and would quit his job.

What was happening? Psychologist Paul Buchanan, director of the human-relations program at China Lake at that time, explained the problem to Alyce and me as one of *homeostasis in group relations*. Since this has an important correspondence in the problems of individual "psychosomatic health," it is useful to discuss homeostasis at some length.

The concept was first formulated by W. B. Cannon (1932) as a characteristic of physiological systems. It refers to the tendency of an organism to compensate for disturbance, to maintain stability. Homeostatic mechanisms govern the heart, for instance, to prevent it from going too fast or too slow. Homeostasis includes the ability of the organism to adapt to its surroundings. It is more than mere inertia, which is the passive tendency of a body to resist change. Homeostasis is an active tendency to restore equilibrium, to maintain steady states in the face of constant change.

In a physiological sense we could not survive without homeostasis, but it is important to know that continuous pressure can modify homeostatic balance. Continuous overwork without relaxation at times will push the heart beyond its capacity to rebalance during rest—and then we have trouble. Homeostasis keeps us healthy and bouncing back from the strains and pressures of life—up to a point. If we are continuously reacting to stress, then homeostatic balances gradually shift, for they are not permanently fixed, and the undesirable result in our body is called psychosomatic disease. *If such a "disease" does develop, then homeostasis actively maintains it* until we do something about it.

A wart is a small nonuseful homeostatic entity that does not usually shrink or grow very much, and it resists change actively when you try to get rid of it. If you cut it off, it "tries" to regrow. Habits are also homeostatic, and perhaps in one sense a bad habit is a psychological wart; if destructive enough, it might be called a psychological cancer. Gordon Allport's idea of personality traits developing "functional autonomy" is a concept in this direction.

In any case, as Paul Buchanan said, it appears that every group of people represents a kind of psychological matrix, a psychological summation, that acts to preserve itself against change. It is, no doubt, the individuals in a group who act to resist change, but it appears that the group itself is resisting change. Thus, if a member of the group attended a training laboratory and returned with beautiful ideas of better group functioning, that individual was likely to be unconsciously encapsulated and neutralized by the group so as to prevent change, somewhat as a cyst develops around a foreign object in the body. Homeostatic processes in groups are as clever as the unconscious of individuals in blocking change.

One striking illustration of the effects of group homeostasis occurred at NOTS. A high-level executive got the idea that his organization would be a better tool in his hands if, in the joint effort of its divisions, branches, and sections, it worked more harmoniously, and he insisted on a study of group relations. Almost all of the management team then went through a three-year program in human relations, but the boss himself declined. He said that if he went through the program he might change and then "wouldn't know who" he was. But it would be useful, he insisted, if the group members would become more cooperative and harmonious. The program worked well, and a great deal of creative energy was released. Individuals moved toward increased freedom in comparison with their previous, more restricted behavior, and friction developed between the group and the top executive. The result was that he, who indeed did not change, quit. He did not fit the new functional relationship the group had developed without him.

Another kind of automatic balance that everyone is quite familiar with might be called personal psychological homeostasis. If a person decides to modify a habit, it seems that everything in one's nature conspires to prevent change. Don Juan explained this to Carlos Castaneda when Carlos was trying to develop "lucid dreaming," trying to become fully aware of being himself in his dream. (This is a significant state for expansion of awareness, as will be mentioned later in the discussion of the field of mind theory.) In *Tales of Power* Carlos tells how don Juan warned him that the early stage of developing this ability "consisted of a deadly game that one's mind played with itself, and that some part of myself was going to do everything it could to prevent the fulfillment of my task. That could include, don Juan had said, plunging me into a loss of meaning, melancholy, or even a suicidal depression. I did not go that far, however. My experience was rather on the light, comical side; nonetheless the result was equally frustrating."

In other words, trying to make a psychological change is going to be opposed by the mind itself. Anyone who has tried to break a habit or change his ways knows about that. So do people who have tried to raise their level of craftsmanship or artistry, such as musicians trying to reach a higher degree of mastery.

From the yogic point of view, psychological homeostasis represents not only a psychological state but also a physiological state. That is why fasting, diets, various physical exercises, and emotional- and mental-control exercises are considered necessary, or useful at least, in bringing about personality change and development.

An example of the positive side of homeostasis is provided by the violin virtuoso Jascha Heifetz. He was asked to explain how, with only a week's practice, it was possible for him to play an extremely difficult concerto after having not played it for a year. "It is because it was properly learned in the first place," he said.

Now consider negative homeostasis in the family. If someone has a "usually fatal" disease, the family can hinder that person's recovery. This is not because the family wants the person to die, but because the family succumbs to the "usually fatal" label, adjusts to the inevitability of death, and, at an unconscious level, resists the change that recovery represents. This is one of the most striking findings the Simontons have made in their work with cancer victims.

In the early days at Travis Air Force Base, Carl Simonton reported that he had a few impressive successes with patients who later were told by their families, in effect, "You're crazy, no one can get over cancer that way." In some instances the result of the family rebuff was catastrophic: The cancers returned and the patients soon died. The inevitable but unanswerable question is: To what extent was the unfortunate outcome the result of the family's negative response?

When the Simontons moved their practice to Fort Worth a few years later, they were convinced that it was essential to bring in the family, if at all possible, to explain that the patient's welfare depended on them as well as on the patient.

The problem with the family is the same as the problem with the patient. The same tendency is in all of us, more or less. It is not easy to accept responsibility for future events without feeling guilty for past events, especially when a doctor says, "I have news for you, this family has cancer and this person [the patient] is stuck with it." If we become aware that a family relationship has resulted in undesirable physiological behavior in ourselves or in a family member, we need to forget the blame for the past and instead accept some responsibility for trying to make a change.

The Simontons focus on emotional needs. Carl finds that the greatest single factor predisposing to the development of the disease is the loss of a loved one six to eighteen months prior to the diagnosis. The loss engenders feelings of helplessness and hopelessness, feelings that often precede and accompany cancer. In this situation the attitude of the family is of major concern. If the family does not want to think about interpersonal relations and the possible physiological consequences, then the patient has two big hurdles to leap: his own attitude and the attitude of his family.

It seems evident that the family is an important element in any psychosomatic illness. In the first ten recoveries from Raynaud's disease that were reported to us, three of the patients were mothers who had been rejected by their sons. The emotional trauma suffered by the women was followed within days or weeks by the appearance of Raynaud's disease. The anger and grief they experienced was blocked, not adequately recognized and handled, until temperature training released the vasospasm and simultaneously released the withheld grief.

In recovering from migraine, patients who remember any causes whatsoever almost always remember problems associated with their families. A striking case was recently told to us by Barbara Pearse. One of the patients she worked with was a woman with a ten-year history of migraine. She was under heavy sedation in a hospital because of the migraine problem when, having heard of our project, she sent an inquiry. Although she could not come to Dr. Sargent's office, it was agreed that Barbara could take a temperature trainer to the hospital and work with her every day for at least a week. Barbara hoped that might help.

Barbara reported that for the first few days the patient did not seem to understand what was required, most likely because she was so heavily sedated. At last, after five days, the woman seemed to grasp what she was supposed to do and then began a rapid recovery. After five weeks she no longer required drugs, had no migraine, and looked like an entirely different person, full of energy and eager to live again.

Shortly after the problem seemed to be solved, she showed up at Barbara's office in a very depressed mood and said that she was more unhappy now than when she had had migraine. She had thought that if she could only get rid of migraine, her life would be wonderful. But now her family was falling apart. As soon as she began to get well, fights began in their home. Her teenage daughter had neatly pinpointed the problem when she said, after one particularly bad episode between her parents, "Mother, it's too bad Dad can't act like a normal human being unless you are sick in bed." Family therapy was recommended.

The responsibility for the problem in the preceding case was not solely the patient's. With migraine, as with cancer, we can often say with truth: "This family has migraine, and this person, the patient, is stuck with it." In all these examples, homeostasis is involved, helping or hindering but always acting to maintain the status quo. If we decide to make changes in ourselves, we do well to anticipate rebellion from somewhere within. Likewise, changes in the company, the city, the state, the nation, or the world as a whole will automatically and unconsciously be resisted. The positive side to all this is that persons of innate good will have a potent homeostatic effect on families and on society. Their natural response to problems is toward healing. They seem to resist disruption; they dissolve irreconcilable opposites and synthesize the energies released.

Once we become conscious of the workings of homeostasis, we find it easier to change. As William James put it, we can choose this thought instead of that thought, this emotion instead of that emotion, and eventually this behavior instead of that behavior. That is what biofeedback training is all about: to learn to move our homeostatic balance points in a direction we choose, physically, emotionally, and mentally. One can envision the spreading ripples eventually affecting our society, internal law and order spreading from the individual to the family and to society rather than being imposed from outside by the state.

Self-image and Field-independence

We are dominated by everything with which our self becomes identified. We can dominate, direct and utilize everything from which we disidentify ourselves.

—ROBERTO ASSAGIOLI

This chapter occupies a unique place in the logic of this book. It is here that we begin to unravel the question, Who am I? We will shift from the familiar to the unfamiliar. Up to now, the material that has been covered is what "everybody" knows, even if they don't already know it. The logic, the machines, the techniques have been obvious. Enough research and clinical data have accumulated so that the fact of interrelatedness of body and mind and the demonstration of control through biofeedback training are generally accepted by students across the country. Now we wish to enlarge the horizon and bring in another dimension, an existential, experiential dimension in which parapsychological events are considered relative to the question, Who am I? There is no abrupt change in our orientation, but the focus shifts more pointedly to questions of self and self-image and the impact of these concepts in certain fields.

To begin, it is useful to mention Harold Witkin's concept of *field-independence*. By "field" is meant the environment that surrounds us. To be field-independent means to be significantly independent of the environment. The opposite, field-dependence, means to be significantly dependent on the environment. In the remainder of this chapter, Alyce and I will be talking about three fields in respect to which we must develop independence in order to pursue the question, Who am I?

The idea of independence in three fields, rather than in one field, will be new to many psychologists, but it is an old idea to yogis, and it is the essence of don Juan's teaching of Carlos Castaneda. It is also a fact that multiple levels of independence can be existentially demonstrated by almost anyone who takes the trouble of following various meditative exercises, but more of this later. Let us take a close look at the Witkin studies preparatory to identifying the three fields we have in mind.

In the late 1940s Harold Witkin carried out "an intense study of the way in which people perceive an object in relation to its surroundings, or a part within a larger whole; and the results indicated that, whereas for some people perception of the part was strongly affected by the surrounding field, others were able to escape this influence and to deal with the part as a more-or-less independent unit" (Witkin, 1950). It is the idea of "a part within a larger field" on which we are going to focus attention to throw light on the question, Who am I? Eventually Witkin developed his ideas quite fully in *Psychological Differentiation* (Witkin et al., 1962).

A perceptual test that Witkin devised for evaluating field-dependence/independence is called the rod-and-frame test. A person sitting in a dark room is asked to determine when a phosphorescently luminous rod is vertical, that rod being contained within a phosphorescently luminous frame that is tilted at various angles in respect to the vertical. Subjects are said to be field-dependent if they have a difficult time determining when the rod is vertical (as a result of being influenced by the position of the frame, the field). Subjects are called field-independent if able to determine when the rod is vertical, regardless of the tilt of the frame. The rod-and-frame test involves a simple bit of reality, namely, that people are influenced in varying degrees by the surrounding environment. The test may be simple, but Witkin found that the ability to determine when the rod is vertical is associated with a large number of psychological and physiological characteristics. Repeated studies have shown that people who judge the verticality of the rod with considerable error (field-dependent) on the average have a global, diffuse, inexact perception of themselves and the environment. They lack a firm sense of their own identity, and they seem to lack to some degree the ability to separate emotion from thoughts and ideas.

Field-independent persons are more aware of themselves as individuals separate from the environment. They are more capable of experiencing their self-identity. Thus, those who show in the lab that they have a relatively constant *internal* frame of reference for determining the position of the rod in the rod-and-frame test also show the same characteristic—a relatively constant internal frame of reference—in everyday life and in social situations. Typically, they are less interested in and have less use for guidance from other people.

Witkin did not say that being either field-dependent or field-independent led toward psychological peculiarity. He did, however, describe certain tendencies of each type. Stating it rather baldly, we can say that field-dependent people have identity problems when stressed. They become doubtful that they know who they are. They may panic inside and react with feelings of helplessness and inadequate control. Problems such as alcoholism or obesity may develop. Field-independent persons, on the other hand, when threatened or stressed defend themselves by taking refuge in isolation, or strong argument, or intellectual rationalization. Rather than feeling helpless, they are inclined to develop delusions of power and grandeur.

Field-independent people can have serious problems, but it is evident that a degree of field-independence is required to refrain from reacting to the environment, in contradistinction to acting in the environment. The significance of these ideas for the self-regulation of internal states is apparent, we hope. When we say to patients, "Remember, it is not life that kills us, but our reaction to life," we are suggesting that it is necessary for them to develop more field-independence in order to get their reactions under control. We must learn to perceive ourselves as separate from the environment so that we can perceive the stress, ponder its meaning, examine our feelings, and respond in the most appropriate ways.

According to one view, a person's position on the dependence/independence scale is, for all practical purposes, fixed and unchangeable. This may be partially true if a person believes it to be so and makes no effort to change. In our experience, however, those who are willing to make an effort to alter their level of independence, to increase their areas of freedom and self-control, do succeed to some degree. If psychologists and physicians did not observe much self-regulation of internal states prior to the development of biofeedback-training systems, it was mainly because hardware and techniques simply were not available.

Biofeedback enhances consciousness of what is going on inside the skin, and biofeedback training leads to awareness of what we call the second level of field-independence (the first being Witkin's field-independence—that is, independence from the environment). The second level involves independence from total uncontrolled autonomy of the autonomic nervous system. We want the autonomic nervous system to behave properly and to function automatically without giving us any particular trouble, but if it does cause trouble, as in psychosomatic disease, we want to be able to tell it what to do, how to function, and have it comply. And if we wish to drive a car all night, we want to be able to tell the autonomic system to forgo temporarily its habit of sleeping and provide logistic support to our striate selves. That is, it must supply energy and nervous activation to keep us awake. These are, incidentally, examples of some of the practical goals of yoga.

Going back to Figure 1 of Chapter 4, we said that the outer circle represents the skin, the boundary where the body meets the outside-the-skin environment (Field 1). The small circle contains the central nervous system and is the internal boundary where the central nervous system meets the inside-the-skin environment. Field 2 is the area lying between the small circle and the large circle. It is everything in the body outside of the central nervous system itself.

Witkin's idea of field refers to the perception of relationships outside the skin, starting simply as a rod in a frame and extending to such an elaborate idea as one's self vis-à-vis society. All of his relationships involve the world outside the skin, but it is interesting to note that our perception of a rod in a frame involves the central nervous system. Perception always involves the central nervous system, as we indicated in Chapter 8 when we referred to the sensorium, where all information from the outside world is presented to the perceiver.

Prior to the development of biofeedback, the idea of independence in the world inside the skin, in the field of body processes, was not much thought about in the United States. Such independence lies at the heart of Autogenic Training and yoga, of course, but those systems of self-regulation were not seriously considered by those few psychologists who had even heard of them. Now, however, biofeedback has opened for study a host of relationships—for instance, between changes in field-dependence and the development of skill with various kinds of biofeedback machinery. Such basic studies can be followed by investigations of one's role in society, the kinds of psychosomatic diseases a person develops, and the facility with which research subjects can learn to handle response to stress—all with field-dependence and the development of biofeedback skills as correlated research variables.

The question, Who is the perceiver?, brings us to Field 3, in which we find ourselves imbedded—which is, of course, the central nervous system itself. Since antiquity people have wondered whether there is a little person in there, in the middle of the head, who perceives all the information brought in through sensory channels, but whose experiences are *not* determined entirely by the sensory input. That is, given that the genetic matrix provided by the egg and sperm is the main constructor and maintainer of the central nervous system, using the raw materials in food, are we otherwise controlled entirely by the various known inputs to the central nervous system, namely (1) inputs from the outside world via the five senses, (2) inputs via the proprioceptive senses from the inside-the-skin world of muscles, joints, and tendons, and (3) inputs via the enteroceptive senses from the inside-the-skin world of viscera and other tissues not previously included? Much argument revolves about this point, but in considering it one is struck mainly by its futility, as if discursive intellect could lift itself by its bootstraps, so to speak, and prove that intellect is (or is not) a faculty of a "higher being." Transcendental knowledge is existential rather than logical, according to the philosophies of the Zen Buddhist, the Hindu yogi, the North and South American Indian medicine men, the Tibetan Buddhist, the Sufi, the Cabalist, the Christian mystic, and the Kalahari shaman in Africa.

Clearly, the three fields—the three environments in which we feel that we have our being—have an important influence on our self-image, and that self-image has an important effect on what happens to us, both inside our skins and in the outer world. But is our self-image totally determined by factors beyond our control? Some people feel that if the mind affects the body and the body affects the mind, then a human is a closed loop, incapable of making a change in self-image or in anything else. But, as we have previously said, this is where volition comes into the picture. It seems to be able to effect changes within the dimensions of the mind-body system.

But is volition itself merely part of a large, but still closed, physiological system? Again, as said in the beginning of this book, the *only* data that seem to have an unequivocal bearing on the question of "volition as a metaforce" are from the field of parapsychology. In our minds parapsychology includes transcendental experiences (direct knowing), extrasensory phenomena (direct sensing), and psychokinetic phenomena (direct action through the use of volition). Parapsychological phenomena provide, in our estimation, positive evidence that the "I" in

"Who am I?" has characteristics that are to some extent independent of the three fields.

Why is this important? We believe that the healthy functioning of our body-emotions-mind unit depends on our self-image, and to bring that triple unit under control it is at least necessary to hypothesize that we are not ourselves limited to the machinery that we are attempting to regulate.

What are we then? The most sophisticated answer that we get from the mystics is also the only answer that has metaphysical justification, because of the nature of logic. That answer is "We are what remains after we have identified what we are not," and "what remains" must be experienced to be known. Logic collapses when it reaches the boundary of its domain and experiential knowing starts us on a new line of exploration and discovery. Can we say that, to know our identity, we must stop clinging only to the rules of left-hemisphere functioning and must allow ourselves also to experience right-hemisphere existential synthesis?

Knowing is not the same as believing. When C. G. Jung was asked toward the end of his life if he believed in a spiritual being that transcended the limits of time and space, he answered that believing was useless; it was necessary to know. And he said, "I do not believe, I know."

Buddhist psychology has addressed itself to the problem of self-identity. An ancient manuscript called *The Tibetan Book of the Great Liberation* (W. Y. Evans-Wentz, 1954) analyzes the realms and bodies, or vehicles, of human experience (what we have referred to as the three fields) in order to identify everything that we are not. What is left over after everything that we know, or could ever think of, is called the Void —not a void in the sense of "nothing," but a void in the sense that nothing can be said about it, for language is a function of the discursive part of mind. (Evans-Wentz, who translated this manuscript with the help of his Tibetan teacher, said that the Void referred to by his teacher included at least twenty-eight differentiable kinds of experience.)

This is apropos of the present discussion, because the existence of extrasensory perception implies that the ultimate nature of mind, even if it is not logically explainable, includes at least one additional dimension of substance (in order to receive thought transmission and allow for psychokinesis) beyond the bounds of the presently defined three-dimensional central nervous system. In order to perceive "ahead in time," precognitively, it is probably necessary to hypothesize a second time dimension. This would give a minimum of six dimensions for representing the mind, four in space and two in time.

These ideas are not new, of course. We first read about them in a book titled *An Experiment with Time,* by physicist John Dunne (1928). Ouspensky in *Tertium Organum* (1947) reviews several such ideas, especially the mathematical analogies of Hinton. The increasing reservoir of extrasensory data makes it considerably easier nowadays to discuss the general hypothesis that mind is more comprehensive than body.

When I saw the tower building of the Menninger Foundation in a hypnagogic image in 1952, twelve years in advance of visual seeing, I was apparently using a set of senses peculiar to mind, as distinguished from body senses. The most economical explanation for this kind of phenomenon, it seems to me, is to hypothesize that *mind is an energy structure that includes the brain.* We have been very much impressed by Patanjali's ideas, first expressed some 2,200 years ago (Taimni, 1967) and lately brought to our attention again by Swami Rama. The mind-body problem (Do we have a mind separate from the body?) is in fact no problem at all, according to Patanjali's *Yoga Sutras.* Both of them are substances, energy structures; the body is merely the densest section of mind, in the same way that a magnet may be thought of as the densest section of a magnetic field. This idea is summarized in the line mentioned earlier that crystallized in our discussions with Swami Rama: "All of the body is in the mind, but not all of the mind is in the body."

In other words, there is nothing happening in the body and central nervous system that is not happening in the mind (though mainly in the unconscious, to be sure). The reverse is not true, however, for some things that happen in the mind are not represented in the body, though they are projected as extrasensory impressions by some hypothesized mechanism *into* the brain. That mechanism is presumably part of the mind.

Everything in the West must be useful; otherwise it is under suspicion of not being of value. Therefore, it seems appropriate to review the advantages of independence in the three fields.

First, in the environment: From Witkin's description of the characteristics of field-independent people it seems clear that being field-independent has its uses. Certainly it is desirable to be able to make up our own minds about things and not need a value judgment from the environment in order to decide if what we are doing is what we want to do.

Second, in the body: It seems self-evident that we do not want to be controlled by physiological processes, no matter how much we make use of the body for sensing and for action. Every person is a psychosomatic entity having certain parts that function less than perfectly. Unless the malfunctions become serious enough to make us unhappy, we normally do not pay much attention to this mind-body unity; we merely employ it. Sooner or later, however, we come face to face with some serious functional problem. At that instant we know that we do not want to be controlled by physiological processes. Under these conditions many people resent their slavery to the body but they can do nothing about it.

Third, in the mind: Some people think of humans as learning machines in whom any kind of behavior can be installed by controlling their physiological responses, their emotional responses, and their thoughts. Nazism was a case in fact, and *1984,* the novel by George Orwell, is a case in fiction, as is *Walden II* (1948), by B. F. Skinner. It is more useful to subscribe to an open-ended system, however, and especially to see through the self-limiting theory that says we ourselves cannot voluntarily modify our bodies, emotions, and thoughts.

William James expressed his own "cutting-through" beautifully in his diary entry for April 30, 1870.

> I think that yesterday was a crisis in my life. I finished the first part of Renouvier's "Essais" and see no reason why his definition of Free Will —"the sustaining of a thought *because I choose to* when I might have other thoughts"—need be the definition of an illusion. My first act of free will shall be to believe in free will. . . . Hitherto, when I have felt like taking a free initiative, like daring to act originally, *without carefully waiting for contemplation of the external world to determine all for me* [this emphasis added], suicide seemed the most manly form to put my daring into; now, I will go a step further with my will, not only act with it but believe as well; believe in my individual reality and creative power. . . . I will posit life (the real, the good) in the self-governing *resistance* of the ego to the world." [Murphy and Ballou, 1960]

It is notable that self-induced changes in behavior are ideas first; later, emotional involvement generates enough energy to result in action. Mental flexibility precedes overt responses when old behavior patterns are being replaced. In all this we feel that the central nervous system is uniquely involved, as summarized in Figure 5.

In our estimation, the psychosomatic syndrome with most people includes a case of mistaken identity. In Figure 5 the *self* that does the regulating is logically and existentially not thought, not emotions, not actions. Whatever it is, it exists in, or has extensions in, the realm of parapsychological inputs. The problem is that if we believe we are only our body, then we cannot control it. If we believe that we are our emotions, then we cannot control them. And if we believe we are our thoughts, then they, too, cannot be controlled. It is interesting that Assagioli developed exercises in "disidentification" to handle the problems arising from such identification.

In the theta training program we often give subjects the old yogic instruction for control of thoughts in order to help them move into the

DOMAINS OF SELF-REGULATION			
PHYSICAL	PSYCHOLOGICAL		
	SENSATION AND ACTION	SENSATION, EMOTION, AND ACTION	SENSATION, EMOTION, THOUGHT, AND ACTION
FIELD 3: CENTRAL NERVOUS SYSTEM			FIELD INDEPENDENCE
FIELD 2: ENVIRONMENT INSIDE THE SKIN		PARTIAL FIELD INDEPENDENCE	
FIELD 1: ENVIRONMENT OUTSIDE THE SKIN	FIELD DEPENDENCE		

Figure 5. **Physical and psychological domains in which self-regulation is possible.** Witkin's idea of dependence on, or independence from, the external environment (Field 1) can be generalized to include the internal environment between the skin and the central nervous system (Field 2, roughly the peripheral nervous system), and, further, to include the central nervous system itself (Field 3).

state of theta reverie. Thinking thinks, just as feeling feels; pay no attention. "If thoughts intrude," we tell them, "don't bother about them. Just let them move through your awareness without reacting in any way. Soon the thoughts will run down, as if they are running on little batteries. If we don't interact with them, their energy dissipates."

To summarize this point, in order to come closer to knowing what we are, we determine what we are not. This old idea is effective in helping people master psychosomatic disease with biofeedback training. Somehow the objectivity of the machine makes it possible for them to disidentify, to be field-independent, and that detachment is instrumental in learning to self-regulate.

Transcendental experiences add to our knowledge of what we are and are not. In the study on which the article "Are We a Nation of Mystics?" (The New York Times Magazine, *January 26, 1974) is based, Greeley and McCready used the techniques of a population survey to begin a study of mystical experiences. ". . . Motivated by no more elaborate theoretical concern than curiosity," they inserted a few questions on mystical experience into a survey of ultimate values in a representative national sample of 1,500 adults.*

Based on two pretest surveys and the literature on mysticism, their first and basic question was: "Have you ever had the feeling of being very close to a powerful spiritual force that seemed to lift you out of yourself, an experience that can best be characterized by the word ecstasy?" About six hundred people reported having at least one such experience, three hundred reported having had several, and seventy-five reported having had such experiences often. Two thirds of them rated such episodes as very intense, at the top end of a seven-point intensity scale.

There was neither time nor money to interview the respondents to obtain the experiences in their own words, but a checklist offered choices of what the experience was like. The answers clustered around such expressions as "I couldn't possibly describe"; "the sensation that my personality had been taken over by something much more powerful than I am"; "a sense of a new life or living in a new world"; "a sense I was being bathed in light."

Greeley and McCready found that those who report having mystical experiences are not the socially or economically disadvantaged. They are most likely to be college-educated, to have an income above the $10,000-a-year level (in 1972) and to be psychologically healthy. Their responses on the brief Psychological Well-Being Scale developed by Professor Norman Bradburn indicated that "The relationship between frequent ecstatic experience and psychological well-being was .40, the highest correlation, according to Bradburn, he has ever observed with his scale." The authors found that this correlation could not be explained away as the effects of other variables, such as education, sex, age, or race. After the effects of these factors were statistically removed there still remained a .39 correlation between well-being and frequent ecstatic experiences.

For those who may not be familiar with the use of a correlation coefficient: When multiplied by itself (.40 × .40 = .16), the resulting number shows the "fraction" of well-being (as determined in the Bradburn questionnaire) that can be directly related to ecstatic experiences. In other words, with this questionnaire and with this group of people, 16 percent of the characteristic called "Well-being" could be accounted for by its relation to ecstatic experiences, but not to education, sex, age, or race.

Greeley and McCready were dismayed when their professional colleagues dismissed their findings with abrupt certainty, saying "Those people can't be having religious experiences." They responded, "Maybe not, but they're having something; and whatever the hell it is they are having, it correlates with mental health at a very high level. If we had found any other correlate, the mental health establishment would be knocking down our doors demanding to know more. If anything else but 'ecstasy' were that good for you, it would sell as if it wouldn't be on the market next year. . . . We thought the funding agencies responsible for mental-health research would be intrigued by the . . . correlation we had discovered between ecstasy and mental health. It turned out they simply didn't believe us. Such scientific objectivity is intriguing."

Greeley and McCready report three general kinds of responses to the research findings among their colleagues and friends. First, skepticism, to the extent of attacking their findings as "impossible and misleading." Second, an eager search for "natural" explanations, such as tachycardia, electrical discharges in the nervous system, inherited shapes of nerve endings, fatigue, etc. And third, a quite surprisingly large number of people who came into the office or telephoned or wrote saying, "I wonder if you'd be interested in some experiences I've had . . ."

After more than twenty random interviews with volunteers from this last group, Greeley and McCready found that, "Like the mystics of clas-

sic tradition, the interviewees perceived the phenomenon as fundamentally cognitive. They saw . . . the way.things really are. The core of the event is knowing. . . . The joy, peace, heat, light . . . are perceived as the result of knowledge. . . ." The friends and colleagues who reported such experiences were seen to be "creative, happy, dynamic individuals."

Respondents from both groups, the national sample and the volunteers, insisted that the experience(s) was an important thing in their lives, that their behavior and many of their decisions were based on it. A quest for self-identity, an answer to the question, Who am I?, underlies the meaning of life for many people. Transcendental experiences often provide clues. A new self-image may emerge, and a change in the image of the universe, seeing it as benign and seeing oneself as one with it.

Evidence similar to that gathered by Greeley and McCready is being assessed by the Religious Experience Research Group at Oxford. See also Inglorious Wordsworths *(Pafford, 1974).*

It seems to us that an important element in the effectiveness of any system for bringing about physiological change is a change in self-image. Carl Simonton mentioned to us one day that he was very much interested in biofeedback training. This was not because it would necessarily have direct application in his treatment of cancer, but because it would have a bearing on the self-image of the cancer patient. The problem with the 80 percent of patients who would not try the training program was that they did not believe it was possible to change *any* physiological process. They felt too helpless and hopeless even to try. With biofeedback, however, the demonstration that it is possible to control one's temperature (for example) is so simple that the self-image automatically begins to change without the person's thinking much about it. After that it is easier to begin creating a positive image in which the cancer may be in some way driven out or eradicated.

Prison is one of the most striking environments in which self-image with respect to the three fields is important. Prisoners are generally not satisfied with their self-image. Often they are willing to try a system for changing it, such as the one developed by our daughter Patricia Norris, director of our biofeedback seminars and workshops. Independence is desired of the environment, of the body, and also of the time and space limitations of the central nervous system itself. Prisoners who have been contacted concerning the possibility of setting up meditation programs in prisons have said that nowhere but in a monastery is the atmosphere so restrictive, and therefore conducive to pondering the question, *Who am I?* In his autobiography Malcolm X said that until he found himself in prison, he literally had not begun to find himself. Perhaps he was one in a million, but many of the prisoners who have heard of biofeedback have been interested in the possibility of learning how to cope with the stresses of the surrounding environment and with boredom, one of the major stresses of prison.

In a monastery one turns away from the outside world, choosing instead the innate attractiveness of the inner domain. In a prison one is forcibly excluded from the larger outside world; in such circumstances the attractiveness of the inner domain may be enhanced. Whatever the difference between prison and a monastery, prisoners are becoming increasingly interested in Edgar Cayce, Transcendental Meditation, the yogic philosophy of Ram Dass, and biofeedback training.

Pat Norris has just completed her Ph.D. dissertation on the use of guided imagery and biofeedback for change in self-image in prisoners. In describing the prisoners who were her research subjects, she says,

> I expected to find hardened men, exploitive and tough, who consciously had decided to get theirs the easy way, live off society, make it rich, and so on. Instead, I was finding fearful, angry, guilt-ridden, and impulsive people (mostly young) who perceived themselves as failures, who felt inadequate and had very low self-esteem, and who, most significantly, perceived themselves and were perceived by others in numerous studies as victims! Victims of society, cultural deprivation, poor education and lack of opportunity, broken homes and alcoholic parents, abusive treatment and chaotic instability. . . . Victims of their own defenses, of their identifications, of their self-defeating and self-destructing behavior, of tension and anxiety and low frustration tolerance and poor impulse control. . . ." [Norris, 1976]

In developing a self-image rehabilitation program for these prisoners, Pat began with Psychosynthesis (using the consciousness-expansion techniques of Roberto Assagioli). She thought that it would be useful, and perhaps necessary if true rehabilitation was to take place, to enhance in these individuals an expanded sense of self. Having been a subject in our theta pilot group, Pat felt that the guided-imagery techniques of Psychosynthesis, when combined with the self-regulation techniques of biofeedback, would potentiate each other. That is, each would tend to increase the effectiveness of the other, a multiplication rather than a simple addition of effects. The training program, therefore, consisted mainly of temperature training and guided imagery (relaxation followed by visualization of symbolic images that seem to have a powerful effect on one's life). Concerning results, Pat writes:

> There were two major categories of psychological effects [of the training]. (1) Memories associated with the original conflicts that started the functional disorders began to emerge, and (2) people's reports suggested that the effects of gaining control over one physiological function (temperature) were *generalizing* and they were gaining a feeling of mastery over other areas of functioning. . . . As they gain some competence in relaxing, subjects are encouraged to experiment internally with their feelings by recalling incidents which have produced anxiety, anger, embarrassment for them in the past, while watching the temperature meter dial and maintaining a relaxed state. Emphasis is placed on being aware, "owning" one's feelings rather than trying to deny or repress feelings, in order to have control. . . .
>
> By this point, participants are eager to explore, through visualization, guided imagery, and psychological exercises, their own psyches. Because of the meaningful, deeply experiential nature of the biofeedback training—the "proof" of their capacity to change—much of the usual resistance to self-exploration is eroded. They no longer can accept the commonly held notion that we have no control over the way we feel.

Please note that this last idea, that a person "no longer can accept the commonly held notion that we have no control over the way we feel," is essentially the basis for establishing field-independence in Field 2, the body. It is an explosive experience to discover that one need not be a victim, not only of problems with the world but of destructive and agonizing feelings inside the skin.

We have said that both monks and prisoners are motivated to seek self-awareness. St. Thomas Aquinas went through three levels of identification in his life. First, like any child, he was dependent on the world, but as he grew up and explored religion, he established independence from Field 1, the outside world. Later, through the practice of physical austerities he established a degree of independence in Field 2, the body. For most of his life he was dominated by ideas, "stuck" in Field 3, and identified himself relative to what he perceived in the intellectual domain. Ultimately he broke through that also. At the very end of his life,

Thomas Aquinas had an experience which his biographer described as follows:

> The writing career of Thomas came suddenly to an end on December 6, 1273. While saying mass that morning a great change came over him, and afterwards he ceased to write or dictate. Urged by his companion to complete the *Summa,* he replied: "I can do no more; such things have been revealed to me that all I have written seems as straw, and I now await the end of my life." [Aquinas, 1952]

One of our associates, Paul Kurtz, director of the Alcoholism and Chemical Addiction Unit of St. Cloud Hospital, St. Cloud, Minnesota, has become aware of the field-independence problems in drug addicts and alcoholics. In his paper "Turning on without chemicals" (1973), he points out that since about 1950 there have been indications that while many Westerners have begun to search for the "missing elements" within themselves, "some persons have come to look at chemical dependence, not as a moral or ethical problem, not even as a handicap, but have dared to look at it as another kind of attempt to discover the buried, inhibited side of ourselves."

He points to William James's experience with nitrous oxide and mescaline and reminds us that there have been many—from Baudelaire to James to Aldous Huxley—who have detailed the "unique quality of experiences with mind-altering chemicals." Edgar Allan Poe wrote about the grotesqueries and mysteries evolving in his tortured alcoholic imagination. Indians have used peyote to worship a power greater than themselves.

Kurtz concludes that though this is not all bad, "there are at least three good reasons for looking elsewhere for means and methods of opening our [hidden selves]." A major problem with the ecstasy experienced with drugs is that it is frequently "followed by extreme depression and despair." In addition, our bodies develop a tolerance, so that we need more and more in order to get an effect we value. Lastly, many chemicals actually cause organic destruction of brain cells, which cannot be regenerated or replaced.

Kurtz goes on to say that some of the best ways of achieving freedom without using drugs are through meditation, biofeedback, and Alcoholics Anonymous. He points out that the essential features of Alcoholics Anonymous include ego reduction, the acceptance of a power greater than self, and "spiritual awakening." He quotes the last step of AA procedures as "having had a spiritual awakening as the result of these steps, we tried to carry the message to alcoholics and to practice these principles in all our affairs." To us a "spiritual awakening" is not an emotional retreat into dogma but an existential event, and often is the beginning of independence in Field 3.

The examples we have discussed show how the principle of field-independence extends through all levels of one's awareness. What can be said as we work with these levels is: We are not merely what society says we are, as children, as adults, or as old people. That is the first level of field-independence: independence from what we perceive outside the skin. Further, we are not merely what our bodies say we are, not in the voluntary nervous system or in the involuntary nervous system. Not only are we not our emotions (which are presumably connected with the autonomic nervous system and its ramifications throughout the body), but we are also not our thoughts. The question remains, then: Who are we?

In Chapter 11, on Swami Rama, Jack Schwarz, Rolling Thunder, and others, we do not treat society, the body, emotions, and thoughts as unimportant. On the contrary, those fields are of utmost importance, because they are the "fields of life," without which there would be no awareness, no discrimination, and no development or evolution. What *is* important, however, is that we not identify ourselves only in terms of these fields, but move on just as those named above are moving on, to the development of volition. As we do this, the question of our identity becomes increasingly existential and less rhetorical.

The people named above are not totally bound by the three fields. They are involved in these ordinary levels of experience, of course, but they also are aware of additional levels: a cosmic level (Field 4) and a universal level (Field 5), for want of better names. Fields 4 and 5 are especially associated with parapsychology and the basic questions of self-identity. All of us are immersed in these levels, although we are usually not conscious of them until we quiet the body, the emotions, and the thoughts simultaneously. We will speak of these ideas at length later in discussing the field of mind. Partial awareness in these levels contributed something, we believe, to the integrative experiences of the college students who participated in our theta training program.

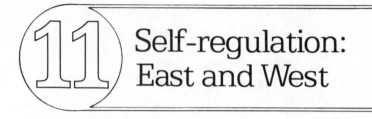

Self-regulation: East and West

It is probably true quite generally that in the history of human thinking the most fruitful developments take place at those points where two different lines of thought meet. These lines may have their roots in quite different parts of human culture, in different times or different cultural environments or different religious traditions: hence if they actually meet, that is, if they are at least so much related to each other that a real interaction can take place, then one may hope that new and interesting developments may follow.

—WERNER HEISENBERG

The mystical experiences described by the Medicine Men, when they will speak of such things—which is not often because of the ridicule with which such theories are received by most whites—are identical with those recorded among other nations which have developed elaborate occult traditions. . . . It is more than interesting . . . that they should describe their occult power in exactly the same way as do these other, far separated races.

—MANLY HALL

The word "magicians" is used here not in the sense of the supernatural, for there can be no such thing as a supernatural power or event. Neither is it used in the sense of sleight-of-hand artists, who are popularly called magicians. Rather, we are going to talk about *people whose skill in self-regulation seems magical*—that is to say, unaccountable. But it is a fact that, with some effort, the average person can master some of the same feats of physiological self-regulation.

Before introducing our subjects and telling what we learned from them, we wish to state our views about the difference between seemingly magical skills and trickery. It is the difference between a yogi who can stop his heart from pumping blood through direct control of the autonomic nervous system and a yogi who claims to be doing this but is in actuality squeezing the circulatory apparatus with voluntary muscles of the chest and abdomen, forcibly altering heart function. Likewise, it is the difference between Uri Geller and a sleight-of-hand artist. Stage magicians are admittedly tricksters, and cannot perform in a laboratory setting without their props. On the other hand, Uri Geller—like Ingo Swann and many others who can demonstrate parapsychological phenomena—has been observed and studied in laboratory settings. The hand can indeed be quicker than the eye, but it is not quicker than the oscilloscope and the metal detector. Things that appear to be unaccountable are not always the results of trickery, as the history of science amply demonstrates. Things found to be unaccountable under rigorous scientific scrutiny ought at least to suggest that science's ability to account for everything may be imperfect.

Alyce and I do not know Uri Geller, but we have talked to several of the physicists, both in England and in the United States, who have conducted research with him. We believe they are not lying, nor have they been fooled concerning the phenomena associated with Uri Geller's presence in their labs. No sleight-of-hand master can do difficult tricks without years of preparation, including both staging and practice. No magician can walk into my laboratory and forthwith operate my polygraph, my electrometer, my densitometer, my monochrometer, my photogalvanometer, my Geiger counter, or any of the other pieces of gear that are found in scientific laboratories. It is impossible without their having prepared the lab in advance, and it is presumptuous nonsense for anyone to maintain otherwise. There is nothing a sleight-of-hand magician can carry that will manipulate plastic, glass, iron, aluminum, paper, and various other materials at a distance; nothing, for instance, that will turn Geiger counters on and off.

In May of 1974, while in England, Alyce and I had a chance to talk with physicists Ted Bastion, John Taylor, and others about children in the British TV audiences who, after seeing Uri Geller bend tableware, found that they could do the same thing. It does not seem strange to us that children should be talented in this way. Almost all of the poltergeist phenomena that have been studied in the last hundred years have taken place in the presence of young people at about the age of puberty. It is as if at that particular age there is an excess of "bioplasmic" energy, which in our estimation is the energy which underlies the "personal power" referred to by don Juan. (More on this later.) There seems little doubt that some kind of as-yet-unaccounted-for energy is connected with human bodies. That by itself is interesting. What is doubly interesting is that under certain conditions this energy can be manipulated by mind. For instance, in "poltergeist kids" the phenomena are spontaneous, not under their control; but those who watched Uri Geller on television tried to bend silverware by willing it, and some of them succeeded.

Edgar Cayce was one of the poltergeist kids, and so was Harry Helson, the psychologist whom Gardner Murphy suggested I talk to about my mathematical paper on the adaptation law for vision. While driving to Manhattan, Kansas, to meet Harry, Gardner told me that some unusual things had happened in Harry's life, which Harry might tell me about if I asked. Responding to my queries, Harry said that generally he did not talk about his early experiences for fear of upsetting his colleagues, but it was a fact that he had been a poltergeist kid. When he was young a number of things happened that could not be explained: Chairs rocked, doors slammed, coal flew out of the coal scuttle and banged into the walls, cans slid off shelves. His parents were relieved when the phenomena stopped.

How many of these children are there in the United States? Hundreds? Thousands? Whatever the number, such phenomena should be investigated because, aside from all other implications, they provide an important bearing on the question, Who are we? Moreover, questions of science should be studied by scientists and not taken up as causes by the media and by sleight-of-hand magicians.

Returning to the theme of this chapter, we point out again that research in our voluntary-controls program has not focused on parapsychology, but has been concerned almost entirely with the physiological domain and its self-regulation by volition. It was natural, therefore, for us to be interested in persons like Swami Rama, a yoga teacher from India; Jack Schwarz, whom we think of as a Western Sufi; Rolling Thunder, a Native American medicine man; and some yogis and meditators whom we studied in India with a portable psychophysiology laboratory. We focused almost exclusively in the physiological and psychological domains, not because we were not interested in the study of extrasensory perception and psychokinesis (we believe those areas may be important for the average person to know about), but because the first need is to be able to self-regulate. Personal well-being and satisfactory handling of one's life should come first, we believe.

In studying people who show unusual inside-the-skin (INS) self-regulation, however, we observed that they almost always show unusual awareness of unconscious processes, both in themselves and in others. Sometimes they appeared to have psychokinetic talents as well. Should we be surprised at this? Since it appears that these people have learned to control "personal power," and have also become aware of normally unconscious processes, it seems reasonable to us that their volitional skills might include the regulation of outside-the-skin (OUTS) energies and an ability to demonstrate psychokinetic phenomena. Our experiences with these people indicate that these INS and OUTS issues are interrelated. In Chapter 14 we discuss this interrelatedness at length.

Swami Rama

As already noted, Alyce and Dale Walters and I began research in self-regulation of autonomic processes in the mid-1960s. Through a publication of the Menninger Foundation which is sent to psychiatric alumni, our voluntary-controls program came to the attention of Dr. Daniel Ferguson, at that time chief of the medical hygiene clinic of the Veterans Administration Hospital in St. Paul, Minnesota. In the fall of 1969 Dr. Ferguson telephoned me and said that he had become acquainted with a yogi named Swami Rama, who had demonstrated in the hospital an ability to obliterate his pulse. Dan suggested that with our psychophysiology equipment it might be possible to obtain a record of what the Swami was actually doing. Would we like to conduct such a project? If we were interested, he would take the responsibility of bringing Swami Rama to the laboratory for a couple of days. Our lab schedule was fully booked at the time, and Swami Rama tended to travel only "when the spirit listeth," but arrangements were finally made and over the Easter weekend, March 28–30, 1970, a number of experiments were performed.

During the first day we familiarized the Swami with the routine of being wired up and had a chance to become acquainted with him. He was forty-five years of age, tall and well built. He reminded me of an Italian Renaissance nobleman. At six feet one inch and one hundred and seventy pounds, and with a lot of energy for debate and persuasion, he was a formidable figure. Uncertain about what he intended to demonstrate and not wanting to upset him with demands, we asked him to tell us what he would like to do.

On the second day, Sunday, we attached a minimum number of transducers to the Swami's body in order to minimize the laboratory-induced "electric chair" effect. The Swami said he would cause the left side of his right hand (hypothenar eminence) to increase in temperature several degrees above the right side (thenar eminence). Thermistors were attached to the palm of the right hand in the positions shown in Figure 6, and an electrocardiographic signal was obtained from between the right ear and the left wrist. Alyce and I remained with the Swami in the experimental room (located about fifteen feet from the polygraph room) and noted that during this demonstration he did not move his hands. They were placed palms up on a board in front of him.

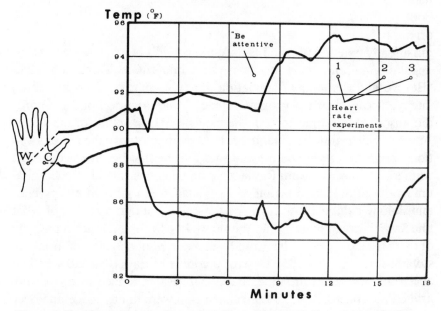

Figure 6. **Simultaneous warming and cooling of the hand.** Swami Rama's demonstration of voluntary control of blood flow in the right hand caused the left side to become pink and the right side gray. The three heart-rate experiments are shown in Figure 7.

Figure 6 shows what happened in this hand-temperature experiment. The Swami increased the temperature difference between the left and right sides of his hand in two stages. The first began shortly after the arbitrary zero time and the second started when he said, "Be attentive, I will do something." The thermistor on the little finger side of the hand (labeled "W" for warm) started at a temperature of 90°F and after a few minutes had drifted up to 91°F. The temperature of the thermistor on the thumb side of the hand (labeled "C" for cool) started at about 88°F and after a few minutes had drifted up to 89°F.

The Swami and I had been talking about blood-flow control just before the zero time on the graph. I said that it was about time for us to start this experiment, and he answered abruptly, "I have already begun." Associated with our polygraph record was a voice-actuated relay which made a mark on the edge of the record so that we could identify places in the record where talking occurred. When we later looked at the record, we noticed that where he said he had already begun, deviations had started in the record. In the first minute the temperature dropped in both thermistors. Then the W thermistor reversed and went up to its original reading and the C thermistor continued to drop. After three minutes they were about 7°F apart.

We continued talking for a few minutes. Suddenly the Swami said, "Be attentive, I will do something." Caught by surprise, I said over the intercom, "Be attentive." I could not think of anything else to say and did not know what he was going to do.

The record shows that the temperature began going up at both locations on the palm of his hand, and then the C thermistor went down to where it had been but the W thermistor kept increasing in temperature until it reached 95°F. Eventually the two thermistors were 11°F apart, an increase of 9°F over the original temperature difference. The Swami told us that this differential control of temperature in one hand was one of the most difficult things that he had learned to do, more difficult than stopping his heart. That seemed unlikely to me at first, but on thinking about it I realized that the neural controls over the radial and ulnar arteries in the wrist and over the arterial shunts in the hand probably were located within a few millimeters of each other in a section of the central nervous system. The Swami's demonstration showed exquisite differential control over this normally uncontrolled piece of the neural apparatus.

After talking another two or three minutes, the Swami abruptly ordered, "Test my heart immediately." A few minutes later he said, "What is my heart doing now?" I labeled these on the records as "heart rate experiment #1" and "heart rate experiment #2" (Figure 7). They were the Swami's experiments, not ours. He already knew what he could do, and apparently was calibrating our laboratory for his own information. Shortly after the second heart-rate experiment he said he wished to be released. Thinking that he wished to be released from the neces-

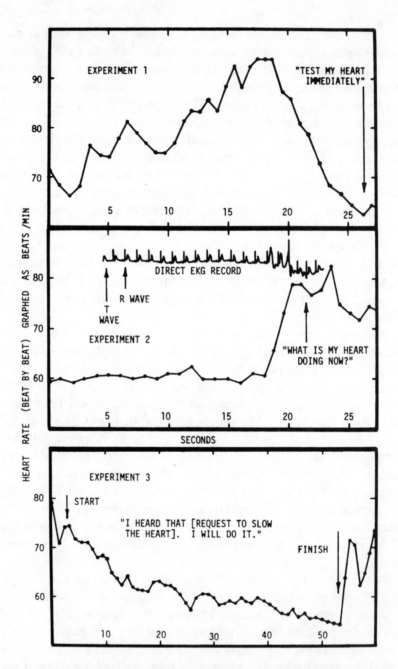

Figure 7. **Voluntary heart control.** Swami Rama's first two demonstrations were unexpected. He asked for heart information. The third "experiment" was requested by Dale Walters over the intercom.

sity of maintaining the temperature difference between the two spots on his hands, I said, "You can now relax the temperature control of your hands." Shortly thereafter the record showed that the temperature of the C thermistor began to increase (Figure 6).

The third heart-rate experiment might be called ours; at least, we requested it. Dale Walters called over the intercom and said, "Ask the Swami to slow his heart." The Swami heard that and said, "I will do it." Figure 7, showing a summary of all three heart-rate experiments, indicates that his heart slowed continuously for about fifty seconds, from seventy-four beats per minute to fifty-two beats per minute.

Heart experiment #1, increasing the rate momentarily, was interesting, but I was not particularly impressed by it, because I had noticed that I could do this myself. Experiment #2 was much more difficult, the Swami said, because of the sudden change that takes place in the heart. Experiment #3 was impressive, because most Westerners, even if they can speed their hearts, cannot start at a normal resting rate and decrease it by twenty-one beats in one minute, at will.

With reference to Experiment #2 of Figure 7, by coincidence the Swami was "doing something with his heart," thereby making it possible for us to observe an unusual occurrence. Our cardiotachometer (for recording heart rate) can be switched to direct display of the electrical EKG signal, and it happened that just a few seconds before the Swami asked for his heart to be monitored, Dale Walters in the control room had switched the cardiotachometer to direct display. The normal *flub-dup, flub-dup* of the heart, heard through a stethoscope, is seen on an oscilloscope or on an EKG chart as R and T waves, shown by arrows on the diagram, above the rate record. In the normal heart record, using the electrical pickup from right ear to left hand, the R wave is taller than the T wave, as shown in the diagram. But note that just before the heart rate suddenly increases, the T wave becomes larger than the R wave. Since the T wave and the R wave represent functions of different parts of the heart, the record indicates that the Swami had developed differential control over sections of the heart, just as he had developed differential control over blood flow in his hands. We mentioned this to the Swami, who said only that this particular demonstration was somewhat risky.

After concluding the laboratory work on Sunday, Alyce and I invited Dr. Ferguson and the Swami to dinner with us at a local smorgasbord place. While chatting about yogic methods for self-regulation, the

Swami surprised us by saying, "I am sorry I didn't stop my heart for you. I know you wanted to see that."

"Oh, that's all right," I said, "you can do it next time."

"No, I will do it tomorrow."

"But you can't do that," explained Alyce. "You just finished telling us that a person shouldn't stop his heart unless he has fasted for three days. And here we are eating dinner."

"That's all right," he said, "I want to find out what I can do. Anything I can do with three days of preparation, my teacher can do in three seconds without any preparation. I have never been wired up like this before, and I would like to find out what I can do."

We attempted to dissuade him, but the Swami was insistent. "I'll sign papers saying that the Menninger Foundation is not responsible for my death," he said, somewhat haughtily. Nothing we said impressed him. At last we gave up. "Don't worry," he said, "I know what I am doing. I can stop my heart for three or four minutes, and also do something no other yogi can do. I can carry on a conversation at the same time. How long a time would be required to demonstrate heart stopping on the machine, since I have not fasted?" I said we would be very much impressed if he did it for ten seconds.

We had earlier scheduled Swami for a lecture in the research department the next morning at ten o'clock; then he and Dr. Ferguson were to catch a plane back to Minneapolis. I called Dale that night and told him we would try to run the "heart-stopping" demonstration at nine o'clock in the morning.

The next day, as I was taking Swami Rama with wires draped over his shoulders into the experimental room, he turned and said to Alyce, "When my heart stops, call over the intercom and say, 'That's all.' " I asked why he wanted that, and he said, "Since I am not prepared in the ordinary way for this experiment, I do not want to do it too long. I want to be reminded to stop so that I will not forget what I want to do. I do not want to damage my subtle heart." I asked him to explain that, and he said that the heart seen in surgery is only the physical appearance of the heart. The way he described it, the real heart is a large energy structure, of which the physical heart is only the dense section.

These two statements by the Swami—that he wanted to be reminded not to stay in the state too long and that he did not want to damage his subtle heart—seem very significant. That he wanted to be reminded of what he was doing implied to me that when he "put" himself into the state in which the "heart stopped," he might be unaware of what his conscious intentions were. In other words, in order to exert control he was going to try to be conscious in a state that was normally unconscious. Heart patients demonstrate many peculiar stress-related heart behaviors, but not with conscious control; the heart is under the control of unconscious mechanisms in the subcortical areas of the brain. I sometimes tell these people that they are "half yogis." By reacting to stress in a certain way they cause heart problems, but, unlike the Swami, they do not know how to go into the normally unconscious domain and straighten out the problem. What the Swami was proposing to demonstrate was, in my estimation, of considerable significance to psychosomatic medicine. Not only could the Swami get into this "somewhat risky" state, but presumably he would get out of it. The question I planned to ask Swami was "How did you get into that state, and how did you get out of it?"

The Swami's second statement, about the subtle heart, is representative of the general yogic idea of the subtle body, of which the physical body is supposedly a representation in the sensory domain. Since this subtle heart is allegedly controlled by mind, the demonstration would be consistent with the field of mind theory that we had been thinking about.

The experiment was about to begin. I was the only one in the experimental room with the Swami. Dale Walters, Alyce, and Dr. Ferguson, and later Dr. Sargent and a few other observers, were in the control room. I seated the Swami in the large armchair, which was barely big enough for him to sit in the lotus position—legs crisscrossed and folded so that the top sides of his feet rested on his thighs—and began talking about heart control. Presently the Swami said that he was going to be quiet for a moment in preparation for the demonstration. Then he said, "I am going to give a shock, do not be alarmed." I thought that he was going to shock his nervous system in some way, but later he said he meant that he was going to shock the doctors and the others in the polygraph room watching the paper record, and he did not want to frighten them.

We sat silently for perhaps two minutes. Then, to my surprise, I heard Alyce say on the intercom, "That's all." I was surprised, because the Swami had not twitched so much as an eyelash to indicate that he was conducting his demonstration. After a short period of time he drew in his solar plexus for a few seconds, then exhaled and looked at me. I could tell from his expression, the glint in his eyes, that from his point of view the demonstration had been a success.

I began asking how one stops the heart when Alyce called over the intercom and said, "The heart record does not look as we had anticipated. I think you should look at it." I excused myself and went into the control room, and was surprised to see the record shown in Figure 8.

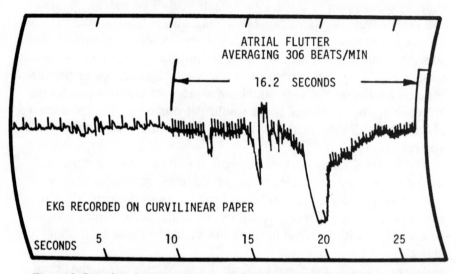

ATRIAL FLUTTER
AVERAGING 306 BEATS/MIN

16.2 SECONDS

EKG RECORDED ON CURVILINEAR PAPER

SECONDS 5   10   15   20   25

Figure 8. **Stopping the heart from pumping blood.** Swami Rama was motionless during the demonstration. After 16.2 seconds of "atrial flutter" Alyce called over the intercom and said, "That's all." Then the Swami drew in his diaphragm, and the resultant muscle tension drove the pen to the edge of the EKG channel. Erratic movements of the pen during the 16.2-second period of atrial flutter were caused by invisible muscle tensions.

Dr. Sargent said that it appeared to be a kind of fibrillation. All of us had previously thought that if Swami succeeded in his demonstration the heart would miss a few beats, and the pen would draw a straight line.

I returned to the experimental room and told Swami that his heart had not stopped in the way we had expected but instead had begun beating at five times its normal rate. He looked puzzled, then said, "Well, you know when you stop your heart this way it still flutters in there." He fluttered his hands in demonstration. We had not known that, but in retrospect I could easily see that the Swami's method, which causes obliteration of the pulse, might be identified as "heart stopping" by observers not using an EKG machine.

Dr. Sargent felt it might be useful to show the records to a cardiologist at the Kansas University Medical Center. He contacted Dr. Marvin Dunne. Dr. Dunne showed us slides made from patients' EKG records in which the same phenomenon was demonstrated and identified the state as "atrial flutter." A section of the heart "flutters" (he happened to use the same word as the Swami used) in an oscillatory mode at its maximum rate, the chambers not filling properly, the valves not working properly, the blood pressure dropping. Suddenly he stopped and said, "What happened to this man, anyway?" "Nothing," I answered. "We took his wires off and he went upstairs and gave his lecture."

Swami Rama and Daniel Ferguson returned to Minneapolis that afternoon, and our lab began to return to normal. Before the Swami left, however, he agreed to return for an extended series of experiments. He said that his teacher had asked him to come to the United States to demonstrate to medical people that the mind can control the body and he would come back for further demonstrations.

Two weeks later he sent me the following letter:

April 16, 1970

Most Blessed Dr. Green,

Thank you very much for your sincere efforts in promoting the Truth. I like to give you a few suggestions for the future tests, in the Lab.

1.) Methods of Concentration and Meditation
    a. Gaze outside in distance or one foot in distance.
    b. Gaze on the tip of the nose, on the nostrils, gaze on space between the two eyebrows.
    c. Concentration on different chakras, and if possible, the variation of the stability of mind can be recorded according to the plexus, and I want to know the brain waves.
    d. Concentration with breathing will be very fruitful. Inhalation in the bellows.
    e. Rhythmic breathing in retention and in making breathing finer.
    f. Concentration on a very minute object within. Concentration on a very big and wide object.
    g. Concentration on withdrawing the senses from outer objects. Concentration in nothingness. Concentration towards negativity. Concentration on positive thinking. Concentration on assimilation the forces of mind. Concentration on expanding the mind. Concen-

tration on the control of conscious mind. Concentration on silencing the conscious mind and bringing forward the subconscious mind.

h. Studying the mind and heart completely in conscious condition.
i. The effects of samadhi can be demonstrated if you have any machine to test.
j. Samadhi with seed and without seed.
k. Samadhi in a plastic capsule which should be sealed. Or samadhi in buried condition.

2.) Heart Tests
a. Slowing down beats to twenty and immediately jumping to 250.
b. Complete stoppage of heartbeat without muscle contraction.
c. Complete stoppage of heart from one and one half to three minutes with will power.
d. Heart stop through rhythmic way of pranayama by controlling vagus nerves.
e. Heart stop with lowest temperature can be examined.

3.) Blood Flow, Temperature, on the Right Side of Body and Reversing Up to Two to Three Degrees Fahrenheit.
a. Creating artificial tumors and dissolving them with will power.
b. The Blood Cell Experiment.
c. Piercing the needle on any part of flesh without bleeding or any damage.

4.) Respiratory Tests
a. You can make any mask for nostrils and mouth and verify the retention of breath.
b. There should be two masks; one for nose and mouth, and another for the eyes. So that close up to ten feet object can be located after closing the eyes, or any book can be read. Note: There are four methods in seeing the things after closing them. The first: after closing the eyes, anything can be visualized clearly at any distance, but eyes should be properly sealed and closed.
c. Through touching the closed envelope can be read, but eyes should be closed.
d. Anything can be read from one room to another, but eyes should be closed.

5.) Moving Things From One Place To Another
a. All the spiritual and psychic as well as physical demonstrations will be done in the lab ONLY, and not before or definitely not in public lecture. Those who are anxious to know the results should come to the lab and only lab. It should be available exclusively for Doctors and Scientists.

b. The experiment of Prana-Solar Science can be done on sunny days and we will fix up the date when I come.

c. I thank you very much for your achievements and I hope you keep in touch through letters before we meet.

I will be sending the lab report from London with film to you. If you wish, I will bring another Swami to give more elaborate tests in the field of respiratory system and heart and weight control.

I forgot to mention the sound experiments, which will be very interesting in studying the brain's vibrations and other internal states.

It is most amazing that people do not understand the power of mind over body. My effort is sincere and you will see that there is nothing unscientific in it. Of course, I find some difficulty in explaining certain things which I can do, but cannot explain how they are done.

Doctor, meditation alone is real life. There is nothing higher than meditation, that is my experience in life.

Please give my regards to Mrs. Green. Love little kiddies.

Let me thank you again for your kind and gentle behavior.

My present address will be: care of American Express, London, ENGLAND.

Please remember me to the members of your Lab.

Thy Own Self,
Swami Rama

We needed funds to continue the work with Swami Rama. With this letter and the results of the previous demonstrations in hand, I prepared a grant proposal for a private foundation. The funds were granted, forty-two thousand dollars over the next year to carry out the various tests and demonstrations described in Swami's letter.

Items (1.i) through (1.k) were to be demonstrations, he said, in which there would be no breathing. Item (2.d) was a demonstration he had already performed for us. Items (4.b) through (4.d) were to be performed while holding his breath. These last items reminded me of Madame Blavatsky's comment, about 1885, that to receive or transmit mental information in the most efficient way it was necessary to hold one's breath. It also reminded me of the Tibetan Buddhist idea that one can maintain a thought without change as long as one does not take a breath. That does not mean that everyone who can hold his breath can maintain a constant thought, but whose who can "hold a thought" may be using breath control as part of the technique.

Swami Rama returned to India after our March sessions. Alyce and

I, meanwhile, were invited to organize the first Transpersonal Psychology section of the annual meeting of the Association for Humanistic Psychology, to be held at Miami Beach in September (1970). We invited Swami Rama to speak, and he accepted, arriving back in the U.S. just in time to make his presentation. After that he came to Topeka, and we began the research program described in his letter.

At the very first, we conducted Swami Rama through five fifteen-minute EEG feedback sessions with alpha and theta so that he could correlate his states of consciousness with their associated brain-wave patterns. Then we began work in items (1.a) through (1.g). When he visualized "a wide object within," such as "blue sky with a small white cloud occasionally drifting by," Swami Rama produced alpha rhythm. A focus on "nothingness" also was associated with alpha. The Swami observed, "I can tell you, alpha is nothing."

To us, the most interesting of these brain-wave experiments was the last part of item (1.g): "silencing the conscious mind and bringing forward the subconscious mind." When the Swami did that we observed theta waves in significant amounts in his brain-wave pattern for the first time. When I asked him afterward what that state was like, he said it was unpleasant and noisy. "All of the things that other people wanted me to do, all of the things that I wanted to do, all of the things I should have done but didn't do, came up and began screaming at me at the same time. It is very noisy and very unpleasant. Usually I keep that turned off, but it is useful to look in there once in a while to see what is there."

These comments were certainly interesting. The states of consciousness associated with theta waves were *not* obnoxious to most people we had tested. But then, unlike the Swami, hardly anyone uses a combination of repression and sublimation to bring body energies and psychic energies under control. The Swami felt that the presence of theta was not healthy because of these discomforts. Concerning his own health, we had a dim idea of the strenuous method of training he had undertaken. His comment gave us additional information on the possible kinds of awareness associated with the conscious theta state. Persons who have not repressed their physiological and psychological tendencies, for whatever reason, may not be disturbed by what is in the unconscious. But, on the other hand, if they have made no effort at all to sublimate the energies, it is probable that they have developed little self-control. This possibility would make an interesting research project.

After five weeks the Swami left for a week for lecture engagements in Chicago and Minneapolis. He was back for a few days and then off again for another ten days. Gradually it became apparent that the seminars and lectures he was giving in various cities were making it almost impossible to keep to a laboratory schedule. Unfortunately, we conducted only about one third of the experiments outlined in his letter.

We had planned to study items (1.i) through (1.k) toward the latter part of our time together, scheduling the simpler things for the first weeks of our research and the more complex things later. In retrospect it is clear that we went at it in exactly the wrong way, at least with Swami Rama. He had been practicing his austerities before he came to Topeka and was keyed up for the demonstrations in the laboratory. If after a short period of adjustment to the research setting we had challenged him to do the most difficult things, he would have immediately attempted to demonstrate them. As it was, however, life at the laboratory became more and more boring to him, and his enthusiasm for the research began to diminish. He mentioned this indirectly on occasion, we realized later, but the significance of what he was saying wasn't immediately apparent to us. He was indirectly telling us that his ability to do things depended upon a kind of emotional activation, or excitement. It depended to some extent upon being challenged, to "put up or shut up," as they say.

For instance, one day after returning from Chicago, where he had given public lectures, he showed me a Polaroid picture in which most of his chest was obscured by a disc of pale pink light. I asked for an explanation, and he said that he had mentioned during a lecture that it was possible to turn on the subtle energy in a chakra so intensely that it would become visible to the naked eye. On hearing that, a skeptical physician in the audience had demanded that the Swami demonstrate it so he could take a picture with a Polaroid camera. The Swami said several pictures were taken and that I could keep that one. I asked him why he found it more difficult to do these things in the laboratory than in public and he responded with flashing eyes, "When I am challenged all of my powers come up and I can do everything."

The blood-cell experiment (3.b) is worth discussing even though we did not see it demonstrated because Swami did not complete the experiments planned. In explaining it he said that just before taking a blood sample we were to say, "20 percent," "40 percent," "100 percent," or "zero," or any other number. Then a drop of his blood would be extricated and put on a microscope slide and the fraction of dead white blood cells could be counted. He would kill, he said, whatever fraction was commanded at the time of the sampling.

I asked how he could kill individual cells. After long discussion ("long" because the Swami told of following procedures from the Sanskrit scriptures involving processes with which he was not totally familiar), I pieced together the following picture.

The body and the mind are both energy structures. In fact, the body is a subsection of the mind. Almost all of the body is in the unconscious, however, and thereby beyond ordinary control. In order to control cells of the body it is necessary to control "cells" of the unconscious. If one can extend conscious control over all parts of the unconscious, then all parts of the body come under control. If the mind is withdrawn from a particular section of the unconscious, the corresponding area of the body dies. That is how death is defined, according to theory. Organized tissues which are bereft of organizing mind fall back into the cosmic pool of physical matter, which is in a general state of disorganization, and the pattern gradually dissolves.

This explanation from Swami Rama is, I discovered later, essentially the same as that given by Patanjali in his *Yoga Sutras,* composed twenty-two centuries ago. Everything consists of "mind and its modifications" (Taimni, 1967). I first read that sutra in 1950, but it had no particular impact at that time.

We did not get to arrange a proper demonstration of item (3.a), "creating artificial tumors," which had been scheduled near the end of the series. I can report informally, however, what the Swami did in this regard. One day Swami and I began discussing tumors. I explained our research with blood-flow control and mentioned my idea that, because the vascular "tree" in tumors includes smooth muscles in blood vessel walls—which are presumably controlled from a hypothalamic center—it seemed reasonable to hypothesize that tumors could be volitionally starved through blood-flow control and reabsorbed by the body.

"Oh yes," Swami Rama said, "all of the soft tissues of the body are easy to manipulate."

I asked what he meant. He jumped up and said, "Press on this muscle with your thumb." It was a large volume of muscle in the right buttock, the gluteus maximus, just behind the hip bone. He said, "Do you feel any lumps in there?" I said, "No." Then he said, "Wait just a second," and he turned his face to the left, away from me for three or four seconds. Then he said, "Feel it again."

I pressed the muscle again and discovered a lump about the size of a bird's egg in the muscle. I said, "What is that, a tense muscle, a charley horse?"

The Swami said, "No, it's a cyst." I asked, "What's in it?" He said, "I don't know." "Would you be willing to have it X-rayed?" After a pause, he said, "I don't know. My teacher said that it was possible for X-rays to make changes in cells that I might not be able to control." I said, "How about a biopsy?" He replied, "Maybe."

Then he said, "Feel it again." I pressed the muscle again and the lump was gone. I said, "It's gone." He replied, "Just a second. I will make another one." He looked to the left side again for three or four seconds, then said, "There's another one." I pressed again with my thumb and found another lump, but in a different place—up against the hipbone. It was vertically longer and also narrower, and as I pressed it against the bone it slipped this way and that, as might be expected of a cyst.

It was unfortunate that this demonstration was not done in the laboratory, where medical doctors would have been available to give their opinions. To me, it seemed to be a striking example of mind-body coordination.

I asked the Swami if he could produce such a cyst in an area that would be easier to observe. Yes, he said, when he was in Germany he had produced a cyst several times on his wrist for physicians. He showed me a small scar. He had given permission for them to excise one of the cysts, which they still had in Germany in a bottle. I asked what the doctors said to him when he manufactured cysts suddenly like that. "They said, 'Swami, you are a very unusual man!' " The Swami continued with a disgusted expression, "I was trying to tell them something and all they said was, 'Swami, you are a very unusual man.' They did not think about what it meant."

Now let us discuss the "moving object" experiment (item 5), which we had planned to study at the end of the series with Swami Rama. One day when one of the physicians and I were interviewing the Swami in my office, he mentioned the fact that he could move objects by mind. Instantly, the doctor said, "You mean you can do it just like that, right now?" The Swami said, "Yes, there's nothing to it. I can do it in five minutes." The doctor said, "Show me."

The Swami jumped up and said, "I'll do it in your office." I interrupted and said, with some irritation, "I thought you said none of this would take place except in the laboratory. We are not planning any such demonstrations until next year. We are not set up to do any of this."

The Swami looked very bothered, but said, "I have been challenged. I have to do it now."

So the three of us went to the doctor's office. At the Swami's request, I hung a pencil on a string from the corner of the desk. He knelt down close to the pencil and began saying a mantra very fast, with considerable breath force. Soon the pencil rotated.

Before my colleague could say anything, I pointed out that obviously the pencil would move, if for no reason other than because his breath was pushing it. To conduct the experiment properly, I said, we would have to make certain that no air currents were involved.

The Swami jumped up and said, "All right, I will do it again." I could set it up, he said, under laboratory conditions, and he would wear a mask to prevent air currents and would be several feet away from the object. And he would "make it move."

I asked him when to schedule the demonstration, and there was a long period of thinking. I asked what he was doing and he said he was calculating when he would be ready. It was necessary to say his mantra many times over a period of days in order to make the demonstration under those conditions. Finally he said that he would be ready in nine days. The time was agreed upon with the doctor, but an additional five-day delay was necessary because of his patient schedules.

I arranged the experiment in a small room in the basement of the research building, blocking air vents to prevent air currents and arranging chairs so six observers and I would have a good look at the Swami and the object he would try to move.

I bought some aluminum knitting needles, ground their tips to points, and glued two of them together at right angles in the form of an X. A small hole was drilled through the place where the needles intersected and the assembly was set on a vertical axle, a steel pin that extended from a plastic block, as shown in Figure 9. The plastic block was glued to a 360° protractor so that "before" and "after" readings could be taken of the position of the needle assembly. A small bead under the needle assembly provided ample friction to prevent motion due to air currents and yet was free enough to allow easy movement. I hung a

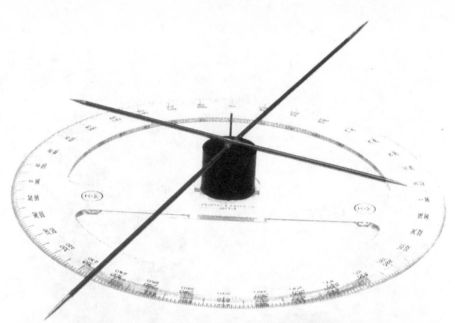

Figure 9. **Needle assembly for psychokinetic demonstration.** Two aluminum knitting needles (14 inches and 7 inches long) were glued together at a 90° angle to provide observers with a good perspective.

floodlight from the ceiling over the lamp table on which the fixture was placed, as shown in Figure 10.

I questioned the Swami about the long delay required for saying his mantra. He said that it was necessary to say it 140,000 times. I asked him why so many times were necessary and he said, "Because it says so in the Sanskrit records." I asked what would happen if he said it only 130,000 times, and he said, "I don't know, but I am afraid to try."

As the days passed the Swami was in seclusion a good deal of the time, practicing breathing exercises and repeating the mantra. Tension increased at our house every day until the day of the experiment. That morning when the Swami came out of his room he was completely at ease and said that he felt certain now that the demonstration would be a success. He said he had contacted his teacher and the teacher had said, "You have been trained to do this, do it." "But," the Swami continued, "there will be trouble about the mask."

I had obtained a painter's mask with a foam-rubber insert through which to breathe, and when I first showed it to the Swami he said that it would not be adequate.

"How could anybody complain about this?" I said. "You can't blow air through it, that's for sure."

Figure 10. **Room arrangements for the psychokinetic demonstration with Swami Rama.**

But he said, "Cover the mask with something to make it more sure."
I obtained a plexiglass plate and bolted it across the foam-rubber insert
so that if any air could be blown through the foam rubber it would be
deflected away and down, as shown in Figure 11.

Just as we were leaving the house to go to the lab, the Swami said
again that there was going to be trouble about air currents. "Someone
in the group is going to say that I did it with air currents. Go back and
get a sheet to tie around me, up to my eyes and over the mask, just so
I can see out."

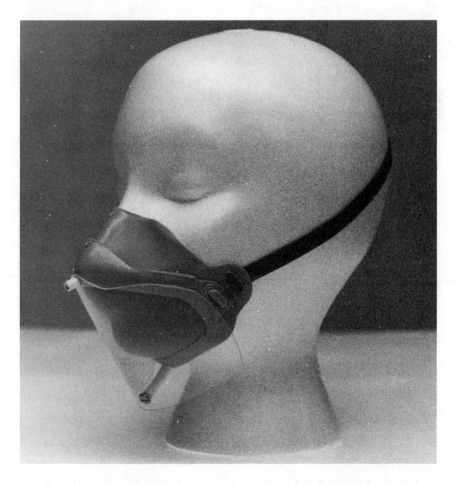

Figure 11. **Face mask used to block air currents during psychokinetic demonstration.** A foam-rubber insert in the mask, under the plexiglass cover plate, permitted respiration.

We were late, however, and I knew that the participating doctors had patients scheduled immediately after the experiment. I did not want to take more precautions. I said, "I really don't care to try to cover more eventualities. There is no way to satisfy every person. I am satisfied with this mask. As far as I am concerned, there is absolutely no way in which air currents can be manipulated through this mask to control the knitting needles five feet away. There isn't time to make more arrangements. Let's go." So we went to the lab.

Doug Boyd had burned a lot of incense in the experimental room for the Swami, and I hoped the observers could tolerate it.

The Swami sat with his back to the wall on the couch shown in Figure 10, facing the low table with the needle assembly on it. Doug's chair was placed at the end of the couch. The Swami had asked that Doug sit there with a wooden stick to prop him up if he should fall to the left, toward the "negative" side, he said. It was important not to touch him with the hand, only with the stick. I lit a candle that the Swami requested for focusing attention and placed it on the floor, lining it up according to the Swami's instructions so that the flame was seen by him above the left tip of the long needle. The short needle pointed at the couch.

While the Swami meditated, Doug waited by the door to the experimental room and I notified the other observers to join us. I first passed the mask around so everyone could look at it and try it on if desired. They looked at the protractor and needles and sat down while I put the mask over the Swami's nose and mouth and adjusted it. After getting into a comfortable cross-legged position and sitting silently for three or four minutes, the Swami remarked that the candle flickered sometimes (which I had noticed) and said that it was distracting him. I rose and blew out the candle. I asked him if we could record his mantra. He said no recordings could be made. (No one would have understood any recording, in fact, because he muttered at such tremendous speed.)

After another brief silence he began. The mantra was quite long, possibly fifteen seconds, and was concluded with a loud exclamation, a word of command, at which time the needle rotated a small amount: The point he was focusing his eyes on moved toward him. We sat for a moment in silence, and then I got up and examined the needle. It had moved ten degrees.

The Swami asked if I wanted him to do it again. I said yes, and the performance was repeated. The needle moved another ten degrees toward him. We talked for a while in the group, looked at the mask again, glanced at the protractor, and went back upstairs.

I immediately sought out the doctor with whom the first "demonstration" had been conducted and asked him how he felt about this one. He said, "I believe that he did it with air currents."

"But," I objected, "air currents as an explanation are not reasonable."

He said, "Let's face it. This is probably the most remarkable person you or I will ever see. He can control blood flow in the palm of his hand, he can stop his heart from pumping blood. He can do things with his breath that you and I can't even imagine. I think he did it with air currents."

"But how?" I replied.

"How do I know? Maybe he bounced air off his chest."

"But," I continued, "how could he do that? He was totally covered over in his white gown—even his hands were covered."

"Don't ask me to explain, but I still think he did it with air."

Entertained by the accuracy of the Swami's prediction, I went to his office in the research building and said, "You were right, Dr. X feels that it was done with air currents." Swami seemed irritated and said, "I told you so." He offered to do another demonstration, behind a large board, but Dr. X was already busy with his patients and this could not be arranged.

Concerning ESP-type events, we had a number of personal illustrations with the Swami, but nothing that took place in the laboratory while he was wired up. On one occasion when Alyce, the Swami, and I were eating lunch at home, Pat Norris telephoned. She asked the Swami if she could talk to him for a few minutes at 1:30 P.M. He said yes. Turning from the phone, he asked me to find a paper and pencil for him. Then he sat on a couch in the corner of the living room and began thinking and writing while Alyce and I cleared away the dishes. I kept wondering what he was doing. Glancing his way, I noticed that he had put the piece of paper face down on a chair. Just as we were leaving to return to the office, Pat arrived.

Later that day I asked Pat what kind of conversation she had with the Swami, and she said that an odd thing had occurred. The instant she came into the house he said, "Ask me a question." She said, "What do you mean, ask you a question?" And he said, "Just ask me a question, something important." At first she could not think of anything, but finally she asked, "Should Peter [her son] go to a private school?" Then he said, "Ask me another question." And she said, "Should I return to college to get a Ph.D.?" And he said, "Ask another question." Pat said that he kept asking for questions until she had asked seven questions. When she was through with the last one he grabbed the paper and handed it to her. Most of her questions (and some suggestions) were written there. One was wrong and one was only partly related to the subject, but the others were correct. She said this was a real surprise.

In November 1970 I was invited to attend a conference on yoga and science, to be held in New Delhi. I did not want to go but when the Swami heard about it he said that he wanted to attend, and wanted to take some biofeedback machinery with him. I had misgivings about his leaving the United States before we had finished our research, but he was eager to go. I asked why he wanted to have biofeedback machines; he could already control physiological functions. He said these machines were going to be useful for "training young yogis and eliminating fakers." I gathered from him that one of the main problems in India is that some people are yogis only by repute and a skillful con man can generate a huge following without ever having to perform. Physiological detectors would make short work of these people, he felt. Complying, we built some special biofeedback machines for Swami to take to India in a foam-lined suitcase.

Swami Rama did not return to our lab after his visit to the conference in New Delhi. Instead, he sent a letter stating that after serious thought he had decided not to return to the Menninger Foundation. His main purpose in being with scientists could not be accomplished in the United States, he said, because he wanted to make experiments in the therapeutic use of yoga, which he felt would be easier to do in India and would be "more useful to humanity." Swami Rama did return to the United States, however, to continue lecturing and teaching and to establish a center of his own.

Rolling Thunder

We met Rolling Thunder in 1971 at the third annual Council Grove Conference on the Voluntary Control of Internal States. Elmer and I had organized the first such conference in 1969, in response to the decision of a group of eight people brought together through the efforts of Helen Bonny. The group included Helen, John Lilly, Kenneth God-

frey, Stanislav Grof, Pauline McKririck, Walter Pahnke, Elmer, and me. We were professionally concerned that the accelerating search for "expanded consciousness" might be getting out of hand. People in all walks of life, and especially young persons, were acting with abandon in their use of such things as psychedelic drugs, marijuana, hypnosis, and sensory deprivation. Aside from danger to users, the group feared that public reaction would adversely affect scientific research in these areas.

We gathered at White Memorial Camp, Council Grove, Kansas. The outcome of several days of discussion was the decision to plan an invitational conference for the following spring to be held in the same simple, quiet, free-from-distraction place. We all suggested names of people who we felt would be both contributors and receivers in an open dialogue on the development of a "science of consciousness." Elmer and I were particularly interested in voluntary methods for the study of consciousness and upon request contributed the name of our project at the Menninger Foundation to the conference, Voluntary Control of Internal States. (This, incidentally, was the title of our 1967 NIMH research grant, which was, to the best of our knowledge, the first biofeedback research project supported by government funds.)

The Council Grove Conferences, as they have come to be informally called, cut across cultural boundaries, discipline boundaries, and religious boundaries, to look at contributions to the concept of consciousness by Zen Buddhism, Tibetan Buddhism, Integral Yoga, Sufism, Mystic Christianity, hypnosis, Autogenic Training, sensory deprivation, psychedelic-drug experience, and biofeedback training. We were looking for "invariant relationships" by going over the common ground of the various systems, which is surprisingly great. There is not sufficient space to review the Council Grove Conferences, but some references include papers by ourselves (Green and Green, 1969), Fadiman (1969, 1970), and Harman (1969).

Stanley Krippner, organizer of the third conference, brought still another consciousness approach to Council Grove: the American Indian tradition. He invited Rolling Thunder, a man of Cherokee blood, trained from boyhood to be a medicine man. We were very much interested in what he might have to say that could be compared with concepts from other cultures.

The first time I saw Rolling Thunder, he was standing at the window of the conference hall, gazing across the Kansas prairies. He wore a plaid flannel shirt, tan workman's pants, and an old straw hat with an

---

eagle feather stuck upright in the hat band. When he turned around I was impressed by the quiet strength of his face. The faint squint of his eyes gave him a thoughtful look, the look of a man accustomed to peering into far places.

I joined him where he stood. Somehow a conversation started, and he told me something of how one becomes a medicine man. If that is the destiny of the individual, it is known when one is born and the child is treated accordingly. When still very young, Rolling Thunder was sent from time to time to live with various medicine men. He would serve them, carry water and wood, and do other chores, and he was encouraged to listen as they sat long hours talking of spiritual things with the elders or with other medicine men. Sometimes he was allowed to watch or help in some small way as they did their medicine.

He went alone into the mountains when he was thirteen to find his own individual identity. There he had his dream, a vision that led to his name, Rolling Thunder. He told something of the strictness of the training he had to undergo to learn the self-discipline necessary to handle the powers of a medicine man. As he talked I was struck again and again with similarities between the training of this American Indian to become a medicine man and the training of East Indian yogis.

Rolling Thunder said almost nothing during the first three days of the conference. He had not yet agreed to speak to the group; he was taking the medicine man's traditional three days to make an important decision. But he could be seen watching people keenly and listening thoughtfully as he stood at the edge of some discussion group. Occasionally he would talk briefly with a small group of two or three people. By the end of the third day, Rolling Thunder had made his decision— he would speak to the conference. Surprisingly, he also agreed to do a healing ceremony. One of the conference participants had been kicked with a spiked shoe in a soccer game shortly before coming to Council Grove. The wound on his leg was now clearly infected—inflamed, swollen, and painful. During a discussion as to whether he should leave the conference to seek medical care in Topeka or Kansas City, someone suggested that Rolling Thunder was a healer—maybe he could help. He was asked, and he agreed.

Stanley Krippner introduced Rolling Thunder to the conference audience by telling us about his first meeting with Rolling Thunder and about watching him as he healed a young woman with an injured back. He expressed gratitude to Rolling Thunder for his willingness to share what he could with us and asked that all observe an Indian tradition of not interrupting or asking questions of a speaker until his talk is finished.

Rolling Thunder walked with slow, deliberate steps to the platform and stood for a moment looking at us as we looked at him. Then he said this was the first time he had spoken to a group of white people about spiritual things, that just ten years earlier it would have been impossible. Now things were changing, especially among the young white people who seemed to like Indians and want to learn more from them. He told of his feelings as he walked among us during the three days he took to make his decision to speak to us. He said, "I felt much good will. You are spiritual people." And so he had told Stanley Krippner that he would speak to us and do a healing ceremony for the injured young man. But he added very firmly that he would reveal none of the medicine man's sacred secrets, they could not yet be revealed, but he would speak as clearly as he could about what he felt was proper for him to say.

Rolling Thunder told us something of the ritual of gathering herbs or any plant or part of plants for healing purposes (he called them "helpers"). It is a spiritual procedure, he said. The plants are not gathered indiscriminately. There are ways of knowing which are the right ones to take, and the plants are told what they are to be used for and that only those that are needed will be taken. The plants are thanked for being of service. In this way, harmony is maintained between the Indians and nature. Their relationship to animals and to everything in nature is guided by similar attitudes and procedures.

He would give us something we could take with us, Rolling Thunder said, and he told us how to make water into medicine. Sometimes Indians are caught without medicine when they need to cure a fever or some other illness. They fill a glass of water and pray over it when the sun is coming up. Then the Great Spirit's power is strong for bringing forth new life. The prayer is begun when the sun begins to rise and ends when the bottom of the sun is seen. "Let the rays of the sun hit that water and you can make medicine out of it if you want to do that and you need the medicine."

I listened with surprise to Rolling Thunder's formula for making water into medicine. Swami Rama had told me an East Indian ritual for doing the same thing, and it also made me think of the Christian tradition of Holy Water and of Dr. Justa Smith's biochemical research on the effects on plants of water that had been blessed (Smith, 1972).

Rolling Thunder talked about the Great Spirit, the source of the medicine man's powers, and the one and only sovereign he answers to. He spoke about nature and said that it is nature's law that keeps all things in balance so that everything that is done must in time bring its just results, good or bad. He spoke of the Earth as a being, the mother who nurtures us all, plants, animals, and humans, and makes us all brothers. He questioned the right of anyone to own a part of the Earth. How can anyone own a part of the mother of us all?

In a very moving way, Rolling Thunder expressed the belief that the Native Americans, the traditional Indians, are the caretakers of our land and that the Indian tradition can teach us not only how properly to use its great gifts but also how to nurture it.

When Rolling Thunder had finished what he wanted to say, he looked out at the audience again for a long silent moment, then said, "Thank you." He answered a few questions and went to his cabin. In two hours the healing ritual was to begin.

People gathered quietly for the healing ceremony. Cameras and tape recorders had been put away. The patient, a young fellow with long hair and a beard, sat at the front of the room. The right leg of his trousers was rolled up to the knee. Those of us sitting in the front rows could see the wounded area. It looked swollen and discolored. Several members of the conference, including Elmer, stepped up and examined the wound. They found the area surrounding it red and hot and hard to the touch.

Soon Rolling Thunder walked down the center aisle. He wore his old straw hat with the eagle feather in it and carried a small battered suitcase. He approached the patient and said something quietly. The young man removed his shoes.

Rolling Thunder kneeled down, opened his suitcase, and took out his pipe and tobacco and what looked like a part of an eagle's wing or several large eagle feathers fastened together. He took off his hat, placed it on the suitcase, and moved a bowl of raw meat (which had been brought at his request) toward his patient's feet. He stood up, filled his pipe, and took out a match. Turning to us, he explained that when he is with his own people his assistants get things ready for him, even lighting his pipe, but here he must do it himself. He put the pipe to his mouth, struck the match, and took several deep puffs. When he was sure the pipe was well lit, he took it from his mouth and looked out over the audience. Everything was very quiet. Rolling Thunder began his healing ritual.

He drew deeply on his pipe; then, blowing smoke to the east and gesturing with his pipe, he said, "To the east, where the sun rises." Then he faced north, drew deeply again, lifted his pipe in that direction, and said, "To the north, where the cold comes from," and he continued the procedure to each direction: "To the south, where the light comes from"; "To the west, where the sun sets"; upward "to the Father Sun" and downward "to the Mother Earth."

Rolling Thunder turned toward his patient, handed him the pipe, and told him to take three deep puffs. The young man drew deeply on the pipe and handed it back. Rolling Thunder asked him why he wanted to be healed, what he was going to do, was there anything else he wanted to say? The young man explained about his injury and said he was worried about it. Again Rolling Thunder asked him what he was going to do, why it was important that this infection should be taken away. This time the young man explained that he was involved in an important project and he needed to be well. It was evident that Rolling Thunder accepted the answer as sufficient. Turning his back toward the audience, he faced his patient squarely and began an odd, high-pitched cry. There followed a strange sequence of actions in which, with his mouth, he seemed to be symbolically drawing the infection into himself and dispelling it. Then he picked up the eagle wing and used it like a brush, as if sweeping something away from the patient's body, from his head to his feet, but without touching the body or the clothes. Occasionally he would stop to shake the brush vigorously over the bowl of meat, as if gathering something undesirable from a subtle body surrounding the man and casting it away.

Presently, the healing ceremony was over. Rolling Thunder picked up his suitcase and hat and walked out of the conference room.

Again the people who had examined the wound before the ceremony went up to look at it. The consensus was that it seemed somewhat less swollen, some of the redness was gone, and the flesh around the wound was less rigid. The young man said the pain was gone. During the coffee hour following the evening meeting we noticed he was playing ping-pong.

The next day the wound seemed to be healing satisfactorily. What had seemed to be a serious infection the night before no longer appeared threatening. There was no pain, and the tissues surrounding the wound were flexible and soft to the touch. Pain is notoriously controllable through suggestion (the healing ritual was a powerful suggestion), and the absence of pain may be explainable in that way. The rapid change in the tissues might seem more difficult to explain. Since we did not study Rolling Thunder's healing techniques in our laboratory, there is little we can say of a technical nature.

Our brief contact with Rolling Thunder at the conference aroused our curiosity. He and Swami Rama were strikingly different personalities, but we were keenly aware of certain basic similarities in their concepts of Nature and Spirit and man's relation to them.

We had invited Doug Boyd to the conference to hear Rolling Thunder's afternoon talk and watch the healing ceremony. Although we had no plan for a laboratory study of Rolling Thunder, we were interested in a personal observation of his work over a period of time, if such a thing was possible. We had a rather vague idea that Doug might be able to help with such a study, and Elmer suggested the possibility at the time. Some weeks later Doug said to Elmer that when he finished the transcripts of his work with Swami Rama he would like to go out to Nevada to see Rolling Thunder. Thus did the wheels begin to turn, eventually to result in the book Rolling Thunder *(1974), detailing Doug's observations.*

We had a number of opportunities to talk with Rolling Thunder during the time Doug was working with him, and from those contacts and Doug's observations we learned a great deal more about the similarities between the teachings of the traditional Native American and the yogic philosophies of the East, including:

1. The unity of all things. Everything is a manifestation of spirit, whether called the Great Spirit of the American Indian or the Brahman of the East Indian.

2. All things have a form of consciousness.

3. There are forces of light (good) and forces of darkness (evil).

4. The existence of spiritual cause and effect (karma) and rebirth (reincarnation).

5. Man's inner nature is identical with the nature of the universe (man is the microcosm, the universe the macrocosm).

6. There are subtle energies that can be directed by volition and there are centers of such energies in the human body.

7. Psychic powers are both natural and potential in every person. They are not necessarily spiritual.

8. Discipline and purification of body and mind are requirements for spiritual development.

9. The principle of harmlessness.

10. The principle of service.

One of the major problems in working with unusual people is the difficulty of separating cultural peculiarities in their teachings from the essence of their teachings. We have thought that if it were possible to study a large enough group of accomplished individuals from a number of different cultures, we would be able to construct a Venn diagram that would identify the culture-free area. For instance, in Figure 12, the encompassing circle represents "knowledge, experience, and explanations in the domain of mind and nature." In this area, the behaviors and awareness of Swami Rama, Jack Schwarz, and Rolling Thunder are illustrated as overlapping. From a theoretical point of view, the region in which all three coincide is expected to be relatively culture-free.

Jack Schwarz

Most people in the West have heard of yogis. The Sunday supplements for more than a hundred years have contained delectable tales of Oriental magicians who performed amazing feats of self-control and healing, and who exerted power over animals and nature. We have "yogis" aplenty in the U.S. nowadays, ranging all the way from hawkers of kundalini powers (who often seem to have no particular power themselves) to the renowned teacher Maharishi Mahesh Yogi, the founder of Transcendental Meditation. His adaptations of raja yoga were thoughtfully prepared for conditions in the West, and have probably helped more Westerners to become involved in "finding themselves" than any other system from India.

By contrast, the Sufi tradition from the Middle East (called "West Asia" in India, by the way) is an esoteric branch of Islam relatively unknown in the West. In essence, Sufism, Tibetan Buddhism, and esoteric Indian yoga bear resemblance. They are so similar that Idries Shah himself, a noted Sufi who has written many books on the subject, defines Sufism in such a way that all yogis are included, and also included are

---

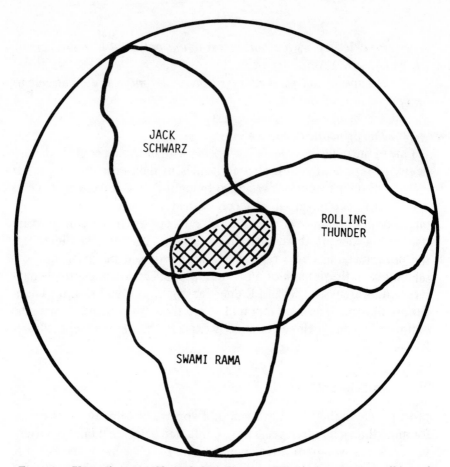

Figure 12. **Venn diagram of knowledge of nature.** The circle represents *all* knowledge and awareness, and the irregular shapes represent the awarenesses of Jack Schwarz, Rolling Thunder, and Swami Rama. The crosshatched area, where their descriptions of nature and their demonstrations agree, represents information that is relatively culture-free.

all persons, of no matter what culture or tradition, who have developed unusual powers of self-regulation and an unusual awareness of other people at a normally unconscious level. From that point of view, Jack Schwarz is a Sufi.

I first heard of him in the spring of 1971, while lecturing in California at the Esalen Institute. Paul Herbert, who recorded lectures for Esalen, asked me if I had ever heard of one Jack Schwarz, who was very much like Swami Rama. Paul's description of Jack intrigued me. He gave me

Jack's phone number and said that it might be useful if I were to tell him about our laboratory. Not long after, I called him.

The first thing I noticed, aside from the fact that Jack spoke English with a slight foreign accent, was that he had a big sense of humor, a good sign. (Who can be more depressing than a deadly serious "spiritual" man? If a sense of humor is lacking he may not know who he is, or may be caught in an "ego trip.") I told Jack about our lab and said that if he ever came through the middle part of the country on his travels, we would be glad to show him what we were doing.

I thought no more about Jack until several months later. My secretary called me and said a man by the name of Jack Schwarz was on the line. "He said that you invited him to come to the laboratory." Almost the first thing Jack said when I answered was that he had some time free between two sets of lectures he was giving on the West Coast and if I wanted him to be a subject at the laboratory he could arrive on the day after Thanksgiving and stay until December 8. We had an unusually heavy lab schedule at that time and I doubted if we would be able to get together, but when I looked at my calendar, those particular days were the only ones that were free until Christmas. I didn't have the slightest idea what Jack would do in our lab, but we quickly made arrangements, and on the night of Thanksgiving I drove to the Kansas City airport to meet him.

Alyce and I had invited him to our house, with the idea that it would provide a somewhat quieter environment than a hotel and would also give us a chance to get acquainted. Jack was an interesting conversationalist, and before we knew it, it was two A.M. I apologized for keeping him up so late, and he said he seldom slept for more than two or three hours a night anyway, but that *we* probably wanted to get some sleep.

Both Swami Rama and Jack Schwarz seemed to need no more than two or three hours sleep each night. Swami had said that it is necessary when going to sleep for the mind and brain to be quiet at the same time, otherwise a perfect rest is not assured. Alyce and I had on a few occasions slept as little as twenty-five hours per week for a short period of time, and sometimes less. For example, during the month in which I was doing my research and writing my dissertation at the University of Chicago, I slept about four hours per night. But we did not make a habit of it, as Swami and Jack did.

Jack's ability to go without sleep has impressed me. Jack has attended three Council Grove Conferences, at which, because of his unusual ability to be aware of trends in people's lives, many of the other participants wanted to talk privately with him. To accommodate these requests, Jack scheduled his time until about five o'clock in the morning. During two of the five-day conferences, I realized from talking with other people that some nights he didn't sleep at all. Curious as to how many hours Jack was getting, I checked every day and found that during one conference he slept a total of seven hours and at another only a little more.

Jack does not recommend, however, that people try this before they have learned to "discharge the stress of the day, and then recharge." One must learn a certain kind of meditation, but even then it isn't simple. Both psychological and physiological factors are involved, and it might take ten years before a person can cut sleeping time from eight hours to six hours, and another ten years to go from six to four hours. The main problem is to learn how to use "the electricity of the body," and not dissipate it through what don Juan, Castaneda's teacher, would call "indulging." The point here is that it is not just a simple procedure that is followed but a way of life, and that way of life represents a big change for the average person.

In that first long talk with Jack we learned that he was forty-six years old and had been born in Holland, in the same region as the famous Dutch psychics Peter Hurkos and Gerald Croisette. Was there something about the Dutch soil or air or water that tended to develop awareness of normally unconscious processes? Swami Rama developed his talents over a period of many years, he said, especially the years from eighteen to thirty-one, but Croisette, Hurkos, and Schwarz developed unusual talents without following any particular training program.

When Jack was in his early teens he saw a stage hypnotist enter a self-induced trance and then push pins into his arm while he talked about the power of mind to control pain and bleeding. Jack had the normal response to pain until he saw that demonstration, and then, for no particular reason, he knew that he would be able to do the same thing. He got some pins and tried it, and sure enough he could turn pain off. What a conversation piece, he thought. Jack said that at first he never tired of amazing his friends. He developed a cocky attitude, in spite of the fact that he had not had to develop his skills, but "woke up one morning and found all the diplomas were on the wall." He could stop pain, stop bleeding, influence people through hypnosis, remove pains in other people by putting his hands on them and thinking about the pain going away, and could often "guess" other people's thoughts precisely.

It is of interest that Swami Rama, Rolling Thunder, and Jack Schwarz are all practitioners of "unconventional healing." These men, who have unusual control of their own bodies and unusual awareness of the problems of other people, believe that good health will be difficult to achieve on a large scale until Western scientific medicine makes room for methods that, for countless generations of human life, were often the only ways of healing. They believe that skillful general practitioners trained in Western medicine often know much about, or unconsciously use, some of these unconventional methods, such as healing by the "laying on of hands."

We did not make a focused effort to interrogate Jack when we began the laboratory work. As with Swami Rama, we asked him to tell us what he would like to demonstrate while wired up. Jack wanted to start with a demonstration of control of bleeding. Dale and Alyce wired him in the same way we prepared college-student subjects in other research. When he sat down in the experimental room he produced an envelope with two 6-inch steel sailmaker's needles. He said he would push the needles through his biceps and demonstrate bleeding control.

During a preliminary period of the test we had trouble with the polygraph. A broken wire had to be tracked down and repaired, so we asked Jack to allow himself to just relax and be comfortable. Jack's heart had been beating at an average rate of about eighty-five beats per minute, but in the few minutes we were working with the polygraph, his heart rate dropped down into the sixties. There was no tension or nervousness. In this Jack demonstrated the consistency of his control—a control, we have observed, that he can turn on at will.

Jack was wired to record the behavior of a number of physiological variables that give indications of stress reactions: heart rate, breathing rate, galvanic skin response, skin temperature, and brain waves. While we were adjusting the equipment near him, one of his needles rolled off the board on which his hands were placed and fell to the floor. As I picked it up I realized that we had not sterilized the needles, and I asked if he wanted me to do anything about it. He said, "No, I often sterilize my needle by putting it on the floor and rolling it under my shoe."

Jack produced beta waves almost all of the time that he was sitting in the chair in the experimental room. We considered this quite normal under the circumstances, because we expected him to be activated. When he put the tip of the needle to his biceps, however, his brain-wave record began to show alpha. This was exactly the opposite from what the average person could be expected to do. A person sitting in a quiet room with nothing to do will usually begin to produce alpha, but if he were asked to push a needle through his arm he would be expected to abruptly "block" alpha and produce beta. But Jack did exactly the opposite.

Later we heard of a similar finding by Erik Peper. He told us that his subject, Ramon Torres from Peru, had demonstrated the same kind of brain-wave pattern when he pushed a bicycle spoke through his cheeks. As soon as he touched the spoke to his cheek he went from beta into alpha and did not go back into beta until the bicycle spoke had been removed from the other side.

Upon reflection, we can say that this appearance of alpha brain waves during the control of pain makes good sense. We all know that pain is seldom experienced if attention is turned away from the sensation. As noted in Chapter 2, the perception of pain was the subject of my doctoral dissertation at the University of Chicago. In my research there, subjects who did not feel the pain of an electrical stimulator were the ones whose attention was continuously focused elsewhere, on impressions from the eyes and ears, and from whole-body vibration. By contrast, those who felt the pain continuously reported that they were unaware of the lights, sounds, and vibrations which bombarded them. Their attention was on the pain itself. What Jack Schwarz and Peper's subject demonstrated was the ability voluntarily to turn attention away from sensory inputs associated with pain. In that condition they appeared to be free of pain. Figure 13 (a) shows Jack being wired up and Figure 13 (b) shows him pushing the 6-inch steel needle through his arm. Figure 13 (c) shows the needle buried about half an inch deep in his biceps.

Before Jack began pulling the needle out of his arm, Figure 13 (d), I decided that it would be useful for the record if it were demonstrated that Jack could bleed in a normal way. It had occurred to me that even if Jack did this demonstration a hundred times we really would not know if he had control of bleeding or merely had a peculiar skin. From a medical point of view, it would be more economical to assume that Jack had an anomalous skin, if he did not bleed, than that he had control of bleeding.

In order to control bleeding it is necessary to control a normally unconscious process. All yogis who demonstrate unusual powers of self-regulation apparently have achieved a kind of coordination between conscious and unconscious. In effect, I decided to interfere with that coordination. Just as Jack was preparing to pull the needle out of his arm, I interrupted him and said, "Jack, tell me, is it going to bleed now?" He looked quite surprised and uncertain, like a man balancing on one finger when someone says, "Are you going to fall now?" I suspect that no one had ever interrupted him like that.

Jack said, "I don't think it's going to bleed." But when he pulled the needle out, it bled freely. The photographer put down his camera, and he and I began mopping up the blood with paper tissues. Bleeding was continuous for about ten seconds, and then I heard Jack say very softly, "Now it stops." Much to my surprise, the hole in the skin that I was dabbing closed up as if drawn by purse strings. It took about one second to close, and not another drop of blood appeared.

We were very much impressed, and I said to Jack, "I am glad to see that you are normal and can bleed, and can also stop bleeding. How about doing it again, but this time don't bleed at all." There was a pause. Many seconds went by, and I began to wonder if I had said something wrong, when Jack said, "Okay, I'll do it again." He pushed the needle through a different place in his arm, as shown in Figure 13 (f), and allowed it to remain buried in the muscle for a half minute or so, Figure 13 (g). Though I squeezed his arm, no blood came out when the needle was removed, Figure 13 (h).

When the test was concluded we talked for a while, and I asked Jack why he had paused so long before he agreed to do the second demonstration. He said he wanted me to understand that he did not force his body to do any of these things. He asked it to. He had to ask his subconscious and wait for an answer. When it said "Yes" to him, he said "Okay" to me.

Jack also mentioned that in a demonstration of this kind he thought of his arm as an object not attached to him, and pushed the needle through it as if it were the arm of a stuffed chair. Detachment is a well-known method for yogic control of pain, but achieving it is not easy. The kind of detachment Jack uses is evidently associated with the production of alpha waves in the brain-wave record, as we have already mentioned, and no doubt something similar is responsible for the continuous production of alpha waves in the yogi masters who did not

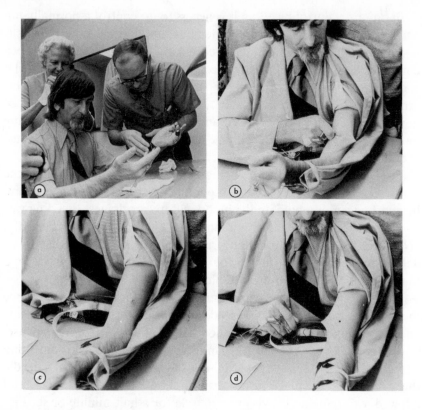

Figure 13. **Voluntary control of bleeding.** Jack Schwarz (a) is "wired" for psycho-physiological recording in preparation for driving an unsterilized knitting needle through his biceps (b). The needle was buried about one half inch deep in the muscle (c). The first wounds released about one half cubic centimeter of blood when the needle was withdrawn from the arm (d). The blood, which was continuously being wiped up, appeared to stop in about one second when Jack said

come out of the brain-wave state, or show any sign of activated beta-wave awareness even when touched by hot glass test tubes in the experiment by Anand referred to earlier (see Chapter 8).

In Jack's first trial with the needle, the alpha in his record increased from about zero up to 10 percent, but during the second trial it increased from zero up to about 60 percent. That is, during the time when the needle was embedded in his arm, 60 percent of the brain-wave record from his left occiput showed the presence of alpha. As said be-

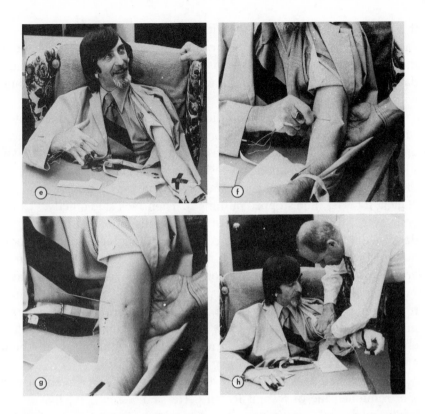

it would cease (e). When asked if he would repeat the demonstration, now that bleeding control had been established, Jack obliged by driving the needle through the biceps again (f and g). No bleeding occurred this time, and no blood could be squeezed from the arm (h). Jack reported feeling mechanical pressure but no pain, and showed no particular signs of pain in heart rate, respiration, galvanic skin response, hand temperature, and brain-wave records.

fore, we interpret this to mean that Jack was exercising "attention control."

A year later Jack demonstrated this pain and bleeding control again at the Veterans Administration Hospital in Topeka at a meeting of physicians arranged by Dr. Stuart Twemlow. In order to make the demonstration clearly visible to the large audience, a closed-circuit TV system was used. When Jack put his needles on the floor, rubbed his shoes on them, and said he was sterilizing his equipment, I noticed that the physicians observing in the video room became unusually silent. Jack pushed a needle through his arm, and for a minute we talked about the previous times we had done this in our lab at the Menninger Foundation, in which he had done it once with bleeding and a second time without bleeding.

During the discussion that followed Stuart Twemlow interrupted suddenly and said, "We need a control subject. I'll be it. Let me have one of those needles, Jack." I was much impressed by Stuart. After some delaying conversation and hesitation, he began to drive the needle through his forearm. When it was about halfway through he said, "Ouch, it hurts," and stopped pushing it. Then Jack said quietly, "Close your eyes, Stuart, and think about the jonquils blooming at the front door of the building." Stuart closed his eyes, and Jack stood up, took hold of the needle, and pushed it the rest of the way through Stuart's arm. Then he said, "Okay, it's done." Stuart looked down and said, "Wow, look at that!" When Stuart pulled the needle out, the two puncture wounds bled for a short time. They subsequently healed without infection, but I noticed when I saw Stuart two days later that considerable subdermal bleeding had occurred, leaving a sizable black-and-blue area across his forearm.

When I asked Jack how he prevented infections, he gave an answer that reminded me of Swami Rama's. He said, essentially, that if the body understands that it is not to interact with or react to any foreign material, there is no way that an infection can start. He said he had done this demonstration hundreds of times and had never had an infection from it. The skin of his arm was free of marks and as smooth as a baby's.

Apropos of Jack's comment on infection, when we were conducting a biofeedback workshop in Australia, Alyce and I met a physician who, hearing about Jack's explanation, told us that he had been using hypnosis (which is a method of attention control) for the relief of excessive pain in many of his patients. Some time ago he had decided that it would be useful to be able to demonstrate pain and bleeding control by doing it himself. Coincidentally, he chose to use the same method as Jack. He did this many times and never developed an infection. Then one time, during a demonstration at a hospital, just as he was about to push a needle into his arm, the medical director suddenly said, "Stop, you haven't sterilized your needle. I will get one that is sterile." And he obtained a sterile hypodermic needle in a plastic container. On that one and only occasion, our workshop participant said, he got an infection. Question: Did the body get confused, or lose confidence as a visualization of infection was planted by the concerned physician? In order to control germs in a mechanical way, as in an operating room, it is necessary to clean the skin also, and the unconscious (as well as conscious) knew that had not been done. Controlled research with brave subjects might shed some light on the relationship between infection and belief.

Returning to our work in the laboratory with Jack, we had a chance to observe that one of the four wounds had disappeared in twenty-four hours; the other three were not visible after seventy-two hours.

A demonstration that was more impressive as an indication of pain control took place on another day. Jack said that he could anesthetize any part of his body at will, so I asked him to anesthetize his arm and demonstrate pain control while we had him wired up to a variety of physiological indicators that might be expected to show a pain response. Jack held the burning end of a cigarette against the inside of his left forearm three times, and neither his overt behavior nor his physiological records gave any indication of pain. During the burning periods there was a slight increase in heart rate of about three beats per minute above the average of the preceding ten minutes. On the third occasion the burning end of the cigarette was dislodged. It lay like a live coal on Jack's arm for about twenty-five seconds, and when he tried to blow it off, it glowed red hot and stuck to his skin. He had to flick it off with his finger.

No blisters formed in this demonstration, but the top layer of skin was definitely burned. The burn marks were obvious the next day. Jack said that he did not know how his skin was going to react to the thermal insult, though he was certain that he would have no trouble with the pain. When we were taking the wires off, he said that although he had anesthetized only his left forearm, the anesthesia was spreading to his right hand. He could feel a tingling and a small amount of numbness.

The demonstration with burning made us somewhat uneasy, but Jack reassured us. That particular demonstration, he said, was relatively insignificant, even if he was burned. More serious, he said, was the demonstration he had made a few years earlier at a meeting of the Los Angeles County Medical Association, arranged by psychiatrist Dr. Kurt Fantl, who had become acquainted with Jack shortly after Jack arrived in the United States.

At a Council Grove Conference Kurt told me that he had arranged for Jack to demonstrate a variety of physiological controls for his medical colleagues. The demonstrations were so startling, however, that his colleagues boycotted him—quit sending him patients—and he had a strenuous time for a few years following Jack's visit. Jack told us that one of the things he demonstrated on that occasion was "fire control." He put his two hands into a brazier of burning coals held by two medical students with asbestos gloves, picked up a double handful of fire, and carried it around, showing the coals to the doctors; then he put the coals on a newspaper, which burst into flames. Dr. Fantl said that Jack's hands appeared afterward to be normal, not even hot, and with no indication of having been subjected to high temperature.

Jack had an occasional slight limp, which caught my attention. I noticed that, after a long day at the lab and an active evening lecturing to the Ashram Association in Topeka, Jack limped slightly when we returned home. I asked him about this, and he said that whenever he stood for several hours he had a tendency to limp, because his ankle had been damaged during World War II. He took off his shoe and sock and showed that his foot was displaced about a half inch to the side, starting at the ankle joint. During the war he had been a motorcycle courier for a period of time, he said, and was in an accident that smashed his ankle. Because there were no medical facilities immediately available and he was in a hurry and did not want to be incapacitated, he told his foot to stop paining, to heal, and to start walking. He got up and went on his way, pushing the machine ahead of him. He did not have his injury X-rayed for a long time. The doctors later found that the broken bones were so distributed that they could not understand how Jack could walk.

Later on, I spoke to Dr. Kurt Fantl about this. He said that, as part of the demonstration Jack had made before the medical association, he had ordered X-rays of the ankle. He showed them to the doctors present, without identifying the patient. The consensus was, he said, that this man should not be able to walk. Thereupon Dr. Fantl identified Jack as the man with the hopelessly smashed ankle.

Jack said that the most entertaining event involving medical opinions about his ankle happened when he was stationed with Dutch military forces in Indonesia. On the basis of X-rays done there, a doctor decided that an amputation was necessary. Jack had to prove he could walk.

Jack's explanation of the imperfect "ankle repair" was that when he told the body to fix it so he could walk, he forgot to tell it to "put it back the way it was," and the body, lacking a complete instruction, complied only with his functional request.

Demonstrations of physiological self-control are certainly interesting to study, but the conclusion one should draw is not that there are unusual people in the world. Psychosomatic disease provides striking evidence of the power of the mind to influence the body in ordinary persons. Jack feels that he has no more *potential* capability to self-regulate than any-one else. Training programs for psychosomatic self-regulation should be within the reach of everyone.

Part of self-regulation is pain control. Pain is useful, of course, being the psychological part of the great signaling system that tells us when something is wrong. But Jack thinks of pain as if it were an alarm clock. He says that when the alarm has rung you turn it off and do something. "You turn the pain off first," he said, "because it's hard to think as long as that is going on inside your head."

"But even if we learn to control pain," I questioned, "how do you handle the problem itself? Say, for instance, that a knife has slipped and cut your hand. What do you do after you've turned off the pain?" In answer, Jack gave a simple but very interesting description of a way of handling body problems that might be extended to any problem that can be visualized. Jack's method of visualization coincides significantly with the kind of visualization techniques taught to cancer patients by the Simontons. Here follows one of Jack's examples as he described it to me.

If you have a cut in the palm of your hand, sit down in a chair in a quiet, comfortable place and first practice some autogenic exercises for quieting the body and the emotions. Use the heaviness and warmth ex-ercises with eyes closed. Then turn attention inward to the realm of visualization. See yourself sitting in the chair in your mind's eye; then allow your body feeling to merge with the visualized figure so that you feel you *are* the figure sitting in the chair in your mind. Then think of your body and your visualization as if they were identical twins fitted perfectly together. Then look at your hand, not physically, but in your mind's view. See the wounded hand slowly slip like a glove from the body. As it moves away from you it grows larger and larger, until it looks as big as a house at a distance of about thirty feet. It turns verti-cally and slowly settles down on its base at the wrist. Now rise to your feet in your mind-body and walk toward the hand. When you are about halfway there, turn around and look at your other body, sitting in the chair. Say to it, "Cross your legs," and it complies. If it doesn't comply, then go back and sit down and try it again. When you do see it cross its legs, psychological conditions are right, and you turn around and face the hand. As you do that you notice it has a door in it. You walk up, open the door, and go inside. The hand is seen to be hollow, and a ladder is leaning against the wall of the hand on the palm side. When you look up you can see where the gash is. On the floor are some patching materials, some tape and glue. You put them in a bucket that is there and climb up the ladder to the cut and begin repairing it.

You repair it in whatever way seems best to you in your visualization. You might put some glue along the edges of the cut and then put strips of sticky tape across that. Or you may tape it first and then paint it over with glue to hold it tight. After you have made the patch you become quiet and watch it for a few moments to see that it is firm. If it is firm and you know that it is firm, then you come down the ladder. If the patch begins to peel off, remove it and start over again. Do this as many times as are necessary to make the patch stick. Then come down the ladder, put the materials on the floor, go out the door, close it, and walk back to your body, where you turn around and sit down.

You look at your huge mind-hand and notice that there is no wound in it. The hand begins to shrink. As it shrinks it rises and slowly moves toward you. Finally, when it is just the right size, it slips back into place like a glove. The visualization is finished. You thank your body for doing such a good job and visualize yourself as one whole being, body and mind filled with joy and energy. You open your eyes, feeling good. You ignore your hand at first, allowing the body to process the visualization without interference. Later you let yourself look at the hand, but you do not "pick at it" emotionally or mentally, just as the farmer does not dig up his seeds to see if they are sprouting. You repeat the visualization a couple of times each day for as long as is needed. It is useful to remember that practice makes perfect.

My description of Jack's technique ends here, but we feel it important to emphasize, just as the Simontons do, that this visualization technique is to be used in addition to traditional medical precautions—in this case, washing the cut, or having stitches taken if necessary.

As we have mentioned many times, the persons with unusual powers of physiological self-regulation whom we have studied often seem to be aware of problems in other people, even if the other person is not conscious of the problem. Jack had this kind of awareness. He amused us on occasion by saying out loud what we were thinking but not saying, and sometimes we teased him in return by saying that this skill of his ought to make it easier to explain lab procedures to him.

That was all in fun, but we got down to some scientific questions when Jack described a pattern of radiation, called an aura, which he said he could see around the human body. In the aura, he said, physical, emotional, and mental characteristics of individuals were visible as patterns of colored bands, streamers, and areas of light and darkness. He agreed to be wired up on some future occasion while we monitored the physiological correlates of his faculty of "reading an aura."

The subject we picked the morning of that experiment for Jack to "read" was Pam Walters, Dale Walters's wife. Jack had never met Pam before, and when I took her into the experimental room where he was sitting, already wired up and plugged in, I merely said, "Pam, this is Jack. Jack, please meet Pam." After they had greeted each other, Jack said, "Don't tell me anything about yourself. Instead, I'll talk for about half an hour, and then you can ask questions if you like." In the next half-hour Jack gave a detailed description of the major physical, emotional, and mental events that had occurred in Pam's life over the preceding nine years. Dale grew more and more impressed as the session went on, and was nonplused when Jack finally spoke of things that Pam had not yet mentioned to him. Pam had gone to the doctor the preceding day, and Jack told her what the doctor had said.

To me, one of the most interesting of Jack's comments to Pam involved what he called "growth rings." He said that they surrounded the lower half of the body, like the growth rings in a tree. It was by looking at those rings, he said, that he could tell how many years had passed since some event had occurred. For instance, he said that a major event had occurred in June, eight years previously. I asked later how he got the date and he said that he counted eight rings and about half of another ring. Since it was now December, the event must have occurred about June, eight years previously. Jack said that the event involved the most important change in Pam's life. Dale laughed and told Alyce and me that was within a month of when they were married.

In all, Jack talked with Pam about seventy minutes, an unusually long session, he said, because he wanted to give us a good chance to make recordings. In general, the physiological recordings merely reported that Jack was alive and healthy. During most of the session he continuously produced occipital beta, but we observed that when he was not actively speaking, but pausing as if to search for words, ideas, or feelings, the beta was replaced in his record by a burst of alpha and theta. It did not happen often. Most of the time he was as busy as if he were reading a book.

That demonstration raised a number of questions about "projection" that have not been satisfactorily resolved. Many people, including ourselves, have seen auras on occasion, but Jack sees them apparently wherever he chooses to. The question is, Are the auras he sees always radiatory patterns of energy from the human body (remembering the idea that body, emotion, and mind, though different, are constructed of the same basic energy) or are they automatic mental projections of one kind or another that are used psychologically to interpret a "knowing"? Sometimes when we "know" something in this way we tend to "see" it in the same way that we see a memory. We know a memory is inside, of course; but if it is not a memory, the image-making faculty sometimes makes internal things appear to be outside, a projection.

This is one of those problems that cause scientists to misunderstand psychics. Psychologists often have more trouble than other investigators with people like Jack Schwarz, because they rarely know much about energy fields but they know a lot about psychological projection, which they may use as a last refuge for explaining (away) phenomena they do not understand. The question of projection is compounded when Jack says that he sees colored auras around human figures in black-and-white photographs and on black-and-white-television screens.

When questioned, Jack said that he felt that the auras were "there." I asked him to explain how he was able to name a specific disease, as he had done several times with members of our group and with others, merely by "examining" the aura. "It is not easy to believe," I said, "that the name of the disease is spelled out in little letters of light in the aura." Jack laughed and said, "No, that doesn't happen, of course, but after I have seen the auras of three or four hundred people who have a disease of a certain kind, I recognize it, the same as a seasoned doctor would recognize a disease from a particular skin color or skin condition associated with it." "But, how about the cases," I said, "in which you name a disease that you have never heard of or seen before?" Jack had correctly identified a strange disease which had no outer manifestation in a friend of ours. "I saw a dark spot in the aura," Jack said. "I wondered what it meant and the word 'lupus' just came into my mind."

One problem of research is to distinguish, objectively, the things that are "there" from the things that an observer projects there through intuitive knowing. One way might be to work with a large group of psychics and have them examine a number of people with a variety of diseases, describe what they see, and what they interpret it to mean. The extent to which they all saw the same thing might be represented by the overlapping area in the Venn diagram of Figure 12. The extent to which they saw different things but interpreted them in the *same* way would give an indication of areas of "knowing" in which projections of auditory and visual images were idiosyncratic, that is, dependent upon the individual psychic's culture and genetics.

The unusual people we have worked with have extremely strong egos, and it happens that none take kindly to the idea that what they are observing may be projections of imagery from their own selves. Still, it is noticeable that they often "see" different things and contradict one another, although they may agree about meanings. For instance, individuals may see different colors in auras and yet agree in their interpretations of the person's problems. This naturally raises questions about invariance. If the color bands seen in auras are *not* invariant, not independent of the observer's culture, learning, and genetic makeup, then what may be invariant is intuitive knowing.

Over the years since first meeting Jack, we have had a running conversation about this problem of "seeing" and how to separate it from "projecting." Jack makes many significant points in favor of fixed auric patterns. I had my chance to argue the case for a projection factor at an evening meeting once when suddenly Jack called out to a young man in the audience, "You have a question which if you don't ask right now you may explode." The fellow laughed and said, "You're right, what I want to know is . . ." Later, I asked Jack why he acted so suddenly, how did he know that that person was about to "explode." Jack said he saw a yellow question mark hanging over that person's head. "Aha!" I said, "did a piece of the aura get detached and make the form of a question mark?" Jack laughed but he knew what I was referring to.

In some respects it may seem that these concerns are either trivialities or technicalities (aside from being impossibilities), but from a scientific point of view, once a person is beyond the point of denying the factual nature of the data, such questions must be asked in order to reduce confusion and get ideas for future testing. Jack Schwarz is interested in both science and medicine, but he is not analytical in exactly the same way that a scientist is. There is a difference in point of view. For a scientist, the proper logic is to think of every possible explanation for a phenomenon and successively test and eliminate explanations that do not satisfy. Eventually one is driven by the method of exclusions toward a definite conclusion. Notice that I did not say "to a definite conclusion," but only "toward a definite conclusion." This may seem a strange way to proceed, but there is no other way to arrive at scientific conclusions. On the other hand, people who are adept at "seeing," or perceiving in a different way, are almost always impatient with this approach. To them, when something is obvious, it is obvious.

This fundamental difference between scientists and psychics need not cause problems if each takes time to understand the framework in which the other necessarily operates. If the psychic tries to pull apart every perception in order to find out if it is incorrect, so as to better determine the "truth," what is most likely to be pulled apart is the faculty of "seeing." The talent for perceiving might well fade away. On the other hand, if scientists stopped trying to find alternate explanations for the facts, they might get lost in a maze of projected and extrapolated ideas. For both scientists and mystics, however, the area of facts—rather than interpretations—is common ground. Excluding the opinions of fanatics, most of the arguments that we are aware of between the two camps have revolved around interpretations. Because psychics almost always have idiosyncratic factors in their frames of reference, scientists often do not understand them. And psychics do not understand what seems to them to be a destructive attitude on the part of scientists.

Perhaps the best way to bridge the communications gap is for scientists who have a talent for "extended perception" to undergo training and practice in both the observation of normally unseen events and the testing of hypotheses concerning these events. This might be easier than trying to train psychics to be scientists. Science is a way of thinking whereas being psychic is not a way of thinking but a way of perceiving, and it seems easier to expand our modes of perception than to expand our modes of thinking. Charles Tart suggests this same solution to the communications problem in his excellent book, *States of Consciousness* (1975).

Norman Shealy has also written about this problem in his book *Occult Medicine Can Save Your Life*. He describes an experiment that he conducted with medical doctors and a group of eight psychic diagnosticians. He compared their abilities in detecting problems in patients whom he had already exhaustively studied, and he reported that the very best psychics were about on a par with members of the medical profession in identifying physiological disorders. He concluded that it is easier to train a medical doctor to use his intuitive diagnostic capabilities, his "psychic" abilities, than it is to train a psychic to be a doctor. He arrived at this conclusion partly, he told us, because the person who was the best psychic diagnostician of all was also a medical doctor. That person, perhaps understandably, was the best diagnostician in both groups.

What Norman said reminded us of several off-the-record reports from psychiatrists in which they unexpectedly became aware of something that the patient had *not* told them. Inexplicably, something that the patient may have been hiding became as clear as an open book, including names and events, not merely moods and other such global conditions. Such events raise fascinating questions and possibilities, and no doubt science and medicine will have much to say in the future about the proper development of talents so that individuals can combine the best of both "worlds," the rational and the intuitive, in their approach to psychosomatic health.

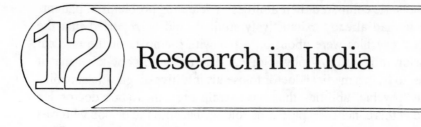

Research in India

Possibly the scientist and the physician could add something by stepping outside the laboratory and the consulting room to reconsider these strangely gifted human beings about us. Where did the mind—call it the spirit if you like—come from? Who can say? It exists.

—WILDER PENFIELD

All men naturally desire to know.

—ARISTOTLE

Before leaving for India in December of 1970, Swami Rama told us of some highly accomplished yogis who lived in the jungle and mountains and avoided society. If we wanted to know something about them we would have to visit India. The idea was appealing, but at the time we could not think seriously about it.

More than a year later, the Swami telephoned from Chicago one day and said he felt we should definitely plan to do some research with yogis in India. After some discussion, we agreed to meet him in New York City and consider the demonstrations that might be possible. Swami said that these people, some of whom were his teachers, were in certain ways more skillful than he. They were specialists, he said, and he was a generalist. He would get promises from the yogis in advance so that five or six of the most talented would be prepared to demonstrate the things he had outlined in his original letter about research at the Menninger Foundation. He said we should visit India in October through January, starting in 1972.

I explained that before we would go we would need to construct a portable psychophysiology lab and that would take both time and money. Unless we were able to obtain research funds for constructing the equipment and to pay the expense of such a trip we could not commit ourselves to go. I would try to get a research grant, but if funds were not received before July 15, 1972, I said, it would be impossible for us to get ready on time. July 15 would be the cutoff day for making a final decision. The Swami said there would be no trouble and that he would see us in India in October 1972. He would meet us in New Delhi and take us to the mountains above Rishikesh, which is on the edge of the foothills of the Himalayas, to visit the yogis.

I proceeded to write research grant proposals in an attempt to raise funds from private foundations, but was unsuccessful. The Swami had in the meantime contacted a number of yogis and had also reserved forest bungalows for our party in various places in northern India. When the Swami found out we were not coming, he had already committed himself, and the result was that he became extremely angry.

Later, in a stormy discussion, I asked why he had made so many definite plans and commitments when he had not received word that we would be able to come. He suddenly volunteered the information then, in a confidential tone, that his teacher had told him we would not come to India until 1973! The Swami's intricate personality made it possible for him to tell something dispassionately and rationally at one level while he was angry at another level. Why, I asked, had he insisted then that we would come in 1972 if his teacher said we would not come until 1973, especially since, according to him, his teacher was never wrong? He shrugged and said, "Well, you know, I never did do what he told me anyway." He had caused his guru very much trouble, he said, and one day when he was feeling apologetic he asked him, "Why are you burdened with such a difficult person?" And the teacher answered with a sigh, "It is my karma."

In January 1973 I wrote to the Swami and told him that at last enough monies had become available for construction of the portable psychophysiology lab. A large fraction of the design was on paper, and I felt it would be possible to construct the equipment by October. Alyce and I told him we would come to India even if we had to borrow travel money personally for the research group. The Menninger Foundation had contributed through the biomedical electronics laboratory in the research department, and would also pay our salaries while we were conducting the research, but there was a shortage of cash for transportation and general expenses of a trip like this one, expected to last three to four months.

The day before we were due to leave Topeka for New Delhi, the shortage was made good by Irving Laucks. At ninety-three years of age, he was one of the most imaginative and energetic people we had ever known. We were doubly indebted to this gentleman, because he had also supplied several thousand dollars from the Laucks Foundation in 1969 to bring people from India and Japan for the first Council Grove Conference.

Since 1969 Mr. Laucks had on occasion talked with us about what he felt was the biggest difficulty in science: the insufficiency of facts about subtle human energies. He felt the way to get high-level scientists involved in the study of psycho-energies was to find a yogi who could levitate and either bring him to the U.S. for a demonstration on national television or at least get movies of such an occurrence in India. Mr. Laucks always mentioned this rather whimsically, I thought, but there was also a measure of certainty that something important would happen in science if top-flight physicists were to witness and verify such a demonstration. Before we left for India he reminded me: "Look for a yogi who can levitate in public." I told him I doubted that we would find any such people, but we would do our best.

Because his 1972 plans for us did not materialize, the Swami may have thought that our 1973 plans would not work out either. Thus, even though he made preparations five months in advance to meet us in Delhi and have us speak at the All India Yoga Conference in Kanpur that he was arranging, he had contacted no yogis. Fortunately, I realized that this was the situation well before our departure date, and wrote letters to the heads of various ashrams in India and to medical doctors we knew were interested in the study of yoga. The final schedule allowed only about two weeks for northern India in the vicinity of Rishikesh, where Swami Rama had his ashram.

The major emphasis in grant proposals I wrote at the time was on the production of a documentary movie, for we wanted to have good film as well as good physiological records. We hoped to obtain scientific data, but we also felt that the trip could bring seed ideas to the attention of researchers and clinicians in both India and the United States, and to accomplish this a movie would be useful. We spoke to film producer Elda Hartley about our plans, and she was very enthusiastic. There was a chance, Elda said, that she might be making a documentary movie for the Theosophical Society at Adyar. Perhaps we could combine our expeditions and spend our time in India together. She would supply the cameras, film, and film crew, and all we would have to provide was automobile transportation in India. All other expenses she would take care of herself. This was a fine opportunity for us. Hartley Productions had put together many excellent movies, ranging from Alan Watts on Zen Buddhism to Ram Dass and yogic meditation to Captain Edgar Mitchell of Apollo 14, who had conducted a parapsychological experiment from space.

To round out the psychophysiological team we asked Dale Walters to come, but his family plans made it impractical. We then considered our daughter Judy, who had been working with psychophysiology instrumentation for several years, starting in an epilepsy research laboratory at Boston University. She was also familiar with biofeedback equipment, since she had helped us conduct several biofeedback workshops. She and Alyce together could run the portable lab, it was decided, while I would observe as much as possible and interact with the yogis we studied. It proved an ideal arrangement.

We also invited two writers to go: Dolly Gattozzi, formerly a science writer for the National Institute of Mental Health, who was planning a sabbatical year, and Doug Boyd, who, as already mentioned, had assisted in the research program with the Swami. Not only would the two writers be additional observers, but both had been students in the yoga study group when Swami Rama had visited our lab in Topeka. Both were conversant, therefore, with the odd problems that can arise in attempting cross-cultural research. They paid their own way.

There is space to describe only the high points of the trip, but it is not exaggerating to say it was the strangest and most strenuous three months we have spent in our entire lives. Perhaps the major miracle that occurred was that our portable lab worked for three months without malfunction. This is seldom found even in the best commercial psychophysiology gear, in which bugs are tracked down and eliminated over a period of months. Because he anticipated failure in one or another channel of the recording machinery, Elmer had designed a certain amount of redundancy into the system. If one device failed another might satisfactorily record the event. Respiration, for instance, was shown on a meter face and was also recorded on magnetic tape. The meter face was photographed by a camera that took a picture once a second. Figure 14 shows the lab set up on the banks of the Ganges in Rishikesh, not far from Swami Rama's ashram, ready to record the physiological behaviors of a man we called the "nail yogi" (Figure 15).

The lab recorded respiration, heart rate, brain waves from the left

Figure 14. **Portable psychophysiology laboratory.** Judy Green adjusts physiological channels to collect data from the "nail yogi" while Dolly Gattozzi (facing camera) watches. The Ganges River is in the background.

occiput, skin potential from the left hand, temperature at two body locations, usually left and right hands, but sometimes the right hand and the forehead. The camera photographed meters or dials showing (1) respiration, (2) temperature, (3) heart rate, (4) a white area on which could be written with grease pencil the date and other pertinent information, and (5) two clocks, one of which told the time of day and the other the time in minutes and seconds since the beginning of a particular test.

Electrical data from heart, brain, and skin, as well as respiration, were recorded on magnetic tape by an ingenious fourteen-pound cassette recorder that made it possible to obtain physiological behaviors and later play them onto polygraph records and onto half-inch magnetic tape for computer analysis. In the psychophysiology laboratory at the Menninger Foundation, we have a PDP-12 computer, with which we are planning to analyze these records.

At the time of this writing, funds have been received from the Insti-

Figure 15. **Sitting on nails.** This yogi had a mantra for anesthetizing the skin.
Photo credit: Tom Kiefer

*tute of Noetic Sciences for the analysis of our Indian data ("noetic"
means "consciousness"). The institute was founded and is directed by
Dr. Ed Mitchell, engineer and former astronaut, who since the flight
of Apollo 14 is devoting time and money to the study of mind-directed
energies both inside and outside the skin. Computer analyses of the
data are not yet available, but the most clear-cut phenomena we recorded have been run from the cassette tapes onto polygraph records,
where they can be "eyeballed," as research jargon has it. Judy's research
project with epileptic patients, involving voluntary control of brain
waves through EEG feedback, uses computer analysis, and the computer programs that handle her data are being adapted for some of the
India data. She is supervising the analysis.*

*Swami Rama had agreed to meet us at New Delhi airport and help
us get through Indian customs. When we landed, three hours behind
schedule, there was Swami Rama in a gleaming white suit, ready to*

shepherd us and another group of about twelve people from Minneapolis and Chicago—American students of Swami Rama who arrived on the same plane. This group was the first contingent of forty students of yoga from the States coming to visit Swami Rama's ashram that month. Except for an argument about a camera, which was solved by the Swami's outshouting the official, we moved through customs with no difficulties.

The Swami had organized a press conference to begin immediately after we and our luggage were deposited at the Lodhi Hotel, and that began a whirlwind of activity, including a visit to the American Embassy and meetings with a number of government and newspaper people. We caught about three hours' sleep the first night in Delhi and were up at four A.M. the next morning for a flight of two hundred miles with Swami and his students to Kanpur (see Figure 16). Here one of Swami's establishments was located. Elmer, Judy, and I were to lecture at the three-day All India Yoga Conference, scheduled to begin that very night. As we stepped down from the plane, a large group of Swami's Kanpur students stepped forward and garlanded us all with malas of golden chrysanthemums.

The first opportunity to test the psychophysiology lab was with a fifteen-year-old "numerical wizard" in Kanpur. We went with Swami Rama to the home of Mr. Karabanda, the municipal tax collector at Kanpur. Mr. Karabanda said we would not be able to forget his name because it meant "true man," the name of one of our presidents, but we have found it easier to remember Truman than Karabanda.

The numerical genius turned out to be an "idiot savant," who had apparently suffered brain damage at birth which subsequently interfered with normal cortical development. He was happy, cooperative, and seemed to have the general mental characteristics of a six-year-old boy, though in equanimity and poise he seemed more like a twenty-year-old.

The demonstration took place in a secluded garden. A rug was spread out on the grass and the boy sat on it, cross-legged. Swami Rama asked questions, and Mr. Karabanda checked the answers. Questions consisted not of arithmetic problems in this particular case, but of naming the days of the week in the preceding few years associated with specific dates, such as what day of the week was January 11, 1969. This boy was famous in Kanpur, and we could see why. He named the day correctly in six out of seven trials. While resting, his heart rate, as shown by the cardiotachometer, averaged about eighty beats per minute. When

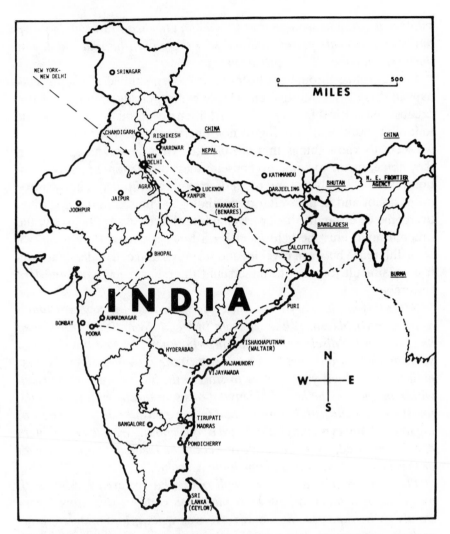

Figure 16. **Seven thousand miles in India.** Starting from New Delhi in October, good weather was almost continuous for three months. Our route loops from Chandigarh in the north to Pondicherry in the south. Backtracking along the east coast took much time and added many miles.

asked a question he would close his eyes and his heart rate would go up to about 120 beats per minute and stay there until he said the day of the week, at which it abruptly dropped.

Idiot savants, throughout history, have been studied at length. Perhaps in these cases intuitive knowledge comes readily to consciousness because the cortical faculty of rational discursive thinking, which seems to inhibit intuitional thinking, is nonfunctional. At unconscious levels we seem to know things that are blocked from consciousness. When they come, or try to come, to consciousness our rational faculty questions, dissects, analyzes, and often destroys. The rational faculty introduces doubt and in the welter of psychological noise, intuition is often overcome or discredited. For psychic intuition to work effectively, the rational mind must be held quiet for a time, it seems. Here again we see a difference between psychics and scientists and can understand why it is so difficult for each to understand the other, even when they try sincerely.

After this preliminary demonstration, we traveled to Swami Rama's ashram in Rishikesh. While we were in Delhi, Swami had introduced us to one of his disciples, Mahatmaji, who knew, he said, many forest yogis and who would get for us subjects of the highest caliber. Mahatmaji found a "nail yogi" for us to start with, but he was not satisfied with him and said he hoped his invitations sent out by runners into the forest would bear fruit before we had to leave Rishikesh. The "yogis of the forest," however, may have heard of our coming with lab equipment and disappeared, for not a single one could be located, either to accept or to reject our invitation to contribute to science.

The "nail yogi" was a very small man who smeared himself with ashes and had taken a vow of silence, although his lips moved constantly as he repeated his mantra. He was willing to demonstrate his ability to sit on nails, and we were glad to have someone to work with in Rishikesh. We unpacked the lab and turned it on, and again it worked —a touch of Topeka on the Ganges.

After that session I said to Swami Rama that if I weighed only eighty pounds and lived outdoors all my life and sat on a bed of nails that were only three quarters of an inch apart and not really as sharp as needles anyway, that I too could probably withstand the pain. He laughed and said that there was more to it than that, for the man had learned a mantra by means of which he was able to anesthetize his skin. Having seen Jack Schwarz do something similar and being aware of the fact that many patients have odd psychosomatic problems in which there is lack of sensitivity in the skin (though sometimes an increased sensitivity), I could believe it, but it seemed a tiresome way to make a living. The nail yogi had his place to sit on the other side of the Ganges, where, with his cup for alms and a modest shrine to his patron deities, he held forth most days of the week.

Harvey Bellin, the director and soundman of Elda Hartley's movie, rode in the car with the nail yogi when they were taking him back to his location across the river. At one point, they did not know which way to go, Harvey said, and to terminate their argument about whether to go straight ahead or to turn right, the nail yogi said one word: "Right."

After Rishikesh we went to a city in northern India called Chandigarh. Many important government laboratories are in Chandigarh, and also one of the few yoga training centers supported by the central government. The director of the training center, Mr. C. Giri, had met us in Kanpur at the yoga conference, and at the urging of Swami Rama and Elda had agreed to try to find some yogis in Chandigarh to be research subjects.

Chandigarh's Yoga Health Training Center is in a way a kind of showcase development, a prototype on which others may be modeled. The purpose of the center is not to develop unusual physiological controls but to educate people in psychosomatic self-regulation for health through yoga. Because of this emphasis on physical health, many of the people who came to the center were interested primarily in hatha yoga (the training of the body) and were not highly concerned with meditative yoga practices. Mr. Giri, however, was familiar with all of the traditions, thus making it possible for his students to study the relationship between mental, emotional, and physiological factors in health.

When we got to Chandigarh Mr. Giri made maximum use of our visit to promote the cause of yoga. He arranged "an informal meeting" with the Central Scientific Organization. When we arrived it turned out to be a full-scale scientific meeting attended by approximately two hundred and fifty physicists, mathematicians, and engineers. We had to be cleared through security in order to get into the laboratory, and it reminded me very much of the Naval Ordnance Test Station at China Lake. Fortunately, we had slides with us of Jack Schwarz and Swami Rama and a seven-minute movie of psychophysiological recording and biofeedback training in the laboratory. After the meeting Dr.

Haresh Vardhan, director of the Central Scientific Organization, gave us tea. Mr. Giri asked him if the organization would be willing to build biofeedback equipment for the Yoga Health Training Center. Dr. Vardhan glanced at some of the circuits and said that it would be quite simple, they could provide anything needed. Mr. Giri said he was certain that through the use of biofeedback the benefits of yoga in physiological self-regulation would become apparent to everyone, and this might help rescue yoga in India from the doldrums.

The second lecture Mr. Giri arranged was at the Graduate Medical College, where about twenty-five physicians examined two biofeedback machines that we had brought along to be exhibited. (They were the machines that had originally been constructed for Swami Rama to take to India at the end of 1970.) One was an alpha-theta brain-wave feedback device, the other a combination machine in which one could choose the feedback of either respiration pattern, temperature, or heart rate. Built into the machine was a little analog computer that converted the raw EKG signal into a fluctuating voltage calibrated in beats per minute. In lectures to medical groups, there were always some in the audience who were hopeful about the possibility of studying and teaching physiological self-regulation, but who had kept quiet about their interest because there was a danger of losing status or not being promoted. Western medicine has swept India to the extent that many Indian doctors are more Western than Westerners themselves, and short shrift is made of any discussion of the regulation of the autonomic nervous system. In fact, some doctors seemed embarrassed by yoga, as if they would like to erase it from their culture. They apparently thought of it as superstition from bygone days. Even with people of this opinion, however, the slides and film seemed persuasive, and the implications of biofeedback training were not treated as inconsequential.

The press conference that Swami had arranged in Delhi the day we landed had made headlines in many large newspapers in India. Wherever we went, therefore, we were expected, and medical people requested lectures. By the time we returned to Delhi at the end of our ninety-day sojourn, we had lectured for about seven hundred and fifty medical people and four hundred engineers and scientists.

Three of six subjects obtained at the Chandigarh Yoga Health Training Center were meditators; that is, they were concerned with states of consciousness without necessarily including the attainment of physiological controls of any kind. In this kind of meditation particular breathing exercises are sometimes used, not for the purpose of generating or demonstrating unusual control of body functions, but for the purpose of energizing the central nervous system through absorption of the pranas that Swami Rama had discussed. The meditating subjects included Pripal Singh, an older man who had practiced for many years, Shila Dugha, a young woman who had meditated for only three months (she came from her job in one of the government offices to accommodate us), and a Mr. Chaudhuri, whose participation as a subject was arranged by his wife. Later the Chaudhuris took us to their home for an Indian tea that must have taken from early morning to prepare. There we learned that Mrs. Chaudhuri was a teacher of Transcendental Meditation.

Another Chandigarh subject was Mr. R. C. Gupta of Simla, whom we had first met at the conference in Kanpur. Mr. Gupta was a long-time yogi, following the discipline of Swami Yogananda, whose book, The Autobiography of a Yogi, *has become a best-seller in the United States. Mr. Gupta demonstrated "bellows-breathing," pranayama (control of breath), and Kriya Yoga, which involves a visualization of pranic energies up and down the chain of chakras that are said to be associated with the major nerve plexuses of the body.*

The fifth of Mr. Giri's subjects was a young man by the name of Mr. Tarmananda. He demonstrated a remarkable yogic exercise called nauli in which the muscles of the abdomen are individually and sequentially contracted and relaxed, resulting in a rotating or churning motion of the abdominal muscles. Elda was especially impressed by the photogenic quality of the demonstration and obtained excellent footage that was later included in the film story.

Before we left Chandigarh, Mr. Giri agreed to be a subject himself, and he also introduced a physicist who was interested in trying the brain-wave feedback machine. I was highly impressed when the latter could easily produce beta, alpha, or theta at will. If alpha and/or theta was present, a high tone and/or a low tone was sounded, but he could turn on either of the two tones or turn them both off at will. When both tones were turned off, we inferred that beta was present. A separate tone had not been included to indicate the presence of beta.

I asked how he had developed such unusual control. I had not yet met anyone who, in two minutes, could produce an abundance of theta waves at will, or turn it off at will. He said that he had meditated most of his life and that the state that he had just demonstrated was of special importance to him. It was a reverie that he could quickly put himself into. In fact, he said, that particular state was one that he had used to solve his doctoral research problem in physics. He said that he put himself into this state and the imagery showed him two significant contributions he could make to the field in which he was working. He quickly checked the ideas, then developed them into his research and doctoral dissertation. He said that throughout his professional life, whenever he was stuck on a problem, he would put himself in this state and examine the images.

He described almost word for word the procedure that I, too, had developed for solving problems. I first used this method in 1946 when I was a graduate student in physics at UCLA, and later used it at the University of Chicago, to develop the single mathematical equation that accounts for both the logarithmic law and the power law for visual sensation (they are special cases of the general law I described mathematically). Awareness of the possible usefulness of theta training for achieving such a state had led us to study "psychophysiological training for creativity," and it was impressive to find someone on the other side of the world who was also aware of the importance of the reverie state for problem solving.

Our next subjects were in the holy city of Varanasi (Benares), a long distance from Chandigarh. Arrangements were made for us at Benares Hindu University by Dr. Uduppa, professor of surgery and director of the Institute of Medical Science, at whose request we lectured to physicians and medical students. One of Dr. Uduppa's associates, Dr. Dubey, accompanied us during much of our visit and guided us to Sarnath, where the Buddha is said to have given his first sermon after he attained enlightenment. Dubey also introduced us to two people at the university who became research subjects.

The first was Ramesh, who demonstrated a variety of hatha yoga postures, or asanas. Ramesh is a teacher of yoga at the university and although he was interested in meditative yoga, his training in hatha yoga focused mainly on exercises in self-control of physiological processes for purposes of enhancing health, rather than demonstrating control of autonomic processes. The name "Ramesh" was given by his teacher. At the university he was known as R. Y. Madhasettiwar, Bachelor of Science, Diploma in Yogic Education, Institute of Medical Sciences.

The second was Dr. H. C. Shukla, head of the Department of Basic

Principles (*systems theory*), *Institute of Medical Sciences. Dr. Shukla, we soon discovered, was thcroughly acquainted with the ancient traditions of India and in addition had had the unusual opportunity and experience of being a student of Sudhei Babu, the remarkable astrologer written about by Paul Brunton in his book* A Search in Secret India (*1972*).

In Dr. Shukla's discussion of his years of learning with Sudhei Babu, he pointed out that the old astrologer had actually transcended astrology, in the sense that the mental and emotional cycles and biorhythms associated with horoscopes were something to be overcome rather than to be a victim of. Sudhei Babu offered a science of "alignment with Nature" through which the cycles and events normally associated with one's psychogenetic structure, so to speak, could be handled from a metadimension, and eventually be replaced by cycles and events of a transcendental order. In modern terms, he was speaking of a subtle form of field-independence, which we will say more about in the chapter on the field-of-mind theory. In advance, it can probably be said that those who say there are no such things as cycles unconsciously allow themselves to be overly influenced by cycles, by ignoring them, and those who cannot make a decision without consulting their horoscopes (cycles) suffer from the same problem, only from the other side: They are overly influenced through giving them too much significance. Both extremes, caught by the rhythms of nature, are generally ignorant of the "law of volition," to borrow one of Alice Ann Bailey's concepts.

The main problem, according to Shukla's teacher, is to discover this law of volition and *at the same time* learn how to work in harmony with the Divine Mother (nature). Some of the experiences that Dr. Shukla said he had with his teacher were somewhat paralleled by those of Doug Boyd, reported in his book *Rolling Thunder* (it rained when Rolling Thunder performed the appropriate ceremony), and also by the experience that Hans de Meisteuffen reported in his 1953 book, *Wanderlust* (an African witch doctor made it rain in an exactly delineated area). From his teacher Shukla had learned of the electrical structure of the body, the chakra system, and its regulation through pranayama (breathing exercises).

After we had become better acquainted, Dr. Shukla said that in the interest of science he would like to attempt to demonstrate for us the focus of attention in different chakras while wired up. We were pleased to accept his offer but warned him that the brain-wave recording would probably show only continuous beta, implying continuous focus of attention. We had already noticed with a number of people who could visualize intensely that they often produce continuous beta, the indication of an active visual cortex. I have already mentioned that I automatically begin to see visual images if I shut my eyes for a short time, and unless I refrain from examining the images and thus let myself sink into a reverie state, I have trouble producing alpha. People generally, however, find it easy to produce alpha and difficult to stay in beta for long periods of time with their eyes shut. Dr. Shukla understood this, but said that even if nothing except beta were found, that would be useful information. If he were to produce continuous beta in the occipital cortex, we could interpret that to mean continuous active focus of attention.

As previously mentioned, we have not had an opportunity to analyze all the magnetic tape records from India with our PDP-12 computer, but we have run Dr. Shukla's record onto polygraph paper and have observed that a low-amplitude alpha pattern (fifteen to thirty microvolts) was present throughout much of his meditative states. The truly striking feature of the record, however, was the appearance on occasion of bursts of alpha, lasting from two to twenty seconds, in which amplitude increased to two and one half times normal. We knew from previous observation and from conversation with Barbara Brown that altered states of consciousness are often associated with sudden doubling or tripling of alpha amplitude, so this was an especially interesting finding.

Before going to India, Elmer had contacted Dr. Arun K. Sil in Calcutta. His specialty is chest surgery, and one of his avocations is to be the superintendent of the Boy Scouts of West Bengal. He is also founder and director of the Institute of Sports Medicine in Calcutta, an activity that includes considerable yoga training. Because of his connection with yogis, we thought that perhaps a week would be spent in Calcutta with the psychophysiology lab, but it turned out that communication from Kansas to Calcutta was easier than from any place in India to Calcutta. We were unable to get letters, telegrams, or telephone calls to him. Until the day we arrived in Calcutta, he was uncertain whether we were planning to visit him in November or December. Since arranging demonstrations with yogis takes time, we did not even unpack the lab. Instead we talked with Dr. Sil about Aurobindo, who was his teacher, and went with him to see Aurobindo's birthplace in Calcutta, which is now a beautiful ashram and museum.

A letter had arrived for us in care of Dr. Sil from James DeVries of the Aurobindo ashram at Pondicherry. Jim also had been in touch with us before the trip. He had suggested that a few people in the Pondicherry area might be good yoga subjects. His Calcutta letter suggested that it would be useful for us to stop at Puri, about a hundred miles south of Calcutta on the Bay of Bengal, and visit the ashram of which Swami Hariharananda Giri was leader. Jim said that Hariharananda had demonstrated the electrical effect of energizing chakras to such an extent that it made the air glow. Perhaps he would be willing to demonstrate it for us. This was apparently the same phenomenon that Swami Rama had given me a photo of, taken in Chicago. As mentioned before, if there is an electrical energy that can be mobilized by will in the body, it is not impossible to imagine that under certain intense conditions there might be a cold-light emission.

After reaching Puri, making connection with Swami Hariharananda was not easy. He was either meditating or visiting students or conducting a ceremony most of the day, but in the afternoon of the second day Elmer and I had a chance to meet him. Unfortunately, he was leaving in fifteen minutes to perform a ceremony in another city. With so little time, we did not even mention the possibility of the chakra demonstration, but talked generally about our research. He was very much interested in the physiological and biofeedback research that we described and said that he would ask his senior disciple to be a subject, not for physiological self-regulation, but for meditation, in which "attention was focused in the cranium."

Swami Hariharananda's ashram was called Ashram Yagoda, and our subject there was Professor Raghadananda, head of the Department of Orriya Language and Literature, Government Evening College, Puri, Orissa. He wished to conduct the session in a small temple at the back of the ashram.

Much to our surprise, when the door of the tiny temple was opened we saw the back wall lined with photographs and paintings of Swami Yogananda and his teacher, Sri Yukteswar Giri, his teacher's teacher, Maharishi, and their legendary guru, known as Babaji. This was the place where Yogananda had received some of his teaching.

Our subject's heart rate at the beginning of the lab session was about

110 bpm; nevertheless, he showed large-amplitude occipital alpha. He said that he was very activated by a disturbing telegram he had just received, but that he would feel calm after the meditation. The polygraph record showed almost continuous smooth alpha during his entire record, indicating a tranquil mental state, but his heart rate fluctuated continuously between 110 and 135 heartbeats a minute, almost twice as high a rate as we had expected. This unusual finding might well be interpreted as showing that he had developed the ability to quiet his cognitive mental processes even while emotionally activated.

Professor Raghadananda was an enthusiastic advocate of the benefits of meditation, and he referred many times to the fact that Yogananda's work in southern California—setting up the Self Realization Fellowship and establishing the science of kriya yoga—had been beneficially influential in many people's lives. I agreed on that, for the breathing exercises that Yogananda taught had been practiced by my father, my mother, and my brother in the late 1950s as part of their own investigations into procedures that might be useful for meditative reasons as well as for the promotion of sound health. They felt that kriya yoga was of value to them.

We had expected that we would spend quite a bit of time with Professor K. Ramakrishna Rao at Waltair, also on the Bay of Bengal, about two hundred fifty miles south of Puri. As it happened, because of problems in arranging for yogis, again due to lack of communications, we visited him on two separate occasions. There had been a "lightning" (wildcat) strike, and many government employees in communications were refusing to go to work. Letters, telegrams, and telephone calls were not getting through.

Waltair, a suburb of Visakhaputnam, is where Andhra University is located. Dr. Rao, Professor and Chairman of the Department of Psychology and Parapsychology, had been studying yogis for a number of years, but prior to our visit had not included psychophysiological measurements in conjunction with parapsychological investigations. Our second visit was scheduled to coincide with the inauguration of his psychophysiology laboratory. During our first visit we gave lectures for medical people and scientists at the university. Jointly we planned a schedule that allowed three weeks for Dr. Rao to obtain the cooperation of some of the yogis he knew, and to prepare some equipment for a demonstration of yogic control of metabolism inside an airtight box.

In the meantime, Elmer had been in communication with the secre-

tary of Sai Baba, "the miracle worker of South India." He explained the focus of our trip and asked if Sai Baba would consider a scientific demonstration that could be used for teaching purposes in the West. The secretary replied that Sai Baba had a busy schedule but would soon be at a city called Rajamundry. He had arranged for us to see Sai Baba sometime on the third or fourth of January 1974. Since it was now December 14, we agreed with Dr. Rao to return to Waltair immediately after our visit with Sai Baba. In the meantime, we would also visit Mahayogini Rajalakshmi at her university in Tirupati, the Theosophical Society at Adyar, and the Aurobindo ashram at Pondicherry, where Jim DeVries was a teacher of biochemistry at the ashram school.

We arrived at Rajamundry and visited the Sai Baba committee. There, unfortunately, we found out that we would not be allowed to "put wires" on him. Elda would be allowed to take pictures at the mass meeting, but the private meeting with Sai Baba could not be scheduled, even without wires. No time was available.

Sai Baba is the most-talked-of yogi in India, and his followers number in the millions. Everyone we talked to in the vicinity of Rajamundry asked us essentially the same question: "Do you believe that Sai Baba is God?" We also noticed that in their greetings and departures, with palms together bowing, they did not say "Ram, Ram" (God, God) but "Sai Baba." The idea of putting wires on him was blasphemous. It probably would have started a riot!

Rajalakshmi, a biochemist, was the daughter of an Indian prince. As an adolescent, she had gone through an episode like that of Theresa Newman of Austria. She told us about herself and her earlier experiences with kundalini, the subtle energy of the body that is discussed in Chapter 15. She described a peculiar phenomenon which consisted of turning vertically during meditation so that while in the lotus posture she was balanced willy-nilly on the top of her head. She could not account for it, she said, and it happened so often at one time that hair was worn thin on top of her head. Her main sensation was of having no weight, she said. Her description brought to mind a perhaps similar behavior of don Genaro, reported by Carlos Castaneda. He would suddenly roll from a sitting position to balance on the top of his head. Are the "personal power" of don Genaro and the kundalini energy of Rajalakshmi found in the central area of the Venn diagram (Figure 12)? Possibly. In don Genaro's case the behavior was intentional rather than spontaneous. Don Juan interpreted don Genaro's behavior as a way of telling Castaneda that Castaneda's world was really upside down, and that his continuous writing and recording of events was meaningless and nonsensical. (Fortunately for us, Castaneda persevered with his writing, as a good anthropologist should.)

Rajalakshmi teaches biochemistry at the Sri Palmavathi Women's College in Tirupati and has many students of yoga who are psychologists and physicians at the college and medical school of Sri Venkateshwara University. She herself did not want to be a research subject at that time. Some other time, she said, perhaps in the U.S. in a full-fledged investigation, but now she would provide for us only a demonstration of *shaktipat* with two of her Yoga students. *Shaktipat* is the Sanskrit word for "power touch" and seems to be related to the demonstration reported by Castaneda in which don Genaro put his hand on Castaneda's shoulder and a seemingly heavy weight forced him to the ground. A similar effect was often induced by the eye, according to Castaneda. It is reasonable to hypothesize that if the demonstration that Swami Rama gave, using his eyes in the needle-moving experiment, involved the transmission of energy, then that effect might well be felt by a human being.

Rajalakshmi ran a small free clinic in her home. When we stopped by to pick her up for a research session at the university, using one of her disciples as subject, a little boy and his father were there. The child, a five-year-old, was very friendly and curious. He scrambled into the minibus to take a good look at it and us. Rajalakshmi showed us a picture of him when he was about three and a victim of polio; his legs looked pitifully thin and twisted. Now he looked well and was very active, and his legs looked perfectly normal. It is no wonder that he and his father seemed devoted to Rajalakshmi. She said she had accomplished his healing through yoga exercises and techniques.

The university at Tirupati was the most impressive that we saw in India. It was explained to us that a portion of the revenues from the temple on the hill were given by the religious leaders to support the cultural, educational, and medical activities in the town of Tirupati.

We gave one lecture and conducted a seminar for Dr. A.V.S.S. Rama Rao, Principal of the Sri Venkateswara Medical College. I also attended a special ceremony at the Sri Palmavathi Women's College, after which I talked about mind-body coordination and the significance of yoga. Three hundred young ladies at the ceremony and the tea which followed made a sight that I probably will never forget. The anima archetype was in full force. Whether it was the beautiful young women in saris, the exotic culture revealed in the ceremony, a religious one with dancing and celebration, or their gaiety that made such a strong impression is hard to say.

While we were visiting the Women's College Harvey asked one of the teachers if Rajalakshmi had demonstrated levitation at the school. The teacher said yes, she had demonstrated it once before two hundred of the students and faculty. According to her report, Rajalakshmi had risen about eighteen inches while in lotus posture, and had stayed up for about five minutes.

We noticed that the attitude toward Rajalakshmi was one of great respect. She said that possibly her presence made some individuals nervous but that generally, since she taught chemistry and did not fly about, they had accepted her. Rajalakshmi and Yogiraja (who later demonstrated meditation in an airtight box in Professor Rao's laboratory), as well as two or three other yogis we met in that part of India, were all students of the same venerable teacher.

Twice Rajalakshmi demonstrated *shaktipat,* energization of one or another chakra, but she did not feel that the first session was satisfactory. She felt that there was no significant energy flow. She had been seated on a chair in lotus posture, with her hand on the subject's head. Several times he jerked suddenly, but she felt that these were artifacts. The record showed no particular autonomic changes. The second subject (who appears with Rajalakshmi in the Hartley movie, *Biofeedback: The Yoga of the West*) was one of her best students, she said. We were very much impressed by him. He seemed a real yogi, in the sense that a powerful kind of tranquility surrounded him. Perhaps because of this presence of tranquility, we came to have a special feeling of affection for him, though we could not communicate a word. I noticed that when Rajalakshmi touched the top of his head, his heart rate decreased several beats per minute. It would be interesting to conduct such a test in which *shakti* was transferred at a prearranged signal. The hand, never touching, could be maintained in place about an inch from the head. If properly designed, such an experiment might throw light on the idea of energy transference. We have conducted a similar test with Jack Schwarz, in which he indicated with six subjects which way the heart rate would go, up or down. Those data remain to be assessed.

Before leaving Tirupati I took several 35-mm shots of photos that had been made by a newspaper photographer. These show Rajalakshmi in lotus posture about a foot off the ground, from three different positions. She did not claim to have true voluntary control of this phenomenon, in the sense of being able to turn it on and off, but said that this sometimes happened when she achieved a certain psychological state. According to the legend in Tirupati, Rajalakshmi while in her twenties (she was thirty years old when we met her) had remained in this state for many months—some said three years. The past was not of great concern to us at that particular moment, however. From a scientific point of view the only thing of significance would be what she might demonstrate in the future.

One of the impressive things about the trip to India was that, wherever we went, we met only the students of the high-level teachers, not the teachers themselves. Such persons, if living, did not proclaim themselves. No one we talked to (including Rajalakshmi herself, even though obviously revered by many devotees) claimed to be more than the disciple of a teacher. Sai Baba might possibly be an exception to this "hidden teacher" rule; we cannot say.

On December 20 we left Tirupati for Madras and its suburb, Adyar. Because of Elda's arrangement with the Theosophical Society to make a documentary movie during their 1973 International Conference, it was possible for us to stay on the society grounds at Adyar. When Jean Raymond, the recording secretary, learned of our biofeedback research, she invited Alyce and me to speak to the conference on December 31.

While in Madras I contacted a number of the scientists in the biomedical engineering division of the Indian Institute of Technology, including Dr. P. M. Srinidasan and Dr. Dhanjaoonghista. The Institute appears beautifully equipped for studies of every aspect of physical and occupational health, including such diverse subjects as mathematical biology, electrophysiology, and biomechanics. Scientists we met at the IIT easily perceived the cybernetic implications of biofeedback and opined that engineering technology and psychology would be able to collaborate in a very good study of yoga. As they spoke, I visualized the rapidity with which progress could be made in India in the study of yoga with appropriate instrumentation. The culture is favorable, the Sanskrit records are there, and enough high-level yogic practitioners remain of the almost-lost tradition to implement a science of consciousness on a meaningful scale. We understand that an impressive start in the scientific study of mind-body coordination has already been made by Dr. P. V. Karembelkar and his colleagues, in the scientific research department of the Kaivalyadhama S.M.Y.M. Samiti at Lonavla, near Bombay. As of now, however, they represent only "one small clearing in the forest."

While Elda, Harvey, and Tom remained in Adyar to make the theosophical movie, Dolly, Elmer, and I went to Pondicherry to find Jim DeVries and Yogi Gitananda, who Jim felt would be a suitable subject for research.

The stay at Pondicherry was like a sojourn in an altered state. The air of peace and veneration for Aurobindo and the Mother were at a maximum. Aurobindo had died in 1950 and was entombed in the ashram courtyard. The Mother, after a long illness, had died while we were in Chandigarh and was buried in the same mausoleum with Aurobindo. Every day dozens, and sometimes hundreds, of devotees came to meditate at the mausoleum, which had become a shrine.

Jim DeVries, a teacher of chemistry at the ashram school, had been the one to prepare our way in Pondicherry. Some years before we met, Jim decided to devote effort toward the goals of Auroville, the international city founded by Aurobindo and the Mother on the outskirts of Pondicherry. Jim took us to Gitananda's ashram in Pondicherry on December 23, but the yogi had just left for Sri Lanka. Jim was also in touch with a physiologist, Dr. Bhatnagar, professor and head of the Department of Physiology, JIMPER (Medical College) in Pondicherry. He took us there to discuss the yoga research that Dr. Bhatnagar and a small group of his associates had begun with Gitananda's students. They were studying physiological changes in yogis as they progress from the naive beginning state to more practiced states. Again arrangements were made for us to give lectures, private meetings, and a lab demonstration.

During the morning of Christmas Day, Elmer and I talked with a group of young people at the ashram, and in the afternoon we visited Auroville and talked to a gathering of young people there. Both groups were a mixture of Indians and Europeans and Americans. We were impressed by their lively interest in practical matters, their concern with how Indian economics, education, food supply, energy resources, etc., could be improved.

On Christmas Eve, Elmer and I lectured at the ashram for about two hundred people. We described biofeedback research and the theory and philosophy behind it. These ideas were not strange to ashram inhabitants because the combining of science and activity in the world with meditation, and the "bringing down" of Spirit for the transformation of one's life, have been advocated more here than at any other ashram. In his book The Synthesis of Yoga *(1955) Aurobindo visualizes a literal synthesis of the substantial physical, mental, and spiritual energies.*

By the perfection of this synthesis Aurobindo means "a transformation of our imperfect state into the fullness of our real and spiritual personality." He discussed five necessities for such perfection: (1) "a perfect equality," by which he means equanimity, balance, tranquility; (2) "the heightened, enlarged and rectified power of the instruments of our normal nature," the body, the emotions, and the mind; (3) the ability to have and to use properly the universal force or energy. The body "must be capable of being filled and powerfully used by whatever intensity of spiritual or higher mind force or life force . . . thus filled the body must have the capacity to work normally, automatically, rightly, . . . as a perfect . . . instrument of the spirit"; (4) "an understanding of the relation between Spirit and Nature"; and (5) a perfected intelligence, "its sole will must be to make itself an unsullied mirror of truth . . . capable of all variety of understanding . . . open to all its forms."

We learned from Rajalakshmi that Yogiraja Vaidyaraja, the "burying yogi," was going to be our subject with Dr. Rao at Waltair. We arrived there to find that Sri Yogiraja had prepared for the demonstration for several days. He felt that the research was important, but he also felt that it was only a superficial way of understanding the power of the mind. It was, however, for that same reason that he himself had chosen long ago to exhibit the hibernationlike ability that makes it possible for a person to be buried underground for a period of days without harm. Yogiraja was a short man with a tall sense of humor and he treated the inconveniences of being wired up good-naturedly, as a test of his yogic ability to "keep his cool." This was fortunate, for between Dr. Rao's equipment and our own he was covered with more wires than a Christmas tree and there were long delays. When we turned our equipment on, using wall power instead of battery power, Dr. Rao's equipment produced large-size artifacts on several pens. An electrical ground loop existed between our equipment and I was unable to find it, so we decided to run our portable lab on battery power only. Because the test of Yogiraja's ability to maintain autonomic equilibrium while enclosed in an airtight box would take all day, we would have to make use of alternate battery packs, which could be recharged in another building.

The yogic demonstration with physiological recording was the launching of Dr. Rao's psychophysiology laboratory in the Department of Psychology and Parapsychology. As a public-relations event it was certain to be successful, whatever its scientific merits; nevertheless, Dr. Rao (as well as we) wished to obtain as much information as possible and had arranged for blood tests and basal metabolism tests of Yogiraja. After the blood samples had been taken and the wiring completed, a *puja* (devotional) ceremony was conducted by the helpers and colleagues of Yogiraja. Then the glass front was clamped to the box in which he sat, a plywood crate measuring about three and a half by three and a half by five feet (about sixty cubic feet of air), heavily waxed inside and out to prevent the wood from being permeable to air. It was reinforced in places with boards half an inch thick, and it was through one of these that we drilled a hole for the wires.

The plug box of the portable lab was placed so that the wires from Yogiraja could come up out of the airtight crate and plug into it. From there a thirty-foot cable led to the lab, so we were able to observe the physiological variables in an out-of-the-way place. The door of the airtight box was quarter-inch glass plate in a wood frame, forming a side wall. We could see Yogiraja in profile. He sat in lotus posture with his back close to but not touching the wall where the wires came out. The glass door had a strip of quarter-inch polyurethane foam glued around its inside edge. I was satisfied that the box was sealed more tightly than the average refrigerator. We had stuffed polyurethane foam where the wires came through the hole in the box and then sealed over and around the wires, both inside and outside, with electrical tape.

In advance of this kind of demonstration, a yogi fasts for two or three days. Fasting quiets physiological functions and brings the body more easily under control. Yogiraja was not attempting the hibernation state —that was a different process—but instead planned to put his body into a state of lowered metabolic functioning and hold it constant for several hours. During this period of time he would attempt to maintain constancy of mind, emotions, and body by entering a blisslike state of consciousness in which time is said to exist no longer.

Mr. Bose, Dr. Rao's research assistant, had attached two of his physiological pick-ups to Yogiraja with spring clamps. One, to measure GSR, was on the hand; the other clamp (similar to a large earring) was attached to a nostril. It held a thermistor for measuring the temperature of air currents, not for determining the flow of air in a quantitative way but for determining the number of breaths per minute.

Yogiraja immediately settled into a state of calm physiological behavior, but after five hours the clamps attracted his attention and we noticed that he shifted the nostril clamp from the right to the left side.

In order to study the effects of distraction during Yogiraja's demonstration, Dr. Rao included flashing strobe lights and an audio buzzer. Every thirty minutes, twenty-five intense strobe-light pulses at about ten per second were flashed into the box and a loud buzzer was sounded over the intercom. In addition, dozens of dignitaries, both men and women, visited the lab and there was much peering into the box and much talking close to the box, but Yogiraja did not show any signs of response or loss of autonomic control.

After seven hours and twenty minutes he tried to signal on the intercom that he wanted to be let out of the box. Unfortunately, the intercom did not work, but somebody eventually noticed him striking the button and the glass cover was hurriedly removed. As soon as it was off, Yogiraja complained that he had received three electric shocks. This had made him uncomfortable and a little angry, and he had terminated the experiment.

If a switch were defective, it was possible that he had received a nine-volt shock, but we could not later determine the cause. In any event, I was happy that we had used battery power so that no ground-loop currents could be generated through our subject's body between Dr. Rao's equipment and ours.

Shortly after Yogiraja entered the box we observed that his heart rate averaged about eighty beats per minute and his respiration was shallow at about four breaths per minute. One of the physicians who attended the demonstration predicted to us that within three hours the pulse rate would be about one hundred and twenty beats per minute and after four hours Yogiraja would have to leave the box to prevent unconsciousness. We ourselves gave him two hours, then three, then simply waited with growing admiration of his abilities as the afternoon wore on.

The day before the test, Dr. Rao had burned a lighted candle in the closed box as a publicity demonstration. After an hour and a half it had gone out for lack of oxygen. The human body may not use as much oxygen as a candle under normal conditions, but if you can imagine being in a small closet in which a candle could burn for only an hour and a half, it is possible to get a feeling for the conditions of the experiment and the skill of Yogiraja.

After seven and a half hours Yogiraja's pulse rate was averaging about ninety bpm, and his breathing, still shallow, averaged about six breaths per minute. The only sign of autonomic disturbance we noticed occurred toward the end of the session. A very short, rapid, out-and-in respiratory jerk began appearing in each breathing cycle. Air can be rebreathed many times without consuming all the oxygen—only a fraction of the oxygen available in each breath is used—and Elmer hypothesized that Yogiraja's diaphragm was jerking to produce a turbulence in the lungs that would facilitate the gas-exchange process and make respiration more efficient.

At the end of his hours in the box, Yogiraja's knees were almost locked in position, and we had to help him stand up and walk to the adjoining room, where an effort was made to get another basal metabolism reading and blood samples. Word came later from Dr. Rao that it had been impossible to get a blood sample or a satisfactory metabolic reading. Blood flow to the peripheral parts of the body had been reduced to such a level that normal techniques for drawing blood from a vessel in the arm were inadequate.

One of the first things we did on reaching Topeka after the India trip was to make polygraph records of sample sections of Yogiraja's EEG record. We observed that he produced alpha almost continuously. It appears that he remained in a state of constant inward-turned attention, neither coming "out" (into beta) nor going "deeper" (into theta). To us that seems to be an impressive demonstration of self-regulation in the central nervous system, of control of thoughts and emotions. The exact behavior of his occipital cortex, including a minute-by-minute computer analysis, will eventually be at our disposal, but in the meantime we can recognize Yogiraja's demonstration as a significant example of self-mastery. The physiological records cannot show it, but we can attest to the fact that Yogiraja did not lose his sense of humor, "blow his cool." Throughout what was to many of us a grueling ordeal, he looked upon all the events (in which he seemed at least as serious a participant as ourselves) with benign amusement.

Before leaving Waltair, Elmer and I had a special meeting with Yogiraja and the manager of his ashram, Dr. V. S. Rao of Rajanyoga Ashram, Alamuru, East Godavary, Andhra Pradesh. They wanted us to help obtain all possible publicity for their organization, of which Rajalakshmi was also a member. They asked for a resumé of the sealed-box experiment that they could use in promoting yoga both in their organization and if any of their members came to the West.

Elmer wrote the resumé and also used the opportunity to warn against the deterioration of discipline that yogis often experience when they come to the West. Under the conditions of their own culture, it may be possible for them to maintain the austerities and emotional tranquilities necessary to demonstrate physiological self-regulation. But, even as we are ourselves activated and energized by strange sights, sounds, foods, and the like, yogis are too. If they come to the West, it is difficult in the extreme for them to maintain the conditions necessary for demonstrating unusual powers of self-regulation.

One of the major research problems in bringing a yogi from India to the West is that if the cultural problem is not satisfactorily handled and the performer is unable to demonstrate his skill, it is likely to be concluded that yogic self-regulation powers are fictitious.

Behavioral scientists have not been quick to recognize that a yogi's ability to perform is a function of the milieu in which the experiment is conducted. This same factor has demolished a good deal of otherwise well-designed parapsychological research. The attitude of the researchers and the environment in which the psychic must perform are part of the chemistry, so to speak. Since this fact is usually ignored, the conclusion if a demonstrator fails is often that there is no such thing as the power he claims to be able to demonstrate.

Yogiraja told us that he could demonstrate the transmutation of mercury. He could swallow two grams of mercury, which was then "transmuted in his body into energy," he said. Swami Rama had spoken of mercury and strychnine and said that it was through such transmutation that some yogis were able to demonstrate the taking of poisons without any ill effects. Possibly such a demonstration might be scientifically evaluated if the yogi were willing to swallow mercury that had been radioactively "tagged" for tracking throughout the body. There is no way for mercury to be absorbed or dissipated through normal metabolic processes, so such research might throw light on the pranic energy processes which, according to yogic theory, underlie every biochemical process. Prana supposedly includes the energies that control the transmutation of all materials that are swallowed.

Yogiraja said that he was eager to demonstrate that he could indeed transmute two grams of mercury every day. It seems to us that if a carefully controlled test were conducted, he would either succeed or fail. If he failed, that would end the discussion with Yogiraja, but if he succeeded it would open up a new line of research that could have an important bearing on the energy structure of the human frame.

The last of our yogic studies took place in the middle of India at Hyderabad. Dr. Rao had made arrangements with Dr. Reddy, head of the Department of Philosophy at Osmania University in Hyderabad, for us to stay at the university's guest house. Dr. Reddy has authored several books and is a student of Aurobindo's Integral Yoga and a founder of the Institute of Human Study. His family once owned a large area of land in India. It was his older brother who started the program under which wealthy landowners divided their holdings among the landless. Dr. Reddy arranged for us to lecture at the university, and it was he who took us to our first meeting with Dr. G. S. Melkote, founder and president of the Patanjali Yoga Research Institute.

Dr. Melkote is surely one of the most unusual and versatile people we met in India. At age seventy-seven, he is a member of the Indian parliament, a medical doctor, labor leader, philosopher, Sanskrit scholar, and scientist. He has successfully persuaded about thirty physicists, mathematicians, biochemists, physicians, biologists, and psychologists to learn Sanskrit in order to translate the ancient Sanskrit records. They are attempting to reconstruct the "lost knowledge" of body and mind that comprised the science of those who (according to tradition) wrapped their knowledge in an elaborate code in the temples in order to preserve it during "dark ages."

Dr. Melkote believes that the energies of nature are also the energies of mind and body and can be self-directed both for health and for expansion of consciousness into additional dimensions of energy. His concept is very similar to the idea put forth by Arthur Clarke in his novel Childhood's End (*1963*). *Clarke probably thought he was writing merely a story about consciousness expansion and the end of the old civilization, but Melkote would maintain that what Clarke got out of his unconscious was a simulacrum of a factual situation. Melkote says that now is the time for humans to rediscover the old information.*

This time we are at a higher level in the spiral of evolution, and the information can be communicated to humans all over the planet. He is convinced that a scientific team, integrating many disciplines, will eventually be able to piece together a version of the old knowledge that will benefit from the use of research techniques. Part of his medical plan consists of translating additional Sanskrit records that relate to Ayurvedic medicine, the body-health section of the old science, and in his laboratory he has a centrifuge, chromotography equipment, and a battery of other devices by means of which he can analyze the medicines that are manufactured according to the old Sanskrit formulas.

The Patanjali Yoga Research Institute is also a medical clinic, which, when we visited, had treated more than seven thousand patients. Of these, about seventy had diabetes, and Dr. Melkote's records showed some significant changes in liver metabolism as a result of the yoga and Ayurvedic program with which he was experimenting. We invited him to present his material at the 1974 Council Grove Conference, which he did. Following the conference, he toured the country, speaking at a dozen universities.

Co-director of the institute and instructor of yogic techniques is Sri Ramananda Yogi. He is one of the group of yogis whose brain waves during meditation were reported in 1961 by Anand, Chhina, and Singh. In their research sessions Ramananda produced continuous high-amplitude alpha from the occipital region and was able to maintain a state of continuous inner attention even though they attempted to interrupt it with flashing lights, ringing bells, and a hot glass test tube pressed against his hand.

Because of communications problems, Ramananda had not fasted in preparation for a demonstration, but he said that he would be willing to demonstrate the obliteration of a heartbeat on command, and we set up the laboratory to check him. Later, when Judy ran his cassette tape into the polygraph, we observed that at appropriate instants his heart skipped a beat.

Again it is worth noting that yogic techniques for self-regulation of physiological systems have a bearing on psychosomatic problems that people suffer from in the West. Breathing exercises for regulating heart rate could be a major factor in the control of psychosomatic fibrillation, tachycardia, and bradycardia, and the use of particular exercises for controlling specific organs and organ systems presumably would have a bearing on psychosomatic and other disorders in those organs. Yogic exercises *plus* biofeedback could be especially synergistic.

It is only a guess, but it seems to us that biofeedback will probably have considerable impact eventually in the East as well as West in training for self-regulation. Not because biofeedback of itself does something to a person (which it does not), but because doing *anything* in an intelligent way, whether driving a car or regulating the gastrointestinal tract, requires information. Yoga masters in India were apparently not numerous in the past and seem to be even fewer at the present time, with the result that many superstitions have developed. The average patient in India seeks a mixture of old and new remedies and seems to be developing more faith in Western science (using the intervention techniques of drugs and surgery), in contradistinction to Eastern science (using self-regulation techniques for control of mind and body). When West and East get together in medicine, however, then perhaps the best of both worlds can be obtained. Neither one alone seems sufficient. Western medicine is not adequate, because it does not really include mind as a factor in health; therefore, the majority of diseases which are said to be psychosomatic cannot be properly handled. And in Eastern medicine, where mind *is* accepted as a factor in health, the masses of people (who could not control their minds and whose superstitions did little to help them) have suffered from lack of proper intervention, good medical treatment. It seems quite clear from our present vantage point that a combination of intervention and self-reliance (self-regulation of internal states) will eventually be most effective for most people in all countries.

The last display of our equipment in India was made at the request of the American Embassy in Delhi. Unfortunately, Ambassador Moynihan was in Washington at the time of our return to Delhi, but we were very pleased to have about twenty of the officials appear for a two-hour seminar. We reviewed the early research on yogis of Thérèse Brosse, Wenger and Bagchi, Kasamatsu and Hirai, and Anand, Chhina, and Singh, and pointed out that although there was an increase of interest at the present time in both East and West in various kinds of meditation, the efforts to study yogis with psychophysiology equipment had started long ago. We were merely providing an additional link in a long line of research that was beginning to pay off. In fact, the most famous studies of yoga had been made at Lonavala, near Bombay, in the Kaivalyadhama Institute for Yogic Research, Training and Treat-

ment. Dr. P. V. Karembelkar had sent us a large number of research findings. We did not have an opportunity to meet him, but everywhere we went we received the same information: The most intensive research so far done in India had taken place at Lonavala.

Although in our embassy talk we pointed to historical roots and previous research, we focused on biofeedback training as a modern way of implementing what is known of mind-body correlation for the benefit of people everywhere, not just for followers of particular gurus, though they may indeed be living links to hidden truths. It is necessary, we said, to establish mind-body self-regulation as a science and not as a mystique. The trip to India was part of an effort to show that Eastern and Western experts in mind-body control are speaking of the same psychophysiological processes, whatever words they may use in explaining such abilities.

We returned to the U.S. January 24, 1974. Three months earlier, some of the group had suffered culture shock as we began our journey through the towns and villages of India, but I experienced shock mostly on our return to the U.S. Either because of much reading or thinking, I had already adapted to India before going there. What I had not anticipated or adapted to was the effect of returning home: acres of airport concrete almost deserted at eleven P.M., elaborate buildings of metal and glass almost empty of people, the environment seemed unreal and sterile. As long as three months later, while sitting at my desk in the research building, the odd feeling would sometimes come of being in a place where life was partially unreal. I thought about it for weeks and finally realized that the essence of India, to me, was its realness. Both life and death are very present and very obvious. Almost every day as we drove along we saw incapacitated people. Most of them were begging, and some were dying. Some people were dying in public in the river cities of Benares and Hardwar. People had come to the holy Ganges to die. And some were dying in public in Calcutta and other places, for the simple reason of having nowhere else to die.

In India death is different from anything we learn about from our Christian background. The attitude of Indian people toward the forces of nature seemed much closer to that of Rolling Thunder than to our own. In three months I had become so adapted to that feeling that it was a shock to return to the United States, and become aware of what I had previously ignored. Namely, we do not talk about death; we do not think about death; we are unaware of death; we are afraid of death; it is buried in our unconscious, and we do not intend to bring it up and think about it. Elisabeth Kubler-Ross's finding (1969) from counseling eleven hundred dying persons, that fear and guilt plague many dying Westerners, suddenly seemed quite obvious.

In India death is part of life and life after death is part of a growing process, neither eternal hell nor eternal "harps," as is taught in much of our Christian system. As a Tibetan teacher put it about 1880, life in the West became a "struggle for life" because of a belief in hell, and religions through their "hells and damnation inculcated the greatest dread of death." This is still a part of our heritage. Gradually the feeling of unreality faded away in me, but it took several months.

More Roots
and Sources

> ... The essence of science, it seems to me, is an attitude—an attitude of disciplined curiosity. ... There is always the lure of the unexplored and the challenge to develop methods that will make further exploration possible.
>
> —ROBERT MACLEOD

Having discussed swamis, sufis, and medicine men, we wish to mention some additional personal experiences that have shaped our thinking and our lives. It is not that our experiences have been so unique (though some of them may seem strange to the newcomer to the field), but we offer them to show that an overall theory is necessary to encompass such experiences.

The decision to include them was not made easily. Alyce and I discussed the pros and cons again and again. In the end we agreed that we want the reader to know "where we are coming from," as our humanistic colleagues would put it. There is risk involved, of course. For about forty years we refrained from telling people about experiences that did not fit *their* frames of reference. According to don Juan in *Journey to Ixtlan* (Castaneda, 1972), the risk in telling is that if people know about you, they tie you down with their "encumbering thoughts," but "if you have no personal history . . . no one pins you down with their thoughts."

Be that as it may, when we told one of our colleagues at the foundation about some of our experiences, he jokingly (I hope) said, "You'd better watch out or they'll send you to the Menninger Clinic!"

The main risk as we see it, however, is one of "impedance mismatch," not transmitting information in an optimal way. If our meanings are not clear, it is possible for incorrect judgments to be made by the reader about the field-of-mind theory. In keeping with scientific practice, therefore, in this book we are (1) presenting "raw data" (anecdotes and experiences) as well as research findings, (2) presenting a theory, and (3) suggesting that readers construct hypotheses to test the theory and possibly modify it, using experiences and data from their own lives.

My beginnings were very different from Elmer's. My first twelve years were spent on a farm in the midst of the wide prairies and wheat fields of North Dakota. I was next to the youngest in a family of eleven children. I had a brother two years older than I and a sister, the baby of the family, four years younger. Our closest neighbors were one and a quarter miles away, as was our white-painted one-room schoolhouse.

Children today, I suppose, might think of my childhood as lonely and boring. I don't remember it being either. I didn't care for dolls or for household things and spent much time outdoors, sometimes with my brother and sometimes alone, in a large grove of trees and in the barns and pastures with the cattle and horses. I loved the birds, all the baby things that came in the spring, and all the animals. I rode everything I could, horses, cows, my pet calf (until forbidden because of a broken collarbone resulting from a fall), and even the pigs. I loved to lose myself in the tall corn, or lie quietly in the cool damp wheat when it was tall but too green for cutting. Perhaps it is from these childhood experiences that my deep conviction comes—a society that forgets its roots in nature, that moves against rather than with nature (consciously or unconsciously), is an endangered society.

As I grew older I was allowed to work in the fields at times. Driving a horse-drawn rake I gathered the hay into long windrows. It was an "alone" job, and I would sing my heart out to the sky and the fields, hoping the neighbors could hear me each time I approached the boundary of our farm.

I went to high school in Sioux Falls, South Dakota. This gave the married sister that I stayed with a live-in baby sitter and me the advantage of a good high school. After graduating I returned home, but home was no longer the farm. It was during the evening of my second day at home that Dad regretfully told me he would not be able to help me go on to college, as he had planned. I knew that he and Mother had lost money in a bank failure some years before, but I hadn't known that the income from the farm was barely enough to support them.

I went out on the porch and sat in the dark for a while and wept. It isn't easy for the young to give up their dreams. Dad joined me on the porch after a while, and we talked quietly about what I should do. He offered to help me borrow some money from the bank, to sign a note for me so I could go to summer school. We thought credits gained from a summer's course work at a teacher's college, plus some extra rural education credits I had earned during high school, might qualify me for teaching in a country school. To think of teaching didn't seem strange—three older sisters had been teachers.

These plans worked out, and so it happened that in the fall, having just reached the required age of eighteen, I began teaching all eight grades in a little country schoolhouse. What a challenge! Thinking of it now, I know it was impossible, but I did it. I was a good teacher. I tried to keep ahead of my students, especially in the difficult subjects. The most difficult for me was eighth-grade math. I did every assignment two or three days in advance. It was this that brought me my first conscious experience of the power of the unconscious mind.

It was a problem in compound interest. I had tried to solve it and failed. I telephoned my brother, who was always better in math than I, and he and a friend drove out to the farm where I had board and room. We worked until midnight without success. We finally decided I should tell my eighth-grade class (of one) when the problem came up the following day that I believed the answer given in the book was wrong and I would write to the publisher for clarification. My brother and his friend went home and I went to bed, the problem still bothering my mind. About four o'clock in the morning I was suddenly awake and was watching (or somehow knowing) the whole problem being worked out in my mind. I got up and wrote it down and with a feeling of great relief went back to bed.

I taught for two years, and it was with real sadness that I said good-bye to my pupils and the schoolhouse with its potbellied stove. My teaching job had paid my debt at the bank and I had saved what money I could. Now I was off to other things. I visited the admissions office at the University of Minnesota, to inquire not only about admission but also about the possibility of a scholarship, without which I was unable to begin a university program. The man who interviewed me was kind but said there were no scholarships available in the drama department. He suggested I might want to look into the two-year course offered at the MacPhail School of Music and Drama.

That fall I entered MacPhail. I studied under two instructors who greatly influenced my life: Louise Holt and John Seamon Garns. Not only were they exceptional teachers of everything having to do with speech and stage, but they were both deeply interested in spiritual things. My reading was broadened, from Ralph Waldo Emerson to Lao-tse's The Tao, *and from the* Baghavad Gita *to William James. Under their separate inspirations there began in me a hunger for, and a satisfaction in, a search for the meaning of things, which has never left me.*

Before leaving MacPhail I entered tryouts for a company that was a remnant or outgrowth of the old traveling Chautauquas. I became a member of a play group doing one-night stands in tents and small theaters throughout the Midwest, across the central states, and down the East Coast from New York State through the Carolinas.

One late summer afternoon I walked down to the large tent where we were to give that evening's performance, to arrange my wardrobe and lay out my makeup. It was cloudy and a bit muggy, and I felt tired. I stretched out on a cot in the dressing room to rest and fell sound asleep. The next thing I knew, I was leaning against the dressing table with part of the tent top draped over me. While struggling to free myself from the canvas I realized that the heel of one shoe had been broken off. When I got myself free I noticed the whole tent was down, and the big center pole had crushed the cot where I had been sleeping. Later I was told that a small tornado had dipped down, done some damage to two houses, ripped the tent apart, and gone back up into the sky. I had been aware of nothing—I wondered how my unconscious knew and got me off that cot in time.

The life of one-night stands is strange, with both tribulations and joys. Two years seemed enough; at the end of the second year I didn't renew my contract. I went back to Minneapolis, and soon married. But it turned out not to be a good marriage. As time went on it became apparent that we did not value the same things, that we did not want the same things out of life. After the birth of our second child, I sought out Dr. Garns. He had left MacPhail to establish a center and school for the express purpose of building a bridge between psychology, religion, and science. It was good to see him again, to feel his compassion and his quiet wisdom. I was aware of a feeling of relief, a feeling of "coming home."

It was something of the same feeling I had long before when Mrs. Holt had first talked to me about reincarnation and the laws of karma. It began when something happened in one of her classes shortly after the beginning of my first term at MacPhail. It was one of those strange déjà vu events, but with a difference. As often happens in such experiences, I had that lonely feeling that I had been here before. What was different was the deep and sudden feeling of love I felt for Mrs. Holt. She must have sensed something, because she turned and looked at me and said quietly, "We have met before," then went on with her teaching. After class she asked me to come to her office, and she told me her ideas of reincarnation and karma in the simplest terms: how she believed people moved in groups, that they came back to Earth again and again, like going through various grades at school, and that, although she didn't know where or when, she felt we had known each other before. We talked for a long time. I had a feeling of "coming to my own," because what was said made sense of so many things; it seemed so right, as if it were something I had always known but not remembered.

I told Dr. Garns that my marriage was failing and then listened in wonder as he described not only me, whom he had known at MacPhail, but also my husband, whom he did not know, better than I could have described him, and our life better than I could have told it. His suggestion was to try once more, to try throughout the summer.

It was a day in early fall when I knew the marriage was over. Suddenly it was finished; there was nothing left in me to try. I have often wondered if Dr. Garns had foreseen that time when it would be finished, without regret.

I had become quite active in Dr. Garns's center, taking classes, doing some teaching in speech and speech correction, conducting Sunday evening candlelight services, and attending Sunday-morning lectures (while my children, Douglas, three, and Patricia Ann, five years old, were in the center's Sunday school).

Dr. Garns was an exciting speaker and teacher, one of the best I have ever heard. He was an omnivorous reader. His Sunday-morning talks were always stimulating as he shared with us not only his philosophy and spiritual concepts but also the new ideas he was constantly gathering in his areas of special interest. He often read aloud from the latest books on science, psychology, and religion, stacked three deep on the table near his lectern.

Other lecturers and teachers were brought to the center. I remember one especially well, Muzumdar, a man from India who had been one of Dr. Garns's teachers. He was in his early nineties, but you would *never have known it from his black hair and alert eyes and the grace with which he danced a waltz with me at a center party. Like Dr. Garns, Muzumdar had his own miracles of precognition and healing to tell, but the sharpest memory I have of him is when he told me to "develop the will." I was going down the broad stairs at the center as he and Dr. Garns were coming up, engaged in an animated conversation. As we were about to pass he suddenly turned, looked at me with his piercing black eyes, and said, "The will! Develop the will," then resumed his conversation and continued up the stairs.*

Dr. Garns's center was one among a number of such groups in the New Thought Movement flourishing at the time (many of them are still active today, such as Unity and Religious Science). A part of their teaching and practice is healing through affirmation and prayer.

Mrs. Holt believed in the power of humans to heal by thought. I didn't take the classes in healing at the center or belong to a healing group, but I did devise my own way of working for the healing of my children when they were hurt or ill. I would sing to them, sing my visualizations of light and energy correcting the difficulty or healing the body. Often it seemed to work, by bringing relief from pain, release into healing sleep, sometimes the sudden lowering of a high temperature, or quick recovery from a childhood disease.

Two of the more dramatic healings involved Douglas. The first was when he was about two and a half years old. I returned from shopping one day to learn that he had fallen from the back of the davenport and hurt himself. My mother, who was visiting at the time, had put him to bed and was sitting beside him to keep him quiet. She thought he had hurt his shoulder. I sat down on the edge of the bed and sang to him for a while, but when I tried to pick him up he cried. Worried that he might have broken a bone, I called our pediatrician. It was in the days when doctors would make house calls, and Dr. Ted, as we called him, soon came. He examined Doug's shoulder, chest, and back. Doug didn't whimper or cry, but he turned his face toward me, away from Dr. Ted. "Well, nothing broken," the doctor said. "If there were any broken bones he would have cried when I pressed on them. He probably just banged his shoulder—he'll be all right in a day or two."

After Dr. Ted left I sang my healing songs again, but Doug wasn't all right. After several days he still winced when I picked him up. I made an appointment to have his shoulder X-rayed. Dr. Ted was still sure there could be no broken bones, not even a greenstick fracture.

After the X-ray we waited in his office until he came in. He looked surprised. The X-ray showed that the collarbone had been broken, he said—not a greenstick fracture but a break straight across the bone. It was healing perfectly, he said; there was nothing more to be done.

About a year later a similar event occurred. Laura, a friend of mine, and her young son, about Doug's age, were living with us at the time. I was playing in the revival of an old-fashioned melodrama at one of the downtown hotels, and my friend took care of the children when I was gone. One evening Doug was feeling miserable; he had a cold, was running a fever, and had complained of an earache for a day or two. When the pain seemed to increase quite drastically during the evening, Laura called her doctor, who was also a personal friend. When I returned home after the performance, Laura was waiting up for me. She told me the doctor had examined Doug's ear, found it abscessed, and recommended an operation. He would come back at ten o'clock in the morning and take us to the hospital. He had given Doug pain-relief medication, and now Doug was asleep. I went into his room and sat beside him, singing softly for about an hour. He didn't waken. I leaned over his crib and placed my hand gently over his ear. As I did so I saw, just for an instant, a small spot of light where each fingertip touched his head. He still didn't waken, and I left his room quietly and went to bed. As I lay in bed I began questioning myself. I had never seen light during healing before—had it been my imagination? Had it been just the firing of some nerves in my eyes? Or static electricity?

When Doug woke in the morning he seemed his usual good-natured self and had no more fever. The doctor came at ten as he had promised but on examining Doug's ear again he found no sign of the abscess. Doug was well.

What can one say of such events? They can always be explained away. Yet whether I was concentrating on the healing of someone else or, on rare occasions, myself, those times when I could achieve a certain feeling of vibrant aliveness (like Jack Schwarz's joy?) seemed to be followed by success.

It was shortly after Doug's ear trouble that I met Elmer. It was at an annual conference of the International New Thought Alliance held in Minneapolis. Dr. Garns was, in a sense, host to the conference. I worked at one of the book tables, and it was there that I first met Elmer and his parents. The second evening of the conference I was one of the speakers, and it was during my talk, I was told later, that

Elmer's mother, dad, and brother decided I would be "just right" for him.

Soon I knew Elmer, his family, and Dr. Erwood well. Elmer and I spent hours discussing things we had read and things we had experienced, things we knew and things we conjectured might be. He and his family came often to the center and two or three times I was invited to attend special meetings held by Dr. Erwood. The first time, as we sat for meditation in a totally darkened room, I saw the luminous outline of Elmer's head and shoulders, but as if he were leaning forward, not sitting straight beside me, as I thought he was. I moved my hand slowly forward to the blue-white light and touched his shoulder; he had leaned forward, with his elbows on his knees. What I was seeing was probably what has been called the etheric body in theosophical literature, an "energy body" which interpenetrates what we normally see as our physical body and extends slightly beyond it. Within this subtle physical body, it is said in raja yoga, the chakras are located, the "organs of perception and action" through which psychic energies flow.

I have had other "experiences of light." In one sense they seem to have nothing to do with me. I have never made an effort to develop psychic abilities, but some things simply happen and I watch, sometimes in wonder. I am sure many people have experienced this.

One evening, a few years ago, we decided to listen to a new record of E. Power Biggs playing Bach in the Thomaskirche, Bach's own church in Leipzig. I am not particularly fond of organ music, and especially organ music played loud, but Elmer put the speakers on the wooden floor and turned the volume up high. We turned out the lights and stretched out on the floor and listened. It was magnificent; the majestic sounds vibrated through the house and through our bodies. Then I became aware of light flowing from my forehead, mingled gold and purple flowing like a fountain or like soft curled petals from the center of a flower. Truly spellbound, I watched the constant glow of color until the music ended. As I attempted to explain to Elmer what I was experiencing, it slowly faded.

I saw that light again under strange circumstances. One day when we were in India to study yogis, I walked with three friends into the hills above Rishikesh to visit a yogi named Tat Walla Baba. He lived in a cave, wearing only a loincloth winter and summer. We had been told there was usually someone there who could interpret for us and that we could ask questions, but this day there was no one. Tat Walla Baba gestured us in, and we sat on rugs on the dirt floor before the low platform on which he sat. We could not converse with him, so we sat quietly. I closed my eyes in meditation. I felt respect for this tall, well-built, and deeply quiet yogi, but I felt no awe or reverence. Then suddenly I became aware again of the gold and purple light flowing from my forehead, not as brilliant or luminous as before, but there, taking the same shapes. I watched for a few moments and then opened my eyes. The yogi sat quietly. Did he know what I had experienced? Did its happening have anything to do with his presence? Or with my presence in this cave where much meditating had been done? I don't know.

Another experience of light happened in our home at Lake Perry. Our living room faces west and has a wall, all windows and glass doors, opening onto a wide deck overlooking the lake. In certain light the surrounding trees and the sky are so perfectly reflected in the glass that occasionally, much to our distress, a bird flies straight into a window and is hurt. One day this happened again. Elmer and I both recognized the thud of the tiny body hitting the glass, and when we went to look there was the little bird, lying still and crumpled as if it had broken its neck. But what a bird it was. I had never seen one like it, nor have I seen one since, nor have I been able to find it in our bird books. It looked as if it were made of lustrous green velvet. Usually when a bird is hurt we don't go out, for fear that it will struggle to escape and damage itself further, but this time Elmer said, "It's dead, completely dead." I couldn't bear to leave it there. I went out and picked it up; it didn't move. I carried it into the house and sat down, holding it cupped in my two hands. I sat quietly for several minutes. Then I saw light flowing and pulsating around my hands; this time the light was gold mingled with orange. As I was watching I felt the bird stir. Soon it was struggling to be free. I carried a rather deep basket out on the deck and put the bird into it, hoping it would stay still and rest for a while, but no sooner had I stepped away than it flew out of the basket and into a nearby tree. It paused there briefly, as if to recollect itself, and then flew away.

Elmer and I have had some unusual sharing experiences. One was after a mountain climb in the High Sierras. For fourteen days we walked in the high mountains, mostly above timberline in the daytime, coming down to streams or lakes and woods for the evening meal and

nighttime. It was August, spring in the high mountains, and the colum-
bine and shooting stars were out and John Muir's Hanging Meadows
were aflame with bloom.

Physically we came down from the mountains in fourteen days, but
it took longer to come down emotionally and spiritually. On the second
night home from the mountains, I remember becoming aware, while
asleep, of Elmer rolling up his bedroll, tucking it under his arm, and
sliding off the ledge we had been sleeping on. He walked toward a lovely
white waterfall nearby. I joined him. We stood for some seconds
(A minute? I don't know) and then Elmer said, "What's a street light
doing there?" And then we noticed the gate and the picket fence and
realized we were not by a waterfall but in our bedroom, by our white
nylon curtains, looking out into our own yard. The hallucinations or
near-dreams of that mountain world continued for several days. I re-
member the nostalgic feeling that accompanied them, and think it
must be similar to the feelings of nostalgia reported by some people
who have, according to all physical signs, been dead and then returned
from that state.

We have had such sharing experiences a number of times. I remem-
ber a shared dream, both of us dreaming together of putting our shoul-
ders to a small boxcar filled with apples to start it moving down an
orchard track, then coming awake to tell each other about it. I wonder
how often people might dream together and never become aware of it.

Some of my experience parallels that of Alyce, but some is quite
different. I have always had the faculty of "seeing mental pictures" if
I close my eyes for longer than about thirty seconds, so perhaps it is
natural that symbolic imagery should have a special place in my experience.

In the beginning of the book I told about Arthur Jay Green and
some of the ideas and training methods my mother and I got from him
in 1935. In the following year we attended a series of lectures in Duluth
given by a man who was known to me only as Professor Lally. His
business manager later said that he had been a lawyer on the faculty
of a school in Minneapolis. After he received "the call of spirit," he
accepted the responsibility in 1936 of "saving the United States for
God" by running for President. This kind of grandiose behavior (not
necessarily involving politics, however, for sometimes it is science or
religion) is a trait shared by many mediumlike persons. Perhaps it is

because they become aware of trends through their trans-temporal sensitivities and make the mistake of thinking that the development of the trend has something to do with them personally as individuals, with the result that their egos tend to get unbalanced and they become unrealistic.

Our experiences with Professor Lally and with Arthur Green were as different as night and day. Arthur was cheerful, bright, spontaneously joyful, and spoke mainly about the need for developing one's potential for happy equanimity. Professor Lally was gloomy and foreboding, full of spiritual condemnation, and he talked much about becoming "the instrument of spirit." We gradually realized that he was advocating training for becoming a medium. That is why I wish to include here something of what we learned.

Nowadays many persons in our society are subjected to the same pressures that we were bombarded with, though now it is not Professor Lally but his modern counterparts in witchcraft, satanism, voodoo, and a host of groups organized for the purpose of calling UFOs, contacting spirits, and developing mediums. Mediums, incidentally, by self-definition are persons who develop unusual psychic sensitivity so that so-called "noncorporeal entities" (commonly called spirits) can speak through them. The modern movement in mediumship started with the Fox sisters in England in 1849 and eventually led to the establishment of the Spiritualist Church.

As mentioned by Jolande Jacobi (1967), Carl Jung's doctoral thesis was a study of a medium, who he felt was expressing "splinter personalities" rather than spirits. These splinters, in Jacobi's words, were "components of a more comprehensive personality hidden in the unconscious psyche." She quotes Jung: "It is, therefore, conceivable that the phenomena of double consciousness are simply new character formations, *attempts of the future personality to break through,* and that in consequence of special difficulties . . . they get bound up with peculiar disturbances of consciousness." Jacobi goes on to say, "Therefore it remained Jung's untiring scientific and psychotherapeutic endeavor to work out a methodological procedure for bringing these components to consciousness and associating them with the ego, in order to realize the 'greater personality' which is potentially present in every individual."

To Professor Lally, however, the spirits were autonomous beings who lived in what don Juan nowadays has called "a separate reality," though don Juan explains that the separateness is a function only of sensory limitations.

It seems to us that the facts actually include a mixture of both ideas, splinter personalities and autonomous beings. This position does not contradict the major religious beliefs down the centuries, and also makes it possible to account for some of the strange occurrences in the field of parapsychology that are not accounted for by the splinter theory. William James studied a number of mediums in his investigations of life after death, and he too felt that the facts demand a consideration of both ideas (Murphy and Ballou, 1960).

Alyce, Dale Walters, and I get quite a few letters and phone calls from people who say they are mediums and psychics and wish to be research subjects. Since our research is not in that domain, we have declined all such invitations. Interestingly enough, the phenomenon of mediumship seems to be on the increase, especially since the advent of public hypnotic programming of mind-training courses for development of psychic powers.

Professor Lally's method for developing psychic sensitivity combined two normally powerful techniques, both of which failed with my mother and me, so far as we could determine. The first was to sit with closed eyes while he delivered a long, repetitive hypnotic incantation and supplication for becoming "aware." The second, which took place at home in private, was the practice of automatic writing (one's hand, not under voluntary control, is supposed to be able to write messages from the unconscious). The importance of automatic writing in Professor Lally's estimation was that it was training in allowing "spirit to take control."

Our problem with the hypnotic induction was that after a long incantation, sometimes lasting the better part of an hour, we were still waiting for something to happen. Did we fail because of skepticism? Many others succeeded and "went into trance," not recovering until Professor Lally made a special effort afterward to bring them back from the "spiritual journey into other dimensions."

With some class members the attempts at automatic writing were very productive, and hundreds of pages of meandering thoughts were displayed each week at show-and-tell sessions, but for us, again, the results were meager. This caused a kind of embarrassment in me, first because I had nothing to show, and second because my low opinion of the material being produced was not easy to hide. After one entertaining attempt to "allow automatic writing," I gave up entirely. That time, when I came closest to a feeling of automatism in my hand, I got the message "Hallelujah! Hallelujah! Hallelujah, I'm a bum."

The most interesting part of Professor Lally's course was a series of lectures on myths, symbols, and psychic energy. Eventually we stopped attending his classes, shortly after he began a sequence of exercises that were supposed to lead to freedom in "other dimensions" through what Charles Tart in 1969 called OOBEs, out-of-the-body experiences, similar in many respects to one of the modern developments in which one is said to put one's life under the control and guidance of a "master" for a promise of journeys in "other dimensions." The uneasiness I felt about Lally's teachings was amplified by the requirement to believe, not to question, not to think, to go along, and to *allow something else to take over* and make the decisions in one's life. In spite of my skepticism (or perhaps because of it), I learned a lot from the contact with Professor Lally.

After finishing high school I spent a year in Duluth studying music (as well as attending Lally's course). I practiced the piano about five hours a day, with the idea of studying music at college. Music has at least one wonderful characteristic: Is is not concerned with ideas as rational, logical things, but instead represents a gestalt-like kind of awareness, a feeling of things as a whole. A year with music, coupled with a large number of experiments and efforts at existential penetration into the normally unconscious mind, made me feel that science and the psychological domain could be brought together. Perhaps science might be extended to include the psychic energies that Arthur Jay Green and Professor Lally had talked about and demonstrated in various ways. In the fall of 1936 I applied for admission to the University of Minnesota, planning to concentrate in physics.

As I said before, the world of classical physics seemed dull after the theory and practice of self-awareness, so I was interested to learn in 1938 that Dr. Erwood was moving to Minneapolis. At one time, ending in 1928, he had been a minister in the Spiritualist Church. After breaking with the church, he was a traveling lecturer and teacher, visiting European countries and most of the states of the Union. When Dr. Erwood moved to Minneapolis I joined his study group. It focused on mind-body coordination, Eastern and Western approaches to religion, and a consideration of occult phenomena. In retrospect it is clear that the meetings with Dr. Erwood, both in the closed group and in private, formed the most important part of my nonacademic education. After three months of weekly meetings the group was closed to outsiders (except for Alyce's joining the group), and only a small number, about seven or eight, continued to meet together until about February 1940. Dr. Erwood's public lectures around the country also continued, and he had closed study groups in other cities as well.

During the preceding year and a half, during my freshman and sophomore years at the university, I had carried out a study of psychic phenomena in the Spiritualist Church and classified most of the phenomena as projections from the unconscious of the medium, rather than messages from "another dimension." Most of the information I received from these mediums concerning my own life was trivial and inconsequential, and it became clear that the quality of the information was directly related to the mental and emotional qualities of the medium. That is, those ministers who seemed to be mentally oriented, and not mere emotional responders, seemed to be in contact with more intelligent "sources." But none of their "guides" knew as much as I did (in my estimation), even though they were, according to their mediumistic channels, coming directly from "the spirit kingdom."

Notwithstanding, there was no doubt in my mind that in most cases a measure of parapsychological awareness was involved. I would walk in off the street without preliminary contact and ask to talk to the pastor of the church, satisfied that no overt knowledge of my intentions had preceded my visit. Almost always the pastors could give me details about family members and situations—for example, I had one brother; my father managed a department store; my mother was interested in the "spirit world"; my mother had two brothers and one sister; I was a musician and was studying science. In one case I got an accurate description of a girl I had dated a few times, including a description of her genetic background, and was advised to marry her. (The description was accurate, but the advice was foolish.)

I noticed that the "spirits" were not accomplishing much with their advice to churchgoers, and, for all the cosmic consciousness of their "guides," the affairs of the pastors and mediums themselves were not in such good order. The overall impression was one of failure of the church. Perhaps it is changed now, but that's the way it was in the 1930s.

The experience with Dr. Erwood was of a different character. The first time I visited him in his room at the Curtis Hotel in Minneapolis,

I was impressed by his careful, low-key mention of things in my college life and private affairs that I had not shared with my family. I made an appointment to return in a week and talk with him while he was in trance. My mother had said that if Dr. Erwood was willing to "go into trance" I could speak with "his teacher." That experience, and the sequence of such experiences in the next few years of both private and group sessions, amazed me. Dr. Erwood would close his eyes and become quiet. After a minute or two he would give a slight shudder, then open his eyes and begin speaking as the Teacher. I have no way of adequately describing the depth and breadth of information. The Teacher declined to identify himself, saying that all information had to be evaluated in one's own life without recourse to authority, but it was clear even in the first session that, among other things, he knew more about me than I myself knew. Not only did he seem to know everything I knew about myself, my family, and my friends, he was also aware of my dreams, and on occasion would remind me of half-remembered or forgotten images, bringing them back to my awareness.

In the year before meeting Dr. Erwood I had become disenchanted with college reality and had decided that the world of meanings and values did not lie in school. I had begun cutting classes, not studying, and my grades had slipped from A's to B's to C's; finally I got an F. At about the time I met Dr. Erwood I was put on probation. I was on the swimming team, and my coach, Neils Thorpe, tried to get me to pay attention to college business, sleep regularly, and forget "all that other nonsense." I was beset by a variety of emotional states, including guilt, anger, and frustration (the last caused mainly by having to study to learn calculus), and I tried to escape from these pressures partly by living it up with fraternity brothers on weekly, sometimes more frequent, beer busts. What agony! My ability to keep my life together was disintegrating, and the thought of finishing school and finding a job as part of our society repelled me. I decided in the spring of 1938, along with one of my friends, Ronald Hoel, to apply for Naval Air Training. I did not inform my family. Ron had essentially finished college and was accepted, but I was rejected because I was three credits short of having completed two years at the university.

With so many difficulties, and thwarted in my major attempt to escape, I asked the Teacher's advice. Oddly, he would not discuss my shortcomings or deficiencies, but instead focused on the usefulness of both intellectual knowledge and meditation for obtaining self-guidance and self-regulation. When I asked directly for him to discuss with me my greatest defects, that I might focus attention on them better and somehow get my life under control, after a silence he said, "We have noticed that you do not arise in the morning with the greatest of alacrity." According to Webster's, "alacrity" means "cheerful promptness, or readiness." What a joke! This was a most humorous answer, it seemed to me, because that seemed the least of my problems, an effect rather than a cause. It was true that instead of going to school I was sleeping until ten or eleven o'clock, or noon or one o'clock on occasion. I was tired from reading all night, not physical chemistry, but books from the Minneapolis Public Library on spiritualism, mediumship, and psychic phenomena.

I considered his comment to be of little value. Many years passed before I came to realize the powerful effect in one's life of the exercise of will in some relatively trivial matter. If I had forced myself, no matter how tired, to get up every morning and go to school, making that the first item of business rather than the last, most of my troubles would have been forced into proper proportion.

The profound effects of the exercise of volition have been recently emphasized by Roberto Assagioli, the creator of Psychosynthesis. Even making oneself stand on a chair for ten minutes as a simple exercise can have far-reaching consequences. But at the time, the Teacher's suggestion or comment seemed too simple and I disregarded it. Ram Dass, the former Dr. Richard Alpert, who experimented at Harvard in the early 1960s with LSD, had a similar experience with a teacher in India. As Ram Dass tells it (1969, 1971), when he realized that the guru knew everything that he was thinking, day and night, he began to wonder why his defects were never discussed. Ram Dass asked Haridas Baba, another of the guru's disciples and Ram Dass's personal instructor, for an explanation. Haridas merely commented, "That would not help your *sadhana* [spiritual development]." The message is: You already know what is wrong; the task is to plant in mind the constructive ideas, the visualizations, which you want to realize. Eliminate defects by focusing on better procedures. No programming, no hypnosis, no argument or discussion of errors is as useful as a discussion of principles. That is only a general rule, however, because teachers sometimes deviate from that procedure and intervene directly in the lives of students. It happened in Castaneda's experience with don Juan, but even there, don Juan said that beyond a certain point only Carlos could make decisions.

I experienced one intervention that was unexpected and inexplicable. In the spring of 1939 I had resigned from my fraternity after much debate with fraternity brothers and alumni. I was the only member who was on an athletic team and had been picked, they said, for fraternity president in 1940. If I left the fraternity I would be a deserter. I finally convinced them that it was essential for me to live alone and to try to pull my life together, but as soon as I was alone I redoubled my reading and made only slight improvement at school. At some level I had become recalcitrant and was determined to escape, at whatever cost, from college.

Then one day the Teacher said that it had been decided to help me in school because I was in danger of failure. That was a mild summary of the situation, though I had succeeded in getting off probation. I was immensely pleased to hear him say this. I had heard of numerous examples of picking up information directly, without having to study, and on occasion it had happened to me in a very minor way. I interpreted the Teacher's remark to mean that I might be able to get through school without having to study in the usual way, but his next statement was a shock: "Your attention seems to be focused on the development of psychic awareness and it is interfering with your education, so we have decided to turn off your psychic faculties."

I heard this with disbelief. In the first place, how could it be done, and in the second place, I would resist. Within a week, however, everything stopped, and I could not turn it on again no matter how long I meditated. I returned to Dr. Erwood and asked the Teacher how long that state would continue. As long as six months? He laughed and said that it would be a good deal longer than that, but my awareness would return when and if needed.

With that avenue of exploration at least temporarily cut off, my attention gravitated back to physics, and I began to think about the *meanings* of the things I had been learning and was learning. One question interested me very much, for several reasons: How could an energy field be projected that could turn off someone's sensory apparatus? Was I doing it to myself through acceptance of suggestion? There was no doubt that sensory processes of some kind were involved. I understood that in order to have visual imagery it was necessary (or it seemed necessary, at least) to have some kind of neurological firing. If I was not blocking my own imagery, how could it be handled, manipulated, or turned off from outside? I have since learned that the organs of psychic perception—the chakras, as they are called in the East—are supposedly energy structures whose workings can be facilitated or inhibited by a knowledgeable teacher in any of his students. Some of Castaneda's experiences with don Juan would qualify as direct turn-ons or turn-offs of perceptual machinery, especially the solar-plexus chakra.

In the second year of Dr. Erwood's closed group meetings there were demonstrations and discussions of psychokinesis (PK). I was especially impressed by the apparent PK manipulation of a portable phonograph. It had a wind-up spring drive and an electronic amplifier. I was responsible for winding it and handling the one record we used at the beginning of meetings. On occasion it would emit voices in addition to the instrumental music, sometimes with oddly distorted music as a background, sometimes alone, and sometimes the voices were distorted.

I asked the Teacher specific questions about these phenomena, at least as many as I could, for he generally talked more of principles than specifics. He made the following points: (1) "scientists" were using the meetings with Dr. Erwood, during which there was a large accumulation of energy, for experimenting with a communications link; (2) the phenomena were useful because they suggested the idea of *direct* communications, and eventually scientists "on different levels" would come in contact with each other through instruments and humans everywhere would have a chance to investigate for themselves; (3) the meetings were necessarily closed so that conflicts between the "energy bodies" of the group members could be eliminated over a period of time and the group made harmonious; (4) power depended on "harmonious vibration"; (5) except for Dr. Erwood, none of us was "generating" an excess of energy; (6) we were "charged" with a certain kind of energy each week during the group meetings; (7) if we lived in certain ways (similar to don Juan's concept of the "impeccable warrior") we would begin to accumulate energy, mainly by not dissipating it in unessential mental, emotional, and physical behavior (called "indulgences" by don Juan); (8) two good habits were (a) no waste time, and (b) no waste energy; (9) each person would have to be his or her own guru (find the center of his or her own being), because the close relationship that existed in the past between students and teachers would not be possible for the large numbers of individuals who would, in the next fifty years, wish to obtain information; in other words, *each person would have to assume self-responsibility*.

I asked the Teacher where the scientists he spoke of were located.

Were they in another dimension? In what part of the electromagnetic spectrum could they be detected? He did not give a definite answer; instead he said in reply to my question about another dimension, "You could say that." From various other things that he said, however, I became aware of the fact that our perceptual systems were involved and that the energies detected in psychological levels (levels of substance, he said) were projected into understandable forms by our minds. The implication was that images usually seem familiar in shape, emotional tone, and thought because our perceptual systems (which have been constructed and programmed from the time we were conceived) force them to appear that way. In other words, the energy that triggers our sensations is perceived, or interpreted, according to the nature or structure of our perceiving apparatus. What we see and hear (or detect in any way) resemble projections whose apparent character, nature, or identifying features are shaped according to rules laid down in our mind-body structure.

For example, if an extremely powerful magnet is moved across the back of the head so that the magnetic lines of force interact with the visual cortex, we see bands of colored light moving across our field of view. In actuality the magnetic field has no color and isn't a band of light, but its interaction with the brain is interpreted (projected) by the perceptual apparatus in the only way it has been trained to perceive. If you agitate visual nerves you get light; if you agitate auditory nerves you get sound. Everything that we consciously perceive has associated with it some kind of electrochemical activity in our brains, but that activity does not necessarily inform us of the true nature of what we are perceiving, especially if the stimulus is from parapsychological sources.

One idea stressed by the Teacher was that one should not believe but should investigate until experience enables one to know. Prejudgment blocks learning, because it distorts perception, so the word of authorities should be used only as data. Each person necessarily must evaluate, test, and experience for himself, even though guidance or counsel from others is used in developing both self-awareness and self-control. It was advised to accept no teachings in which it was demanded, requested, or even suggested that compliance or obedience to another was necessary before one would be allowed an experience of one kind or another. Such compliance led ultimately to surrender of volition and self-awareness, and our goal was the opposite: to increase both. That did not mean that we did not have to comply with nature in order to gain understanding; on the contrary. Many years later I came across a similar idea from Milarepa, the great Tibetan yogi: "Combine, in a single whole, the goal of aspiration, the meditation, and the practice, and so attain *Understanding by Experimentation*" (Evans-Wentz, 1957; emphasis added).

The first time I talked to the Teacher alone was just before I joined Dr. Erwood's group. He talked about me and my life, about my children, Pat and Doug, and about Elmer. I can't remember now how it was done, it wasn't said in so many words, but when our talk was finished I was aware that in his thoughts Elmer and I would spend our lives together.

This last was a difficult problem for me. Elmer had said from the beginning that he was going to marry me, but he was younger than I, he had not yet graduated from the university, and I had two children. It seemed to me that it would be an unfair burden.

As time went on Elmer and I talked with the Teacher together a number of times. He talked about many possibilities and probabilities in our lives. He talked about reincarnation, how we had returned many times in the same family group, drawn together, held together, learning together through our interweaving karmas. And we would be together again. We did not ask and he did not offer any details as to who or where or when, in the past or in the future.

The ideas of reincarnation and karma were not new to us. "As ye sow so shall ye reap," and from the reaping, "good" and "bad" we learn. This world is our school, and we return as often as necessary to complete the various grades. These concepts seemed to us a reasonable foundation for life.

When Elmer and I talked to the Teacher after we were married, after we did "join forces under one roof," as he had recommended, he talked to us about the children, that they came to be mine "not by chance" and now they were Elmer's "not by chance," that they were not strangers to him. He talked about the children who were then coming into incarnation, that they were "children of a new age" and he stressed the responsibility of parents in guiding them through their childhood. Before and after Sandra and Judy were born, he talked to us about them. Our family of six became a close family. The idea of stepsister, stepbrother, stepchild, stepfather never occurred to us.

As mentioned previously, my attention on studies improved after my attempts to explore in the field of psychic phenomena (after the Teacher's intervention) yielded nothing. The biggest help, however, was meeting Alyce. Within a week it seemed clear, to me at least, that we were going to get married, and I began to think seriously about how to take care of a family. In short, I had a reason for getting my diploma.

The Bachelor of Physics degree was awarded me in 1942 and I immediately began work for Minneapolis-Honeywell in fire-control instruments, time-and-motion studies, and setting up assembly lines. Eventually I moved into the aeronautical division of Honeywell, learned about autopilots and turbo-regulators, and then, as a technical representative with the Air Force, traveled to Air Force bases in Nevada, Idaho, and finally to an island in the Marianas, Tinian. I said good-bye to Dr. Erwood in 1944 and did not see him again. He died in 1947. But while on Tinian I got a letter from the Teacher, dictated to my dad in Duluth. It contained specific information on the handling of sex energy in marriage, and answered some questions that I had not had a chance to ask.

When World War II ended in 1945, Alyce and I found ourselves and our children in a small mountain community of Southern California. Oddly enough, in view of our interests, Krishnamurti and Aldous Huxley also lived in Wrightwood. We became somewhat acquainted with the Huxley family.

At the time I still felt that through the study of physics it might be possible to make headway in the domain of mind-body energies. I applied to UCLA and was admitted as a graduate student in physics. We had enough cash so that I could go to school for one semester, and then it would be necessary to sell our cabin at Wrightwood in order to continue. I was pleased to note that my slump as a student at the University of Minnesota had ended.

During that tour as a graduate student I began to develop a hypnagogic-imagery technique for the solution of problems in physics and mathematics. After filling the mind with background information, the technique is to instruct the unconscious to get the information wherever it is, and to present it in the form of auditory or visual images. Then one becomes quiet physically, emotionally, and mentally and allows it to happen. In 1962, at the University of Chicago, after receiving my doctorate in biopsychology, I used the imagery technique successfully in solving mathematically the hundred-year-old problem in psychophysics that related the intensity of physical stimulus with the intensity of perception in the sensory systems. The debate had swirled around the question of whether or not the mathematical function relating physical stimulus to psychological perception was a logarithmic law (Fechner) or a power law (Stevens). I was able to demonstrate that both laws were correct if they were treated as special cases of a more general law.

A degree of delayed justice was involved in this. I was opposing Stevens and supporting Fechner, the "father of experimental psychology," who had proposed in 1860 (though I did not know it in 1962) that there was a "world mind" (a field of mind) of which our conscious minds were unaware because our "threshold of awareness" was too high and we were too insensitive. That is, at an unconscious level we are all extensions of "one mind substance," but we cannot know it unless we become conscious of the unconscious. Stevens said Fechner had set psychology back one hundred years because his occult theories had confused scientists. For his part, Fechner said that scientists would not understand what he was talking about for one hundred years.

By 1960 the power-law advocates (following Stevens) had almost silenced the adaptation-law people (following Fechner). When I submitted my mathematical paper to *Psychology Review,* the reviewers (power-law people) said that I was in error: "Stevens has already shown that it could not be true." The editor told me he would therefore not publish the article. I replied to each objection the reviewers had made, showing their basic errors and prejudgments, but the editor refused to consider the matter further and did not submit the issue to a new pair of reviewers who could read all the pros and cons. Temporarily stymied, I asked Gardner Murphy for advice. He said that Harry Helson, the adaptation-theory specialist, could help, and together we went to Manhattan, Kansas, to see Dr. Helson.

Helson's advice was to send the paper for an opinion to physicist Deane Judd in the National Bureau of Standards; he had been editor of the *Journal of the Optical Society of America.* I did this and received the following reply: "Although this paper proved not to be easy reading, we [Dr. Gerald Howett and Dr. Judd] found it well worth studying, and believe it should be published." He said that if I would make a few technical changes suggested by Dr. Howett, and change my symbols to conform to optical-science conventions before submitting it to *JOSA,* "I think that the paper would be accepted." Being then involved in the beginning of our biofeedback research, I did not find time to change the symbols in the long mathematical development, and the paper remains unpublished. A short nonmathematical version was published in *Science,* however, in 1962. (For psychologists and students of optics who may be interested, the general law for describing the visual sensation levels that are associated with various levels of light intensity is described in Appendix II.)

The fact that I was able to find my way to the general mathematical solution through the use of hypnagogic imagery was especially exciting to me when Alyce later began telling of her findings in the study of creativity. What I had done intentionally with imagery was similar to the reports of spontaneous imagery in the creativity literature, but so far as I knew no simple system had been developed for teaching people how to turn on this creative technique. This experience with the Fechner/Stevens law, plus Alyce's creativity study and our brain-wave studies, eventually culminated in our decision to form the theta training project.

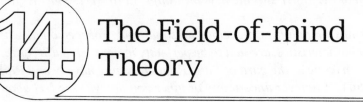

14 The Field-of-mind Theory

The most beautiful thing we can experience is the mysterious. It is the source of all true art and science. He to whom this emotion is a stranger, who can no longer pause to wonder and stand rapt in awe, is as good as dead: his eyes are closed. . . . To know that what is impenetrable to us really exists, manifesting itself as the highest wisdom and the most radiant beauty which our dull faculties can comprehend only in their most primitive forms—this knowledge, this feeling, is at the center of true religiousness. In this sense, and in this sense only, I belong in the ranks of devoutly religious men.

—ALBERT EINSTEIN

The earth and myself are of one mind.

—CHIEF JOSEPH

I mean that if the active mind of a man does communicate with other active minds, even on rare occasions, it could do so only by the transfer of some form of energy from mind to mind directly. Likewise, if the mind of man communicates with the mind of God directly, that also suggests that energy, in some form, passes from spirit to spirit. It is obvious that science can make no statement at present in regard to the question of man's existence after death, although every thoughtful man must ask that question. But, when the nature of the energy that activates the mind is discovered (as I believe it will be), the time may yet come when scientists will be able to make a valid approach to the study of the nature of a spirit other than that of man.

—WILDER PENFIELD

As we pointed out in an article we wrote for the Journal of Transpersonal Psychology, *"On the meaning of transpersonal: Some metaphysical perspectives" (1971), those working toward the development of a science of consciousness find that one of the major difficulties in states-of-consciousness research is that there is no satisfactory vocabulary. It is necessary to use Sanskrit words or to create totally new words, or to use words with which we are already familiar and define them by their usage so that they have specific new meanings. "Transpersonal" is such a word.*

Two kinds or qualities of being, personal and transpersonal, with different characteristics, are said to be perfectly integrated in a "realized being," such a one as the guru of Baba Ram Dass may have been (Ram Dass, 1969). Whatever uncertainty or inner conflict we may feel about the nature of personal and transpersonal roles usually revolves around problems associated with a paradox, "being in the world but not of the world." No wonder, for many teachers have said that such an integrated personal-and-spiritual nature (personal and transpersonal) is the ultimate, or at least penultimate, condition of being (Ghose, 1955; Bailey, 1934; Ramakrishna, 1952).

In Chapter 10 we spoke of Witkin's idea of field-independence/dependence and extended that idea to include not only the external environment (Field 1), but also the internal environment inside the skin (Field 2), and inside the central nervous system, the brain and spinal cord (Field 3). We suggested that in all of these fields it is necessary to develop a measure of independence.

Such independence facilitates a kind of joy. It accompanies self-actualization.

We also pointed out that information can reach us from levels and by communication channels normally called nonsensory. This nonsensory information was called extrasensory by J. B. Rhine (1937). Having talked of those things and outlined the three fields in Figure 5, it is now possible to construct a similar diagram that would include four fields in which it is useful to develop field independence. This diagram, Figure 17 (Green and Green, 1970), can be interpreted to include the basic field-independence features of Figure 5 and, in addition, to suggest in a theoretical or hypothetical sense the existence of additional fields, in each of which we can become aware.

Figure 17 might be called "The Anatomy of a Psyche." The figure was first sketched in 1963 for a psychology course, called Personality Functions, that I taught at the University of Chicago. The purpose in constructing it was to clarify the similarities and differences between the psychological systems of Sigmund Freud and Carl Jung. To wit: Freud limited his concepts to physical, emotional, and mental levels of the diagram: E1, E2, and E3. At one point (with what seems to us great insight) he noted that as far as the human psyche was concerned, he was working only in the "basement." Jung, on the other hand, con-

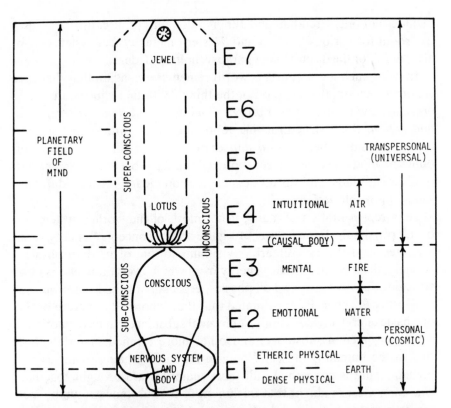

Figure 17. **Symbolic interpretation of human substance and perceptual structure.**
Each line of the vertical cylindrical figure, which represents a human being,
stands for at least three things: a boundary between different organizations of
substance (different kinds of matter), a boundary between different kinds of possible *perception,* and a boundary between different kinds of possible *action.*

cerned himself with all levels of the diagram. In his Psychological Com-
mentary to W. Y. Evans-Wentz's 1957 book *The Tibetan Book of the
Dead* (with which Figure 17 is quite consistent, with its many transpersonal levels of consciousness), Jung wrote: "For years, ever since it
was first published [in 1927], the *Bardo Thödol* [*The Tibetan Book of
the Dead*] has been my constant companion, and to it I owe not only
many stimulating ideas and discoveries, but also many fundamental
insights."

In 1970, the original diagram was elaborated for the section on
Transpersonal Psychology (which we organized) at the annual meeting of the Association for Humanistic Psychology. The diagram now

includes not only Freudian and Jungian domains of discourse, but also has room for various Eastern and Western metaphysical systems. It is also useful for the discussion of parapsychological ideas.

In using such a diagram it is worth remembering again that the map is not the terrain, the name is not the thing. With that caution in mind, one can view Figure 17 as *a proposed model of substance, perception, and action*. Each structural line represents three things: first a conceptual boundary between *substances* organized in different ways or of different kinds, second, a conceptual boundary between *perceptions* of different kinds, and third, a conceptual boundary between different kinds of possible *actions*.

As a representation of many, if not most, of the world's systems of occult physics the basic feature of Figure 17 is a concept of energy (and a related field theory) remarkably similar to that of modern physics. Namely, there is one primary energy from which everything else is constructed. Further, in "psycho"-physics, especially of the kind proposed by Gustav Fechner, it is postulated that the elaborated structure of the one basic energy includes not just physical substance but also emotional substance, mental substance, and other more rarefied materials, and that in the human being (and only in the human being so far as our planetary life is concerned) all these materials are brought together. The early Greeks taught that this union of the substances (symbolized by earth, water, fire, air, and ether) was what made man the microcosm. In him, they said, were found all the materials of the macrocosm, the universe (Hall, 1947).

The individual in Figure 17 is represented by the vertical cylinder that tapers at top and bottom and then is abruptly cut off. This being "cut off" is meant to indicate the existence of an open system, implying that there is more structure if we knew how to diagram it, both above and below. At least, the most respected teachers in all ages and cultures say the system is open. The major *structural* features inside the cylinder of the human psyche are identified as the brain (and nervous system), the Lotus, and the Jewel. The major *perceptual* features are the conscious and the unconscious. The unconscious is comprised of two subdivisions, the subconscious and the superconscious, as shown. The numbers at the right of the psyche represent the traditional seven major energy states, or levels, of conscious awareness in the most advanced realized beings, represented by Buddha and Christ in the East and in the West. Most people, however, are usually aware only of the limited realm inside the balloon-shaped figure labeled Conscious.

The words "personal" and "transpersonal" refer to levels and energies. Roughly speaking, personal includes physical through mental levels, E1–E3, and transpersonal extends from the intuitional level through the entire superconscious range, from E4 through E7. Note that the Conscious covers only a fraction of the area of a psyche in levels E1, E2, and E3, thus implying that usually we are aware only to a limited extent of physical, emotional, and mental events.

Physical events, in level E1, are divided into dense physical and etheric physical in order to account for the pranas of yoga, the psychokinetic energies of parapsychology, the ectoplasm of mediums in the spiritualistic tradition, the "bioplasmas" of Russian researchers, and the hypothesized healing energies of those who heal by touch, by the laying on of hands.

The outline of the brain at the bottom of the drawing represents the brain and nervous system, and is supposedly constructed of *both* dense physical and etheric physical parts. This double composition is an essential feature, since it is the etheric physical (the substance said to be responsible for psychokinetic events) that is supposed to be the transducing agent that allows the pranic organs of perception and action (the seven major chakras of Eastern metaphysical systems) to interact with the neural machine delineated in Western neuroanatomy and neurophysiology.

As mentioned before, until direct existential awareness verifies to us the existence of such energies and structural arrangements as we here outline, their existence can only be inferred from parapsychological data and from the reports of mystics and occultists from various cultures who claim to have experienced or observed these normally unconscious realms of the psyche. Without stopping to justify each line of the diagram, it is useful to itemize some of the general concepts, as follows.

(1) Each of the seven levels is supposed to be a level of substance. The Jewel is thought of as the spiritual essence (or monad) of a psyche and exists as a form of substance. Aurobindo sáys the Jewel is part of the substance of "supermind," and it was this level to which he referred when he said that if one were embarrassed by the word "spirit," then think of spirit as the subtlest form of matter, but if one is not embarrassed by that word then one can think of matter as the densest form

of spirit. Between levels E1 and E7, then, are merely differing grades or densities of matter, or isotopic analogies of matter.

(2) The entire environment outside the psyche, E1 through E7, is called the "planetary field of mind." The planetary field of mind is thought of as the legendary "Being" of esoteric religion in whom we "live and move and have our being."

(3) Like beams of light, the energies of the various levels and their subdivisions can penetrate the same space at the same time. There are no levels in the sense of up and down; there are only kinds of energy, and all kinds are interpenetrated by one another. In the human frame, according to A. T. Barker (1923), all levels are conjoined, and humans are the only creatures who exist in all energy dimensions. Obviously, we do not have exact words for this, nor is this the place to discuss the ramifications of this idea of a spectrum of substances in additional dimensions, but some outstanding references in which both theory and experience are discussed include Bailey (1934), Barker (1923), Blavatsky (1917), Castaneda (1974), Evans-Wentz (1957), Ghose (1951, 1955), Govinda (1960), Hall (1952), Levi (1968), Long (1948), Myers (1954), Ram Dass (1969, 1971), Ramakrishna (1952), Shah (1968), Steiner (1950), Tart (1969), and Teilhard de Chardin (1959). Most of these can be obtained from any bookstore carrying metaphysical works.

The question arises, If these energies exist, why haven't scientists discovered them with their instruments? The answer generally given is very exact, whether right or wrong. The energies of Levels E2 through E7 have not been detected with scientific instruments because these instruments have no parts above the E1 level. Humans have all the parts and can therefore detect a greater spectrum of energies. Instruments are made of minerals, and lack the transducer components needed for detection of E2 through E7 energies. In other words, living beings are coupled to the cosmos better than scientific devices, which are, after all, quite limited tools.

(4) The dense physical is divided into solid, liquid, and gas, as everyone knows, and the etheric physical is said to be of four sorts; household electricity is the densest, and there are three other, more rarefied ethers. None of these is the hypothesized ether of Victorian physics, which was the supposed vibratory medium for light waves (just as air is the vibratory medium for sound waves). On the contrary, these ethers are said to be substances in the same way that electricity and light

are substances. Some psychics and mystics claim that the physical aura they see around the human body is composed of these energies.

(5) The balloon that represents consciousness is tapered in its extension through the brain and spinal cord, implying that a large fraction of the nervous system is unconscious. It is, of course, a basic observation that much of the neural machinery of humans is located in normally unconscious sections of the nervous system.

(6) The E2 and E3 energies (emotional and mental) extend beyond the E1 domain (physical) in accordance with the data from parapsychology. As an aside, it is interesting to note that our food has certain emotional and mental effects, according to this theory, because it has substances in it from many levels in addition to the physical. This is one of the reasons for vegetarianism in many Eastern religions.

(7) The lower part of the cylinder is drawn with heavy lines to indicate that the individual has a tough barrier that blocks direct interaction with the planetary field of mind at personal levels, physical, emotional, and mental.

(8) The conscious is divided from the subconscious by a thin line to indicate that that barrier to awareness is not particularly tough. In some people the barrier is tougher than in others but anyone who can remember a dream or can become aware of hypnagogic imagery has penetrated this barrier. The barrier to the unconscious can be penetrated spontaneously in many places from E1 to E4, so people sometimes unexpectedly and uncontrollably become aware of the contents of their own physiological, emotional, mental, and transpersonal selves. Beginners' trips beyond the barrier are generally into their own normally unconscious levels and not into the planetary field of mind beyond the heavy line in domains E1–E3.

(9) If the tougher barrier (the heavy line) between the personal subconscious and the planetary field of mind is penetrated, there is often an influx of energies that are felt to be representative of the emotions and thoughts of people at a distance, and the person becomes temporarily psychic.

Psychism is conscious awareness of information coming directly into the psyche without passing through the usual sensory neural systems that project into the sensory areas of the brain. How can direct perception occur? Again, right or wrong, a simple answer is given by yogis: *Perception takes place primarily in the etheric physical.* That substance can be agitated by energy from any other level. The coupling of dense physical nerve fibers to etheric physical appears to be relatively strong, while the coupling from other energy levels to etheric physical is progressively weaker from E2 through E7.

(10) These barriers to other levels of consciousness (we may call them energy thresholds) are insisted upon by existentially developed persons of every religion and every major psychological system that we know. Those who have not experienced the puncturing of these barriers, who have not risen above the energy thresholds, generally deny that any field of energy outside their own consciousness can influence them (except through the central nervous system, of course), but this ignorance results from having a limited existential-experiential base. If most people were colorblind, those who could see colors would be hard put to describe what the sensation was like, but the blindness of the majority would not change the experience nor the certainty of it one whit in those who had it.

(11) The conscious balloon is widest at the emotional level, because that seems to describe the average human. That is, the average person is more consciously aware of his own self emotionally than physically or mentally.

(12) Breaking the heavy barrier to consciousness in E2 develops a kind of psychism called instinctual intuition, but according to yogis of all traditions a higher kind of intuition exists at E4. The tunnel experience reported by several of our college students in the theta training program has been experienced by people all over the globe. It has often been interpreted in the West as symbolizing the person's movement through the birth canal into the physical world, but, as represented by the tube at the top of the conscious balloon (where it connects with the Lotus), it symbolizes the tunnel, or canal, leading into the spiritual world. The tunnel experience of any individual will depend on his level of awareness, which may fluctuate in correspondence with the outer-inner aspects of his life. It is presumably here that the Biblical injunction "Ye must be born again" has significance.

(13) In the Orient, the Lotus represents the part of the structure of the psyche that is immortal, while the Jewel is the eternal being. The lotus plant was used as a symbol because it grows in the earth (the physical), rises up through the water (the astral plane, E2 and most of E3) into the air and blooms. In Zen this flower has been called the "True Self"; some Tibetans call it the "Rainbow Body"; Aurobindo calls it the "true psychic being within the heart"; and Ira Progoff (1969,

1970) refers to the "deep level of self" that can be reached by going down the inner well. "Down the well," of course, represents passing through the tunnel to E4 and it means going deep within. The tunnel or well is called in Sanskrit the *antakarana*, or Path. In Christian mysticism this path has been called Jacob's Ladder (see Genesis 28:10–17). In China this path was called the Tao.

To many people who have studied the Chinese Tao, that path was thought to be metaphorical, to mean "the path to follow through life," that is, how to behave as a moral human being. But in the highly developed Tibetan psychophysiological system this morally correct path is a path of substance, a literal structure of substance sometimes called the "causal body" in each person's psyche that connects him as a personal entity with his own transpersonal being.

(14) A region transcending personal boundaries is indicated in the upper half of the diagram, levels E4–E7. These higher levels are not separated with solid lines from the planetary field of mind, but are bounded with dashed lines. The openings are meant to represent a free exchange of energies, E4 to E7, linking each person with Universal rather than Cosmic Nature (which is said to be limited to Levels E1 through E3) and with the transpersonal levels of every other person.

It is said that all humans are brothers and sisters because at transpersonal levels of the unconscious each person is inseparably part of one Being. (Perhaps this is the basic idea in the phrase "Man is made in the image of God.") This possibility may not be recognized if a person has not gone through the tunnel, has not been "reborn in spirit," in the words of Christian mystics. Ira Progoff says that those who go "down the well" become aware of the deeper levels of their being and become aware of and unified with the rest of life. Perhaps these general ideas are what Christ referred to when he said, "I am the Son of God, and ye are my brethren."

The physicist we referred to in another chapter, who went through the tunnel and saw himself standing as an ordinary figure with another brilliantly luminous figure of himself balanced upside down on top of his head, was seeing an image of the personal self with the transpersonal self balanced above it. Through that image he became aware of the transpersonal section of himself that, in a way, was himself, except that it was luminous, was upside down, and radiated so much light that it seemed to be more than he could bear. Again, one is reminded of a Biblical phrase: "As above, so below." And, like a tree reflected in a lake, the image is upside down. To don Juan it is the world of ordinary awareness that is upside down. Interestingly, his concept corresponds to some of the ancient myths in which the tree of life is upside down, with its roots in heaven. Again, a paradox, but by shifting from a personal to a transpersonal frame of reference, all such paradoxes are seen to be resolved as mere artifacts of personal perception. This concept, interestingly enough, was an important part of the "sorcerer's explanation" given by don Juan at the end of Tales of Power.

At this point we trust it is clear that each one of the lines of the structure in the diagram represents a boundary between different kinds of awareness and/or different kinds of substances, and that the "earth, water, fire, and air" of levels E_1 through E_4 identify different substances which correspond to analogous parts of the psyche at different levels.

As already indicated, a significant distinction is made between two major domains, levels E_1–E_3 and levels E_4–E_7. The former domain represents the realm of the personality, the being that originates in the womb and lasts until death, while the latter domain (the structure from the Lotus upwards to the Jewel) represents the realm of the true entity, a being that develops by repeatedly extending itself into personal life to obtain experience. According to The Tibetan Book of the Dead and some other of the world's scriptures, after the death (or shedding) of the physical body a period of time is spent in emotional and mental bodies, until a second "death" takes place and the being passes into transpersonal levels. Eventually, through desire for additional experience (if we can put it that way), it obtains another opportunity to live as a composite structure and is reborn as a personal separate being.

The Lotus is said to be the reflection of the Jewel, and both slowly change as each Lotus goes through thousands of different personal experiences. It is believed in Buddhist lands that eventually Gautama, the Buddha, could remember several hundred of his lives. Be that myth or not, Dr. Ian Stevenson has recently presented persuasive evidence of twenty children who seemed to remember clearly detailed experiences of another life a short time before the present one. He was able to identify and check the accuracy of the experiences or happenings they related (Stevenson, 1966, 1975).

Regardless of myth and research, unless a person has a sense of conviction within himself or herself, the idea of reincarnation is merely an *idea. Nevertheless, from a rational point of view, the idea has some useful characteristics. For one thing, the reincarnation theory makes it possible for people who believe in justice to understand why it may be that some babies are born blind or deformed, while others have healthy bodies. Aurobindo says it well in his discussion of karma and rebirth:*

> *Each being reaps the harvest of his works and deeds. . . . This is the law and chain of Karma . . . it gives a meaning to the total force of our existence, nature, character, action, which is absent from other theories of life . . . a man's past and present Karma must determine his future birth and its happenings and circumstance.*

Yet karma is not the sole arbiter of rebirth and personal evolution, for here too the soul has some choice:

> *It is for experience, for growth of the individual being that the soul enters into rebirth; joy and grief, pain and suffering, fortune and misfortune are parts of that experience, means of that growth; even, the soul may of itself accept or choose poverty, misfortune and suffering as helpful to its growth, stimulants of a rapid development.*

Also, the possibility of changing karma exists:

> *. . . For the principle is not the working out of a mechanism or law, but the development of the nature through cosmic experience so that eventually it may grow out of the ignorance. There must therefore be two elements, Karma as an instrument, but also the secret consciousness and Will within, working through the mind, life and body as the user. When the soul and self emerges, when we become consciously spiritual beings, that change can cancel or wholly remodel the graph of our physical fate.*

Perhaps the most useful feature of the acceptance of the ideas of reincarnation and karma is that a person logically assumes at least partial responsibility for his genetic pattern and social placements. This can be helpful if it leads to development and growth, although in India it led to the suppressive caste system, which shows the absurdity to which an idea can be pushed by logical means, for selfish purposes. The caste system has been outlawed, of course, and caste consciousness is slowly disappearing in India.

Having made the distinction between personal and transpersonal experiences and substance, it is useful to talk for a while about the *extrapersonal*. The "seeing spirits" referred to by mediums, to the extent that such experiences are not projections and images from their own subconscious, are said to be or result from the perception of real but noncorporeal entities, mostly in levels E2 and E3. These two levels combined have been called in many literatures "the astral plane," and it is said to include not just the planetary field of mind of Figure 17, but also a general field of mind that includes all galaxies. This galactic field might be called a cosmic field of mind, in contradistinction to a more limited planetary field (which holds within itself the personal minds that exist within the heavy walls of the individual psyches at levels E2 and E3).

For convenience, we refer to experiences in levels E4–E7 as transpersonal and refer to experiences penetrating the heavy barrier of the psyche in levels E2–E3 as extrapersonal. Extrapersonal, then, refers to psychic nontranspersonal experience. Such experience may be limited to the planetary field for a person, or it may extend to the general cosmic field (using Aurobindo's definition of cosmos as the extent of levels E1–E3 throughout the universe). It is interesting that transpersonal is sometimes linked with the concept of mystical, and extrapersonal is linked with psychic.

Consider some related ideas. Toward the end of the book called *My Story,* Uri Geller (1975) says that the one thing he was sure of about the "beings" who had contacted him from space was that they were not God. He was saying, in other words, that they were cosmic beings of some kind, but not transpersonal. In the book by Andrija Puharich (1974) called *Uri,* it would seem that the "entities" with whom he had much contact were certainly not transpersonal. If anything, they seemed in certain respects to be inferior to humans.

According to Aurobindo, the cosmos (the horizontal extension of E1, E2, and E3) is infinite in extent, and the beings who can be contacted in levels E2 and E3 often do not evolve because they have no "vertical" structure, no extensions into E4 and above. In a diagram such as Figure 17 they exist as horizontal structures at some level at which they are "stuck." Aurobindo and some of the Tibetans maintain that the only kind of psyche that can develop vertically must combine the substances of all levels. Wherever such a form is located, in any galaxy, it must be analogous to the human on planet Earth. regardless of its "shape," its physical configuration.

Most of these ideas are strange to Westerners and are not likely to be experientially tested in the near future, so it might be asked if these general theories can be of any importance. The answer is yes. One reason is that many thousands of people seem to be in the process of developing psychic awareness. Whatever the stimulus or cause, people are becoming aware both of levels of being in themselves and of connections outside themselves of a parapsychological nature which they now must handle. And it is useful to have a theoretical structure in which to fit these experiences. The theory may be modified as experience is gained, but without a theory the bombardment of psychic pressures can seem chaotic, and sometimes intolerable as one seeks to maintain psychological balance and to learn.

While subject to a plethora of psychic bombardments can reality be tested? Can we discriminate between hallucination, "dreaming true" (Muldoon and Carrington, 1958), *seeing* and *dreaming* (Castaneda, 1972), and find any invariant realities in levels E2 and above?

To focus on these questions, consider again the idea of the tunnel, or canal, of "spiritual rebirth." According to yogic theory, the tunnel is an internal structure that develops in each psyche over hundreds of lives, allowing consciousness eventually to expand to include the transpersonal domain as well as the personal. The tunnel leads to the Lotus Being, part of which has been called the "causal body" as long ago as ancient Egypt. By becoming aware of this Lotus Being in ourselves, it is said, we come closer to the answer to the question, Who am I? According to Tibetan Buddhists, the answer is the Jewel, and the foremost Tibetan mantra—*Om mani padme hum*—is sometimes translated as "Hail, O Thou Jewel in the Lotus."

An especially entertaining idea for many Westerners in all of this is the concept of transpersonal substance. If one accepts the concept as a working hypothesis, then the debatable problems of good and evil, right and wrong, morality and immorality, are replaced by operational questions involving the use of energy for the development of transpersonal awareness, transpersonal knowledge. Dogmatic religious concepts are not needed. In the thought of Aurobindo, and in texts of Tibetan Buddhism, these problems exist not as matters of religious dogma but rather as a need for understanding laws of substance. We can think of a need, therefore, for a new psychophysics that includes superphysical energies and states of consciousness.

Accept the hypothesis for a moment and consider how doing so affects the argument in the U.S. about pornography. Those who wish to abolish all restrictions argue that there is no such thing as good or evil, right or wrong. All values are equal, all "moral" and "immoral" ideas are equal, all things are equally good, true, and beautiful. It all depends on your point of view, some say, because there are no absolutes. There is only custom and convention rooted in religious or other dogmas.

From the point of view of substance, however, there *are* some absolutes (some invariant facts) that are capable of experiential verification. Pornography and its effects are focused in levels E_3, E_2, and E_1, and don Juan described such mental and emotional behaviors, and many sentimentalities much milder than pornography, as "indulging." In order to prevent the escape of energies through indulging the "tonal" (roughly, the personal self), it is necessary to turn off oversentimental emotions, said don Juan. According to his teaching, a "warrior" accumulates the "personal power" needed to become aware of the luminous being by living in a nonindulging manner, that is, living without squandering mental, emotional, and physical energy on trivialities. The personal power that is accumulated by austere, nonindulging behavior (as, for example, in cases of East Indian ascetics) is the power that drives consciousness to higher levels, that allows consciousness to overcome specific energy barriers, the thresholds of awareness in Figure 17.

With respect to this power, it is noteworthy that in some of the world's Bibles it is said that the Kingdom of Heaven is taken by force—i.e., with energy. In parallel vein, it is said by most yogis that the kundalini, the basic energy of the etheric-physical level (symbolized by a serpent lying coiled at the base of the spine), must not be allowed to become sidetracked into the second and third chakras, i.e., sex, emotionalism, and sentimentalism. In emotionalism and sentimentalism, which are different from emotion and sentiment, we include selfishness, greed, desire for power, lust, vengeance, and other negative expressions of the second and third chakras, as well as the excessive glamors of doing good, being a success, having pity rather than compassion, etc. Instead, this energy should be channeled into expression in the fourth chakra and above, in the heart, throat, and head. In this theory, the conscious balloon in our diagram is like a rocket in which blastoff can take consciousness to high-level inner space, to the Lotus Being itself, if enough launching energy is accumulated and not wasted in indulging.

Along another vein, the East Indians, the Tibetans, the Chinese, the Japanese have all referred in their esoteric traditions to the essence of a human as a "being of light." It seems no coincidence to us, therefore, that our physicist friend who went through the tunnel saw himself as two beings, one dark and one light (one personal and one transpersonal). In *Tales of Power,* don Juan tells Castaneda that "the double [the luminous being] has inconceivable power" and it is this double "who dreams the self." This could imply that the energy body (the chakras and their interconnections) comprise the true body, which the physical is a reflection of, or it can imply that it is not the personal that creates the transpersonal but the other way around: The transpersonal creates the personal. Because of lack of consciousness (with its consequence, mistaken identity) we usually cannot answer the question, Who am I?, and we fritter away our energy, according to don Juan, through indulging. In this view, correct (moral) behavior is a straightforward matter of energy and conservation of energy according to a karmic balance sheet, rather than a matter of dogmatic moralizing.

Returning to religion, it seems obvious that the founders of the world's major religions were aware of the various energy domains. They talked about them. But how could they transmit a clear, rational understanding of moral behavior to unsophisticated peoples? They could not, of course, and therefore taught with stories and parables that included the idea of the acceptance of transpersonal direction by personal being: "Not my will, but Thine, oh Lord, be done." Nowadays, with our concepts and understanding of fields, energies, and substances, it is not difficult to conceive of the possibility that morals and ethics are not constructs of an anthropomorphic God as much as they are the laws of substance and energy in a universal (transcosmic) field of mind, a transpersonal field of mind.

These ideas have been clearly expressed in the East, and it is entertaining to find a recent and succinct expression of them in the West in the teachings of don Juan. Concerning a situation in which proper behavior was called for, he says to Castaneda, "There is no flaw in the warrior's way [a way of living true]. Follow it and your acts cannot be criticized by anyone. . . . The warrior's way would have been, first, to ask questions without fear and without suspicion . . . or draining yourself . . . [then] assemble what you have learned, without presumptuousness and without piousness. Do that and no one can find flaws in you."

Don Juan's teachings suggest that in order to find out about one's self it is necessary to conserve energy without draining through indulging, and yet without presumptuousness or religiosity.

To us, religiosity and religion are not the same thing. Religiosity means being sentimentally religious, personal rather than transpersonal. We hypothesize that true religion involves awareness of the transpersonal. For those who feel that religion is unnecessary, it is useful to note that according to theory we must conform to certain energy rules in order to develop direct awareness of universal Nature. Nothing could be simpler than that old idea, nor more modern. The moral track that leads to awareness of the "noosphere" of Teilhard de Chardin (1959) and the ethical conformities needed for becoming self-aware in Tibetan Buddhism express the same idea.

The energies of levels E5 through E7 have not been named by us in Figure 17 because no satisfactory words exist in English, unless we use Aurobindo's "overmind," which seems to involve the energies of E4 and E5, and "supermind," roughly E6 and E7. As mentioned before, W. Y. Evans-Wentz was told by his Tibetan teacher that levels E4–E7 are called the Void, because they cannot be explained in verbal language, but can only be experienced. The way to gain such experience was to follow the Path, literally constructing through aspiration and visualization a path of substance at the level of the causal body of Figure 17, thus making conscious contact with the superconscious self.

It is maintained that eventually the personality, the Lotus, and the Jewel, become unified, and the fully integrated person, man or woman, can exist consciously on all levels at the same time. In the Tibetan tradition, if a physical body is retained after full consciousness has been attained, then the perfected human (the Bodhisattva) works in the world to speed the evolution of consciousness in the race. If the physical body is not retained, say various teachers, the perfected "individual," who now has certain universal awarenesses, moves to a series of developmental levels which lie beyond the Jewel.

The completely integrated and realized being develops through the voluntary control of subjective energies. The Lotus and Jewel bodies are present in partially integrated humans all the time, according to Oriental traditions, but we are usually not aware of this until we voluntarily direct our personal energies inward (upward in the diagram).

In esoteric traditions the basic source of energy in humans is through a power center in the "subtle body" (the etheric template of the physical body). As mentioned before, this energy is called kundalini in yogic tradition. In both Integral Yoga and Tibetan Buddhism it is maintained that all energy in every organ is an expression of kundalini. Some writers have equated kundalini with sex energy, but the highest teachers maintain that sex is merely the usual way in which this energy is felt and expressed. If the energy is not used exclusively in personal levels, but also is focused toward awareness at the Lotus level through meditation, there will ensue an activation of specific chakras (etheric organs of the body), which are especially sensitive to superconscious grades of matter.

Perhaps these facts are the reason the world's religions have been much concerned with sex, even though this is not generally understood by religious leaders. The modern tendency to discard ideas of self-regulation, especially self-regulation relating to sex, is likely (in this view) to interfere with transpersonal self-actualization. For anyone who wants to experiment with energies, a two- or three-month effort to direct kundalini to the Lotus level and away from sex is usually educational. Awareness, it is said, goes where this energy is directed, but as the energy (the personal power) builds up, it becomes more and more difficult to control, and large sudden changes in consciousness often ensue, both subconscious in the Freudian sense and superconscious in the Jungian sense. More will be said about this subject in the next chapter, but a book could be written on "the psychophysiology of creativity" and "the psychophysiology of morals."

Mind Training, Hypnosis, and the Development of Psychic Powers

On the one path, he becomes proficient in black magic, which is only the developed powers of the personality, subordinated to the selfish purposes of a man whose motives are those of self interest and worldly ambition. . . . On the other path [of white magic] he subordinates his personality . . . working always in the light of the soul with the soul in all forms, and laying no emphasis upon the ambitions of the personal self. Clear discrimination of these two paths reveal what is called in some occult books that "narrow razor-edged Path" which lies between the two.

—THE TIBETAN

In the search for control over normally unconscious psychological and physiological processes, many people have turned to so-called mind-training programs of various sorts. These programs are related to the self-regulation training programs described in earlier chapters of this book, but they differ in certain important respects. In this chapter we would like to make clear these distinctions, and also to point out the hazards inherent in some of the current popular programs offering the development of psychic powers.

Almost all of the popular commercial mind-training programs use a heavy dose of hypnotic programming. It may not be called hypnosis, and in fact it may be vehemently denied by instructors, but nevertheless many of the courses use hypnotic techniques that are "right out of the book." We have not personally taken one of these courses in order to experience it, but the Attorney General of the State of Kansas sent us an instructors' manual from one of these four-day courses and asked for our evaluation. The hypnotic nature of the procedures was obvious. As an example, twelve times in the four-day course the instructor programmed his trainees with the following statements before bringing them out of a state of suggestion achieved by hypnotic countdown:

"You will continue to listen to my voice. You will continue to follow instructions at all levels of mind, including the outer conscious level. This is for your benefit, you desire it—and this is so." Correspondents from other states have told us that instructors in commercial mind-training courses claim that no one who goes through their course comes out the same. That is not to be wondered at. After a few days of programming during which the trainee is in a suggestive state much of the time, it is almost certain that behavioral and perceptual changes will occur. The changes may not last in every case, but for a period of time "graduates" do not seem the same to themselves and often seem different to friends.

Alyce and I wrote an article criticizing the commercial mind-training programs for lack of responsibility to their customers (Green and Green, 1973a). Immediately we began receiving two kinds of letters, one strongly disagreeing with us and the other strongly agreeing. One woman said that she had suffered from psychosomatic diseases for more than twenty years, had been treated by internists and a psychiatrist, had spent about twenty-five thousand dollars with no positive result, and finally had achieved freedom from those diseases within three weeks as a result of taking a two-hundred-dollar mind-training course. In addition, her husband had been "cured" of an ailment that had bothered him for many years. How dare we criticize something so valuable!

On the other hand, a woman wrote that after her husband had taken the course one of his "imaginary psychic advisers" unexpectedly began speaking to him without being asked. The adviser explained that he (the adviser) was God and that for spiritual reasons the wife also must take the course. When she refused to do this, "God" told him to get a divorce. She and her teenage sons were unable to influence her husband. He also developed some other peculiarities. In desperation she wrote for advice.

The article referred to above is especially germane to "independence in the field of mind," so we excerpt its essential features here before turning to the topic of medical hypnosis.

1. Through hypnosis and through various training programs, including biofeedback, many persons can become aware of normally unconscious processes.

2. Awareness of normally unconscious processes is sometimes accompanied by spontaneous (and sometimes volitional) ESP phenomena.

---

3. Commercial mind-training courses promising ESP powers are using hypnosis as the major method and, advertising to the contrary, subjects are not necessarily in an alpha brain-wave state.

4. Commercial mind-training "teachers" generally deny that they use hypnosis, and by denying or ignoring the risks associated with hypnotic programming are inducing in some persons a form of paranoid neurosis or psychosis, often related to obsession or possession.

5. Hypnotic programming for ESP bears a similarity to some of the methods used for development of trance mediumship, especially the "possession by spirits" of low-grade mediumship.

6. Awareness of normally unconscious processes can be safely taught under the guidance of a counselor, without hypnotic programming, by methods which allow each person to develop according to his own inner needs.

7. Mind-training procedures should be voluntarily modified by those interested in the subject to eliminate psychic hazards. If this is not done, government agencies may summarily ban many research and training programs that otherwise, if carefully developed, might become valuable adjuncts to our education and health systems.

8. The major problems are (a) to determine what techniques are safe as well as efficient for the extension of awareness, (b) to establish standards of qualification and responsibility of teachers, and (c) to offer the benefits of awareness training programs to the public through non-profit institutions.

Many psychologists in the last few years have become interested in research possibilities that a few years back were considered beyond the realm of science, namely, voluntary control of normally unconscious psychological and physiological processes. The first medical approaches to this subject in the West, starting in about 1910, sprang from the researches and developments of Autogenic Training and Psychosynthesis, beginning with Johannes Schultz in Germany (1959) and Roberto Assagioli in Italy (1965), respectively. At about the same time, Edmund Jacobson was beginning to develop in the United States his training program which came to be known as Progressive Relaxation (1938). In other parts of the world, new interpretations of yoga were developing, such as the Integral Yoga of Aurobindo. His *Synthesis of Yoga,* for instance, is concerned with a program for enhancement of consciousness and for control ["transformation"] of normally unconscious processes (1955). The newest development along this line of self-regulation of mind and body, perhaps the most applicable to Westerners in general, has resulted from research in the area of biofeedback training.

The programs mentioned above deal with one's power to modify and control, through volition, one's own mental, emotional, and physiological states, without hypnotic programming by another person, and in all of these developments (except perhaps Progressive Relaxation, which deals primarily with problems of muscle tension) parapsychological events sometimes occur. These events are not, however, the goals of training. The primary goal is self-mastery, and in Psychosynthesis and Integral Yoga the primary goal is self-mastery coupled with the development of awareness of what, in Zen, is called the True Self. Unless this aspect of Self is developed, it is said, psychic powers become an "ego trip." The attainment of psychic powers may follow safely *after* a degree of self-mastery (ego mastery) is achieved, but if paranormal development comes first, psychological problems develop. Aurobindo's way of saying this focuses attention on what he calls the Overmind level of one's being. After achieving awareness of that, he says, one can explore in "astral" dimensions with a measure of safety. Otherwise, it is possible to become involved in psychic (psychological) entanglements and not be able to find one's way, through layers of mental and emotional confusion, back to one's center. The ancient Christian advice concerning these matters was to seek first the Kingdom of Heaven, which was within, it was said, and other things would follow in due course.

These considerations seem to have an especially important meaning today because we are bombarded by newspaper advertisements of entrepreneurs who (for a fee) will develop psychic powers in us, through hypnosis. It is denied that hypnosis is the technique employed, because "hypnosis" is a "bad word." Instead it is called "conditioning," "programming," "brain-wave training," "alpha training," etc., but nevertheless, it *is* hypnosis. On this professionals agree, though they do not always agree on how hypnosis works (Hilgard, 1965; Gill and Brenman, 1959). The "countdown" induction procedure used in commercial mind-training "programming" is a classical hypnotic technique.

Hypnosis is an extremely powerful tool for control of physiological and psychological states. It is well known that through hypnosis painless surgery can be performed, people can be made to see things that are not there, and not see things that are there, but it is not generally realized, even by professionals, that through hypnosis parapsychological sensitivity can be enhanced. Frederick Myers, in 1901, clearly summarized the major findings of hypnosis experimentation in the last century and showed that hypnosis and parapsychology are not necessarily two separate subjects (Myers, 1954). More recently, Beloff, in an analysis of the paranormal, ventures the opinion that "hypnotism may not be just a psychological phenomenon but may have a certain paranormal component as well." The points being made here are that hypnosis *can* involve the paranormal, and the paranormal is being invoked by hypnosis in some of those who take commercial mind-training courses, opinions of noninvestigators notwithstanding.

The question might now be raised, So what? What difference does it make? This question can be answered in at least three ways, depending on whether one looks at commercial mind training (1) from a traditional *psychological* point of view, that is, treat the various phenomena that result from the program as figments of the imagination; (2) from a *psychosomatic* point of view, in which the power of mind over events inside the skin is accepted, but parapsychological events are considered to be figments of the imagination; or (3) from a *parapsychological* point of view, in which the phenomena of hypnosis are seen as consistent with research data from various psychological, psychosomatic, and parapsychological studies.

But before these points of view can be considered it is necessary to identify some of the phenomena that are claimed by commercial mind training teachers and by many of their students, namely:

(a) A person can "go down" into his own "unconscious" and while in that deep "level" can program his own physiological and psychological processes so that various diseases in him that have not yielded to standard medical treatment can be brought under control.

(b) While at his deep "level," a person can become aware of physical, emotional, and mental states and diseases in other people and can correctly diagnose ailments.

(c) While at his "level," a person can learn to manipulate the physical, emotional, and mental natures of other persons, sick or healthy, and thereby modify their behavior.

(d) While at his "level," a person can learn to manipulate nature so that coincidences, "accidents," or lack of accidents, can come under his control. This is, essentially, a promise of psychokinetic powers.

Now from a traditional *psychological* point of view, the above ideas are sheer nonsense, some would say "sheer madness." From that point of view, the tens of thousands who have taken mind-training courses and are convinced of the reality of some or all of the above claims have been programmed into a serious delusional system and can be expected sooner or later, if rationality is not reestablished, to develop, in consequence, some degree of neurosis or psychosis.

From a *psychosomatic* point of view it might be acceptable to hypothesize that one could learn to manipulate certain normally unconscious psychological processes whose physiological correlates are thereby brought under control; that is, item (a) above might be accepted, but items (b) through (d) would be considered to be belief in sheer nonsense, which, if persisted in, would probably lead to mental or physical breakdown.

From the *parapsychological* point of view, none of the items listed above is at variance with data accumulated in the last fifty years indicating that such events are possible, or at least worthy of hypothesis testing, even though not statistically probable.

From the parapsychological viewpoint, the main questions that must be raised about commercial mind-training programs are, judged by professionals rather than entrepreneurs, (1) what is actually happening to students in regard to psychological, psychosomatic, and parapsychological events and accomplishments, (2) what are the dangers of hypnotic programming for the purpose of enhancing psychic development, (3) what is the level of responsibility of program organizers and associated teachers, (4) what mind-training techniques are safe as well as efficient in bringing a person to a level of psychic development that is not inappropriate for him, (5) what is the most responsible way of presenting mind training and its various benefits to the public, and (5) how is the mind-training movement to be regulated in the interest of public welfare. Concerning these questions, the following comments might be made.

Hypnotic programming as used in the commercial courses has several defects, namely: (a) Many people are psychically catapulted, so to speak, into existential realms in which they cannot protect themselves from dangers arising either from within their own unconscious, or from psychic manipulation by other persons, or from "extrapersonal" sources (dangers inherent in so-called astral dimensions). There is not time here to review the history of spiritualism since 1849 and the psychic disasters that often resulted from dabbling in the area of trance medium-ship, but mental hospitals, even today, contain many people who "hear voices." These people usually cannot turn the voices off, cannot separate fact from fiction, have lost their reality-testing powers, and often are obliged to act out, against their will, instructions they are "given." (b) Commercial mind-training students are often "programmed" in ways not appropriate to their own needs, nor at their own proper rates. What is proper for one can be disastrous for another. This hazard arises because, apart from the dangers of hypnotic penetration into astral levels of being, (c) many mind-training teachers are incompetent to work with people in matters where psychological and physical health are at stake. For example, former salesmen who have had a few courses in hypnotic programming are not qualified to work in this very delicate area of the human psyche, with its psychosomatic correlates. (d) And, most seriously, psychic submission may be enhanced in astral dimensions, rather than powers of self-volition. This is the consensus of Eastern teachers who, it must be conceded, reflect much experimentation and experience over the centuries with training methods for self-mastery. It is admitted that psychosomatic *self*-regulation achieved by any volitional method is slow compared to submitting oneself to hypnotic instruction, turning the control of one's mind over to another person, but it is also maintained by the most accomplished teachers that the power of psychic self-determination is the sine qua non for safety in astral dimensions.

Concerning safety in astral dimensions, possibly the greatest specific danger associated with hypnotic submission in commercial mind-training programs lies in the developing, or obtaining, of psychic "advisers." They are the male and female assistants who "know everything," who at the deep "level" of mind advise the student, and sometimes tell him what to do. Students of the mind-training programs might consider being on guard against the possibility of mediumistic "possession" through the agency of the advisers.

Another point: Mind-training teachers often maintain that no harm can be done to another person by themselves or by their students because they are programmed with the idea that if these "powers" are used for ignoble or selfish purposes they will be lost, but this is likely to be nonsense. Posthypnotic suggestions are notorious for their impermanence, so if real psychic "powers" are developed in students it can be assumed that hypnotically imposed restrictions on the use of such powers will not be long-lasting.

The examples given above indicate that whether one chooses to examine commercial mind-training methods from either the traditional psychological point of view or from the parapsychological point of view, there is risk involved for students. We do not presume to be able to answer all the questions raised, but when over one hundred thousand persons have already been processed through such mind-training programs (including two thousand high-school girls at a school in Philadelphia in October 1972), some questions should be asked. In view of the hazards associated with hypnotic programming in commercial mind-training courses, the present writers believe that hypnosis as a technique for inducing self-awareness and parapsychological faculties is not adequately safe and should be discarded.

Does this mean that there is no use for hypnosis? Not at all, no more than that there is no use for surgery. But even as surgery has particular use in *acute* situations, where something must be done or else unbearable pain, or permanent damage, or death may occur, so also with hypnosis. For *chronic* situations, however, those which are characteristic of most psychosomatic diseases, nonhypnotic volitional training programs such as those employing biofeedback are more desirable. For exploring in psychic domains, new and safe training methods are being developed by Dialogue House and Psychosynthesis, for example, and through research in brain-wave training. Other safe methods also exist, as is well known, such as various forms of yogic meditation. In all of these methods, both old and new, accent is placed on learning to handle psychological and physiological problems through voluntary control and at a rate consistent with one's capacity for self-protection.

Spiritual teachers concerned with the development of inner awareness have always excluded hypnosis as a technique, both in the East and in the West, not because it was not understood, but because it *was* understood. Self-development and programming by another were considered antithetical. There is no logical reason to assume that things are now different, merely because we are in the twentieth century and people are in a hurry, wish to have immediate results, and perhaps even hope to get something without effort. Hypnotic programming (like LSD) has convinced many people that an inner terrain exists, and in this way it has been instrumental in drawing attention to an important dimension of human life, but it is also important that we now look at the entire area of "inner exploration" and, in as balanced a way as possible, evaluate the many programs that are being offered for penetration into hitherto arcane dimensions of the psyche. Commercialism should not enter into such a vitally important matter. Commercialism often results in (a) false and misleading use of such scientific terms as "alpha and theta brain-wave training," and distortion of what is actually accomplished by such training, (b) exaggerated claims for "powers" that can be obtained by anyone who pays the price and takes the course, (c) stressing of powers not appropriate to certain persons, such as the ability to diagnose and treat diseases, (d) undue emphasis on large enrollment in courses in order to earn more money, rather than to be of service. Large enrollment interferes with one-to-one contact between teachers and students, so that whatever problems arise are unlikely to be properly handled even if the teacher had the necessary skill.

In short, commercialism in the mind-training field does not lead in the direction of high responsibility and service, and this raises the very important question about the manner in which regulation can best be established in the mind-training movement. We are of the opinion that if responsible control is not established quite soon by those already involved, government agencies will step in and provide regulation in the interest of public welfare.

In our estimation, a list of positive guidelines to follow in establishing an ideal training method might include the following items:

(1) Make it possible for each person to discover "himself" at a proper rate, that is, penetrate into the unconscious at a rate consistent with his ability to keep his feet on the ground, keep his reality-testing powers intact. This means that those for whom psychic unfoldment would lead to destructive neuroses or psychoses should achieve only those insights and awarenesses which, in the usual therapeutic sense, would help integrate and bring under control various discordant sections of the personality.

(2) The student should be shielded by the training method from imperfections of the teacher that might otherwise become part of the student's "psychic atmosphere" and hinder his progress.

(3) Teachers should be ranked or evaluated according to their level of insight and awareness so that as each student progresses existentially he has a properly qualified *human* adviser with whom to talk.

(4) The student should be passed on from teacher to teacher, so to

speak, as rapidly as his experiences require more advanced advice or suggestion (not programming).

(5) Training centers for self-awareness should be located within access of anyone interested in participating in the program and should be established on a *nonprofit* basis.

Not everyone will agree with the many points of caution stressed above, thinking them excessively conservative perhaps. But consider what one psychiatrist recently told me. In a group of thirty persons who took a popular mind-training course in which he participated, four trainees became psychotic. Two of them ended up in hospitals. He felt that possibly the difficulty was caused by a psychologically disturbed instructor, who, he said, had a very bad effect on the group. That was an especially interesting observation because some yogis say that a kind of "psychic pollution" can result from projection to another person of emotional and mental substance. Another psychotherapist who works with encounter groups put it in a succinct way. He said that if a leader is unbalanced, then "madness is contagious."

Although this doctor was not thinking of direct transference of psychic energy, Jack Schwarz has mentioned that in his experience with psychic phenomena, problems in the unconscious of the trainer can be transmitted to the client, especially during hypnosis. This is the reverse of the case in which the unconscious problems of the patient can be absorbed by the psychiatrist, to the latter's detriment. If we accept the idea of extrasensory perception and extrasensory projection (including psychokinesis), then we must accept the idea of psychic contamination by "schizophrenic teachers" (rather like "typhoid Marys") in levels E2 and E3 of the field-of-mind diagram. From this point of view, the Freudian concepts of transference and counter-transference involve transfers of psychic substance back and forth between patient and therapist.

The psychiatrist mentioned above who took the commercial mind-training course also pointed out that people who are on the verge of psychosis, and who do not have enough money to visit a clinical psychologist or a psychiatrist, often seek help wherever they can get it, and they are attracted to programs that offer quick surcease from, or victory over, their problems. In other words, he was saying that the training program may not have caused the psychoses, but only revealed them. If this is a possibility (which we accept), then it is clear that a few weeks of training in hypnotic programming, after experience limited mainly to selling shoes, real estate, or automobiles, which is the background of many mind-training instructors, is not adequate for handling such responsibility. Ministers, physicians, psychologists, psychiatrists, and others in the helping professions may be able to handle the responsibility, but even they, when they plunge into the extrasensory domain, often are not properly prepared.

One idea that is promulgated in a number of commercial mind-training courses is so-called psychic control of another person. This may seem like a sheer impossibility to some, but to one acquainted with the phenomena of ESP and psychokinesis it is not implausible. Frederick Myers reviewed the results of experimentation with hypnosis in the last century and reported studies by physicians in which hypnosis at a distance was apparently demonstrated (1954). More recently, reports of Russian experiments with hypnosis (Ostrander and Schroeder, 1970) have mentioned similar findings. Mind-training instructors often claim that if you wish to influence a person to take a certain course of action with which he does not agree, you can influence him psychically by going down to your deep state, your "alpha level" (erroneously identified with alpha brain waves), and modify the other person's unconscious, planting therein the ideas you want him to carry out. Many yogis and psychics, in addition to people who have taken mind-training courses, say that they have learned to do such things. To the extent that it is possible, it is quite unethical, and it certainly is an attempted invasion of privacy. Even the common boast of mind-training graduates that they can "demonstrate a parking place" has a tinge of the unethical about it. But are these promises of "powers" nonsense? If they are nonsense, some of the true believers are going to need psychotherapy as a consequence of exposure to the training. If it is not nonsense, they may have power-trip and ego-aggrandizement problems to solve.

When people ask for advice about taking commercial mind-training courses, we answer that we cannot decide for them. I, for instance, learned a great deal from Professor Lally. The experience was enlightening. Even though there were risks which I did not then recognize, I do not regret the experience. It seems to us that the main problem is to preserve one's own integrity, one's own ethics, one's own sense of values, and to reject the conventional nonsense that if you succeed in developing a psychic power of some kind in a mind-training course you will be able to use it only for the good. According to Eastern tradition, the attainment of psychic powers (*siddhis*) was for centuries (and largely remains) a closely guarded secret because such powers, like money, can be used in whatever way one desires.

Hypnosis used in a *medical* context, however, can be a valuable tool in the hands of a skilled therapist, especially in helping the body recover from physical injury. (It has not proven equally useful, though, with psychological problems.) One surgeon who attended a biofeedback workshop and seminar told us that for a period of time he consistently used post-surgical hypnosis to accelerate the healing process. A standard hypnotic induction was not necessary, he said, because he visited the intensive-care ward at about the time patients would begin to recover from anesthesia. After testing reflexes to make certain that the patient was coming to consciousness, he would begin talking in a very low voice, telling the patient how well the operation had gone, how nicely the body had responded, how well the repairs were made. He planted the idea that there would be little pain, and possibly none at all; the tissues would recover very quickly; there would be no infection; the patient would be walking in a very short time. Nurses in intensive care soon noticed that his patients recovered more rapidly than others and asked him to work with other patients too. He did this to some extent, he said, and recoveries from surgery were generally rapid.

In the last century, in the days before anesthetics, Esdaile reported very much the same findings. He reportedly performed three thousand major surgical operations in India, using only hypnosis for pain and bleeding control. His infection rates were lower and his recovery rates faster than those later associated with anesthetics, and to us the reason seems obvious. In hypnosis the body-programming power of mind is mobilized rather than ignored. When the body is in a trancelike state, either through general anesthesia or through hypnotic induction, it will often accept a healing *suggestion*. In cases in which surgery is performed without getting the willing consent of the patient, however, as is often the case with children, who are sometimes taken to the operating room in great fear (a powerful negative influence), it is not surprising that difficult post-surgery problems might crop up. In fact, a few cases have been reported in which post-operative healing problems were traced to accidental negative suggestions made by surgical personnel. Under hypnotic regression to the time of surgery, patients remembered comments made in the operating room while the conscious was "asleep" but the unconscious was "listening." For instance, one patient in intensive care, who was hypnotically regressed to the time of surgery in order to determine the cause of her lack of healing, remembered someone saying, "If this one ever leaves here, it will be feet first."

The physician referred to above said that news of the procedure he was using with the intensive-care cases soon reached the ears of other doctors and finally came to the attention of the medical director of the hospital, who became angry and forbade his using such procedures in the future. The director's argument was that since the patient had not given permission for such a procedure in advance, it was unethical. One would think that there would be little trouble in getting such permission in advance, but the opportunity to do that was denied the doctor, and that potent technique for accelerating healing was discontinued in that hospital.

In modern practice, hypnotic suggestion is used in a very "permissive" way compared to the old notion of an authoritative doctor ordering the hypnotized patient to do things. Modern hypnotherapists are aware of the fact that unless the unconscious of the patient agrees, results will be unpredictable. It was this unpredictability that led Freud and other researchers to abandon hypnosis as a useful medical tool but, fortunately, it led Johannes Schultz, the founder of Autogenic Training, to think. He concluded that if the power to regulate the unconscious were turned over to the patient, some of the undesirable effects of authoritarian hypnotic procedures could be avoided.

It must be clear by now that we feel there are some specific dangers in the areas of psychic development. The major recommendation of teachers in whom we have confidence seems to be to develop a universal awareness (levels E4 and above on the field-of-mind diagram). Don Juan summarized it neatly when he told Castaneda that in the separate reality there were an infinite number of paths, but only those that "have heart" are of any value. In Tibetan Buddhism and in Indian yoga, "having heart" refers to the development of the fourth chakra, the heart chakra. The development of the fourth chakra is referred to by Aurobindo as the development of "the true psychic being within the heart." Jesus commented on it, "As a man thinketh in his heart, so is he." In esoteric Christian terminology, this development of the fourth chakra, the symbolic radiant heart on the robe of Jesus, represents an at-one-ment of the personal self with its own Christ nature, the Lotus self, that center of each person which leads to transpersonal and universal awareness.

Again, most interesting in the development of universal awareness is the concept of sacrifice, an idea that is anathema to many philosophers because it appears to militate against self-interest. But the idea of sacrifice consists mainly in the acceptance by the isolated personality of transpersonal goals and alignment with transpersonal Nature, rather than fighting for the self-centered personality itself. Those who work in the Peace Corps, or VISTA, or in many of the national and international organizations around the world in which human welfare is a genuine goal, often have foregone personal comfort for something that is to them more fascinating and productive. There is reward in working for transpersonal goals, and the individual and society both benefit. Nonindulging obviously involves the sacrifice of one thing for another. Even such a worthwhile accomplishment as "right human relations" usually involves sacrifice of the path of least resistance, which means sacrifice of indulging.

The Teacher Alyce and I previously spoke of provided a few simple rules which he said tended to insure right human relations and guard against delusion and undesirable psychic involvements. The first focuses on right attitude. "Regardless of the attitudes of other people toward you, your attitude toward them must be right." The point of this is not just to be kind to other people and have them like us, though that is pleasant. The important issue is to become akarmic. This rule prevents a person from being trapped in automatic cycles of cause and effect; that is, it frees one from karma. We must consciously act rather than react. It is reaction that blocks us from being free agents. If we react rather than act, we are not really choosing.

The second of the Teacher's rules concerns compassionate nonattachment. In visualizing a specific goal or desired event, inside or outside the skin, the creation of the image is followed by the positive statement "May that which is best for me [or the other person, or group] and all mankind come about." This decoupling keeps us from becoming engrossed in our ego involvements, and allows unconscious transpersonal sections of ourselves to influence events. Paradoxically, we can work intensely for a specific goal and at the same time be detached.

What this means is that we can learn to work without needing positive and negative rewards and reinforcements to keep us going and in a good mood.

Sometimes the application of this rule of compassionate nonattachment has unexpected consequences. It has been reported by some of the best-known spiritual healers that sometimes when they work for a sick person whose condition has been stationary for a long time, the person suddenly dies. These healers almost always use a nonattached approach to their energy transfer. Yogananda reported an interesting case of this in his autobiography. He had been involved with a sick deer that he was trying to heal with infusion of psychic energy. Then he had a dream in which the deer came to him and said that he was interfering with its death. To Yogananda, this dream was an important learning experience. He realized that it was presumptuous of him to decide that the deer *must* be saved. He had formed an emotional attachment to the animal and temporarily had forgotten the yogic tradition of working selflessly without demanding the fruits of work as a fee.

A third rule of the Teacher involves right consciousness, paraphrased as follows: "Do not wrestle in darkness but flood every situation with light." This is a visualization of a beam of white light coming down from the stars like a searchlight. If a so-called negative condition exists internally in one's own nature, then this beam of light, which is thought of as coming from the Jewel through the Lotus into the personal self, accelerates change. It tends to incinerate undesirable emotional and mental habits.

What Next?

The Nobel prize winners in physics and chemistry for 1972 were asked what the awards in their fields would be given for in the year 2000. They both simultaneously answered "For the study of man's consciousness. This is the new frontier."

—Institute of Noetic Sciences

The dawn of brilliant epochs is shadowed by massive obscurantism . . . rooted in human nature . . . the refusal to speculate freely on the limitations of traditional methods. . . .

The rejection of any source of evidence is always treason to that ultimate rationalism which urges forward science and philosophy alike.

—ALFRED NORTH WHITEHEAD

We are at the beginning of a dramatic cultural change, but whether it will come with a traumatic dissolution of old concepts or through a more gentle evolution of the new cannot yet be determined. Of the many factors that are playing a part, two forces at work in our society are prominent, both stimulated by technology and the priority we have given science in all aspects of our existence.

One force is dissatisfaction with our social life, politics, economics and ecology, education, medicine, psychology, religion, and with science itself.

The other force is renewed belief in humanity: belief that humans are capable of building toward a unified and caring society, in which each person has an opportunity to become an integrated physical, emotional, mental, and spiritual being, to release the potential for expanded awareness, choice, and change. Many are refusing to accept any longer the image of humans as body only, with all other qualities explainable as "nothing but" epiphenomena of the physical.

A return to humanistic and spiritual values, concepts with which this country began, will result from a conscious awakening of society as a whole. Since change does not usually happen in "society as a whole" unless forced by dictatorial means, it becomes the responsibility of each individual who senses the new image of man/woman to be a catalyst in awakening others to that image.

The present problems of economics and ecology, so closely bound together that they cannot be considered separately, are results of the success of the technology that flowed from science—a success so fabulous that, observing it, we stood in awe. Believing that science would eradicate the traditional enemies of humanity—poverty, hunger, disease, and war—we gave it full reign. And science's technology did great things; never have so many had so much. This is true in spite of the fact that many have had little and the gap between rich and poor grows wider. But the creators of our technology have tended to erode the image of man. They thought with intellect, not with "heart," and followed such slogans as "Anything that can be done should be done" and "Values have no place in science." Technicians in science, government, and industry strove to master rather than serve man and the planet. We forgot that power without wisdom destroys, that "man does not live by bread alone"—no matter how fancy the bread.

Revolt against our "economics" shows up in myriad ways, involved, we believe, with the conscious or unconscious search for something to satisfy the hunger of that part of the human not sustained by bread alone. Many young people have chosen the way of "dropping out," quitting school or jobs, rejecting the "moral principles" they have been taught.

Others not so young, have dropped out in other ways, leaving their universities or work in the city to move "back to nature," withdrawing their contribution to a materialism they no longer believe in. Such withdrawal from the materialistic system may be a first movement toward a more "frugal society," to use Willis Harman's term (1975), toward the "small is beautiful" philosophy of E. F. Schumacher (1973). The great mass of people "stay put," of course, in their schools, jobs, and professions. But this does not mean that they are not questioning the conventional values of Western society and changing the "inner aspects" of their lives.

Dissatisfaction is a force that pushes for change, and we have seen some of its results in the investigations and examinations going on in our political system, in the questioning of the concept of "more and bigger" by many members of our society, and in the daily demands for more sound economic-ecological practices. But the energy of hope— rekindled by all that illuminates the possibilities of self-knowledge and self-direction—is a more promising force.

There is promise of a fundamental humanistic change in education, from elementary school through the university, to include training in self-awareness and self-regulation. In confluent education, heart and mind, emotions and intellect, are combined to enrich both. If biofeed- back training is added, and students are in touch with their physiologi- cal nature, it gives an opportunity for integration of the personality: emotions, mind and body. If the transpersonal (spiritual) aspects are added, integration of the whole person may ensue.

Another promising sign is the increasing numbers of people attracted to and finding renewal in movements such as Psychosynthesis and Dia- logue House. These developments can be thought of as a kind of trans- personal education also, not neglecting body and emotions but striving to bring them into a new harmony with the transpersonal aspects of one's nature, seeking to add discipline, discrimination, and balance to the expansion of experience.

Holistic medicine is developing rapidly (Miller et al., 1975), and as patients and doctors increasingly become partners in establish- ing and maintaining health, the responsibility for success will be shoul- dered more and more by the individual, and the impossible burden of total responsibility for mass public health will be removed from the medical system. In this there is promise of more freedom for every medical professional, for more joy in their work and for more health, freedom, and joy at less cost for their patients.

Studies of the various aspects and levels of consciousness, if carried out (Tart, 1975; Ornstein, 1972), will give us enlightenment about ourselves and each other. And as the meaning of the new physics and the new psychophysics permeates us (Capra, 1975), we, as a society, will have a more caring and joyful attitude toward the Nature that sur- rounds us.

Permeating the major movements noted above is an undercurrent of change in consciousness that bears on the question, Who am I? This question has new connotations when we begin to consider that mind and nature are not truly separate, even as mind and body are not separ- ate. Even though the question has a new context, it remains unanswer-

---

able in words. Words are only symbols. They are part of the map and not part of the terrain, even though such maps are useful.

In a way, every branch of science is a specialized map, and a science of consciousness is an attempt at the ultimate map. It inquires into the mind of the map maker. And when we add to science a new psychophysics, as part of a science of mind, a science of consciousness, we add a new factor into physics, namely the intercoupling effects of mind and matter. This psychophysics will constitute, literally, a new dimension in science. It will be at least as map-shaking as the change from Ptolemy to Copernicus, or from Newton to Einstein (Harman, 1969).

In one sense this is not new, only regenerated. Fechner's basic view of nature and mind as it first appeared in 1860 was essentially the same view we have outlined above (Fechner, 1966). He realized that *mind* would have to take its place as a force in nature, both inside and outside the skin. He was certainly correct in saying it would be a hundred years before scientists began to understand what he was trying to say. And we can add that it might be another hundred years before satisfactory equations are developed to describe the coupling functions between physical matter and mind-directed force.

Considering the acceleration of interest in states of consciousness, it is possible that the general theory of the interlocking machinery of personality, body-emotions-thought, will be quite clearly formulated by the next century, and then the question, Who am I?, will more definitely shift, at least in the minds of educated people, to the transpersonal self, to the levels of experience in the so-called Void, about which "naught can be said."

That is probably far in the future, however, and in the meantime we have a very practical problem to handle: What to do about the psychic breakthrough that is sweeping the planet? Somewhere in the developing science of consciousness it will be necessary to pin down the sources of psychic phenomena and to determine our human place in the cosmos, in the cosmic extensions of body, emotions, and mind that are symbolized by Levels 1–3 of the field-of-mind diagram, Figure 17.

Eastern and Western "magicians" can help in this task. Generally not straitjacketed by intellectualized theories, they can function as cosmic eyes and ears, as sensitive instruments for examining the cosmos. We must neither believe nor disbelieve what they tell us, but merely plug the information, however strange, into our computers to make a Venn-like probability analysis (ascribing probabilities to points in the Venn diagram of Figure 12). These sensitive humans can be explorers in inner space for humanity as a whole. Hopefully, they will achieve a respected place in science and be neither adulated nor despised, as is the case too often at present.

To evaluate the observations of future sensitives, we can examine and classify their reports, and match them with data and probabilities already in our computer bank, probabilities originally computed from similar reports made by other explorers. As in all sciences, their agreement with others in the interpretation of relatively well-understood phenomena will tend to provide a "confidence level," a calibration, an estimate of their reliability in respect to "far-out" hypotheses. The rudiments of this procedure for evaluation of reports by explorers in inner space have already been implemented by engineer Robert Monroe (1971, 1976).

What about contact with extraterrestrial intelligences? Astronomer Stephen Dole has noted that this planet travels in a galaxy that probably contains more than 600,000,000 other earthlike life-bearing planets. One of Dole's colleagues, Carl Sagan, estimates that at least 1,000,000 of these bear intelligent life and support advanced civilizations (Sagan, *The Cosmic Connection,* 1973). And, as Isaac Asimov reminds us, there are *billions* of other galaxies. These life-bearing planets in our galaxy are estimated to be 27 light-years apart on the average (approximately 150,000,000,000,000 miles), a distance so vast that NASA-type physical vehicles can be ruled out as possible modes for contact. But even in our present rudimentary state of a science of consciousness, it is clear that physical limitations do not properly apply to mind. If, as previously mentioned, mind is not limited by c (the velocity of light, the limiting velocity for objects that exist in physical time and space), then new possibilities open up in science for communication between us and others in the cosmos.

If Sagan and others are right about the likelihood of other advanced civilizations, then we can conclude that we live in a cosmos that contains a network of intelligences and oddly enough, just at this moment (in the planetary sense) it seems we are becoming aware of this. If there is a shred of possibility here, what better step can we take than to investigate and try to determine the probabilities of inner-space contact with selected scientists who already know something from their own experiential base? If such a group found enough data indicating a likelihood of a cosmic connection, even though that likelihood were not large (as computed by a national science-of-conscious-ness computer bank), then for our own safety we should take the pos-sibility seriously and look further into the matter. Aside from safety, and our innate curiosity, possibly we can tap into a network of intel-ligences who may have something useful for us. That can be determined only if we take rational steps to evaluate data. In other words, whether regarded from a positive or negative point of view concerning dangers or benefits, we should make an investigation.

At least fifty scientists in the United States, Europe, Britain, Japan, India, Australia, and Canada have had sufficient experience (and are sufficiently sophisticated in the psychological domain) to be able to constitute such a committee. The problem will not be to find committee members, but to obtain funds to begin such an investigation. Since committee members will presumably already be aware from personal experience and/or previous scientific investigation that the mind-matter interaction is real, their task will be to find the best scientific examples of phenomena and report on the data and on their inter-pretation to scientists at large. If within two or three years a convincing display were compiled, then we would hope as a next step to see a large effort implemented for basic research in a few laboratories.

Willis Harman has already initiated planning action along similar lines by calling for both private and national funds for research in consciousness. He proposes that scientists involved in the study of consciousness generate a research blueprint for funding organizations. When, early in 1975, he asked us to comment on and participate in his proposal, we were impressed by the similarity between our own in-terest in stimulating a "new psychophysics" and his general proposal. It goes without saying that we want the scientific community to look with favor on these ideas.

Returning to earth, we quote from Chapter 1: "We still must send our children to school, pay taxes, earn a living, and do everything else that mundane life demands." These necessities can be leavened, how-ever, by an improved self-image. Not only do we have some powers of self-regulation and self-fulfillment, but we have transpersonal con-nections that reveal the beauty of an open-ended universe—a stimulat-ing prospect.

Appendix I
Breathing Exercises
and Autogenic Phrases

Assume a comfortable position. Keep the body still. Do not strain the lungs by exhaling or inhaling more deeply than is comfortable. The capacity of the lungs and the control of the breath will increase as you progress.

Take five slow, full breaths, exhaling and inhaling through both nostrils. Then begin "equalized" breathing.

Equalized or Even Breathing: Exhale and inhale through both nostrils slowly and smoothly, with no pause between the exhalations and inhalations. Concentrate attention on the flow of breath past the space between the nostrils. If the mind wanders, bring it back to the space between the nostrils. Continue for four minutes. Breathe slowly, but not so slowly that the diaphragm jerks in order to get more air into the lungs.

Now forget the breathing entirely and focus attention on the autogenic exercises for quieting the body (low muscle tension), quieting the emotions (warmth in the hands), and quieting the mind (inward-turned attention).

Quiet the Body: Take time to visualize, imagine, and feel the relaxation of each part of the body as you silently repeat the phrases; then just "let it happen":

> I feel quite quiet . . . I am beginning to feel quite relaxed . . . My feet, my ankles, my knees and my hips feel heavy, relaxed and comfortable . . . The whole central portion of my body feels relaxed and quiet . . . My hands, my arms, and my shoulders feel heavy, relaxed and comfortable . . . My neck, my jaws, and my forehead feel relaxed. They feel

comfortable and smooth . . . My whole body feels quiet, comfortable, and relaxed . . .

Quiet the Emotions: As you remain comfortable and relaxed, use the following phrases in the same manner as above, visualizing, imagining and feeling the warmth:

> My arms and hands are heavy and warm . . . I feel quite quiet . . . My arms and hands are relaxed, relaxed and warm . . . My hands are warm . . . Warmth is flowing into my hands, they are warm . . . warm . . . My hands are warm . . . relaxed and warm.

Quiet the Mind and Turn Attention Inward: On each phrase imagine and feel the quietness and the withdrawal of the attention inward:

> I feel quite quiet . . . My mind is quiet . . . I withdraw my thoughts from the surroundings and I feel serene and still . . . Deep within myself I can visualize and experience myself as relaxed, comfortable and still . . . I am alert but in an easy, quiet, inward-turned way . . . My mind is calm and quiet . . . I feel an inward quietness . . .

Maintain the inward quietness for about two minutes. Reactivate by taking five slow, full breaths. Stretch and feel energy flowing through your body.

At the end of your practice, record the session in your logbook by answering the following:

1. What were your physical sensations as you went through today's practice?
2. What were your feelings?
3. What were your thoughts? Were they in words or images, or both?

Appendix II
Mathematical Model
for Visual Intensity

Equation (1) below is the solution to the 100-year-old debate in psychophysics about visual brightness and its dependence on stimulus intensity. Was the relationship a *power law,* as S. S. Stevens said in his paper, "To honor Fechner and repeal his law" (1961), or was it a *logarithmic law,* as proposed by Fechner in 1860? As I was able to show, both Fechner and Stevens were right, but only under certain conditions. The power law and the logarithmic law are special cases of a more general law, equation (1). In dealing with the contradictory empirical data of Fechner and Stevens (generated by operational differences in their research methods), it seemed to me that such good observers could not possibly be wrong in their observations, only in their interpretations. Incidentally, I found it necessary to solve this problem graphically (Figure 18) in writing my Ph.D. thesis (on the detection of pain thresholds), and did not complete the mathematical description until the following year, stimulated by a criticism of an article I published in *Science* (Green, 1962). Someone said that the graphic solution shown in *Science* was not a "proof" because it was not done mathematically.

To describe the development of the following equations would take many pages, so only the conclusions are shown herein. The general equation for visual brightness (ψ) when looking at a white light is:

$$\log\psi = n(N_e - 100) + \log\psi_{100} \tag{1}$$

This equation describes, for example, the sensation of changing brightness after entering a dark theater from broad daylight, and, conversely, after coming out of a dark theater into daylight. In equation (1):

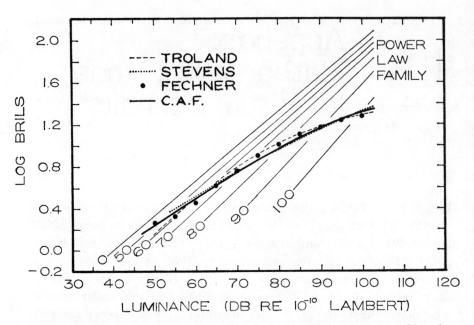

Figure 18. This graph demonstrates the solution to the hundred-year-old problem in psychophysics relating physical intensity of white light, N (on the horizontal axis, in decibels), to the subjective sensation of brightness, ψ (shown on the vertical axis as log ψ). Both the power law (shown by the family of solid curves) and the discriminability law (dashed line) are special cases of the more general "law" of the text.

$$\psi_{100} = 100 - 1.253 \times 10^{-3} A^{2.40} \qquad (2)$$
$$n = .0333 + 2.566 \times 10^{-11} A^{4.31} \qquad (3)$$
$$N_e = 10 \log (I_t - .011 I_A 0.67) + 100 \qquad (4)$$

In the above four equations:

(ψ) is the general changing sensation of brightness, expressed in brils.

(ψ_{100}) is the sensation of brightness when the eye is exposed for one second to a white light of 100 db (1 lambert) intensity, after previous adaptation to a white light of A db.

(n) is the general slope of the straight portion of the family of power functions (solid lines) shown in Figure 18.

(N_e) is the effective level of physical-stimulus intensity in decibels (db) when 100 db is equivalent to one lambert, a unit of physical stimulus intensity in optics.

(A) is the normally changing adaptation level of the eye, in decibels, and, by definition, $A = 10 \log I_A + 100$ decibels, where (I_A) is the changing adaptation level expressed in lamberts.

The adaptation level normally changes in response to a sudden increase or decrease in light intensity according to the following expression:

$$I_A = I_f + (I_1 - I_f) e^{-Kt}, \text{ and} \qquad (5)$$
$$A = 10 \log [I_f + (I_1 - I_f) e^{-Kt}] + 100$$

where (I_f) is the final intensity of the light, in lamberts; (I_1) is the intensity of the light to which the eye is adapted; (K) is the time constant of adaptation (related to the time it takes for 63.2% of adaptation to take place); and (t) represents time in seconds after a change in stimulus intensity occurs.

Although it is not needed for obtaining the power law and logarithmic functions, the value of (K) can be approximated from

$$K = 6.37 \, (12.1 + a \, I_f) \, 10^{-4} \qquad (6)$$

where (a) is the area of the pupil in square millimeters.

From examining these equations it is clear that the sensation of brightness, ψ of Eq (1), can be written in terms of (t), (K), (I_f) and (I_1). In psychophysical studies both (I_f) and (I_1) are given various values as parameters, and the research subject who evaluates brightness for the experimenter looks through a small artificial pupil so as to make (K) a parameter, dependent only on I_f. Time (t) is then the controlling factor after a change in physical stimulus intensity from I_1 to I_f.

To generate mathematically the power functions which were empirically obtained by Stevens, it is merely necessary to let $t = 0$ in the above equations, so $e^{-Kt} = 1.0$. This is necessary because Stevens exposed the eye to changes in brightness for a period of only one second. This is too short a time to allow any significant adaptation to take place in the eye. Thus, in Stevens's research, the sensation of brightness was determined *before adaptation* occurred.

To get Fechner's logarithmic equation, on the other hand, it is merely necessary to insert $t = \infty$ in the equations, so $e^{-Kt} = 0$. This results from the operational fact that Fechner's research was conducted under essentially total adaptation. After half an hour the eye approaches closely to its final state of adaptation. Fechner's technique involved the determination of just noticeable differences in brightness (jnd's), essentially maintaining a state of continuous adaptation. In other words, in contradistinction to Stevens, he made his measurement after adaptation occurred.

The difference between the power and logarithmic laws of visual intensity is seen by everyone in the difference in visual brightness one second after emerging from a dark theater into sunlight, and the visual brightness half an hour later after the eye has adapted to the bright light.

The mathematical effects of the different operational conditions described above for Fechner and Stevens are obtained from the appropriate version of Eq (5) and then used in the preceding equations.

When $t = 0$, $I_A = I_1$. A fixed value of I_1 can now be substituted for the variable I_A in Eq 4, and (A) in Eqs (2) and (3) becomes $A = 10 \log I_1 + 100$.

The family of power functions is literally generated by assigning a series of values to initial and final stimulus intensities, calculating ψ_{100}, n, and N_e, and using the derived values in Eq. 1 to obtain $\log \psi$.

When $t = \infty$, then $I_A = I_f$ and $A = 10 \log I_f + 100$ in Eq 5 and the single logarithmic function is generated from substituting values from Eqs. (2), (3), and (4) in Eq. (1).

It is interesting that the hundred-year battle about the power and logarithmic function resulted from scientists not taking proper account of different research procedures.

The three names on Figure 18, Troland, Stevens, and Fechner, refer to the various curves shown. Stevens's curve (dotted line) was called the "terminal brightness function," but in his articles (1961) he did not recognize it as Fechner's logarithmic law, and in fact he makes the statement that "A power function, not a log function, describes the operating characteristic of a sensory system." The terminal brightness function also corresponds with Troland's graphical law for visual function. C.A.F. refers to the "continuous adaptation function," the Fechnerian function which I derived from a study of Stevens' power-law data.

Of special significance for this book is the fact that I guided myself through the development of these ideas by the intentional use of hypnagogic imagery. Whenever I was "stuck" I made my mind a blank and asked the unconscious to get the information I needed from wherever it was, from my own mind, or the collective mind, or from the "future" if that was possible. I believe that this technique, which I developed over a period of years, is not unique to me, but can be learned by anyone who takes time and makes the effort.

Bibliography

ALLEN, GAY WILSON. *William James: A Biography*. New York: Viking, 1969.

ALLPORT, GORDON W. *The Nature of Personality: Selected Papers*. Cambridge, Mass.: Addison-Wesley, 1950.

ANAND, B. K., G. S. CHHINA, and B. SINGH. Some aspects of electroencephalographic studies in yogis. *Electroenceph. Clin. Neurophysiol.*, 1961, 13, 452–456.

AQUINAS, THOMAS. Biographical Note in *The Summa Theologia*, Vol. I. Chicago: Encyclopedia Britannica, Inc., 1952. (Also in Vol. 19 of Great Books of the Western World.)

ASSAGIOLI, ROBERTO. *Psychosynthesis*. New York: Hobbs, Dorman, 1965; Viking, 1971.

———. *The Act of Will*. New York: Viking Press, 1973.

BAILEY, A. A. *A Treatise on White Magic*. New York: Lucis Publishing Co., 1934.

BARBER, T. X., et al., eds. *Biofeedback and Self Control*. A series of annuals beginning in 1971 in which leading articles in the field are republished each year. Chicago: Aldine-Atherton.

BARKER, A. TREVOR, ed. *The Mahatma Letters to A. P. Sinnett*. London: Rider and Co., 1923.

BASMAJIAN, JOHN V. *Muscles Alive: Their Functions Revealed by Electromyography*. Baltimore: Williams & Wilkins, 1962.

———. Control and training of individual motor units. *Science,* 1963, 141, 440–441.

BECK, A. T. Role of fantasies in psychotherapy and psychopathology. *J. of Nerv. & Men. Disease,* 1970, 150, 1.

BENSON, HERBERT. *The Relaxation Response*. New York: Morrow, 1975.

BLAVATSKY, H. P. *The Secret Doctrine*. Point Loma, Calif.: The Aryan Theosophical Press, 1917.

BOYD, DOUG. *Rolling Thunder*. New York: Random House, 1974.

———. *Swami*. New York: Random House, 1976.

BRENER, J. M., and R. A. KLEINMAN. Learned control of decreases in systolic blood pressure. *Nature,* 226, 1063–1064, 1970.

Brown, Barbara B. Recognition of aspects of consciousness through association with EEG alpha activity represented by a light signal. *Psychophysiology,* 1970, 6, 442–452.

―――――. *New Mind, New Body.* New York: Harper & Row, 1974.

Brudny, Joseph. Spasmodic torticollis: Treatment by feedback display of the EMG. *Arch. Phys. Med. Rehab.,* 55, 403–408, 1974.

―――――, Julius Korein, et al. Sensory feedback therapy as a modality of treatment in central nervous system disorders of voluntary movement. *Neurology,* 24, 925–932, 1974.

Brunton, Paul. *A Search in Secret India.* New York: Weiser, 1972.

Budzynski, Thomas H., Johann M. Stoyva, and Charles S. Adler. Feedback-induced muscle relaxation: Application to tension headache. *Behav. Ther. Exp. Psychiat.,* 1, 205–211, 1970.

―――――, and Daniel J. Mullaney. EMG biofeedback and tension headache: A controlled outcome study. *Psychosomatic Medicine,* 35:484–496, 1973.

Cannon, Walter B. *The Wisdom of the Body.* New York: Norton, 1932.

Capra, Fritjof. *The Tao of Physics.* Berkeley, Calif.: Shambhala, 1975.

Castaneda, Carlos. *The Teachings of Don Juan: A Yaqui Way of Knowledge.* New York: Ballantine, 1968.

―――――. *A Separate Reality: Further Conversations with Don Juan.* New York: Simon and Schuster, 1971.

―――――. *Journey to Ixtlan: The Lessons of Don Juan.* New York: Simon and Schuster, 1972.

―――――. *Tales of Power.* New York: Simon and Schuster, 1974.

Chappell, M. N., and T. T. Stevenson. Group psychological training in some organic conditions. *Mental Hygiene,* 1936, 20, 588–597.

Clarke, Arthur C. *Childhood's End.* New York: Harcourt Brace-Jovanovich, 1963.

Cocteau, Jean. The process of inspiration. In B. Ghiselin, ed., *The Creative Process: A Symposium.* Berkeley and Los Angeles: University of California Press, 1952.

Desoille, R. *The Directed Daydream.* Psychosynthesis Research Foundation, New York, 1966.

Dunne, John. *An Experiment with Time.* Atlantic Highlands, N.J.: Humanities Press, Inc., 1928.

Engel, Bernard T. Personal communication, 1970.

―――――. Operant conditioning of heart rate in patients with premature ventricular contractions. *Psychosom. Med.,* 33, 301–321, 1971.

―――――. Visceral control: Some implications for psychiatry. Paper presented at the American Psychiatric Conference, Anaheim, Calif., 1975.

―――――, Parviz Nikoomanesh, and Marvin M. Schuster. Operant conditioning of rectosphincteric responses in the treatment of fecal incontinence. *New England J. of Med.,* 290, 646–649, 1974.

EVANS-WENTZ, W. Y. *The Tibetan Book of the Dead.* London: Oxford, 1927. New York, Oxford University Press, 1957.

————. *The Tibetan Book of the Great Liberation.* New York: Oxford University Press, 1954.

EVERSAUL, GEORGE. Practical and potential applications of feedback thermometer training and nutrition in crises and preventive medicine. (Paper presented at the annual meeting of the International Academy for Preventive Medicine, Hollywood, Florida, 1975.)

FADIMAN, JAMES. The Council Grove Conference on altered states of consciousness. *J. Humanistic Psych.,* 9, 135–137, 1969.

————. The second Council Grove Conference on altered states of consciousness. *J. Trans. Psychology,* 2, 169–174, 1970.

FECHNER, GUSTAV. *Elements of Psychophysics, Vol. I.* New York: Holt, Rinehart and Winston, 1966. (H. E. Adler, translator; D. H. Howes and E. G. Boring, editors.)

FINLEY, W. W., H. A. SMITH, and M. D. ETHERTON. Reduction of seizures and normalization of EEG in a severe epileptic following sensorimotor biofeedback training: Preliminary report. *Biological Psychology,* 2, 189–203, 1975.

FRIEDMAN, ARNOLD P. Migraine headaches. *J. of the American Med. Assoc.,* Vol. 222, 1399–1402, 1972.

FURMAN, SEYMOUR. Intestinal biofeedback in functional diarrhea: A preliminary report. *J. Behav. Ther. & Exp. Psychiat.,* 4, 317–321, 1973.

GELDARD, FRANK A. *The Human Senses.* New York, Wiley & Sons, 1953.

GELLER, URI. *My Story.* New York: Praeger, 1975.

GHOSE, AUROBINDO. *The Life Divine.* New York, The Sri Aurobindo Library (1951), pp. 718–721. (Available from the California Institute of Asian Studies, San Francisco.)

————. *The Synthesis of Yoga.* Pondicherry, India: Sri Aurobindo Ashram Press, 1955. (Available from the California Institute of Asian Studies, San Francisco.)

————. *On Yoga II, Tome One; On Yoga II, Tome Two.* Pondicherry, India, Sri Aurobindo Ashram, 1958. (Aurobindo's letters to his disciples.)

GLADMAN, ARTHUR E., and NORMA ESTRADA. Biofeedback in clinical practice. (Unpublished report, 1974.)

GILL, MERTON M., and MARGARET BRENMAN. *Hypnosis and Related States.* New York, John Wiley & Sons, Inc., 1959.

GOLDBERGER, E. Simple method of producing dream-like images in the waking state. *Psychosomatic Medicine,* 1952, 19, 127–133.

GOVINDA, LAMA ANAGARIKA. *Foundations of Tibetan Mysticism.* New York: Dutton, 1960.

GREELEY, ANDREW, and WILLIAM MCCREADY. Are We a Nation of Mystics? *The New York Times Magazine,* January 26, 1974.

GREEN, ALYCE M., and ELMER E. GREEN. Biofeedback: research and therapy. In Nils Jacobson, ed., *New Ways to Health.* Stockholm: Natur och Kultur, 1975.

————, and E. DALE WALTERS. Psychophysiological training for inner awareness. Paper presented at the Association for Humanistic Society Conference, Miami, 1970.

————. Psychophysiological training for creativity. Paper presented at the American Psychological Association Annual Meeting, Washington, D.C., 1971.

————. Brain-wave training, imagery, creativity and integrative experiences. Paper presented at Biofeedback Research Society Annual Conference, Colorado Springs, 1974.

GREEN, ELMER E. A preliminary study of sensory barrage using pain threshold as an indicator. Doctoral dissertation, University of Chicago, 1962a.

————. Correspondence between Stevens' terminal brightness function and the discriminability law. *Science,* 138, 1274–1275, 1962b.

————. A mathematical model for skin potential analysis. *Bio-Med. Comp.,* 1, 103–114, 1970.

————, and ALYCE M. GREEN. Conference on voluntary control of internal states. *Psychologia,* 12, 107–108, 1969.

————. On the meaning of transpersonal: Some metaphysical perspectives. *J. Transpers. Psych.,* 3, 1, 1971.

————. Mind Training, ESP, hypnosis, and voluntary control of internal states, *APM Report, Acad. Parapsych. & Medicine,* Los Altos, CA., Vol. I, #3, Spring, 1973a.

————. The ins and outs of mind-body energy. *Science Year, 1974,* World Book Science Annual, Chicago, Field Enterprises Educational Corporation, 1973b.

————. Regulating our mind-body processes. *Fields Within Fields Within Fields,* 10, 16–24, The World Institute Council, Winter, 1973–74.

————. Biofeedback: Rationale and applications. In Benjamin B. Wolman, ed., *International Encyclopedia of Neurology, Psychiatry, Psychoanalysis and Psychology.* 1976. (Available from the editor, 10 West 66th St., New York, N.Y.)

————, and E. DALE WALTERS. Feedback technique for deep relaxation. *Psychophysiology,* 6, 371–377, 1969.

————. Biofeedback for mind-body self-regulation: Healing and creativity. In *Biofeedback and Self-Control,* 1972. Shapiro, et al. (Eds.). Aldine Publishing Co., 1973.

GREEN, JUDITH A. Brain-wave training for seizure reduction in epilepsy. Doctoral dissertation, Union Graduate School, 1976.

HALL, MANLY P. *Man: The Grand Symbol of the Mysteries,* 5th Ed. Los Angeles: Philosophical Res. Soc., 1947. (First published in 1932.)

––––––. *The Secret Teachings of all Ages,* 10th Ed. Los Angeles: Philosophical Res. Soc., 1952. (First published in 1925.)

HARDYCK, CURTIS D., and LEWIS F. PETRINOVICH. Treatment of subvocal speech during reading. *Journal of Reading,* February 1961.

––––––, and DELBERT W. ELLSWORTH. Feedback of speech muscle activity during silent reading: Rapid extinction. *Science,* 154, 1467–1468, 1966.

HARMAN, WILLIS N. The new Copernican revolution. In *Stanford Today,* Winter 1969.

––––––. The great legitimacy challenge: A note on interpreting the present and assessing the future. Unpublished report, Stanford Research Institute, 1975.

HARTLEY, ELDA. *Biofeedback: The Yoga of the West.* (Film.) Hartley Productions, 1974. (Address: Cat Rock Road, Cos Cob, Conn.)

HAUGEN, G. B., H. H. DIXON, and H. A. DICKEL. *A Therapy for Anxiety Tension Reduction.* New York: MacMillan Co., 1963.

HEFFERLINE, RALPH F. In *Gestalt Therapy: Excitement and Growth in the Human Personality.* New York: Julian Press, 1951.

––––––. Learning theory and clinical psychology. In Arthur J. Backrach, ed., *Experimental Foundations of Clinical Psychology.* New York: Basic Books, Inc., 1962.

HILGARD, ERNEST R. *Hypnotic Susceptibility.* New York: Harcourt, Brace & World, Inc., 1965.

HNATIOW, MICHAEL, and PETER J. LANG. Learned stabilization of cardiac rate. *Psychophysiology,* 1, 330–336, 1965.

JACKSON, PHILIP W., and JACOB W. GETZELLS. *Creativity and Intelligence: Explorations with Gifted Students.* New York: John Wiley & Sons, Inc., 1962.

JACOBI, JOLANDE. *The Way of Individuation.* New York: Harcourt, Brace & World, Inc., 1967.

JACOBSON, EDMUND. *Progressive Relaxation.* Chicago: University of Chicago Press, 1938; paperback, 1974.

JAMES, WILLIAM. In Gardner Murphy and Robert O. Ballou, eds., *William James on Psychical Research.* New York: The Viking Press, 1960, 6–7.

––––––. *The Principles of Psychology.* New York: Dover Publications, Inc., 1950, Vol. I, 258.

KAMIYA, JOE. Conditioned discrimination of the EEG alpha rhythm in humans. Paper presented at the Western Psychological Association, San Francisco, 1962.

_____. Conscious control of brain waves. *Psychology Today,* 1, 11, 57–60, 1968.

KANT, IMMANUEL. *Critique of Pure Reason.* New York: St. Martin's, 1929.

KAPLAN, B. J. Biofeedback in epileptics: Equivocal relationship of reinforced EEG frequency to seizure reduction. *Epilepsia,* 16, 477–485, 1975.

KASAMATSU, A., and T. HIRAI. Science of Zazen. *Psychologia,* 6, 86–91, 1963.

KHAN, AMAN U. Present status of psychosomatic aspects of asthma. *Psychosomatics,* Vol. 14: 195–200, 1973.

KOESTLER, ARTHUR. *The Act of Creation.* New York: The Macmillan Co., 1964.

KORZYBSKI, ALFRED. *Science and Sanity.* Lakeville, Conn.: International Non-Aristotelian Publishing Co., 1948.

KOTSES, HARRY, KATHLEEN D. GLAUS, PAUL L. CRAWFORD, and JACK E. EDWARDS. The effect of operant conditioning of the frontalis muscle on peak expiratory flow in asthmatic children. Proceedings of the Biofeedback Research Society, Colorado Springs, 1976.

KUBIE, LAWRENCE S. The use of induced hypnagogic reveries in the recovery of repressed amnesic data. *Bulletin of the Menninger Clinic,* 7, 172–183, 1943.

_____. *Neurotic Distortions of the Creative Process.* Lawrence, Kans.: University of Kansas Press, 1958.

KUBLER-ROSS, ELISABETH. *On Death and Dying.* New York: Macmillan, 1969.

KURTZ, PAUL S. Turning on without chemicals. *J. of Bio-Feedback,* 1, 88–103, 1973.

LEUNER, H. Guided affective imagery, a method of intensive psychotherapy. *American Journal of Psychotherapy,* 1, 23, 1969.

LEVI, ELIPHAS. *Transcendental Magic: Its Doctrine and Ritual.* London: Rider, 1968.

LILLY, JOHN C. *The Center of the Cyclone.* New York: Julian Press, 1972.

LONG, M. *The Secret Science Behind Miracles.* Vista, Calif.: Huna Research Publication, 1948.

LUBAR, J. F., and W. W. BAHLER. Behavior management of epileptic seizures following EEG biofeedback training of the sensorimotor rhythm. *Biofeedback and Self-Regulation,* 1, 77–104, 1976.

LUCE, GAY, and ANTOINETTE A. GATTOZZI. The use of biofeedback training in enabling patients to control autonomic functions. *N.I.M.H. Mental Health Program Reports,* 5, 1971.

LUTHE, WOLFGANG. *Autogenic Training*. New York & London: Grune and Stratton, 1965.

————. *Autogenic Therapy*, Vols. I–VI. New York: Grune and Stratton, 1969.

————. Autogenic training: Method, research and application in medicine. In J. Kamiya et al., eds., *Biofeedback and Self-Control*. Chicago and New York: Aldine-Atherton, 1971.

MACKINNON, D. W. Creativity and transliminal experiences. Address given at the American Psychological Association Convention, Los Angeles, 1964.

MACLEAN, PAUL D. Psychosomatic disease and the "visceral brain." *Psychosomatic Medicine*, 2, 338–353, 1949.

MARINACCI, ALBERTO. The basic principles underlying neuromuscular re-education. In *Applied Electromyography*. London: Lea and Febiger, 1968.

MAY, ROLLO. The nature of creativity. In Harold H. Anderson, ed., *Creativity and its Cultivation*. New York: Harper and Bros., 1959.

MCKELLAR, PETER. *Imagination and Thinking: A Psychological Analysis*. New York: Basic Books, 1957.

————, and LORNA SIMPSON. Between wakefulness and sleep: Hypnagogic imagery. *British Journal of Psychiatry*, Vol. 45, 266–276, 1954.

MEISTEUFFEN, HANS. *Wanderlust*. (Victor Rosen, translator.) New York: McGraw-Hill, 1953.

MILLER, N., and L. DI CARA. Instrumental learning of urine formation by rats; changes in renal blood flow. *American Journal of Physiology*, 1968, 215:677–683.

MILLER, STUART, NAOMI REMEN, ALLEN BARBOUR, SARA MILLER, and DALE GARRELL. *Dimensions of Humanistic Medicine*. San Francisco: Institute for the Study of Medicine, 1975.

MONROE, ROBERT A. *Journeys Out of the Body*. New York: Doubleday, 1971.

————. Report at Council Grove Conference. Council Grove, Kansas, 1976.

MOWRER, O. H., and W. M. MOWRER. Enuresis: A method for its study and treatment. *American Journal of Orthopsychiatry*, 8, 436–459, 1938.

MULDOON, SYLVAN, and HEREWARD CARRINGTON. *The Projection of the Astral Body*. London: Rider, 1958.

MULHOLLAND, THOMAS, and C. R. EVANS. Oculomotor function and the alpha activation cycle. *Nature*, 211, 1278–9, 1966.

MULHOLLAND, THOMAS, and S. RUNNALS. Evaluation of attention and alertness with a stimulus-brain feedback loop. *Electroencephalography and Clinical Neurophysiology*, 14, 847–52, 1962.

MURPHY, GARDNER. *The Challenge of Psychical Research.* New York: Harper & Brothers, 1961.

———, and ROBERT O. BALLOU. *William James on Psychical Research.* New York: Viking Press, 1960, pp. 6–7.

MYERS, FREDERICK W. H. *Human Personality and Its Survival of Bodily Death.* New York: Longmans, Green & Co., 1954.

NORRIS, PATRICIA. Biofeedback applications in a consciousness training program. (Paper presented at the Biofeedback Society Conference, Monterey, Calif., 1974.)

———. Working with prisoners, or there's nobody else here. Unpublished doctoral dissertation, 1976.

ORNSTEIN, ROBERT E. *The Psychology of Consciousness.* San Francisco: Freeman, 1972.

ORWELL, GEORGE. *1984.* New York: New American Library, 1971.

OSTRANDER, SHELIA, and LYNN SCHROEDER. *Psychic Discoveries Behind the Iron Curtain.* New York: Bantam, 1971; Prentice-Hall, 1970.

OUSPENSKY, P. D. *Tertium Organum.* New York: Knopf, 1947; Random House, 1970.

PAFFORD, MICHAEL. *Inglorious Wordsworth.* London: Madder & Stoughton, 1974.

PAPEZ, J. W. A proposed mechanism of emotion. *Archives of Neurology and Psychiatry,* 28, 725–743, 1937.

PAUL, G. L. *Insight Vs. Desensitization in Psychiatry.* Stanford: Stanford University Press, 1966.

PERLS, FREDERICK, RALPH HEFFERLINE, and PAUL GOODMAN. *Gestalt Therapy: Excitement and Growth in the Human Personality.* New York: Julian Press, 1951.

POIRIER, FERDINAND. Traitement de l'epilepsie par retroaction sonore. *La Clinique D. Epilepsie de Montreal.* Paper presented at the Biofeedback Research Society Conference, 1972.

———. Personal communication, 1973.

PROGOFF, IRA. *The Well and the Cathedral.* New York: Dialogue House Library, 1970.

———. *Depth Psychology and Modern Man.* New York: Dialogue House Library, 1970.

———. *At a Journal Workshop.* New York: Dialogue House Library, 1975.

PUHARICH, ANDRIJA. *Uri.* New York: Doubleday-Anchor, 1974.

RAMAKRISHNA. *The Gospel of Sri Ramakrishna.* New York: Ramakrishna-Vivekananda Center, 1952. (Swami Nikhilananda, compiler and translator.)

RAM DASS. The transformation of a man from scientist to mystic, a personal chronicle. Lecture given at the annual meeting of the Association for Humanistic Psychology, Silver Spring, Md., August 1969.

————. *Be Here Now*. New Mexico: Lama Foundation, 1971.

RHINE, J. B. *New Frontiers of the Mind*. New York: Farrar & Rhinehart, 1937.

RICHARDSON, ALAN. *Mental Imagery*. New York: Springer, 1969.

ROGERS, C. *Client Centered Therapy*. Boston: Houghton Mifflin, 1951.

RUGG, HAROLD. *Imagination*. New York: Harper & Row, 1963.

SAGAN, CARL. *The Cosmic Connection*. New York: Doubleday, 1973.

SARGENT, JOSEPH D., ELMER E. GREEN, and E. DALE WALTERS. The use of autogenic feedback training in a pilot study of migraine and tension headaches. *Headache*, 12, 120–125, 1972.

————. Preliminary report on the use of autogenic feedback training in the treatment of migraine and tension headaches. *Psychosomatic Medicine*, 35, 129–135, 1973.

————. Psychosomatic self-regulation of migraine and tension headaches. *Seminars in Psychiatry*, 5, 415–442, 1973.

SCHULTZ, JOHANNES. The clinical importance of "inward seeing" in autogenic training. *British Journal of Medical Hypnotism*, 11, 26–28, 1960.

————, and WOLFGANG LUTHE. *Autogenic Training: A Psychophysiologic Approach in Psychotherapy*. New York: Grune & Stratton, 1959.

SCHUMACHER, E. F. *Small Is Beautiful*. London: Blond & Briggs, 1973.

SCHUMACHER, G. A., and H. G. WOLFF. Experimental studies of headache. *Archives of Neurological Psychiatry*, 45, 199, 1941.

SCHWARTZ, GARY E., and DAVID SHAPIRO. Biofeedback and essential hypertension: Current findings and theoretical concerns. *Seminars in Psychiatry*, 5, 493–503, 1973.

SCOFIELD, C. I. Holy Bible. Authorized King James version. The New Scofield Reference Bible. New York: Oxford University Press, 1967.

SHAH, IDRIES. *The Way of the Sufi*. London: Jonathan Cape, 1968.

————. *The Sufis*. New York: Doubleday, 1971.

SHEALY, C. NORMAN, and ARTHUR S. FREESE. *Occult Medicine Can Save Your Life*. New York: Dial, 1975.

SIMONTON, O. CARL, and STEPHANIE SIMONTON. Belief systems and management of the emotional aspects of malignancy. *Journal of Transpersonal Psychology*, 7, 29–47, 1975.

SKINNER, B. F. *Beyond Freedom and Dignity*. New York: Knopf, 1972.

————. *Walden Two*. New York: Macmillan, 1948.

SMITH, M. JUSTA. Research into the phenomenon of healing. Paper presented at the Conference on Psychic Healing and Self Healing, sponsored by the Association for Humanistic Psychology, 1972.

STEINER, RUDOLF. *Occult Science: An Outline.* 2nd Ed. New York: Anthroposophic Press, 1950.

STERMAN, MAURICE B. Neurophysiologic and clinical studies of sensorimotor cortex EEG feedback training: Some effects on epilepsy. *Seminars in Psychiatry,* 5, 507–525, 1974.

STEVENS, S. S. To honor Fechner and repeal his law. *Science,* 1961, 133, 80–86.

STEVENSON, IAN. *Twenty Cases Suggestive of Reincarnation.* New York: American Society of Psychical Research, 1966.

————. *Cases of the Reincarnation Type, Vol. 1, Ten Cases in India.* University Press of Virginia, 1975.

SUGRUE, THOMAS. *There Is a River—The Story of Edgar Cayce.* New York: Holt, 1942; Dell, 1970.

SWANN, INGO. *To Kiss Earth Good-bye.* New York: Hawthorn, 1975.

TAIMNI, I. K. *The Science of Yoga.* Wheaton, Ill.: Theosophical Publishing House, 1967.

TART, CHARLES T. A psychophysiological study of out-of-the-body experiences in a selected subject. In Tart, ed., *Altered States of Consciousness: A Book of Readings.* New York: Wiley, 1969.

————. *States of Consciousness.* New York: Dutton, 1975.

TEILHARD DE CHARDIN, PIERRE. *The Phenomenon of Man.* New York: Harper, 1959.

TROLAND, L. T. *Mystery of Mind.* New York: D. Van Nostrand Co., Inc., 1926.

TRUSSELL, WILLIAM. Personal communication, The Children's Hospital of The Menninger Foundation, 1974.

TWEMLOW, STUART. Personal communication, The Veterans' Hospital, Topeka, Ks., 1974.

VAN DER BERG, J. H. An existential explanation of the guided daydream in psychotherapy. *Review of Existential Psychology and Psychology,* 1962, II, #1.

WALKUP, L. E. Creativity in science through visualization. *Perceptual Motor Skills,* 21, 35–41, 1965.

WALLACE, ROBERT KEITH. Physiological effects of transcendental meditation. *Science,* 167, 1751–1754, 1970.

————, and HERBERT BENSON. The physiology of meditation. *Scientific American,* February, 1972.

WALLACH, M. A., and N. KOGAN. *Modes of Thinking in Young Children.* New York: Holt, Rinehart & Winston, Inc., 1965.

WEIS, T., and BERNARD T. ENGEL. Operant conditioning of heart rate in patients with premature ventricular contractions. *Psychosomatic Medicine,* 33, 301–321, 1971.

WICKRAMASEKERA, IAN. Electromyographic feedback training and tension headache: Preliminary observations. *American Journal of Clinical Hypnosis,* 15, 83–85, 1972.

WITKIN, H. A. Individual differences in ease of perception of embedded figures. *Journal of Personality,* 1–15, 1950.

———, R. B. DYK, H. F. PATTERSON, D. R. GOODENOUGH, and S. A. KEMP. *Psychological Differentiation.* New York: Wiley & Sons, 1962.

WOLFF, H. G. *Headache and Other Head Pain,* 2nd ed. New York: Oxford University Press, 1963.

WOLPE, J., and A. A. LAZARUS. *Behavior Therapy Techniques: A Guide to the Treatment of Neuroses.* New York: Pergamon Press, 1966.

WYLER, A. R. Operant conditioning of epileptic neurons in monkeys and its theoretical application to EEG operant conditioning in humans. Paper presented at the Biofeedback Research Society Conference, Colorado Springs, Col., 1976.

———, J. S. LOCKARD, A. A. WARD, and C. A. FINCH. Conditioned EEG desynchronization and seizure occurrence in patients. *Electroencephalography and Clinical Neurophysiology* (in press, 1976).

Index

Action-perception-substance model, 300–15
Alcoholics Anonymous, 192–3
All India Yoga Conference (1973), 246, 250
Allport, Gordon, 161, 174
Alpha waves, 44, 118, 208, 258; frequencies of, 120, 135–6; and meditation, 123, 254–6, 258–60, 272; and pain control, 156, 229–33; and Schwarz, 229–33, 240
American Society for Psychical Research, 21
"Analyzer" (cortex), 122
Anand, B. K., 123, 232, 272, 273
"Anatomy of a Psyche" (diagram), 300–15
Anesthesia, 235–6, 327
Ankle repair, of Schwarz, 237
Antakarana (Path), 307
Anxiety, 27, 44, 102–3
"Are We a Nation of Mystics?" (Greeley and McCready), 187–9
Asanas, 256
Asimov, Isaac, 335
Assagioli, Roberto, 151, 186, 190, 291, 318
Association for Humanistic Psychology, 301

Association for Research and Enlightenment Clinic (ARE), 84
Asthma, 27, 94–7
Astral plane, 306, 310
Astrology, 257
Atrial flutter, 205
Attention control, pain control as, 156, 229–34
Attitude, 88; and biofeedback training, 66–8; and cancer remission, 169–70, 175–6; and kidney damage, 114; right, 329
Aura (in epileptic seizures), 104
Auric patterns, 239–41, 305
Aurobindo, 63, 153, 258–9, 265–6, 271, 300, 303–4, 306, 309–11, 314, 318–19, 328
Autobiography of a Yogi, The (Gupta), 255
Autogenic feedback training, 33–41
Autogenic Training, 25, 115–16, 150, 318; and biofeedback, 28–41; development of, 26–7
Autogenic Training (Schultz and Luthe), 15–16, 115
Autohypnosis, 26
Automatic writing, 287–8
Autonomic nervous system, 16, 49–50, 54, 73; and biofeedback training,

Habits, 173–4
Hair-color change, 8
Hall, Manly Palmer, 162, 302, 304
Hallucinations, 26
Halstead, Ward C., 14, 16, 69
Hand-warming, 28, 33–41, 44, 48–9,
    157–8, 198–201; side effects of, 37–
    40, 76–9, 83–4, 86–7. *See also*
    Temperature-training
Hardyck, Curtis, 44
Haridas Baba, 291
Hariharananda Giri, Swami, 259
Harman, Willis, 219, 332, 334, 336
Hartley, Elda, 246, 253, 255, 261, 264
Haugen, G. B., 44, 102–3
"Head-stands," 261–2
Headaches, 26, 27. *See also* Migraine;
    Tension headache
Healing: by Alyce Green, 281–2; and
    hypnosis, 327–8; psychic, 11–12,
    229, 303, 330; by Rolling Thunder,
    220, 222–4; self-, 11, 237–8
Heart: and biofeedback, 74–9; stop-
    ping of, voluntarily, 199–204, 272;
    subtle, 202–3; voluntary rate control
    in, 27, 43–4, 53, 74–9, 199–205, 229
Heaviness, and autohypnosis, 26
Hefferline, Ralph, 23, 162–4
Heifetz, Jascha, 175
Helson, Harry, 196, 297
Hemiparesis, 99
Hemorrhoids, 157
Herbert, Paul, 226
Herbs, as medicine, 221
Hilgard, Ernest R., 319
Hinton, James, 184
Hirai, T., 123, 273
Hnatiow, Michael, 44, 74
Hoel, Ronald, 290
Hogan, Ben, 60
Holt, Louise, 278, 279–80
Holt, Robert R., 146
Holy Water, 221
Homeostasis, 53, 89, 172–7; in fami-
    lies, 172, 175–7; in group relations,
    172–3, 174–6; negative, 175–6;

psychological, 174–5; self-regula-
    tion and, 115, 173–4; side effects of,
    116
Hormones, 27, 114
Horowitz, 152
Howerton, James, 90
Howett, Dr. Gerald, 297
Human Senses, The (Geldard), 13
Humanity, belief in, as motivation,
    331–3
Hurkos, Peter, 228
Huxley, Aldous, 192, 296
Hypertension, 79–89
Hypnagogic images, 44, 120, 124–34,
    150, 296–7; and psychotherapy,
    149–52; and theta waves, 120, 124–
    34, 137–8, 140–9
"Hypnagogic reverie," 44
Hypnapompic images, 120
Hypnosis, 164–5, 323; medical, 327–8;
    in mind-training programs, 316–18,
    319–23, 326; and pain control, 234,
    327–8; and parapsychology, 319–20
Hypothalamus, 50–2, 114
Hypothenar eminence, 198–201

Identity: and central nervous system,
    155; don Juan on, 161; and experi-
    ential knowing, 183; and field-
    independence, 178, 182, 192; and
    parapsychology, 182–3; and psy-
    chosomatic disease, 186; search for,
    333–6; and volition, 182–3
Idiot savants, 250–2
Imagery: archetypal, 145; and
    creativity, 125–7, 142–3, 149, 152;
    and psychotherapy, 149–52. *See
    also* Hypnagogic images
Imagery: The Return of the Ostracized
    (Holt), 146
Incontinence, 92–3
Independence: from body, 180–1, 185,
    193, 300; from environment, 178–
    80, 184–5, 193, 300; from mind,

Independence (*cont.*)
182, 185, 193, 300, 317. *See also*
Free will; Volition
India, research in, 244–75
Indian Institute of Technology, 264
Infection, prevention of, 234–5
Inglorious Wordsworths (Pafford),
189
INS (inside-the-skin) experience, 51–
2, 55, 196–7
Instinctual intuition, 306
Institute of Human Study, 271
Institute of Noetic Sciences, 248–9
Integral Yoga, 271, 315, 318, 319
Integrative experiences, and theta
training, 142–3, 149–52
"Internal scanning techniques," 127
International New Thought Alliance,
282
Intuition, 306

Jackson, Philip, 16
Jacobi, Jolande, 286
Jacob's Ladder, 307
Jacobson, Edmund, 163, 318
James, William, 64–5, 127, 177, 185,
192, 287
Jesus Christ, 302, 307, 326
Jewel, in field-of-mind theory, 302,
303, 306, 308, 314
*Journal of the Optical Society of
America*, 297
Journal of Transpersonal Psychology,
299
Journey to Ixtlan (Castaneda), 276
Juan, don, 7, 62, 154, 161, 174–5, 257,
276, 287, 291, 293, 308, 312–13,
328
Judd, Deane, 297
Jung, Carl, 8, 10, 63–4, 145, 183, 286,
300–1

Kamiya, Joe, 44, 118
Kant, Immanuel, 154

Kaplan, B. J., 104
Karabanda, Mr., 250
Karembelkar, Dr. P. V., 265, 274
Karma, 295, 309, 329
Kasamatsu, A., 123, 273
Kekulé, Friedrich, 126, 149
Khan, Aman, 96–7
Kidneys, 86, 114–15
Kleinman, R. A., 80–2
Knights of the Round Table, The
(Cocteau), 125
Koestler, Arthur, 126–7
Kogan, N., 142
Korein, Julius, 99
Korzybski, Alfred, 70
Kotes, Harry, 97
Krippner, Stanley, 219, 220
Krishnamurti, 296
Kriya Yoga, 255, 260
Kubie, Lawrence, 44, 127, 150–1, 152
Kubler-Ross, Elisabeth, 275
Kundalini, 261, 315
Kurtz, Paul, 192–3

Labile hypertension, 81, 88
Lally, Professor, 285–8, 326
Lang, Peter, 44, 74, 90
Laucks, Irving, 246
Law of volition, 257
"Laying on of hands," 229. *See also*
Healing
Lazarus, A.A., 151
Leukocytes, 111, 209–10
Leuner, H., 151
Levi, Eliphas, 304
Levitation, 263, 264
Lilly, John, 66, 218
Limbic system, 51–2, 114
Liver metabolism, 272
Long, M., 304
Lotus, in field-of-mind theory, 302,
306–7, 308, 311, 314, 329
Lubar, J. F., 104
Luce, Gay, 96

New Thought Movement, 281
Newman, Theresa, 261
Nikoomanesh, Parviz, 92
1984 (Orwell), 185
Noncorporeal entities, 286, 310
Nonsensory information, 300
Noosphere, 314
Norris, Pat, 83, 189, 190–1, 217–18, 280, 295
"Numerical wizard," 250–2

Occipital cortex, 118, 119–20, 154
Occult Medicine May Save Your Life (Shealy and Freese), 156, 242–3
Olwine, Margaret, 83–5
OOBEs (out-of-the-body experiences), 288
Operant (instrumental) conditioning, 29, 103
Operationalism, in research, 65–6, 70
Optic nerve, 154
Ornstein, Robert, 69, 333
Orwell, George, 185
Oscilloscope, 30
Ostrander, Sheila, 326
Ouspenski, P. D., 184
OUTS (outside-the-skin) experience, 50, 51, 197
Overmind, 153, 314, 319

Pafford, Michael, 189
Pahnke, Walter, 219
Pain control, 15, 224, 237; and alpha, 229–33; and hypnosis, 234, 327; for paraplegics, 156
Papez, J. W., 51
Paradoxical sleep, 123
Paraplegics, and body consciousness, 155–6
Parapsychology: and energy, 22; and hypnosis, 319–20; and identity, 182–3. *See also* ESP; PK

Parasympathetic nervous system, 49, 73
Patanjali, 63, 184, 210
Patanjali Yoga Research Institute, 271, 272
Path, 307
Paul, G. L., 151
Pearse, Barbara, 41, 176–7
Peper, Erik, 169, 230
Perception, 120; and brain activity, 129, 154–5; and central nervous system, 167, 181; and electrochemical activity, 294; and etheric physical, 305–6; and field-(in)-dependence, 179–80; of pain, 230
Perception-substance-action model, 300–15
Peripheral nervous system, 49, 155
Perls, Fritz, 162
Personal experience, 300, 303, 307–8
Personality, and cancer, 170–1, 176
Personality change: and biofeedback, 71, 78–9, 91; and theta training, 142–4, 149
Petrinovich, Lewis, 44
Petroni, Lillian, 35–6, 45
pH feedback, 93–4
Phantom limb, 155–6
Physical events, in field-of-mind model, 303
Physical therapy, 109
Pituitary gland, 51–2, 114
PK (psychokinesis), 11–12, 182, 293, 303; and energy, 22; with Swami Rama, 211–17; and volition, 61–2
Planetary field of mind, 304, 305, 310
Poincaré, Jules, 125, 149
Poirier, Fernand, 105–6
Pornography, 312
"Power touch," 262, 263
Pranas, 303
Pranayama, 255, 257
Precognition, 17–19; and theta training, 147–8
"Primary neural nucleus," 61

Prisoners, self-image of, 189–91
Progoff, Ira, 151, 157, 306–7
Progressive Relaxation, 44, 163, 318, 319
Progressive Relaxation (Jacobson), 163
Projection, psychological, 240–1, 289
"Prophylactic rest—autohypnosis," 26
Proprioceptive feedback, 108, 182
Psyche, proposed anatomy of, 300–15
Psychic development, 305–6, 316; dangers of, 328–30
Psychic healing. *See* Healing
Psychic pollution, 325
Psychic submission, 322, 326
Psychics, experimental difficulties with, 240–3
Psychokinetic phenomena. *See* PK
Psychological Differentiation (Witkin), 179
Psychological homeostasis, 174–5
Psychology of Consciousness, The (Ornstein), 69
Psychology Review, 297
Psychopathology, and theta, 142–3
Psychophysics, 65–6, 70, 334, 336
Psychophysiological principle, 33–4, 45, 58–9, 66, 71; illustration of, 46, 49–52
Psychophysiological Research Society, 44
Psychosis, and mind-training programs, 318, 325
Psychosomatic disease, 56, 71, 186; and family, 89–90, 175–7; and homeostasis, 173; and self-regulation, 272; unconscious nature of, 60, 68–9; and visualization, 168–9
Psychosomatic health, 71; and body consciousness, 156, 164; and homeostasis, 173–4
Psychosomatic self-regulation, 34, 42, 45–52, 59, 68, 272; as continual process, 96, 97; and homeostasis, 115; illustration of, 47; and volition, 58–62. *See also* Self-regulation

Psychosynthesis, 151, 190, 291, 318, 319, 323, 333
Psychotherapy, hypnagogic reverie in, 149–52
Puharich, Andrija, 310
PVC control, 74–5

R waves, 75, 201
Raghadananda, Professor, 259–60
"Rainbow Body," (Lotus), 306
Rajalakshmi, Mahayogini, 261–4, 266, 270
Ram Dass, Baba, 190, 247, 291, 300, 304
Rama, Swami, 62, 138, 158–61, 196, 227; and Indian research, 244–6, 249–52; self-regulation of, 197–218; and "traveling through the body," 159–61, 167
Ramakrishna, 300, 304
Ramananda Yogi, Sri, 272
Ramano, Jacques, 6–7
Ramesh, 256
Rao, Dr. A. V. S. S. Rama, 262
Rao, Dr. K. Ramakrishna, 260–1, 266–9
Rao, Dr. V. S., 270
Raymond, Jean, 264
Raynaud's disease, 40–1, 50, 89, 115, 163, 176
Reaction time, and theta, 127–8
Recall. *See* Memory
Reddy, Dr., 271
Reich, Wilhelm, 10
Reincarnation, 295, 308–9
Relaxation Response, The (Benson), 115
Religion, 313–14, 315
Religiosity, 314
Religious Experience Research Group, 189
REM (rapid eye movement) sleep, 123
Rennick, Dr. Philip, 18–19
Renouvier, Charles, 65, 185

Respiration control, 27, 43; and
asthma, 95–7
Retina, as transducer, 13
Reverie: and creativity, 124–7, 256;
hypnagogic, 44; integrative, 150–2;
and psychotherapy, 149–52; and
theta, 120, 123, 124–34, 137–8,
140–9
Rhine, J. B., 22, 62, 300
Richardson, Alan, 143
Right attitude, 329
Right brain/left brain, 69–71
Right consciousness, 330
Rod-and-frame test, 179
Rods and cones, 154
Rogers, Carl, 13–14, 172
Rolling Thunder, 62, 196, 218–25, 257
Rolling Thunder (Boyd), 224, 257
Roosevelt, Franklin D., 60
Rosencranz, 163
Rugg, Harold, 127

Sacrifice, 329
Sagan, Carl, 335
Sai Baba, 261, 264
Sargent, Joseph, 36–9, 41, 204–5
Schizophrenics, brain-waves of, 122
Schroeder, Lynn, 326
Schultz, Johannes H., 26, 27, 43, 53,
114, 157, 318, 328
Schumacher, E. F., 332
Schuster, Marvin, 92
Schwartz, Gary, 80, 82–3, 89
Schwarz, Jack, 62, 196, 263, 325;
self-regulation of, 225–41
Science, 298
Science and Sanity (Korzybski), 70
Science of consciousness, 65–6, 219;
motivations for, 331–6; vocabulary
for, 299–300
Scientific research: in consciousness,
65–6, 219, 299–300, 331–6; and
culture, 270; in India, 244–75;
instruments for, 247–9, 304. (*See*

also Transducers); operationalism
and existentialism in, 65–6, 70; on
psychics, 240–3
Search in Secret India, A (Brunton),
257
Secondary gain, from illness, 171
Self-healing, 11; visualization for,
237–8. *See also* Healing
Self-image: and cancer, 170–1; and
field-independence, 179–93; and
physiological change, 189–90; of
prisoners, 189–91
Self Realization Fellowship, 260
Self-regulation, 11, 194–7; and consciousness, 25, 273; and detachment,
56, 187; INS and, 196–7; pain con-
trol as, 237; and psychosomatic
disease, 272; and Rolling Thunder,
218–25; of Schwarz, 225–41; by
Swami Rama, 197–218; and visual-
izations, 8, 11, 15, 25, 33–4, 48–9;
and volition, 59–62. *See also* Psycho-
somatic self-regulation; Voluntary
control
Sensorimotor rhythm (SMR), 103–4
Sensorium, 154–5, 181
Sensory deprivation, and theta, 127–8
Sensory feedback therapy, 98. *See also*
Biofeedback training
Sex energy, 315
Shah, Idries, 225, 304
Shaktipat, 262, 263
Shapiro, David, 80, 82–3, 89
Sharing experiences, 284–5
Shealy, Dr. Norman, 156, 242–3
Shukla, Dr. H. C., 256–8
Sil, Dr. Arun K., 258–9
Simonton, Carl, 111, 169–71, 175–6,
189
Simonton, Stephanie, 111, 169–71,
175–6, 189
Simpson, Lorna, 143
Singh, B., 123, 272, 273
Singh, Pripal, 255
Single motor unit firing, 31–2, 98, 106,
109

Theta waves: and ESP events, 136–7, 138–40, 146–9; frequencies of, 120, 135–6; and meditation, 123, 127, 254–6; pilot research on, 134–40; and Schwarz, 240; and Swami Rama, 208; and "traveling through the body," 159–61
Thomas Aquinas, Saint, 191–2
Thorpe, Neils, 290
Thyroid malfunctioning, 115
Tibetan Book of the Dead, 301, 308
Tibetan Book of the Great Liberation, 183
Tibetan Buddhism, 183, 207, 225, 306–7, 311, 314–15, 328
Torres, Ramon, 230
Torticollis, 98–9
Trances, and unconscious, 165, 166–8
Transcendental experiences, 182; study of, 187–9
Transcendental Meditation (TM), 190, 225
Transducers, 110–14, 116; inorganic, 12; for pH feedback, 93–4
Transference, 10, 325
"Transliminal experience," 127
Transpersonal experience, 300, 303, 307–8, 310
Transpersonal Psychology, 301
"Traveling through the body," 159–61, 167
Troland, L. T., 8
"True Self" (Lotus), 306
Trussell, William, 151
Tumo (Vital Heat), 16
Tumors, control of, 111–12, 210–11
Tunnel experience, 306, 311
"Turning on without chemicals," (Kurtz), 192
Twemlow, Stuart, 151, 233–4

Uduppa, Dr., 256
Ulcers, 90, 93–4, 157
Unconscious: autonomous entities in

the, 161; communication with, 165–8; control of, and death, 210; in field-of-mind theory, 302, 305; physical location of, 69; and psychosomatic disease, 60, 68–9
Universal Nature, 193, 307
Uri (Puharich), 310

Vachon, Louis, 96
Van der Berg, J. H., 151
Vardhan, Dr. Haresh, 254
Vasoconstriction, 36, 80–1
Vasodilation, 36
Vasomotor system, 27, 36–41
Vegetarianism, 305
Vision, 44, 109–10, 119–20
Visual intensity law, 256, 296–8
Visualizations: and asthma control, 95; and body consciousness, 166–71; of body feeling, 157–8; and cancer remission, 169–71; and creativity, 125–7; idiosyncratic, 113; negative, 170–1; and passive volition, 54; for self-healing, 237–8; and self-regulation, 8, 11, 15, 25, 33–4, 48–9
Vogt, Oscar, 26
Void (Buddhist concept), 183, 314, 334
Volition, 14, 43, 329; active, 54; as exercise, 291; and identity, 182–3; law of, 257; as a metaforce, 58–71; passive, 33, 54–5; and self-regulation, 59–62; and voluntary control, 52–3. *See also* Free will
Voluntary control: approaches for, 218–19; and body feeling, 157–8; and field-independence, 180–1; and volition, 52–3. *See also* Self-regulation

Walden II (Skinner), 185
Walkup, L. E., 125–6

Elmer Green, Ph.D., Director of the Voluntary

Controls Program, Research Department, the Menninger Foundation, received a B. Physics degree from the University of Minnesota in 1942 and worked as a physicist in electronics and computing before returning to graduate school at the University of Chicago, where he received his Ph.D. in Biopsychology in 1962. He was a Research Associate in the Department of Medicine, University of Chicago, 1962 through 1963, and in 1964 he established a psychophysiology laboratory at the Menninger Foundation.

His research has combined the disciplines of Autogenic Training and biofeedback training and has included physiological studies of yogis in India (1974). His present focus of attention is on "biofeedback and the image-making faculty" and their use in the establishment and maintenance of psychosomatic health. Dr. Green is on the board of directors of the Biofeedback Society, the Psychosynthesis Institute, the Institute of Transpersonal Psychology, and the advisory board of the Canadian Institute of Psychosynthesis.

Alyce Green, Co-Director of the Voluntary Controls Pro-

gram, Research Department, the Menninger Foundation, obtained her B.A. degree in psychology from the University of Chicago in 1962 and did graduate studies in counseling and creativity. Her laboratory work on creativity at the Menninger Foundation has focused on "Alpha-Theta Brain-wave Feedback, Reverie and Imagery," funded in 1972 and 1973 primarily by the National Institute of Mental Health. She is presently involved in exploring brain-wave training for psychotherapy, an outcome of the "creativity" research.

Alyce Green was one of three Menninger psychophysiologists who studied yogic control of physiological processes in India (1974). She was first president of the Association of Transpersonal Psychology and is a member of the advisory board of *The Journal of Transpersonal Psychology* and the new journal *Synthesis*. She is a member of the Advisory Council of Planetary Citizens and is on the board of directors of the Academy of Parapsychology and Medicine.